D0033655

Women in the Field

WOMEN IN THE FIELD

ANTHROPOLOGICAL EXPERIENCES

Second Edition, Expanded and Updated

EDITED BY
Peggy Golde

UNIVERSITY OF CALIFORNIA PRESS
Berkeley • Los Angeles • London

University of California Press
Berkeley and Los Angeles, California

University of California Press, Ltd.
London, England

Copyright © 1970, 1986 by Peggy Golde

Second edition, expanded and updated

Library of Congress Cataloging in Publication Data

Women in the field.

  Bibliography: p.
  1. Anthropologists, Women.   2. Ethnology—Field work.   I. Golde,
Peggy, 1930–
GN20.W65   1986   306'.088042   86–6947
ISBN 0–520–05421–0 (alk. paper)
ISBN 0–520–05422–9 (pbk.: alk. paper)

Printed in the United States of America

1 2 3 4 5 6 7 8 9

Contents

Preface to the Second Edition

A t the time the first edition of *Women in the Field* was in the process of publication, the feminist movement was gaining momentum. Late 1969 saw the beginning of women's studies; today, according to Paula R. Holleran, there are some 300,000 courses and 600 programs in women's studies in the United States alone.[1]

Despite the historical importance of 1969, this book was not conceived in a feminist furor, although anthropology as a discipline was lagging behind. In January 1979, *Anthropology Newsletter* published a report of its Ad Hoc Committee which concluded that there had been "a consistent pattern of discrimination in the hiring and promotion of female anthropologists with qualifications equal to male anthropologists."

A more detailed picture had been presented in Roger Sanjek's paper in the December 1978 *American Anthropologist* (vol. 80, no. 4), entitled "The Position of Women in the Major Departments of Anthropology, 1967–76" (p. 894). Sanjek's most telling comments regarding the context of employment before 1970 were concerned with a declining proportion of women in the top departments and a total lack of women in half of the twenty two departments surveyed (Stanford, for example, had no women of junior rank in anthropology until I joined the department in 1967).

Things have certainly changed since 1969, with the pressures for change having come from within the field of anthropology itself, from the Department of Health, Education and Welfare (now the Department of Health and Human Services), and perhaps from the feminist movement as well.

In my introduction to the first edition of this book, I wrote about my need to provide an arena in which anthropologists could "present personal and human reactions to field work" and could consider where the influence of the researcher's gender might affect the results of the research (p. 2). This updated volume gives us the opportunity to expand the bibliography for use in women's studies programs. The new bibliography demonstrates the impact of the first edition through the large number of books presented which focus on field work, on women, and on cross-cultural orientation.

---

1. Holleran, Paula R., "The Feminist Curriculum: Issues for Survival in Academe," *Journal of Thought,* vol. 20, no. 3, Fall 1985, Special Topic Edition: Feminist Education-Editor, Barbara Hillyer Davis), pp. 25–36.

There was no need to update the introduction, since it was based on common themes found in the original essays and has withstood the test of time. Two new essays have been added, and these provide an accidental bonus in their common demonstration of the value of returning to the field after a lapse of time. (In my original essay I mentioned the villagers' negative reaction to my return for a brief visit, a reaction that surprised and saddened me.) That negativism is not apparent in these new essays. A different insight results from these anthropologists' perceptions of the effect of return. This insight enables one to appreciate the impact of the passage of time on the deepening, enriching, and strengthening of trust and on the quality of sharing that is possible only with repeated encounters.

The place itself changes in historical time; the ethnographer, too, changes because of her own experiences (Diane Freedman's article is the most poignant example of this observation). Obviously, the ethnographer has over time developed new "eyes" with which to behold her subjects—the participant observer is aging at a different rate from those being observed.

What is different about the female anthropologist who is going into the field today is that she is more likely to travel with a nonanthropologist husband. The authors of both new essays were married to men who were in other disciplines when they first entered their communities. The first edition dealt primarily with unmarried women confronting an unknown situation at a time when it was considered unusual for a woman to travel great distances alone to establish a temporary living situation for conducting a strange kind of work never fully grasped by her hosts.

Having edited the first volume, I have certainly been aware of changes in women's roles and of the need for the work of anthropologists to be better understood and appreciated. Over time it became clear that a new edition of the book was needed because colleagues teaching both undergraduate and graduate students were finding it impossible to collect enough copies of the original book, which had gone out of print. Some of these colleagues wrote testimonials concerning the significance of the book, referring to it as a "classic," the first work to focus on the importance of gender in field work and the first to stress the impact of subjectivity when entering an unfamiliar site for a field study.

Freedman's chapter depicts the implications for Americans who bring their own culture and political orientation to groups with totally foreign ways of life. Her essay illustrates dramatically how an anthropologist can successfully maneuver the rapids of a precarious political situation. Even though Freedman's dissertation was concerned not with politics but with the arts (specifically, dance) and thus posed no threat to the Romanian government, she became entangled in a cat's cradle of bureaucracy, embassies, and intricate negotiations surrounding her entry into Romania.

Freedman also recounts her experiences in returning to the field one year after the death of her husband from cancer, and her essay thus provides a literary model for conveying a painful subjective experience. She went back to the Transylvanian village in a new role, that of a widow in mourning.

The field of anthropology is changing toward a greater acceptance of subjectivity and a wider focus on human problems that were formerly the domain only of the psychologist and the sociologist. Consider the 1983 *Abstracts* from the Annual Meeting of the American Anthropological Association, which include categories of papers that would best qualify as clinical anthropology: for example, perception of gender, drug and alcohol use, bereavement, family studies, and mental health.

This second edition also shows a movement toward the recognition of anthropologists as reflective, sensitive human beings, not exploitive social scientists mining other cultures for the gold of new knowledge.

Margaret Mead's shadow is cast strongly over many conceptions in this edition, not least in the essay by Rena Lederman, chiefly by virtue of the common interest of the two women in Papua New Guinea. Mead's death in November 1978 left a noticeable rent in the fabric of female anthropologists.

Lederman's contribution here is a many-faceted field account dealing with economic aspects, women's status, gender ideology, and the interaction between a reflexive orientation and the use of textual materials.[2] The sum total of these many facets is an essay reflecting feminist research and theory.

In the fulfilling of her present teaching responsibilities at Princeton University, Lederman no doubt draws heavily on the research described here, especially in her course on the "Anthropology of Gender." The entire essay is ideal for its position in this second edition of *Women in the Field,* as I first conceptualized its ethnographic goals (see the introduction).

Anthropologists are still using the same tools to accomplish ethnographies: participant observation, cameras, tape recorders, and typewriters. Recently, they have also begun using portable, battery-powered computers for instant data analysis.

Other tools are the self and the ability to empathize with other peoples, along with the ability to write descriptively about inner feelings. The latter was attempted with reluctance by some of the women writing in the first book. Since it is not taught in graduate school and is not common in the writing of most anthropologists, such "diary-style" writing will probably always present some difficulty.

In sum, the general situation of professional women has been greatly changed

2. Marcus, George, E., and Dick Cushman, "Ethnographies as Texts." 1982. In Bernard Siegel et al. (eds.), *Annual Review of Anthropology,* Vol. II. Palo Alto, California: Annual Reviews Inc.

in the past fifteen years or so, and it will no doubt continue to move toward a situation of complete equality of regard for the work of such women as they become full professors and heads of departments in the major universities in this country.

P.G.

Introduction

PEGGY GOLDE

In the field of anthropology there has been little public discussion of the subjective aspects of field work, perhaps because it would have been considered unessential or irrelevant to the communication of information about other cultures, the central scientific task. This attitude could adequately serve the discipline in the past, while it was still small enough for graduate training to rely on close personal exchanges to rectify gaps in the literature and when anthropologists were oriented toward building an alliance with the sciences and attempting to separate from the humanities. The growth of anthropology, both in the number of anthropologists and of independent departments in universities and colleges throughout the country, has resulted in wider audiences and the possibility of commitment at an earlier stage in college education. Consequently, there is need to make the work of the anthropologist more vivid as a career choice to an ever growing number of young students.

The student often reads an ethnography as a fait accompli with no clear idea of how the picture of another culture was achieved, and with an inadequate grasp of the process of interaction between researcher and community members and of the problems, pitfalls, and procedures of the anthropologist as "photographer." When, as a first-year graduate student, I read *Return to Laughter* by Elenore Smith Bowen (1954), I recognized something I had been missing in most anthropological works. The fictionalized description of becoming acclimated to life in an African village, which included the author's transitory emotional reactions as well as more deeply felt and enduring responses, was alive and compelling; it served as a constant reassurance when I subsequently engaged in my own field work. The impact of the book on me was the stimulus for this volume and provided evidence of the potential value of such a volume for students of anthropology. As I wrote to the contributors to this collection, our book could "present in an open, direct, and immediate fashion a variety of models that the students could, as it were, try on for size."

This volume was conceived in 1965,[1] influenced not only by Bowen's work, but by other books as well: Margaret Mead's *An Anthropologist at Work: Writings of Ruth Benedict* (1959); *Reflections on Community Studies,* edited by Vidich, Bensman, and Stein (1964); and *Sociologists at Work,* edited by Phillip E. Hammond (1964). Since that time still other works have appeared that have exposed to view the researcher's self, notably *Stranger and Friend* by Hortense Powdermaker (1967) and *A Diary in the Strict Sense of the Term* by Malinowski (1967).

Beside the need to present personal and human reactions to field work, the second issue to which this volume is directed is how the characteristics of the ethnographer may indirectly and inadvertently affect the process of research. Several recent works in the field of psychology examine the influence of the experimenter on the results of his research (Rosenthal, 1966; Friedman, 1967), and their publication signifies to me a changing attitude, a growing recognition of the value and importance of considering social-science research as the process and product of interaction between the questioner and the questioned and of the need to subject this process to scrutiny.[2] In the same vein Powdermaker notes, "A scientific discussion of field work method should include considerable detail about the observer: the role he plays, his personality and other relevant facts concerning his position and functioning in the society studied." (1967, p. 9). Facts about the observer-observed interaction have relevance not only for field work methods, but, as the subsequent chapters will illustrate, for theories of cultural dynamics as well.

Given this over-all task, what is the rationale for focusing on women and excluding the field experiences of men? First, sex is the simplest variable to hold constant. If our goal is to analyze and evaluate the influence of the researcher on the data being studied, it would seem most economical to begin by looking at a shared characteristic inherent in the researcher—one

1. In 1965–1966 I was in residence at the Center for Advanced Study in the Behavioral Sciences, Stanford, California. At that time I began to work on an article with Ann Fischer (Fischer and Golde, 1968) that made us both acutely aware of the positive and negative aspects of the professional woman's role in anthropology. Though the idea for the book had been germinating below ground for some time, doubtless these discussions and ruminations caused it to surface.

2. At the time of writing, *Anthropologists in the Field,* edited by D. G. Jongmans and P. C. W. Gutkind (1967) had just come to my attention through a book review by Dennison Nash in the *American Anthropologist* (Vol. 70, pp. 768–769). Nash opens his review with the comment, "If self-consciousness is a sign of maturity, then this volume is one indication of the coming-of-age of a social anthropology that has begun to raise serious questions about its own activities." Nash describes the volume as a collection of personal accounts that explore the ethnographer's role.

that is highly visible or unusual and consequently likely to be noted and responded to. Femininity meets these criteria best precisely because response to it is likely to be clear and direct; all cultures, having two sexes, can be expected to have developed attitudes about women, and in most nonliterate cultures it is an unusual event to be visited by a woman who engages in activities not associated with the usual women's roles.

I envisioned this book as an informal cross-cultural study of attitudes about the sex of the "outsider" who eventually becomes, through a set of mutual adjustments, an "insider." I hoped it would provide data to partially answer the question, "Is there any theoretical knowledge to be gained from examining the responses of a variety of culturally distinct human groups to the common stimulus of the female stranger?" The latter part of this introduction will be concerned more specifically with how this collection speaks to the question of the common aspects of the response.

Second, I assumed that simply growing up as women in American society would have made the contributors aware of the kinds of subtle and conflicting pressures that may be exerted on women. Their own personal adaptation as professionals would have demanded that they develop heightened sensitivities about sex role, and I believed that this awareness, including an acceptance of "perceptiveness about feelings" as appropriate to the feminine role, would make the assessment of the influence of sex easier for women than it would have been for men. I also hoped that if these assumptions were correct, the resulting information about the consequences of gender might sensitize male anthropologists to the problem and implications of sex roles and provide data they could use to contrast and compare with the responses they themselves elicit as researchers. Systematic comparisons of this kind are necessary if we are to establish the extent to which aspects of responses and roles are determined by the sex of the investigator, not only because of the nature of the responses of the society being studied, but because of sex role training, attitudes, and biases transmitted to each sex in our own culture. Therefore, I also hoped that the volume would emerge as an ethnography of ethnographers, with each participant acting as a "native informant" reporting on her subjective view of her own world, values, and aims and on how her work might reflect her sex identification as well as her professional training. Through these accounts the reader would be provided the opportunity of meeting and getting to know a number of anthropologists in a special way; in these pages the reader would be able to sense the kind of people they are, how they have reacted to their own experiences, and to discover aspects of a basic outlook they may share.

Before dealing explicitly with some of the commonalities exhibited in the chapters, I would like to include here a good part of the original letter of invitation sent to the contributors; it provides a concise way of presenting the aims of this collection and serves as a frame in which to gauge its success in achieving these aims.

It is my hope that each contribution will portray the subjective impact of moving into a new culture, presenting an individual sightline on a unique experience. At the same time, the pooling of these reminiscences may illuminate the recurring problems, choices, and solutions that are common to the encounter between the woman as a stranger and a foreign culture.

Ideally each narrative would move back and forth among different levels, interweaving three separate but related kinds of materials and reference points: (1) personal and subjective, (2) ethnographic, and (3) theoretical or methodological.

First and foremost the account should be personal, tracing the inward history of the field experience, perhaps beginning with prior expectations, apprehensions, hopes, and ambitions. It might encompass the chance happenings, the frustrations and rewards, the unsought insights, the stumbled-upon understandings, the never-resolved misunderstandings—whatever characterized the sequence of the human interchange between you as outsider and those with whom you made your home. It might include answers to the questions your friends and acquaintances were most interested in when you returned: "What was it like? Was it difficult making friends? Weren't you lonely? Were you ever frightened? What did you do for fun? How did you arrange a place to live?" I do not intend that you search for the sensational or the exotic; on the contrary, it is my belief that a realistic description of the trivia of daily living can give an intimate picture of the process of adjustment to another culture and, simultaneously, a sense of the characteristic profile of that culture. It is also my feeling that the best way to transmit what it means to be an anthropologist (how we do our work, how we respond to the strange and different and come to understand it, how we balance objectivity, distance, and respect with our own personal values) is to describe the process from the self's point of view, thus enabling others to "live" vicariously through the experience.

Obviously, in the course of such a narrative, many ethnographic details perforce will enter. What happened to you happened in a particular locale, in a given context, and it would be meaningful to try to make explicit when the bits of interchange were influenced less by the impact of you as a person than by forces existing within the culture, such as traditional attitudes toward women, the existing social structure and norms of managing novel situations, the history of previous contacts, the current political climate, or whatever might have been relevant to your experience. These are meant to be only suggestions of the kinds of factors that may have intruded, that may have shaped the course and nature of your relationships, and the kind of work you could and could not do.

Last on the above list, the theoretical or methodological aspect, may well come last in your write-up as well, in the form of generalizations, conclusions, suggestions for future research questions, or an explicit contribution to role theory, field technique, what-have-you. My hope is that the task I have set will result in a human document, meaningful in its own terms, but also as a systematic self-conscious scrutiny of how the chief instrument of research, the anthropologist herself, may alter that which is being studied and may be changed in turn. There is need for more open speculation and consideration of such issues as: how were my data affected by the kind of person I am, by my sex or other apparent attributes, and how did my presence alter, positively or negatively, the flux of life under observation? Through the attempt to analyze the rapport-building process and the creation of your role, the natural history of adjustment and acceptance that characterize field work may become visible.

As this letter indicates, I hoped that one of the consequences of gathering these accounts would be to illuminate common responses to the female ethnographer that might stand as generalizations or that might be framed as hypotheses for future testing. However, my attempt to present an array of work situations and a wide representation of geographical locations has worked somewhat against the achievement of these theoretical objectives. On the other hand, the variety does accurately convey the range of research activities within the field of anthropology that women may engage in, and despite the diversity, several recurring themes appear that can be identified and that deserve comment and further consideration. Some of these themes have been made explicit by individual authors, some are based on my own interpretation of the combined data. These themes, as I label them, are protection, initial suspicion, conformity, reciprocity, and culture shock.

"Protection" refers to the motive that underlies specific behavior triggered by the perception of female sex identity. At the core of this behavior seems to be an assessment of the vulnerability of the woman seen in terms of relative physical weakness, lesser resourcefulness in confronting unforeseen hazards, or openness to sexual attack. Protection arises as an issue even before the ethnographer takes up residence in a new community; it is first clearly seen in the reactions of the several worlds—academic, political, administrative—she passes through before arriving at her final destination. Protection also operates in varying degrees, depending on the circumstances, after she moves into the new culture.

To perceive vulnerability is to simultaneously perceive provocation, for if to be vulnerable is to be susceptible to exploitation, this very defenselessness is perceived as a potential challenge to take advantage of it. Protection, then, has a double aim—the direct need to insure the safety of the woman, and the protection of others through the prevention of situations that might provoke others to exploit her. Protection is expressed as apprehension that the woman may get into difficulties from which she will not have the skill, knowledge, or leverage to extricate herself. In other words, one facet of the perception of the woman reflects her presumed naïveté as an "innocent abroad" who may become a dupe for those who will be ready to capitalize on her incapacity and inexperience. Provocativeness also contains a sexual element per se, a dimension that has both passive and active faces. In the frame of some cultures, the fact of a woman's accessibility may be considered provocative in itself, while in others it may be imagined that her sexual interest will lead her actively to tempt men into liaisons. (The field worker who is physically attractive in terms of the prevailing aesthetic standards of the community she is studying will pose a greater threat and will suffer these suspicions to a greater degree.) Perceptions of provocativeness are manifest in the exaggeration of dangers by those who act as gatekeepers to the field. Once in the field, gossip and rumors, insinuations of wrongdoing, overt and disguised sexual encounters initiated by men, and active attempts to control and limit the woman's freedom of movement are further expressions of this attitude. (See contributions by Golde, Nader, Landes, Weidman, Fischer.) Such behaviors not only reveal these attitudes, but they also serve as mechanisms of social control. They contain a message that may be manifestly solicitous, but at the same time constitutes a veiled warning to both the field worker and the community that the limits of tolerance may not be pushed too far.

The techniques devised to actually provide protection or simply to symbolize it, reduce either the woman's accessibility or her desirability. These include finding a man or men whose role enables them to serve as protectors; moving in with a family; taking or being assigned an already existing role that minimizes or neutralizes sexuality or is a traditionally protected one, such as "child," "sister," "grandmother"; working chiefly with the women and children of the community or living in the field with a husband or a team of fellow workers (Thompson, Marshall, Friedl, Fischer, Mead). The vulnerability associated with femininity is less an issue for the older woman or for those to whom has been ascribed high status or power (Du Bois, Fischer, Mead). Age implies a decreased interest in sex as well as a lessening of desirability, while status and power function as built-in protection. The theme of protection in these essays is most elaborated in the accounts of those women who were relatively young, unmarried, or alone when they did their field work (Briggs, Golde, Nader, Marshall, Weidman, Fischer, Mead); they express their concern for their own well-being and also about the responsibility they inadvertently thrust on the local authorities. Insuring her own safety means freedom from anxiety about it, and this seems to be the issue for the female anthropologist. In arranging her household, and recognizing that she cannot be self-sufficient and that she requires help in managing her daily life, she surrounds herself with symbolic "chaperones" because they serve as shield and reassurance both for her and the community.

Protection has positive as well as negative implications; the same feeling can contribute to bonds of attachment between the anthropologist and the community. When, in crisis situations, the community demonstrates responsibility, protectiveness, and possessiveness toward the ethnographer, it is not only a source of deep emotional gratification for her, but it is also an observable demonstration to everyone involved of the extent of its commitment.

Initial suspicion is a more expectable response to an outsider than is ready, congenial, unequivocal acceptance. If a community is conceived as a system of defined roles and organized relationships based on predictable behaviors, then it is likely that any intruder would be initially perceived as a potential threat to the order, and in turn, that defensive behaviors would be set in motion to preserve the integrity of the system. The stranger is threatening on two counts: first, she is strange, unknown, different, unprepared for; and second, she can neither be relied upon to behave in familiar ways nor trusted to respect people's needs and feelings. A strange woman may be less frightening than a man because her attributes of womanhood already suggest a good deal of information, as I have outlined above, and because a man would be presumed to be more potentially aggressive.

To anticipate critics who may suggest that I am being ethnocentric in these statements about the relatively unthreatening image of the woman, I cite D'Andrade (1966), who writes, in his review of the cultural expressions of sex differences, "The cross-cultural mode is that males are more sexually active, more dominant, more deferred to, more aggressive, less responsible, less nurturant, and less expressive than females." However, he does qualify this statement by pointing out that it is not universally applicable, since "occasionally the trend is actually reversed" (p. 201). For biological reasons alone—childbearing, lesser strength and size—one may expect the majority of societies to shape the woman's role as less aggressive than that of the male. Other supporting evidence can be found in Barry, Bacon, and Child (1957), who found cross-cultural differences in the socialization of male and female children. Their study, based on ethnographic data from 110 societies, revealed that girls are trained to be nurturant, responsible, and obedient, while boys are trained for self-reliance.

The community's defensive behaviors are reflected in early questioning of the researcher's motives, in rumors that represent attempts to explain her presence, in petty and large resistances of all kinds, and in the accusation that she is a "spy"—that is, a person who obtains information, without revealing her own identity and goals, that she will ultimately use against people (Golde, Nader, Landes, Du Bois, Friedl, Weidman, Fischer). These accusations and suspicions have frequently been explained as reactions to an ambiguous figure or as the result of prior negative contact with foreigners. I do not discount the operation of such factors, but whatever historical reality and present ambiguities may exist, these creations can also be viewed as mechanisms for the defense and preservation of a group. They operate through the behavior of members of the group who act to protect and conserve what is familiar and what constitutes the group identity.

Clearly, some threat, real or imagined, must be perceived before this kind of behavior would be set in motion; and the fact that Margaret Mead reports a lack of suspicion of women anthropologists working in New Guinea may suggest that the people felt no threat because they were so proud and certain of their identity or because the status of European women was such as to preclude such behavior. Another seeming exception is described by Gloria Marshall; she found no suspicion of her in the community in which she lived, rather, she was first treated as an honored guest (as are all strangers to Yoruba society) and later as "a child who had come home." However, it must be noted that she resembled her hosts physically and observed the traditional respect forms; she comments that "the fact that I was black seemed to be more important than my nationality in determining the way they responded to me." The community members were able to reduce the threat implied by this foreign woman's residence by convincing themselves that she really was not a stranger at all; despite the fact that she could not trace her genealogy, they seemed to want to believe that she was "undoubtedly a Yoruba."

The third theme, conformity, is differentiated from initial suspicion in that the latter relates to the perception of the stranger, whereas conformity centers on the problem of the stranger who has become familiar but does not always conform to expectations. After the researcher has been accepted to some degree, the unstated message of the host community is, "If you want to live with us, act like us." The dilemma for the anthropologist lies in balancing the community's need to absorb and control her with her own need for independence of action. Because she has a task to accomplish, some of her behavior will almost certainly lead to flouting some of the culture's traditional expectations of women's behavior. Since women in most cultures are permitted less leeway than men, less deviance in their role performance, any nonconformity on the part of the female researcher will seem noteworthy. Obviously the degree of disruption produced by non-conforming behavior will vary with the culture and the variety of its available roles; what is of more interest is how the researcher overcomes these obstacles and fulfills her goals, despite the pressures put on her, and how the community resolves the issue of her nonconformity.

Though the researcher may try to create a role for herself that is to some extent new to the host society, any viable creation must be an amalgam of the new with previously existing duties, activities, and expectations. The society then can adapt by making the field worker the sole exemplar of the innovated role, or it can simply assign her an existing variant or deviant role. Ruth Landes talks about the availability in urban Brazil of the variant roles of "artist" or "prostitute" in which she was cast; but in the end the deviant role of "Communist" seemed to have more explanatory power in accounting for her behavior and in justifying the actions taken by her hosts. Jean Briggs describes aspects of the deviant roles between which she moved: "mentally retarded" and "child." Since her behavior did not always fit what was expected of a "daughter," her "family" had to look for other explanations or pre-existing models to make her behavior meaningful to them. Similarly, both Hazel Weidman and Laura Nader were at times suspected of being "men" because of dissonant aspects of their appearance or because they exhibited certain inclinations and qualities usually associated with men; the only way to make sense of these anomalies was to entertain the belief they might actually be men. The deviant role "crazy" was not applied to any of these women, as far as we can tell from their accounts, probably because they were generally competent, were recognized as coming from another culture, and brought recommendations from the outside world that signified they were valuable and responsible.

It seems clear that the greater the extent to which the anthropologist can remain outside the existing system of roles and expectations, the freer she will be to pursue her own goals; to the extent that she attempts to conform to a structural role, as did Ernestine Friedl and Jean Briggs, she becomes more constrained. The judicious balancing of demands—which to recognize and which to reject or ignore—is a problem all anthropologists must face, but paradoxically, again it may ultimately be less problematic for women than for men. The appearance of the woman in the field may initially be more difficult to understand and rationalize, because of the disparity between her behavior and that of the women in the community, but once this hurdle has been overcome, she may have more freedom of movement among age and sex groups within a culture than would a man (Nader, Du Bois, Mead).

However, easy access to people does not imply easy access to information and experiences. There are hints of this difficulty in Ann Fischer's account, when she describes the different information she and her husband were given by informants. Ernestine Friedl, and Margaret Mead as well, describe interactions of their husbands with village men in which they could not join. Gloria Marshall points out that she was never permitted to witness ceremonies normally barred to women.

A further aspect of deviance associated with sex is marital status. If the field worker is single, the community will be concerned about why she is not married; if she is married but her husband is not with her, people will wonder about that situation; if she is with her husband, attention will focus on why she has no children. These questions are irksome rather than troubling, but they do require the researcher to search for explanations that are meaningful to informants. On the other hand, these questions themselves constitute useful information because they reveal implicit expectations, areas of concern, and the specific nature of the discrepancies between the people and the ethnographer. The stranger is not perceived merely as threatening, but also as an object of curiosity and attention; this curiosity is directed toward learning about another life and to establishing just how human the researcher is, how many traits she shares with the local people. Such questions provide the opportunity of exchanging many kinds of information (including photographs), which give the people some means of elaborating their image of the researcher and making more real the background from which she comes, all of which tend to reduce psychological distance.

The theme of reciprocity, implicit in these essays, is the least well-documented in the following chapters; it is so unconscious, so deeply entrenched in all of us, that it remains unrecognized unless it becomes dramatized by events. The issue for the ethnographer is, "How can I repay these people who give me so much?" while the issue for the community is, "What does she give that makes up for the trouble she causes, for the fact that she is not like us and cannot contribute what we are accustomed to expect?" Reciprocity in some form can be the anthropologist's means of demonstrating her value, her importance, her membership in the community, and of counteracting the negative effects of her differences. Some of the researchers gave lessons in English, others did favors, provided medicine, gave food, drink, or material goods (Golde, Nader, Codere, Marshall, Weidman). Whether female anthropologists feel the need to "repay" to a greater extent than do males cannot be determined from these chapters. On the one hand, it could be argued that reciprocity would be less of an issue for women from our culture because they are more accustomed to being protected as part of their role. They do not feel an obligation to make some kind of return, nor would it be expected. On the other hand, their very dependence on the largesse of others may make them more sensitive to the costs involved and may heighten the urgency to "make it up."

Culture shock, the last theme, is a familiar one to anthropologists. In an article written in 1951, Cora Du Bois wrote, "Some twenty years ago, I remember first chatting with colleagues about the peculiar emotional state we anthropologists developed when we were working in the field" (p. 22). She described this state as "culture shock," a term which she credits to Ruth Benedict (private communication); by 1940, it was so well accepted by social scientists that it needed no citation.[3] Du Bois describes it as a syndrome "precipitated by the anxiety that results from losing all your familiar cues," which includes frustration, repressed or expressed aggression against the source of discomfort, an irrational fervor for the familiar and comforting, and disproportionate anger at trivial interferences. Kalervo Oberg (1954) paraphrases Du Bois when he states that culture shock is the anxiety that "results from losing all our familiar signs and symbols of social intercourse." He isolates and describes stages in the process, and though he is writing about visiting technical personnel in a foreign country rather than about anthropological field work, there seem to be emotional parallels. The first, or "honeymoon," phase, lasting from a few days to weeks or months, is characterized by fascination with the new. This positive attitude is succeeded by a hostile and aggressive phase, which is a reaction to the difficulties of adjustment and to an imagined lack of understanding and concern on the part of others. This second stage Oberg labels the "crisis," the point at which the visitor may so reject the entire experience that he returns to his home. If, however, the visitor traverses this crisis phase and begins to acquire the language and to find his way in the new culture, the third, or "recovery," stage is entered. The fourth and final stage, that of "adjustment," is achieved through learning the cues that guide behavior and accepting the alien customs. He observes that "Understanding the ways of a people is essential but this does not mean that you have to give up your own. What happens is that you have developed two patterns of behavior" (p. 11).

Aspects of culture shock are clearly revealed in the accounts of first field experiences included in this volume (Briggs, Golde, Nader, Weidman, Fischer). It is generally the initial encounter that most exemplifies the frustration, anxiety, paranoid-like perceptions, inner complaints, and depression characteristic of the syndrome. Laura Thompson writes that there is never again "anything like one's first field trip," and perhaps that is when the lesson—heightened by novelty, impressed through high arousal—is irrevocably learned. That lesson, the learning of culture, is not an intellectually dispassionate one, nor is it even necessarily mediated by words; it is

3. J. B. Holt, in "Holiness Religion: Cultural Shock and Social Reorganization," *Am. Soc. Rev.*, 5 (1940), 740–747, speaks of culture shock as arising from the precipitation of a rural person into an urban situation. His definition of shock includes the "loosening of mores from strict social control" and "disruption of habits," but he gives no citation for his usage.

direct intuitive learning that seeps through all the senses, as it did when we were children being socialized into our own world. Field work can be a replication, condensed in time, of childhood learning, with its attendant anxieties, mystification, impotence, and occasional and gradual mastery. We might label this "initiation anxiety," expecting to find perplexity, feelings of powerlessness, unsureness, and strain accompanying the process of being inducted into any ongoing, structured situation that is new, whether it be going to college, taking a new job, moving to a new place, or joining a new group.

Culture shock is certainly due in part to an inadequate set of meanings with which to interpret the behavior of others, but the concept includes the notion of threat to one's own system of meanings and values, and consequently to one's own identity. There is discomfort and anxiety in trying to balance a different way of seeing the world with one's own established perceptions, particularly if these "two patterns of behavior" are incompatible.

The severity of the experience of dislocation will thus depend not only on the individual and his previous exposure to total novelty, but also on the degree to which the new beliefs, values, norms, and style of behavior conflict with the individual's own core values and emotional profile. The conflict may be experienced in its more extreme form as abhorrence, disgust, anger, frustration, intolerance, oppression; or it may emerge as impatience, bewilderment, disapproval in its milder form. Conversely, the same range of feelings may inadvertently be triggered in others reacting to the field worker's behavior, so that she has to deal with their disapproval without always understanding its source. It can happen that what one has deeply accepted as proper, valuable, correct for oneself may be disvalued by another culture; what one disvalues for oneself may be preferred by that culture. This opposition can produce profoundly disturbing reactions.

Ann Fischer reacted negatively to the unfavorable status of women in Japan, and in New England she feared offending the sensibilities of women who didn't like being asked too many questions. Laura Nader was oppressed by the attitude of inferiority she observed in the Talean townspeople and found respite with the people of Juquila, whose self-esteem and pride were more consonant with her own notion of how people should be and feel. Jean Briggs, identifying with the needs and feelings of the Eskimo, burst out angrily at those she thought were trying to exploit her friends, forgetting the importance of repressing overt anger; she was behaving in terms of her own needs, her own definition of what was honorable behavior, but the Eskimo disapproved her explosiveness as "annoying" and "improper." Hazel Weidman felt impatience with Burmese ways, with its ideal of interpersonal behavior that inhibits the expression of feelings that might trouble another. The breakdown in communication resulting from this inhibition led her to feel betrayed and deceived in a relationship with a Burmese that she had thought was based on openness and honesty. The verbal ambiguity she discovered in Burmese responses caused anxiety because she was uncertain how to interpret their meanings; but even when she learned to play the game, she did not like the rules.

As Ruth Landes and Margaret Mead suggest, the anthropologist, through field work, lives more than one life. It is just this "total human experience," in Helen Codere's words, this total immersion, this giving over of oneself to a differently organized reality, that leads the women writing here to attribute to this experience pervasive and compelling consequences. Note the phrases they use indicating that what happens in the field is ultimately related to the self: Weidman speaks of the "conflict about a self," Landes describes the lure of field work as the "lure of self," Nader mentions "knowledge of self," Du Bois writes that field work requires a "continuing willingness to immerse one's self in an infinitely varied series of life ways," and Codere talks about a "change in character that comes about in so total and intense a learning experience." All the women share an essentially positive evaluation of their experience, even those who wrestled with painful ambivalence, feeling they had been beneficially augmented and altered, both as people and as anthropologists, by their journey into an alien world. It is this attitude which may make possible the final goal of ethnography, in Malinowski's words,

> . . . to grasp the native's point of view, his relation to life, to realize *his* vision of *his* world. We have to study man, and we must study what concerns him most intimately, that is, the hold which life has on him [1961, p. 25].

Equally clear in the following chapters is a strong commitment to an intellectual problem, an investment in discovery that includes the self but is aimed at a target defined more broadly than Malinowski's goal. That target is the uncovering of principles, of regularities, of relationships between events, forces, attitudes, meanings and consequences. The anthropologist is first and foremost a scientist—using the particular to illustrate the general, focusing on a particular group of human beings to understand the processes that operate in any human group, analyzing the specific situation with its unique constellation of characteristics in order to place it on some continuum of other instances. The ultimate target of the discipline of social anthropology is the ability to explain human behavior and what we call social facts or phenomena. This means the ability to grasp the structure of what is, the development of that structure, the factors that keep it the way it is or cause it to change, and ultimately the ability to predict the conditions under which specifiable changes will take place.

The ability to relate one's own research to a larger body of findings, and to evaluate its significance and accomplishment in terms of the larger goal described above, differentiates the anthropologist from the novelist or the journalist. Progress toward that goal is measured not only in the accumulation of data, but also in the development of new techniques for getting information and new strategies for studying old problems. This interplay of problems and methods is well illustrated in the chapters of Codere, Du Bois and Thompson. Codere, faced with the challenge of chronicling a revolution and its consequences in East Central Africa, had to devise techniques that would permit her to tap attitudes formed within the context of a dynamic and fast-moving social phenomenon. Questionnaires, diaries, life histories, and a photographic projective technique were among the means she utilized.

Du Bois' project, like Codere's, was not cast in the traditional mold of the anthropological study of a small homogeneous group, but was an attempt to capitalize on a fortuitous set of characteristics. In her "natural laboratory" in Bhubaneswar, a newly-established capital city located in a small area populated by traditional villages, she found a perfect setting in which to study confrontation of modern and traditional lifeways. Recognizing that no single investigator could hope to grasp the intricacy of the multifaceted subject, her research became the fulcrum of a training project for graduate students, each of whom could benefit from and could contribute to the total study.

The anthropologist's search for new means includes learning and adapting techniques from other disciplines. Thompson's description of her multi-disciplinary project to study the impact of United States government policy changes on six Indian tribes documents a search for means to establish the connections between culture and personality, to spotlight the relation between covert cultural meaning and external, observable behavior. Children's games, school performance, language, and culture-free psychological tests became windows through which she could view the ethos of a people.

The chapters by Fischer and Mead have been placed last because they are not oriented to one locale or one research problem but instead compare field experiences that varied in space, time, and circumstances. Their chapters reflect and summarize the entire collection, providing a controlled comparison of cultural responses to a researcher-female-stranger, synthesizing from their own experiences a number of the issues and observations discussed by the other contributors. The peoples they studied also represent the two extremes of the continuum of human societies described within these covers: from the people of New Guinea, the most technologically

primitive, to the peoples of Japan and the United States, the most technologically advanced.

This collection was not meant to be merely a book that opens to view
the subjective impact of living in an alien culture, through it may be read as
such, nor is it merely about the field techniques used by anthropologists to
reveal the anatomy of another culture, though it will provide insights into
that process. It is not solely an attempt to examine systematically the effect
of the researcher's sex on the role she plays in the community being studied,
though this was one of the stated goals, nor is it only a documentation of
cross-cultural attitudes toward women, though the dedicated reader directing his attention to that issue will discover a wealth of pertinent information. The collection cannot be described by any one of these separate categories because, I hope and believe, it overlaps them all.

Kapluna Daughter

JEAN BRIGGS is professor of anthropology at Memorial University of Newfoundland. Since writing NEVER IN ANGER, from which this chapter is excerpted, she has made nine additional field trips to the Canadian Arctic. She has published papers on various aspects of Inuit (Eskimo) psychology and socialization and is currently working on a book about Inuit interpersonal games as well as on two Inuit dialect dictionaries. Professor Briggs has held visiting appointments at the University of Tromsö (Norway) and at the Hebrew University of Jerusalem, and she recently began field work with the Bedouin.

"It's very cold down there—*very cold*. If I were going to be at Back River this winter, I would like to adopt you and try to keep you alive."

My Eskimo visitor, Unai,[1] dramatized her words with shivers as we sat drinking tea in the warm nursing station in Gjoa Haven. It was only mid-August, but already the wind that intruded through the cracks in the window frame was bitter, and the ground was white with a dusting of new snow. Last winter's ice, great broken sheets of it, still clogged the harbor, so that the plane I was waiting for was unable to get through to us. I was on my way to spend a year and a half with the Utkuhiksalingmiut, a small group of Eskimos who lived in Chantrey Inlet at the mouth of the Back River on the northern rim of the American continent. They were the most remote group of Eskimos that I could find on the map of the Canadian Arctic, a people who in many ways lived much as they had in the days before *kaplunas* (white men) appeared in the north. They were nomadic; they lived in snowhouses in winter, in tents in summer; and their diet consisted very largely of fish—trout and whitefish—supplemented now and again by a few caribou.

Their contact with kaplunas had been relatively slight. Two or three of the older people had been hospitalized in Edmonton, and a few of the adolescents attended the government boarding school in Inuvik, on the Alaskan border. Apart from these children—who were away at school during much of my stay—nobody in Chantrey Inlet spoke any English. The nearest resident kaplunas—and, for that matter, the nearest other Eskimos—lived in the small mission-and-trading settlement of Gjoa Haven, 150

The research on which this chapter is based was supported by the Wenner-Gren Foundation, the Northern Co-ordination and Research Centre of the Department of Northern Affairs and National Resources (now the Department of Indian Affairs and Northern Development) of the Canadian Government, and the National Institute of Mental Health of the United States Government (Pre-doctoral Research Fellowship No. 5 F1 MH-20, 701-02 BEH with Research Grant Attachment No. MH-07951-01).

1. All personal names in the text are pseudonyms.

19

miles to the north. Under the best conditions one could travel from Chantrey Inlet to Gjoa Haven and back in a week by dog sled, but usually the round trip took closer to a week and a half or two weeks; in summer Chantrey Inlet was cut off entirely by the open water of Simpson Strait, which lies between Back River, on the mainland, and Gjoa Haven, on King William Island.

Unai's words presaged the most important influence on the course of my life at Back River: my adoption as a "daughter" in the household of an Utkuhiksalingmiut family. It is an aspect of this adoptive relationship that I have chosen to describe here. In addition to conveying something of the flavor and value of Utkuhiksalingmiut life, the story will illustrate certain of the complexities that can develop in relationships between an anthropologist and his hosts.

One of the questions I am asked most frequently about my life at Back River is, "Were you accepted?" People seem to expect a straightforward yes-or-no answer, but in fact there is no such easy response. What is meant by "accepted"? What kind of communication, what kind of exchange of services, can be called "acceptance"? One may be differently "accepted" in different seasons and by different people. When I left for the field, I, like my questioners, was naïve enough to believe that "rapport" was something that was built up, gradually and painstakingly, over a period of weeks or months and then ran on its own momentum until the end of one's stay, barring untoward accidents or carelessness. I discovered, to my sorrow, that the situation wasn't quite so simple. But that knowledge grew only gradually out of a variety of incidents. The relationship that I shall describe was one of the most salient for the growth of my understanding.

It is not my intention, however, to focus solely on my own problems of adjustment. Questions about "acceptance" often ignore the fact that the hosts must also rearrange their lives, at some cost to themselves, to include the anthropologist and to solve the problems created by the latter's presence. The disruption may be more or less severe, depending on the nature of the role that the anthropologist adopts (or is assigned) in the society and on the congeniality of his personality and work habits. Thus, adoption of an intimate role by an uncongenial person may be highly disruptive. The relationship on which this paper focuses is of this nature; it will illustrate some of the special difficulties that my Utkuhiksalingmiut hosts encountered in incorporating an anthropologist of very un-Eskimo temperament into the role of "household daughter" in a ten-foot iglu. It will also illustrate behavior characteristic of my Eskimo family's attempts to cope with these difficulties.

In conclusion I shall make a few observations concerning the anomalous nature of the anthropologist's situation and the part that this oddness plays in creating the problems that plague both anthropologist and hosts.

I arrived in Chantrey Inlet at the end of August 1963 on the plane that the Canadian government sent in once a year to collect the three or four schoolchildren who wished to go to Inuvik. I had with me letters of introduction from the Anglican deacon and his wife in Gjoa Haven, Eskimos from the eastern Arctic who served as missionaries not only to the Anglican Eskimos in Gjoa Haven, but also to the Utkuhiksalingmiut. The letters— written in the syllabic script in which the Utkuhiksalingmiut, like most other Canadian Eskimos, are literate—said that I would like to live with the Utkuhiksalingmiut for a year or so, learning the Eskimo language and skills: how to scrape skins and sew them, how to catch fish and preserve them or boil the oil out of them for use in lighting and heating the winter iglus. They asked the Eskimos to help me with words and fish and promised that in return I would help them with tea and kerosene. They told the people that I was kind and that they should not be shy and afraid of me: "She is a little bit shy herself"; and assured them that they need not feel— as they often do feel toward kaplunas—that they had to comply with my every wish. They said, finally, that I wished to be adopted into an Eskimo family and to live with them in their iglu as a "daughter." In Gjoa Haven, when I had told Ikajuqtuq, the deacon's wife, that I wished to be adopted, she had assumed that I meant in the role of a wife, and she had assured me that I would have no difficulty in finding a husband. I had corrected her, and in order to forestall any similar errors, her husband, Naklirohuktuq, had specified in his letter that I wished to have an Eskimo mother as well as an Eskimo father.

I had a number of reasons for wishing to be adopted, and there were several precedents for adoption as well: four other kaplunas of my acquaintance, both scholars and laymen, who had wintered with Eskimos had done so as "sons," sharing the iglus of their Eskimo families. Living with others would be warmer than living alone, I thought (Ikajuqtuq and Naklirohuktuq agreed); and I thought vaguely that it might be "safer" if one family had specific responsibility for me. The idea had romantic appeal, too; I saw it as a fulfillment of a childhood wish to "be" an Eskimo, and I expected no "rapport problems," since on two previous trips to the Alaskan Arctic I had identified strongly with the Eskimo villagers with whom I had lived. To be sure, there were also arguments against adoption: I had qualms concerning the loss of an "objective" position in the community, drains on my supplies that would result from contributing to the maintenance of a family household, and loss of privacy with resultant difficulties in working. Still, when the moment of decision came, the balance lay in favor of adoption.

There were two suitable fathers among the Utkuhiksalingmiut (that is, two household heads who had wives alive and at home), and these two were both more than eager to adopt me—presumably motivated at least in part by the benefits that a rich kapluna daughter would provide in the form of tea, tobacco, kerosene, and sundry other goods. One, however—an intelligent, vigorous man named Inuttiaq—far outdid the other in the imagination and persistence with which he "courted" me for a daughter. He and his gently smiling wife, Allaq, and their two little daughters paid me lengthy visits in my tent several times a day, and always he waited on me or told Allaq to do so. He lit the primus stove or pumped it up, fetched water, filleted my fish. He anticipated my every wish and some that I did not have at all. More, he was a jolly and ingenious language teacher, acting out words and patiently repeating them until my stumbling tongue managed to produce some half-intelligible variant of the proper sounds. Most gratifying of all, both he and Allaq were astonishingly quick to understand my halting attempts to communicate, and in this respect they contrasted vividly with Nilaak, the other possible "father" and his wife. There was no question which family I preferred. Fortunately, Inuttiaq also occupied a much more central position among the Utkuhiksalingmiut than did Nilaak. He had many more close kin and therefore always moved in a relatively large circle. He was also the Anglican lay leader of the group; he conducted the tri-weekly church services and read prayers over the sick at their request. Nilaak, on the other hand, lived to one side (and sometimes across the river) with his wife and daughter and participated relatively little in community life. I was convinced that both anthropology and I would benefit more if I were adopted by Inuttiaq.

From the moment that the adoption was settled, I was "Inuttiaq's daughter" in the camp. Inuttiaq and his relatives with much amusement drilled me in the use of kin terms appropriate to my position, just as they drilled his three-year-old daughter, who was learning to speak. They took charge of my material welfare and of my education in language and skills. Inuttiaq's wife, Allaq, also to some extent took charge of my daily activities, as it was proper that a mother should. She told me what the day's job for the women of the family was going to be: gathering birch twigs for fuel, scraping caribou hides in preparation for the making of winter clothing, or skinning the fish bellies out of which oil was to be boiled. The decision to participate or not was left to me, but if I did join the women—and I usually did—she made sure that my share of the work was well within the limits of my ability and stamina. "We will be walking very far tomorrow to get birch twigs," she would say; "you will be too tired." If I went anyway, it was always silently arranged that my load should be the lightest, and if I wandered out of sight of the other women in my search for birch bushes, someone always followed behind—sent by Allaq, as I discovered months later—to make sure that I didn't get lost.

Though sometimes Allaq's protectiveness was so discreet that it escaped my notice, often enough I was aware of it and was immensely warmed by it. I was warmed, too, by the smiles of approval with which Inuttiaq greeted me when I helped with the work—smiles that other people noticed and remarked on: "He is watching his daughter." But it was still early autumn, and I was still living in my solitary tent at a little distance from the three Eskimo tents. Grateful as I was for my family's protectiveness, and increasingly comfortable as I felt with them, the thought of actually moving in with them, as it had been arranged I would do when they built their winter quarters, nevertheless filled me with trepidation. It was primarily the loss of privacy I dreaded—the loss of the solitary late evening hours to which I looked forward as a respite from the efforts of the day. The endless struggle to understand the flow of speech was exhausting, as was the attempt to play an unfamiliar role all day long, constantly attempting to react in ways that would be acceptable to my hosts instead of in ways that came naturally to me, and unremittingly keeping alert to cues that would tell me whether or not I had succeeded. Most difficult of all was the attempt to maintain an appearance of quiet, even cheerfulness, like that which the Eskimos displayed both to me and to one another. The evening was a time of recuperation—a time to read Jane Austen, to indulge in secret feasts of half-frozen dates and chocolate, and simply to think kapluna thoughts, uninterrupted. Books, food, and thoughts all provided a much needed link with the world I had left behind, and I feared that if I lost this kapluna interlude, the days would be insupportable.

Curiously, the effect of the move when it came in October was the opposite of what I had expected. I basked in the warm protectiveness of Inuttiaq's household, and what solitude I needed I found on the river in the mornings, when I jigged for salmon trout through the ice with Inuttiaq, or, to my surprise, in the iglu itself, in the afternoons, when the room was full of visitors and I retired into myself, lulled and shielded by the flow of quiet, incomprehensible speech. In many ways life in Inuttiaq's household was easier for me than life in my solitary tent had been. For one thing, it was no longer necessary for me to play hostess. Although Inuttiaq's iglu that autumn was the social center of the camp—and I suspected it was because of my novel presence—nevertheless I could withdraw, in a manner of speaking, into my corner and let Inuttiaq and Allaq entertain our visitors. I thus had privacy without the chill of isolation. Then, too, Inuttiaq and Allaq did their utmost to make me feel welcome. I sensed it in the responsibility they assumed for my welfare, more than ever teaching me how to do things, feeding me, and protecting me from the dangerous effects of my ignorance of the land and climate. I sensed it also in the many considerate allowances that they made on my behalf in the ordering of household life, assuring me from the first that, if I wished, I might type, or keep my lamp lit later than they at night, or "sometimes" eat kapluna food without offering it to them, "because you are a kapluna." They even said they were lonely when I spent an evening visiting in another iglu. That was the most heartwarming of all.

Their treatment of me seemed to be partly parental; on many occasions the care taken on my behalf and the services performed for me were the same as those performed for Inuttiaq's other daughters, six-year-old Raigili and three-year-old Saarak. But in these early days the graciousness that Inuttiaq and Allaq showed me was also in part the behavior of kind hosts toward a guest, a stranger, who is to be treated with formal courtesy. Even their parental behavior—their compliance with my wish to be treated as a daughter—can be seen, I think, partly as submission to the demands of a stranger. Such obligingness is characteristic of Utkuhiksalingmiut in dealing with kaplunas, and perhaps with Eskimo strangers as well. It is motivated partly by fear, partly by a wish to appear unfrightening themselves so that the stranger will treat them well and gratefully, and partly by the very strong value that the Utkuhiksalingmiut place on protectiveness as a virtue in its own right.

The graciousness was very seductive. I came to expect the courtesies that I received and even to resent it a bit when they were not forthcoming, though at the same time I told myself that such feelings were shameful. However, as time passed and I became an established presence in the household, I was less and less often accorded special privileges, except insofar as my ineptitude made services necessary. Allaq still mended my skin boots for me and stretched them when they shrank in drying; my stitches were not small enough and my jaws not strong enough. She continued to fillet my fish when it was frozen nearly as hard as wood. But in other respects Allaq, and especially Inuttiaq—who was far less shy than his wife—more and more attempted to assimilate me into a proper adult parent-daughter relationship. I was expected to help with the household work to the best of my ability—to make tea or bannock and to fetch water; and I was expected to obey unquestioningly when Inuttiaq told me to do something or made a decision on my behalf.

Unfortunately I found it impossible to learn to behave in every respect like an Utkuhiksalingmiut daughter. Inuttiaq lectured me in general terms on the subject of filial obedience, and once in a while I think he tried to shame me into good behavior by offering himself as a model of virtue— volunteering, for example, to make bannock for me if I were slow in making it for him. But to little avail. Sometimes I was genuinely blind and deaf to his lessons, unaccustomed as I was to Utkuhiksalingmiut subtlety. At other times I saw what was wanted but resisted for reasons I will describe in a moment. Inevitably conflicts, covert but pervasive, developed, both regarding the performance of household chores and regarding the related matter of obedience to Inuttiaq. There were other kinds of conflict, too, but it is impossible to describe them all here.

The causes of the conflicts I have mentioned were three. First was the fact that some feminine skills were hard for me to learn. Overtly my Utkuhiksalingmiut parents were very tolerant of the lack of skill that they rightly attributed to kapluna ignorance and perhaps also to kapluna lack of intelligence, or *ihuma*. However, perhaps because of an assumption that kaplunas were unable to learn, if I was at all slow to understand Allaq's instructions and demonstrations, she easily gave up trying to teach me, preferring instead to continue to serve me. And though she stretched my boots and cut my fish with the most cheerful manner, after a while her added chores may well have been burdensome to her.

A second cause of the conflicts is implied in the difference between the way "daughterliness" is defined in Utkuhiksalingmiut society and the way it is defined in our society. Some of Inuttiaq's and Allaq's assumptions about the nature of parental and daughterly virtue were at variance with mine; in consequence not only did I have to learn new patterns, I also had to unlearn old ones. Hardest of all to learn was subordination, unquestioning obedience to paternal authority. Sometimes I could not help resisting, privately but intensely, when Inuttiaq told me to "make tea," to "go home," to "hurry up," or to "pray." I was irritated even by the fact that after the first weeks of gracious formality had passed, he began to address me in the imperative form, which is often used in speaking to women, children, and young people. Rationally I knew that I should have welcomed this sign of "acceptance," but I could not be pleased. My irritation was due partly to the fact that subordination threatened my accustomed—and highly valued— —independence, but it was aggravated by a fear that the restrictions placed on me interfered with my work.

And herein lay the third cause of the conflicts: I found it hard sometimes to be simultaneously a docile and helpful daughter and a conscientious anthropologist. Though Allaq appeared to accept my domestic clumsiness as inevitable, she may have felt less tolerant on the occasions when it was not lack of skill that prevented me from helping her but anxiety over the pocketful of trouser-smudged, disorganized field notes that cried out to be typed. A number of times, when I could have helped to gut fish or to carry in snow to repair the sleeping platform or floor or could have offered to fetch water or make tea, I sat and wrote instead or sorted vocabulary— tiny slips of paper spread precariously over my sleeping bag and lap. It was sometimes professional anxiety that prompted me to disobey Inuttiaq, too, and I am sure that on such occasions, as on others, he must have found my insubordination not only "bad," but completely incomprehensible. My behavior at moving time is an example. My gear, minimal though it was by kapluna standards, placed a severe strain on Inuttiaq when we moved camp. Whereas the sleds of others were loaded to little more than knee height, the load on Inuttiaq's sled was shoulder high. From his point of view it was only reasonable that he should instruct me to leave my heavy tape recorder and my metal box of field notes on the top of a small knoll, as the Utkuhiksalingmiut cached their own belongings, while we moved downstream, not to return until after the flood season. I, however, questioned whether the water might rise over the knoll, and Inuttiaq's silent scrutiny seemed to say that he considered my inquiry a reflection on his judgment.

I do not mean to create the impression that life in Inuttiaq's household during that first winter was continuous turmoil. There were many days, even weeks, when I, at least, felt the situation to be very peaceful and enjoyable. I was grateful for the warmth of my parents' company and care; it was good to feel that I belonged somewhere, that I was part of a family, even on a make-believe basis. But the rewards of my presence for Inuttiaq and his real family were of a different, and probably of a lesser, order. Because Inuttiaq's purchases in Gjoa Haven were supplemented by mine, our household was richer than others in store goods: tea, tobacco, flour, jam, dry milk, raisins, and kerosene. All the men made periodic trips to Gjoa Haven during the winter, to trade white fox skins for such store foods, but the amounts they bought were always quickly used up, so that periods of scarcity alternated regularly with the periods of plenty. Inuttiaq's household was the only one in which supplies were, on the whole, plentiful enough to last from trip to trip. But I am afraid that Inuttiaq's and Allaq's initial enthusiasm for material luxury may rather quickly have dampened in the face of the unanticipated difficulties that my presence created. And apart from these material benefits, and at first perhaps the novelty (and prestige?) of having a kapluna daughter, it is hard to see what Inuttiaq's family gained in return for the burden they carried. I played "Tavern in the Town" and "Santa Lucia" on my recorder; Inuttiaq enjoyed that and once in a while asked me to play for guests. I helped inefficiently in the mornings to remove the whitefish from the family nets and to drag them home, harnessed with Allaq to the sled. I assisted—erratically, as I have mentioned—with the other domestic chores; and in late winter, when the sun returned and Inuttiaq began again to jig for salmon trout, I usually fished with him. That is all that occurs to me, and a trivial contribution it must have been from my family's point of view.

It was hard for me to know at the time, however, just what their reactions to me were, because the tensions that existed were nearly all covert. It is characteristic of Utkuhiksalingmiut never to confront one another openly in irritation. Hostility is ignored or turned into a joke; at worst it becomes the subject of gossip behind the offender's back. I, too, did my best to smother my annoyance and frustration, but my attempts were not wholly successful. My training in self-control was less perfect than that of the Utkuhiksalingmiut, and at the same time the strains were greater than those I was accustomed to dealing with in my own world. Moreover, the most potentially gratifying of the outlets utilized by the Utkuhiksalingmiut—gossip—was not open to me as an anthropologist. I did my best to learn with the children when they were taught to turn annoyance into amusement, but laughter didn't come easily.

I knew that my feelings were not always perfectly concealed; the Utkuhiksalingmiut are acutely sensitive to subtle indications of mood. They heard the coldness in my voice when I said, "I don't understand," noted the length of a solitary walk I took across the tundra or the fact that I went to bed early and read with my back turned to the others. Later, Inuttiaq might give me a lecture—phrased, as always, in the most general terms—about the fate of those who lose their tempers: Satan uses them for firewood. Or he might offer me an especially choice bit of fish—whether to shame me or to appease me I don't know. The contrast between my irritability and the surface equanimity of others gave me many uncomfortable moments, but I persuaded myself that the effects of my lapses were short-lived. When I laughed again and heard others laugh with me, or when they seemed to accept the generous gestures with which I tried to make amends, I was reassured that no damage had been done. I was wrong. But it was only when I returned to Gjoa Haven on my way home a year later that I learned how severe the tensions had become between November and January of that first winter. Then the deacon's wife, Ikajuqtuq, told me of the report Inuttiaq had made of me in January when he went in to Gjoa Haven to trade: "She is not happy. She gets angry very easily, and I don't think she likes us any more."

At the time I was, as I have said, unaware how severe the tensions in our household had become. But shortly after Inuttiaq's return from Gjoa Haven in January, conflict did erupt into the open in an incident that illustrates clearly the nature of the tensions between us, and Utkuhiksalingmiut ways of handling such difficult and unprecedented situations.

The two weeks of Inuttiaq's absence in Gjoa Haven had been an especially trying period for me. I had looked forward to them as a much needed interlude in which to type and organize the swelling pile of penciled scrawls that filled my trouser pocket. When Inuttiaq was at home, it was often difficult to maintain the iglu temperature within the range of twenty-seven to thirty-one degrees at which typing was feasible. If I tried to type during the daylight hours of the morning, when the outdoor work was done, my fingers and carbon paper froze as a result of Inuttiaq's drafty comings and goings at jobs that seemed to necessitate propping the door open. But in the sociable afternoon and evening hours the snow dome dripped in the heat and occasionally deposited lumps of slush into my typewriter, and the iglu steamed so that my work was lost in a wet fog as a result of Inuttiaq's demands for tea, boiled fox, bannock, and soup in rapid succession. Allaq never initiated eating orgies, she never suggested that I interrupt my typing to make tea just when the temperature had arrived at twenty-eight, nor did she come and go through the door with such abandon as her husband or sit in the open door to drink her tea. Many were the frustrated moments when I heartily wished him gone; but it was only when he *was* gone that I discovered how completely our comfort depended on his presence. "When the men are away the iglus are cold," the women said; and it was true. The morning drafts that had plagued me before were nothing compared with the chill that resulted when nobody came and went at all. It was partly, of course, that Inuttiaq had taken with him one of our two primus stoves and one of the two kerosene storm lanterns, which ordinarily heated the iglu. But Allaq's behavior during her husband's absence intensified the cold. She never boiled fish, rarely brewed tea, and never lit the lamp to dry clothes— any of which activities would have warmed the iglu. She merely sat in her corner of the sleeping platform, blew on her hands, and remarked that the iglu was cold. It was; it was twenty degrees colder than when Inuttiaq was at home. I fretted and fumed in silent frustration and determined that when he came back I would take drastic steps to improve my working conditions.

I broached the subject to Inuttiaq a few days after his return to camp. He listened attentively to my explanation: I needed a place to work; it was difficult in the iglu; my fingers froze or the dome dripped or people wanted to sleep and I did not like to bother them. I told him that I had thought about going to live for a while in the empty wooden building that stood on a peninsula a few miles from camp. The government had built it as a nursing station, but it had never been used except by me as a cache for my useless belongings. It had a kerosene stove, which would make it luxuriously comfortable—unless the stove was as erratic as the similar stove in the similar nursing station in Gjoa Haven, with which I had once had an unfortunate experience. Inuttiaq agreed that the stove was unpredictable. Instead, he suggested that he take me to the nursing station every morning and fetch me again at night, so that I would not freeze. As often before, he reassured me: "Because you are alone here, you are someone to be taken care of." And, as often before, his solicitude warmed me. "Taking me to the nursing station every day will be a lot of work for you," I said. The round trip took an hour and a half by dog sled, not counting the time and effort involved in harnessing and unharnessing the team. He agreed that it would be a lot of work. "Could you perhaps build me a small iglu?" I asked. It seemed to me that this would be by far the least taxing alternative for him; it would take only an hour or two to build a tiny iglu near our own, which I could use as an "office"; then he need concern himself no further. Lulled by the assurance he had just given me of his desire to take care of me and by the knowledge that the request I made was not time-consuming, I was the more disagreeably startled when he replied with unusual vigor, "I build no iglus. I have to check the nets."

The rage of frustration seized me. He had not given me the true reason for his refusal. It only took two hours to check the nets every second or third day; on the other days, Inuttiaq did nothing at all except eat, drink, visit, and repair an occasional tool. He was offended—but why? I could not imagine. Perhaps he objected to my substituting for his suggestion one of my own, however considerately intended. Whether Inuttiaq read my face I do not know, but he softened his refusal immediately: "Shall Ipuituq or Qajaq"—he named two of the younger men—"build an iglu for you?" Perhaps it would be demeaning for a man of Inuttiaq's status, a mature householder, to build an iglu for a mere daughter. There was something in Inuttiaq's reaction that I did not understand, and a cautioning voice told me to contain my ethnocentric judgment and my anger. I thought of the small double-walled tent that I had brought with me for emergency use. It was stored in the nursing station. "They say my tent is very warm in winter," I said. Inuttiaq smoked silently. After a while he asked, "Shall they build you an iglu tomorrow?" My voice shook with exasperation: "Who knows?" I turned my head, rummaging—for nothing—in the knapsack that I kept beside my sleeping bag until the intensity of my feeling should subside.

Later, when Inuttiaq was smoking his last pipe in bed, I raised the subject again, my manner, I hoped, a successful facsimile of cheerfulness and firmness. "I would like to try the tent and see whether it's warm, as I have heard. We can bring it here, and then if it's not warm, I won't freeze; I'll come indoors." Allaq laughed, Inuttiaq accepted my suggestion, and I relaxed with relief, restored to real cheer by Inuttiaq's offer to fetch the tent from the nursing station the following day—if it stormed, so that he could not go on the trapping trip he had planned.

My cheer was premature. The next day Inuttiaq did not go trapping and he did not fetch the tent; he checked the nets. I helped without comment. The tent was not mentioned that day or the next, until in the evening, unable to contain myself longer, I asked Inuttiaq, in the most gracious voice I could muster, when he thought he might get my tent. "Tomorrow," he said. "You and Allaq will do it while I check the nets."

Morning arrived; the tent was mentioned in the breakfast conversation between Inuttiaq and Allaq. I could not catch the gist of the exchange, but when Inuttiaq inquired of a neighbor child who came in whether any of the young men of the camp were going near the nursing station that day and was told that they were not, I realized that once more the tent would not be brought. As usual, I was not informed of the decision. Had I been a good daughter, I would have trusted Inuttiaq to keep my interests in mind and to fetch my tent in his own time, when convenient opportunity arose. Unfortunately I did not trust Inuttiaq to do any such thing. The repeated delays had convinced me—whether rightly or wrongly, I do not know—that he had no intention of bringing me my tent.

My voice taut with exasperated resolve, I asked what the weather was like outside. I said nothing of my intention; nevertheless, I was surprised when Inuttiaq asked why I wanted to know. "Why?" was ordinarily a rude question; I was forced to ask it frequently myself in the course of my investigations, but I did not expect to be asked in turn. "Who knows why?" I replied. It was a rude evasion, and Inuttiaq said nothing but went out to check the nets. When I began to put on my fur clothing, Allaq too asked what I planned to do; I never wore my furs in the vicinity of camp. "I'm going to walk," I said more gently. I thought her inquiry was probably prompted by concern lest I wander off by myself and come to harm. I was too angry with Inuttiaq to consider that his inquiry might have been similarly motivated.

Like Inuttiaq, Allaq was silent when I evaded her question, and silently she set off for the nets. I went off in the direction of the nursing station, invisible on the horizon. I had no intention of fetching the tent myself—it would have been impossible; but I needed a few hours alone, and vaguely I knew that the direction of my walk would be to Inuttiaq a sign, however futile, that I was in earnest about my tent.

I knew it would be a sign, but I did not dream that he would respond as charitably as he did. I had just arrived at the nursing station and was searching among my few books for a novel to comfort me in my frustration, when I heard the squeak of sled runners on the snow outside and a familiar voice speaking to the dogs: "*Hooooo* [whoa]." Inuttiaq appeared in the doorway. I smiled. He smiled. "Will you want your tent?"

Gratitude and relief erased my anger as Inuttiaq picked up the tent and carried it to the sled. "You were walking," he said, in answer to my thanks. "I felt protective toward you."

It was a truce we had reached, however, not a peace, though I did not realize it at once. Since it was nearly dark when we reached camp, Inuttiaq laid the tent on top of the iglu for the night, to keep it from the dogs. The following morning I went with Inuttiaq to jig for trout up-river, and when we returned I thought that finally the time was ripe for setting up the tent.

Not wanting to push Inuttiaq's benevolence too far, and remembering the force of his response to my query about iglu building, I asked, "Shall I ask Ipuituq to help me put up my tent?" "Yes," said Inuttiaq. There was no warmth in his face; he did not smile, though he did tell me to keep my fur trousers on for warmth while I put up the tent. I obeyed, but the wind had risen while we drank our homecoming tea, so that even in fur trousers tent raising was not feasible that day or the next.

When the wind died two days later, Inuttiaq and I went fishing again, most companionably. Relations seemed so amicable, in fact, that this time on our return I was emboldened to say directly, without mention of Ipuituq, "I would like to put up my tent."

Naïvely, I thought that Inuttiaq would offer to help. He did not. His face was again unsmiling as he answered, "Put it up."

My anger was triggered again. "By myself?" I inquired rudely.

"Yes," said Inuttiaq, equally rudely.

"Thank you very much." I heard the coldness in my voice but did not try to soften it.

Inuttiaq, expressionless, looked at me for a moment, then summoned two young men who were nearby and who came, with a cheer that was in marked contrast to his own manner, to help me set up the tent.

Inuttiaq's attitude toward the raising of the tent puzzled me. I failed to understand why he resisted the plan, unless he thought it ridiculous to set up a tent in winter. I think now that he did consider it foolish, not only because of the frigid temperatures, but also because of the winds, which can have relentless force in January.

But it seems to me now that more was at stake than the feasibility of the project. Inuttiaq was personally affronted by my request. One clue to his reaction I find in a question that I hardly heard at the time. He had wanted to know, after the tent was up, whether I planned to sleep in it or only to work there, and I think he may have felt that my demand for a tent was a sign that I was dissatisfied with him as a father, with his concern for my welfare. He may also have considered an offense against his dignity the suggestion that he himself set up the tent. The thought crossed my mind even at the time, when he substituted younger assistants for himself; but in other seasons, when moving was the order of the day, Inuttiaq readily helped to raise my tent.

I cannot know Inuttiaq's thought, but in retrospect I see so many reasons why he might have opposed my wish that I am no longer astonished that he did resist it. I am surprised only by the extent to which he remained protective throughout the whole episode, while obviously intensely opposed to my wish. Perhaps in part the protective actions were a shield for the hostile feelings, making it possible for Inuttiaq to convince himself that he

was conforming to Utkuhiksalingmiut values of helpfulness and obligingness. Or perhaps—as I believe—he really did feel both protective and
hostile toward me simultaneously. It is possible that his outrage at my
exorbitant demand was due in part precisely to the fact that he knew himself to be a good father to me. In any case, his behavior was a curious blend
of opposites. He chose the site for my tent with care, correcting my own
choice with a more practiced eye to prowling dogs and prevailing wind. He
offered advice on heating the tent, and he filled my primus stove so that it
would be ready for me to use when my two assistants and I had finished
setting the tent up. And when I moved my writing things out of his iglu, he
told me that if I liked, I might write instead of going fishing. "If I catch a
fish, you will eat," he assured me. But he turned his back on the actual
raising of the tent and went home to eat and drink tea.

On the following day I saw his displeasure in another form. It was
Sunday morning and storming; our entrance was buried under drifting
snow. Since there could be no church service, Inuttiaq and Allaq had each,
separately and in mumbling undertones, read a passage from the Bible.
Then Inuttiaq began to read from the prayerbook the story of creation, and
he asked if I would like to learn. I agreed, the more eagerly because I
feared that he had perceived my skepticism toward his religious beliefs and
that this was another hidden source of conflict between us. He lectured me
at length. The story of creation was followed by the story of Adam and Eve
(whose sin was responsible for the division of mankind into kaplunas and
Eskimos), and this story was in turn followed by an exposition of proper
Christian behavior: the keeping of the Sabbath—and of one's temper.
"God is loving," said Inuttiaq, "but only to believers. Satan is angry.
People will go to heaven only if they do not get angry or answer back when
they are scolded." He told me that one should not be attached to earthly
belongings, as I was: "Only God's word should make one feel longing."
Most striking of all was the way Inuttiaq ended his sermon to me. "Naklirohuktuq made me king of the Utkuhiksalingmiut," he said. "He wrote
that to me. He told me that if people—including you—don't want to
believe what I tell them, and don't want to learn about Christianity, then I
should write to him, and he will come quickly. If people don't want to
believe Naklirohuktuq either, then a bigger leader, a kapluna, the king in
Cambridge Bay [the government center for the Central Arctic], will come
in a plane with a big and well-made whip and will whip people. It will hurt a
lot."

Much of this I had heard before, but this version was more dramatic
than previous ones. It made me see, more clearly than I had before, something of Inuttiaq's view of kaplunas generally. I heard the hostility directed
against myself, as well, but again he had softened the latter by blending it

with warmth, in the manner that I found so confusing. He knew that I believed in God, he said, because I helped people, I gave things to people—not just to one or two, which God doesn't want, but to everybody.

The rest of the winter, for a wonder, passed more peacefully, at least on the surface. Partly, I think, this was because I spent a great deal of time closeted in my tent, typing up the notes that had accumulated during the months when conditions in the iglu had prohibited typing. In part the more peaceful atmosphere was also due to the fact that Inuttiaq almost never again permitted his own hostility to emerge so overtly against me. In a flash of the eye; in a silence; in a comment unintelligible to me, at which Allaq laughed; in a surreptitious glance toward a visitor who remained expressionless—in these I saw, or imagined I saw, irritation or disapproval; but the explosions, which still occasionally occurred, were all mine, and Inuttiaq's restraint in the face of them was extraordinary. Most often he was silent; sometimes he offered me something to eat; occasionally he reassured me that I was cared for; and occasionally, as before, he lectured me.

The more even flow of daily life and occasional warm gestures—expressions of gratitude for my material help and the gift of a puppy for the duration of my stay (because all members of a family should own a dog)—lulled me into believing that the hostile feelings that had infected the air earlier in the winter had been forgotten and convinced me that the tensions that I continued to spark from time to time were momentary flashes without lasting effect. I am no longer sure that my peace of mind was justified. In retrospect, it seems to me possible that those warm acts were neither rewards for improved behavior on my part nor evidence of a generous willingness to accept me in spite of my thorny qualities, but, rather, attempts to extract or blunt some of the thorns. I think my Eskimo parents may have hoped that the same techniques of pacification and reassurance that throughout the winter had soothed crises away might also serve to prevent difficulties from arising. If I knew I was cared for, I might not get angry so easily. I thought I heard similar logic in the admonition Inuttiaq once in a while gave his six-year-old daughter when she sulked: "Stop crying, you are loved." Another possible motive may have been a desire to shame me, by virtuous example, into reforming. Perhaps these kind acts even had the effect of nullifying Inuttiaq's and Allaq's own prickly feelings, permitting them to prove to themselves that—as Inuttiaq once said—they didn't get angry, only I did.

But whatever the interpretation of these incidents, it is clear to me now that there remained more of an undercurrent of tension in my relationship with Inuttiaq and Allaq than I perceived at the time. I began to suspect its presence in the spring, when our iglu melted and I moved—at Inuttiaq's orders—back into my own tent; Allaq almost never visited me, as she had done in the first days after my arrival in Chantrey Inlet. More important, these winter tensions, I think, added their residue of hostility to a crisis situation that developed at the end of the summer. This crisis introduced a new phase in my relations not merely with Inuttiaq and Allaq, but with all the other Utkuhiksalingmiut as well—a phase in which I ceased to be treated as an educable child and was instead treated as an incorrigible offender, who had unfortunately to be endured but who could not be incorporated into the social life of the group.

The crisis was brought about by the visit to Chantrey Inlet of a party of kapluna sports fishermen. Every July and August in recent years Chantrey Inlet has been visited by sportsmen from the provinces and from the United States, who charter bush planes from private sports airlines and fly up to the Arctic for a week's fishing. Every year the sportsmen who come to Chantrey Inlet ask permission to borrow the Eskimos' canoes. These canoes were given to the Utkuhiksalingmiut by the Canadian government after the famine of 1958 and are indispensable to the present economy of the Eskimos. In 1958 the disappearance of the caribou herds from the Chantrey Inlet area forced the Eskimos to begin to rely much more completely on fish than they had formerly done. In consequence they had to accumulate and store quantities of fish during seasons when they were plentiful; to facilitate this procedure, the government introduced fish nets and canoes. Originally there had been six canoes, one for each of the Utkuhiksalingmiut families, but by the time I arrived in Chantrey Inlet only two of these remained in usable condition.

The first parties that came asked, through me, if they might borrow both canoes, and the Utkuhiksalingmiut, who for various reasons rarely if ever refuse such requests, had acquiesced, at some cost to themselves. They sat stranded on the shore, unable to fish; unable to fetch the occasional bird that they shot on the water; unable to fetch a resupply of sugar for their tea from the cache on the nearby island; and worst of all, perhaps, unable to visit the odd strangers who were camped out of sight across the river. Ultimately these kaplunas left and were replaced by another group, which asked to borrow only one canoe. But relief was short-lived; trolling up and down the unfamiliar river in the late twilight, the kaplunas were unfortunate enough to run the canoe on a rock and tear a large hole in the canvas, whereupon they returned that canoe and announced to the men through sign language that, since the boat was unusable, they were now obliged to borrow the other: Inuttiaq's. When I arrived on the scene, the kaplunas were attaching their outboard to the canoe, as Inuttiaq and the other Utkuhiksalingmiut men watched.

I exploded. Unsmilingly and in a cold voice I told the kaplunas' guide a variety of things that I thought he should know: that if he borrowed the second canoe we would be without a fishing boat; that if this boat also was damaged, we would be in a very difficult position, since a previous guide had forgotten to bring the repair materials that Inuttiaq had traded for; and that we would be unable to buy materials ourselves until the strait froze in November. I also pointed out the island where our supplies of tea, sugar, and kerosene were cached and mentioned our inability to reach it except by canoe. Then, armed with the memory that Inuttiaq had earlier, before the arrival of this party of kaplunas, instructed me in vivid language never again to allow anyone to borrow his canoe, I told the kaplunas that the owner of that second canoe did not wish to lend it.

The kapluna guide was not unreasonable; he agreed at once that the loan of the boat was the owner's option: "It's his canoe, after all." Slightly mollified, I turned to Inuttiaq who stood nearby, expressionless like the other Utkuhiksalingmiut. "Do you want me to tell him you don't want to lend your canoe?" I asked in Eskimo. "He will not borrow it if you say you don't want to lend it."

Inuttiaq's expression dismayed me, but I didn't know how to read it; I knew only that it registered strong feeling, as did his voice, which was unusually loud: "Let him have his will!"

That incident brought to a head months of uneasiness on the part of the Utkuhiksalingmiut concerning my volatility. I had spoken unbidden and in anger; that much the Eskimos knew. The words they couldn't understand, but it didn't matter; the anger itself was inexcusable. The punishment was ostracism. So subtly was it expressed, however, that I didn't at first realize my situation. My work seemed somehow more difficult than usual, I felt tired and depressed—"bushed" perhaps, I thought—in need of a vacation. Visitors seemed to come less frequently to my tent; when they did come, they looked in, smiled, and moved on instead of coming in to chat; but I thought that was because they saw I was busy with my notes, and on the whole I was glad to be left with my thoughts. When I did go out to sit with the others on the beach, I was welcomed with smiles, as always. And I would have continued to think that my difficulties were all of my own imagining had I not come into possession of a letter that Allaq's father, Pala, had written to the deacon, Naklirohuktuq, the day after the kaplunas left. Pala had intended to send it out on the plane that was daily expected to come and pick up the schoolchildren; he had kept it for a time, but then—fearing that when the plane finally came, he would forget the letter—he had given it to me to hold along with my own correspondence. The letter was in syllabics, of course; in an amoral spirit I decided to read it, to test my skill in reading Eskimo. I did not anticipate the contents: "Yiini [that was my name] lied to the kaplunas. She gets angry very easily. She ought not to be here studying Eskimos. She is very annoying; she scolds more and more and gets angry easily. Because she is so annoying, we wish more and more that she would leave."

So there was a reason why my work was going poorly! And my low spirits were not all due to my long isolation from my own world and my mailless summer, as I had thought. I was shocked at the drastic effect of my "righteous" outburst to the kaplunas and perhaps even more shocked that in the week and a half since the event I had noticed no change in the habitually warm, friendly, considerate behavior of the Utkuhiksalingmiut. Now, watching more closely, I did see, or thought I saw, minute signs that told me how I was regarded. Now and then one of the warm smiles seemed a little dimmer than usual, the answer to a question a little shorter or more evasive. And in subtle ways it seemed that I was being encouraged to stay in my tent. By faithfully bringing me tea every time it was brewed, the others forestalled my coming to drink it with them outdoors or in their tents, and they did not invite me to join them as they used to do. But so covert were these small withdrawals that I was never quite sure whether I was imagining them.

It was in October, when the autumn iglus were built, that the change in the Eskimos' feelings really became apparent. I was not at all sure that Inuttiaq would invite me to move in with his family again as he had done the year before, but I need not have worried; his hostility did not take such a crass form. However, the quality of life in the iglu was in striking contrast with the previous year. Whereas then Inuttiaq's iglu had been the social center of the camp, now family and visitors congregated next door, in Allaq's father's iglu. Inuttiaq and Allaq—the children too—spent the better part of every day at Pala's. Even in the early mornings, when the family woke, and at night when we were preparing for bed, I was isolated. It was as though I were not there. If I made a remark to Inuttiaq or Allaq, the person addressed responded with his usual smile, but I had to initiate almost all communication. As a rule, if I did not speak, no one spoke to me. If I offered to fetch water or make tea (which I seldom did) my offer was usually accepted, but no one ever asked me to perform these services. The pointedness of this avoidance was driven home one day when we were cooking. I do not recall what was being made or who had initiated the cooking; I think it likely that I had done so, since the primus stood on the floor in front of me, instead of in its usual place near Allaq. Nevertheless, when the pressure began to run down, unnoticed by me, Inuttiaq turned not to me but to Allaq: "Pump up the primus." And she had to get up and come over to my side of the iglu to pump up the stove. Had he spoken to me, I would only have had to lean over to do it. Too late I realized the dignity inherent in the Utkuhiksalingmiut pattern of authority, in which the woman is obedient to the man. I envied Allaq the satisfaction of knowing that she was appreciated because she did well and docilely what Inuttiaq told her to do.

Invisible as I felt in the iglu, the other occupants gave evidence that they found my presence, however walled off I was by our mutual silence, extremely irritating. One day, about a week after we had moved into the autumn iglus, Inuttiaq even suggested that when we moved into winter iglus later on, I should be physically walled off to a degree. Often when Utku-hiksalingmiut build their permanent winter iglus, they attach to one side a small chamber, called a *hiqluaq,* in which to store the fish they net. The hiqluaq opens into the interior of the iglu by way of a hole just big enough to crawl through. Inuttiaq's idea was to build such a chamber for me to live in; after I left, he would use it in the orthodox manner, for fish storage.

But in spite of all these tensions, I was still treated with the most impeccable semblance of solicitude. I was amazed that it should be so—that although my company was anathema, nevertheless people still took care to give me plentiful amounts of the foods I liked best, to warn me away from thin ice, and to caution me when my nose began to freeze. The Utku-hiksalingmiut saw themselves—and wanted me to see them—as virtuously solicitous, no matter what provocations I might give them to be otherwise. Allaq's sister expressed this ethos of concern explicitly in a letter to Ikajuqtuq in Gjoa Haven: "Because she is a kapluna and a woman, we have tried to be good to her here, and though she is sometimes very annoying . . . we still try to help her."

It was at the end of August that the incident with the kapluna fishermen occurred, and it was the end of November before I was finally able to explain myself to the Utkuhiksalingmiut. I had wanted from the beginning, of course, to confront them with an explanation of my behavior, but I had feared that such un-Eskimo directness would only shock them the more. Instead, I had written my version of the story to Ikajuqtuq, had told her about my attempt to protect the Utkuhiksalingmiut from the impositions of the kaplunas, and had asked her if she could help to explain my behavior to the Eskimos. My letter went out to Gjoa Haven, along with Pala's, when the school plane came in September. Unfortunately there was no way in which Ikajuqtuq could reply until the strait froze in November, enabling the men to make the long trip out to Gjoa Haven to trade. But when Inuttiaq, accompanied as usual by Allaq's brother, Mannik, finally went out, they brought back from the deacon and his wife a response that surpassed my most sanguine expectations. Inuttiaq reported to his family: "Naklirohuk-tuq says that the kaplunas almost shot us when Yiini wasn't there." The exaggeration was characteristic of Inuttiaq's lurid style of fantasy. He turned to me: "Did you write that to Naklirohuktuq?" I denied it—and later, in Gjoa Haven, Naklirohuktuq denied having made such a statement to Inuttiaq—but I did confirm the gist of Inuttiaq's report: that I had tried to protect the Eskimos. I described what it was that I had written to Ikajuqtuq, and I explained something of the reasons for my anger at the kaplunas.

The effect was magical. The wall of ice that had stood between me and the community suddenly disappeared. I became consultant on the moral qualities of fishing guides; people talked to me voluntarily, offered me vocabulary, included me in their jokes and in their anecdotes of the day's activities; and Inuttiaq informed me that the following day he and I were going fishing. Most heart-warming of all is the memory of an afternoon soon after the men had returned. The iglu was filled with visitors, and the hum of the primus on which tea was brewing mingled with the low voices of Inuttiaq and his guests. I knew every detail of the scene even as I bent over my writing, and I paid no attention until suddenly my mind caught on the sound of my name: "I consider Yiini a member of my family again." Was that what Inuttiaq had said? I looked up, inquiring. "I consider you a family member again," he repeated. His diction was clear, as it was only when he wanted to be sure that I understood. And he called me "daughter," as he had not done since August.

Not that I had suddenly become a wholly acceptable housemate; that could never be. I was not and could never become an Utkuhiksalingmiutaq, nor could I ever be a "daughter" to Inuttiaq and Allaq as they understood that role. Inuttiaq made this quite clear one day about this time, when we were both sitting, silently working, in the iglu. "I think you're a leader in your country," he said suddenly. The remark had no obvious context; it must mean, I thought, that he had never reconciled himself to my intractable behavior. There was also the slightly wild look that I caught in his eye when I said I thought that I might someday return to Chantrey Inlet. The look vanished when Allaq explained that I meant to return after I had been to my own country, not merely to Gjoa Haven. "Yes," he said then; "we will adopt you again—or others may want to: Nilaak, perhaps—or Mannik, if he marries." And later, when we were talking about the possibility of other "learners" coming to Chantrey Inlet, Inuttiaq said, "We would be happier to have a woman come than a man—a woman like you, who doesn't want to be a wife. Maybe *you* are the only acceptable kapluna."

But it was the letters that Allaq and Inuttiaq wrote me when I left Chantrey Inlet in January that expressed most vividly and succinctly what it meant to them to have a kapluna daughter. They both said, "I didn't think I'd care when you left, but I did."

In very abbreviated form, then, this is the story of the relationship between an Eskimo "father" and "mother" and their kapluna "daughter." In some respects the story is specific to the personalities involved. I have not dwelt here on matters of personality, but they were important. Had the anthropologist been more amenable to direction, or her adoptive father less personally affronted by resistance to his authority, much of the conflict of wills might have been avoided. Tension might have been less severe, too, if each person had been less perceptive of the moods, the unspoken reactions, of the other.

In other respects the course of events was determined by the contrast between specifically Utkuhiksalingmiut or Eskimo values on the one hand and kapluna behavior and values on the other hand. Whereas in the New England culture in which I grew up the direct expression of ill feeling is per-mitted, albeit to a limited extent, in the Utkuhiksalingmiut view to lose one's temper or even to admit and try to explain the existence of bad feeling under any circumstances is deplorable. A good person is con-sistently warm, protective, and concerned for others; hostility, when it exists, is concealed under cover of the most impeccable concern (perhaps even more impeccable than usual). So strong is this ethic that even when hostility is expressed, it may appear on the surface as protectiveness: "You can't come fishing with me because you'll hurt yourself on the sharp rocks."

But in still other respects the story of Inuttiaq, Allaq, and Yiini may have implications applicable to relationships between anthropologists and their hosts elsewhere, and in conclusion I should like to raise a few ques-tions concerning these more general implications.

These speculations concern the process by which a resident foreigner is incorporated into the conceptual world of his hosts and in turn learns the role or roles assigned to him. The relationships between an anthropologist and his hosts are in some respects like all other human relationships. They are not static but dynamic, and their development can be viewed as a process of progressive conceptualization. Both parties are continually at-tempting to interpret and predict (and in the case of the hosts, perhaps, to mold) the behavior of the other. But I think we sometimes forget, when talking about anthropologists in the field, that the conceptualization prob-lems are not all on the side of the anthropologist.

I observed three more or less distinct phases in the Utkuhiksalingmiut's view of me. During the first period I was a stranger and a guest, and I was treated with the formal courtesy and deference that the Utkuhiksalingmiut ordinarily accord to such persons. I was referred to as a kapluna, a white person, and addressed by my personal name—"Yiini" in the Eskimos' speech. Much of the time during this period the Eskimos must have been at a loss what to make of my behavior, and often when I did something that under other circumstances they might have defined as reprehensible—when

I went to bed early, nursing a bad humor, or when I was silent in depression—they gave me the benefit of the doubt; they asked me if I were tired and considerately lessened my work load or withdrew so that I might "sleep."

Gradually, however, this first phase gave way to a second, in which my immediate family (though not others in the community) treated me in some respects as a daughter and a child. My parents replaced the name "Yiini" with the term "daughter" when speaking, and sometimes when referring, to me, and my two small sisters called me "elder sister." Inuttiaq—though never Allaq—also began to use the imperative forms of speech that he used in addressing his other daughters and his wife. Even an appropriate age was invented for me: I had to be younger than Allaq—if only by one season—though all the evidence pointed to my being in fact slightly older than she was. Both parents directed my daily activities, and I was expected to obey them as a daughter should. When I did not, efforts were made to teach me better behavior through lecturing or shaming, the former a technique that was otherwise only used in teaching small children. My moodiness was no longer interpreted charitably, and efforts were made to educate me out of that behavior, too.

Categorization of me as a "child" was probably determined by a combination of factors: I had introduced myself as one who wanted to "learn" from the Utkuhiksalingmiut, and I had asked to be adopted as a "daughter"; I was also obviously ignorant of Utkuhiksalingmiut proprieties and skills. The fact that I am a woman may also have facilitated my categorization as a child in several respects. For one thing, among the Utkuhiksalingmiut a woman's technical skill—skin sewing—is very difficult to learn. I never mastered more than the most rudimentary, clumsy stitching; my work was so poor that when I mended my skin boots, Allaq considered it necessary to redo the job. Moreover, in order to be considered properly adult, a woman must have children, and I had none. For these reasons the role of an adult woman was virtually closed to me, whereas had I been a man, I might have earned an adult role as a fisherman and hunter, as some male kaplunas who have lived among Eskimos appear to have done.

There is another way, too, in which my femininity may have facilitated classification as a child. Since children everywhere are characterized by behavior that is more uncontrolledly expressive than that of adults, any kind of expressiveness, any absence of restraint, that is foreign to one's own patterns is, I think, likely to be perceived as childish, provided certain conditions are met. The adult must be perceived as not knowing, rather than as deliberately flouting, the correct patterns (as a criminal would do); he must be perceived as capable of learning proper behavior (unlike a mentally defective person); and, in the Eskimo case, his lack of restraint must be perceived as harmless and inconsequential, even though unpleasant.[2] The fact that I am a woman and thus physically unthreatening may have made it easier for the Utkuhiksalingmiut to view my ill temper, as I think they did, like that of a child. Had I been a man, I think they might have seen my temper as dangerous, even potentially lethal—anything but childish.

The third phase, in which I was treated as an incorrigible offender, replaced the "child" phase, I think, when it became apparent to the Utkuhiksalingmiut that I was uneducable. Inuttiaq no longer lectured me or used any other method to teach me. I was called "Yiini" again instead of "daughter," and daughterly services were no longer asked of me. In fact, nothing at all was asked of me. Though my physical needs for warmth, food, and protection from danger were still taken care of, socially I was simply "not there." There was one other person in the community who was similarly ostracized: a woman of about my age, who appeared to be of subnormal intelligence. Almost all of her personal qualities—her imperfect speech, clumsy gestures, and domestic incompetence—were subject to comment behind her back, but hostility in her case, as in mine, centered on her volatility—the fact that she was easily upset and was unable to exercise proper restraint in the expression of her feelings. She too was considered uneducable, and I am sure that, like her, I was privately labeled "simple-minded."

In more general terms the sequence of judgments passed on me seemed to be: strange; educable; uneducable in important ways. And each phase, each judgment, was associated with a role familiar to the Utkuhiksalingmiut: stranger; child; simpleton—each role being identifiable in terms of the way I was addressed; the kinds of behavior that were expected of me; the interpretations placed on my misbehavior; and the methods used to control that misbehavior.

In other cases, too, it has happened that native hypotheses concerning the reasons for the anthropologist's unfamiliar behavior have caused the anthropologist to be assigned to certain roles. A vivid example is that of Bowen among the Tiv (Bowen, 1954). The "offender" category in which she was ultimately placed was that of witch rather than that of idiot. However, phases such as I have described need not necessarily occur sequentially; the anthropologist may be judged at one and the same time educable in certain respects, uneducable in others. Neither is it necessarily the case that judgments passed on the anthropologist's behavior will classify him as playing a particular role in the community. Judgments of educability or uneducability, for example, could logically be aspects of any role.

2. This analysis is based in part on Wallace's (1961, p. 135) analysis of the differences between the behavior of the psychotic, the mentally deficient, the foreign, and the criminal. He does not mention children.

Such considerations lead to interesting theoretical questions concerning the selection of a role or roles for the anthropologist. Under what circumstances will he be assigned a role out of his own cultural repertoire: nurse, missionary, government officer; and under what circumstances will a native role or roles be chosen? What kinds of cues in his behavior are attended to? And a related question: In respect to which kinds of behavior is he going to be expected to conform to native standards, and in which respects will his foreignness serve as a legitimate excuse for deviant behavior?

In the event that the anthropologist is assigned a native role, what determines the selection? The choice cannot be automatic, since the anthropologist, as a foreigner, is inevitably an anomaly from the native point of view. He will probably rarely possess all the critical attributes of any category of persons, and therefore when a category or role is chosen, some of his personal attributes may have to be manipulated in order to improve the fit. Parenthetically, observation of the nature of such manipulation should give us insight into the critical attributes of the category. In my case, when I was defined as a daughter, my graying hair was ignored, my age was denied, and kinship status was invented for me that related me to all members of the community.

But even when his attributes have been appropriately altered, the anthropologist will still almost certainly be seen as only a quasi-member of the category. Perhaps he will be considered simultaneously a member of two or more categories that are ordinarily mutually exclusive, such as adult and child or kapluna and daughter. In my case, even though attempts were made to improve the fit between my attributes and the "adopted daughter" category to which I was assigned, I was nevertheless only partially a daughter. For example, Inuttiaq always explained his protectiveness toward me in terms of the fact that I was "a woman and alone," not in terms of the fact that I was his adopted daughter. And I expect that such complex situations are the rule.

What are the consequences of the anthropologist's anomalous situation for his role playing? Although an anthropologist must have a recognized role or roles for the local population to interact with him sensibly and predictably, it will nevertheless be evident from what I have described of my own case that the assignment of a role—especially a native role?—may create as many problems as it solves for both the anthropologist and his hosts. Such problems may be of various kinds. Here I shall limit my remarks to questions concerning the definition and learning of the role.

In my case, the role of daughter was one that was familiar to me in my own culture, and I think it was precisely this fact that was responsible for much of the misunderstanding between my Eskimo parents and me. The label was the same in both cultures, but the proper behavior was quite different; daughterly behavior to me was not at all what Inuttiaq thought of as "daughterly" behavior. Similarly, my notions of proper "fatherly" behavior did not at all coincide with Inuttiaq's ideas. But neither of us initially—and I think Inuttiaq never—fully realized this fact.

One implication of the failure to recognize that two different definitions of the "same" role are theoretically possible is that the existence of such a different definition will be unavailable as an explanation for aberrant role behavior. Instead, any quirks of behavior are likely to be attributed to defective personality. This, I think, is precisely the conclusion Inuttiaq reached concerning me—not at once, but ultimately. As I see it, the difficulties in our relationship took the following course.

1. When Inuttiaq undertook to adopt me, he assumed that I would naturally behave as he was accustomed to having daughters behave. To him, "fatherliness" and "daughterliness" in the Utkuhiksalingmiut sense constituted the natural order of the world. He knew, of course, that as a kapluna I was ignorant of the Eskimo skills that adult daughters have usually mastered, but it is easier to recognize cross-cultural differences in technology and language than differences in the structuring of interpersonal relations; one is far more inclined to think of the latter as given in "human nature."

2. Inuttiaq was wrong, of course, in assuming that my behavior would be that of an Utkuhiksalingmiut daughter. Consequently his first hypothesis was replaced by a second, which I have mentioned: that kaplunas don't (or Yiini doesn't) know how to behave correctly but can learn. Here the underlying assumption may well have been that I was a *tabula rasa*; I only needed his instruction in order to be able to learn. But he was wrong again. For various reasons, none of which were, I think, recognized by Inuttiaq, I didn't learn easily. The first reason why learning must be difficult is that the intruder faces a double task. On the one hand he must discover what has to be learned—that is, what exactly is wrong with his "normal" behavior and what the proper behavior should be. And on the other hand he must overcome resistance to doing what is required—resistance caused by the interference of his old patterns of role behavior. Such interference may be expected to be particularly marked when the role to be learned bears the same name ("daughter") as a role one is accustomed to playing in one's own culture.

Learning will also be difficult and imperfect because the anthropologist is not completely committed to the role he is playing vis-à-vis his hosts. He is simultaneously playing other roles derived from his culture: "medical assistant," perhaps; "charitable person"; and not least, "anthropologist." His professional role especially places demands on him that at times cannot help but conflict with the role he is assigned in the community. He must try to learn all kinds of facts about the community, many of which it may be inappropriate for someone in his assumed native role to know. He must try to maintain sufficient distance from the culture he is studying and from himself so that he can record "objectively" and, hopefully, use his reactions to his experiences as sources of data. And he must try to record and participate simultaneously. The latter problem has been amply illustrated in my case as I have described it above.

3. It was because of these difficulties and others that Inuttiaq's second hypothesis—that I was educable—proved to a large extent wrong. And so he arrived at his third hypothesis (shared, as I have said, by the rest of the community), to the effect that I was a defective person: "bad" and "simpleminded."

This analysis of the relationship between my Eskimo family and me is, of course, far from complete. It is, I repeat, obvious that difficulties of conceptualization are only some of the problems that beset relationships of any kind. It is obvious also that most relationships—and the one described here is no exception—have strongly positive features as well, or they would cease to exist. As for the more general issues of anthropological role playing, the account that I have presented here may serve as a basis for comparison with the experiences of others.

References

BOWEN, ELENORE SMITH. 1954. *Return to Laughter.* New York: Harper & Row.
WALLACE, ANTHONY F. C. 1961. "The Psychic Unity of Human Groups." In Kaplan, Bert (ed.), *Studying Personality Cross-Culturally.* New York: Harper & Row.

Exploring American Indian Communities in Depth

LAURA THOMPSON derives her knowledge of American Indians from her field work with the Papago, Hopi, Navaho, Zuni, and Sioux. She has also studied the Lauans of Fiji, the Chamorros of Guam, and the Icelanders, all in their homelands. Now living in Hawaii, she is writing a book on her experiences and development as a woman anthropologist in the twentieth-century world. Her books include FIJIAN FRONTIER, GUAM AND ITS PEOPLE, THE HOPI WAY *(with Alice Joseph), and* THE SECRET OF CULTURE.

M y initiation into work with American Indians was quite accidental. And yet it developed into what probably has been the most significant professional experience of my life.

Of course, there can never again be anything like one's first field trip. Mine was to Lau, Fiji, at a time (1933–1934) when merely the mechanics of transportation from Suva to the remote eastern islands took weeks. Without access to medical aid, without mail, radio, or telephone, without any communication with the outside world or between islands except by native sailing canoe, an anthropologist could either sink or swim. But regardless of how much I learned about the culture of southern Lau with tools acquired by years of professional training, I felt a certain inadequacy in the actual field situation. Almost immediately I sensed at work in the community forces that I was not equipped to fathom. How can one explore the hidden dimensions of a culture, its invisible persisting ethos? What about the "psychology" of the group? I knew then that somehow I must find a way to gain greater insight into the covert meaning of observed behavior.

The opportunity did not arise for almost a decade. Meanwhile, through travel and field work in Nazi Germany, Guam, Japan, and Hawaii, I had become very much concerned about the growing power and popularity of dictatorships in the world. How could democratic institutions be protected and fostered?

By early 1941 my experiences in Europe and the Orient had convinced me that the United States would soon be drawn into war in the Pacific as well as in Europe. I expected that shortly the Japanese would not only attack but also land on Oahu. It now appears that they could have done so immediately after Pearl Harbor. But my countrymen seemed oblivious to the threat. In Honolulu no one would listen. "You are too near the problem," my friends asserted.

An anthropologist doing field work in Germany, Guam, Japan, and

47

Honolulu in 1934–1941 was near the problem all right, I thought; but was I too near? So I cashed in my savings and set out for Washington. Still no one paid any heed—no one, that is, except the Commissioner of Indian Affairs. This seemed surprising until I gave the situation some thought.

The "Indian problem" during the 1930's and 1940's

Actually, as others have noted, the United States Indian Service during the 1930's and early 1940's resembled a government in microcosm, with virtually all the problems of a small nation. In fact, reservation Indians at that time numbered about 420,000—a larger population than many small nations have today. The Bureau was empowered to cope with the political organization, law, economy, education, and health of its Indian constituents. It had to handle human-relations problems involving differing degrees of authority between Washington and the field, regarding some 150 tribes in 27 states. And it had to deal with the relations between each tribe and its non-Indian neighbors, as well as between the several communities and individuals within a tribe.

Classed as wards of the United States, most of the tribes were related to the federal government by treaty, rather than in the manner of other American minorities. Thus the Indian Service actually represented a government within a government, with congress in the role of final authority. Each of the tribes comprising the Bureau's clientele had its own distinctive institutions and culture, only partly obscured by recent changes. Thus the Indian Service might be conceived as a federal bureau responsible for structuring complex cross-cultural relationships among semi-independent political units.

But no precedent or conceptual model existed in America for this type of semi-autonomous minority-group relationship. On the contrary, for more than a century Indian affairs had been handled in the manner of a dictatorship. Despite treaty obligations, reservation Indians remained outside the United States Constitution until they gained American citizenship in 1924. Even then they were inadequately protected by statute law.

To overcome historical precedent and political inertia, to design a plan of voluntary reorganization for each tribe in relation to Washington, and to implement the plan without pressure or coercion in hundreds of local Indian communities, all required considerable political acumen, legal sophistication, and devotion to the democratic ideal. In the early 1930's this problem had attracted a group of brilliant and dedicated men to the Indian Service: Carson Ryan, Felix Cohen, Walter Woehlke, Ward Shepard, Willard Beatty, and others, under the leadership of Commissioner John Collier. All were profoundly aware of the dangers of dictatorship to the civil liberties of American citizens. These men formulated and, as far as possible, implemented a community-centered policy and program for American Indians. The policy, known as the Indian New Deal, was embodied in law, mainly the Wheeler-Howard Act of 1934.

But there is many a slip 'twixt policy and implementation. How could one be sure that the new policy was a "good" policy—good for the Indians, that is? After eight years of work under the New Deal, the Indian Service group in Washington decided that a comprehensive and objective evaluation of policy and program was needed. Could such questions be answered through the methods of science? It was decided to find out by means of an independent interdisciplinary research project.

The Indian Service situation in the early 1940's represented what is now called a "natural experiment." Both the new and the old policies, including changes in the legal status of individual Indians and of Indian communities, were explicitly stated in numerous documents. The extent of implementation of change at the community level, compared to the situation before the New Deal, could be studied clinically in the field by anthropologists, social scientists, and psychologists. Physical and mental health, community welfare, nutrition, educational aims and achievements, and resources conservation, before and after the change, could be compared. Out of such questioning and thinking was born the Indian Education Research Project (Collier, 1945).

A multidiscipline project

I had left Washington and was studying human development at the University of Chicago when I was asked to serve as coordinator of the project. It seemed a ready-made opportunity for experience of the kind I was seeking. I could not think of a more ideal way to learn how to understand culture and personality in depth than by actually engaging in multidisciplinary field research. The "dictatorship problem" was also involved in this policy-evaluation project.

To insure its scientific integrity and to guard against political pressures, the project was sponsored and financed by the Department of the Interior but was contracted to the University of Chicago's Committee on Human Development. Two research committees were organized: an Indian Bureau Committee, whose function was to facilitate the research, and a Chicago Committee to design, implement, and report on it.

We started in September 1941. Within a few months the country was at war. Most experienced male anthropologists and many women were drafted into war work. Except for military-sponsored projects, anthropological field research was severely curtailed. Yet, despite the war, we thought that the Indians had to be administered to and their problems resolved. And we considered that more knowledge and understanding of "democratic" versus "authoritarian" programs was badly needed, especially at the grass-roots level. Although handicapped by loss of staff personnel and by shortages of equipment and gasoline (and later, the paper on which to publish the findings), we pushed the project ahead. As in other sectors of life at home and abroad, women carried on, and that is how the Indian Education Project happened to be "manned" to a conspicuous degree by women.

Mainly for reasons of our own ignorance, we decided to concentrate on cross-culturally effective field methods and to search for operations that promised to illuminate the problem of personality development in relation to cultural patterning in the situational context of several Indian tribes. We felt woefully inadequate to the task. Since we knew that we needed advice about so-called culture-free psychological tests and other field operations that might prove effective for our purposes, we solicited the help of a glittering array of consultants. These included Ruth Benedict, Margaret Mead, Clyde Kluckhohn, Kurt Lewin, A. I. Hallowell, Fred Eggan, Lawrence K. Frank, Bruno Klopfer, Erik H. Erikson, Grace Arthur, and Eugene Lerner. Although belonging to a diversity of theoretical schools, each was master of one or more field methods.

One of my functions as coordinator was to prepare a tentative research design. I therefore interviewed most of the consultants for ideas regarding field operations, especially "culture-free" psychological tests. These contacts turned out to be a rich educational experience as well as profitable to the project. I believe that they helped to set the high quality level of the research.

Six tribes (Papago, Hopi, Navaho, Zuñi, Zia, and Dakota Sioux) made up our original sample, but we dropped one (Zia) when the Indians objected to being tested. The Research Committee decided that to afford perspective on culture and personality change processes, at least two comparable communities should be studied in each tribe. When possible, one of these communities was chosen as representative of a less acculturated milieu and a second as representative of a more acculturated one.

I was told by an anthropologist who had worked with American Indians that we might as well give up the idea of interviewing Indian children, since they would not respond. It was naïve, she said, to expect that we could give these children psychological tests. Nevertheless, we developed a battery of about a dozen "culture-free" psychological tests, including projective, performance, and guided-interview types as well as medical examinations, to be administered to about 1,000 children, aged six to eighteen years, comprising an age-graded, statistically significant sample from the selected communities. We found that the children not only could be given the whole battery, but that they responded to our field workers' questions again and again with spontaneity. Furthermore, their behavior reinforced the findings from the tests and illustrated many principles of social, cultural, and personality organization manifested in daily life on the reservations. Perhaps the fact that the field staff consisted mostly of women played a role in this success. Young Indians were used to responding to women.

At the suggestion of our Indian Service advisers we decided to divide the labor of field work and to use specialists, including psychiatrists and anthropologists, only when an operation (such as the Rorschach and the TAT tests and medical examinations) required a high degree of specialization. We planned to train all field workers, including resident volunteers from the sample communities, to do most of the actual testing and interviewing under staff supervision. I was told that when it became known that we planned to use teachers, nurses, administrators, and even tribal Indians on the field research teams, the whole project was dismissed as more or less of a joke. This reaction surprised me at the time, but I suppose it was to be expected, since the training of native assistants in the field, now an accepted field procedure, was still in the experimental stage.

Later events proved that our decision had been an astute one. The plan not only solved our wartime manpower shortage problem on the home base, it also served as an in-service training device. In most of the selected communities it simplified the gaining of rapport with the residents, since most of the field workers were already known and trusted by the Indians. It also reduced certain communication difficulties that might be expected in a field project involving thirteen communities whose members spoke half a dozen different languages related to as many different cultures. Except for Hopi and Papago, both of which belong to the Utaztecan linguistic stock, each Indian language was unrelated to the others and, of course, to English, the language of the research staff.

After being trained, the field workers rendered invaluable service to the project. Several volunteers demonstrated so much interest, ability, and aptitude in their field assignments that they were invited to Chicago to participate in the data-processing phase of the research.

I must admit, however, that most Indian Service employees who were asked to "volunteer" for this assignment did not feel free to refuse. Participation in the project required of a schoolteacher, for example, many hours of extracurricular work that was not only new and demanding, but also uncompensated outside of the regular teacher's salary. Many teachers found the training and field work highly rewarding (Kelly, 1954); on the other hand, a few reacted almost traumatically to their first exposure to modern child-development theory. Some had never been in an Indian home, and their initial interview turned out to be quite an ordeal. Then, too, accidents and unforeseen crises occasionally occurred. I was appalled when a shy and apprehensive teacher returned in tears from her first visit to a Papago village. She reported that when she entered the house, she found a group of women clustered around a sick child at one end of the room. The mother came to speak to her, and while the interview was in progress, the child died. I felt there was little I could say to comfort her.

PILOT STUDY ON THE PAPAGO RESERVATION

From the beginning the staff agreed that a pilot study would be necessary to test the usefulness of each field operation in our tentative research design. Thus, before the testing plan was finalized, each test could either be accepted, adapted to the field situation, or rejected altogether. Although the coordinator was put in charge of the pilot study, I requested and received the assistance of the Indian Service anthropologist, Dr. Ruth Underhill, a veteran specialist on Papago culture. Her knowledge and experience turned out to be indispensable to the project. I also enlisted the help of Dr. Alice Joseph, a neuropsychiatrist who was serving as field physician on the Papago reservation. In helping to plan, administer, and analyze the Rorschach test and medical examinations, Dr. Joseph, and also Dr. Dorothea C. Leighton, made unique contributions to the research. They were among the first psychiatrists to engage in actual field work on the reservations.

As the plans neared completion, I could hardly wait to start the field work. But the Research Committee wisely insisted that I was not to leave Chicago until several field guides had been drafted. I hurried the work along, and in February 1942 I departed for Arizona. In contrast to my experiences in the South Seas, transportation presented no problem. I merely went by train from Chicago to Tucson—at that time a three days' journey—and was driven sixty miles westward on an unpaved road to Sells, the seat of the Papago Indian Agency. There a government car was put at my disposal. Lodging also required no effort; instead of having to hire a native cook "boy" and borrow a grass house, as in Lau, I merely settled into a comfortable room in the Indian Service employees' club and ate my meals in the cooperative dining room. Mail was delivered regularly, and an up-to-date hospital was reassuringly near, in case of emergencies.

As I crossed the vast desert of southern Arizona bordering Mexico for the first time, I saw many horses and cattle grazing on sparse open range. Occasionally a water hole appeared, but rarely a human being. Where are the people, I wondered. The Papagos live in isolated villages scattered about one large and two small reservations (total area: 2,851,830 acres). But since their dirt-roofed shelters of wattle and daub or adobe were widely spaced and merged with the landscape, they were inconspicuous. In fact, during the field work it was often difficult to find a village. Many were located on obscure wagon roads far off the beaten track. In summer, with the temperature rising to 120 degrees, "*cherchez la famille*" became a real frustration. In the western, less acculturated parts of the reservation, where precipitation dwindles to an average of five inches a year, the villages were very small and poor. To obtain a group for our sample large enough to represent the less acculturated element in the Papago population (number-ing about 7,000), we had to study eight separate villages (Hickiwan, Guvo, Kuakatch, Emika, Stoa Pitk, Hotason Vo, Totia Tock, and Vaya Chin), compared to the four which comprised our more acculturated eastern unit (Topawa, Komelik, Supi Oidak, and Choulic).

One of my first impressions was of the extraordinary beauty of Papago-land. Broad sandy valleys, decorated with creosote, mesquite, cholla and *suhuaro* (giant cactus), merged into distant blue mountains, which turned pink in the crimson sunset. In April the unwatered desert transformed itself into breathtaking loveliness. Every twig, even the most lifeless, burst into bloom. Incredibly delicate flowers—pink, yellow, and red—appeared on the desert floor and the paloverde trees changed dry stream beds into rivers of gold. Most astonishing of all, wooden ocotillo fences surrounding Pa-pago corrals sprouted gay, bright red blossoms.

Exciting as is the springtime in Papagueria, it is hard to imagine a more dramatic event than the coming of summer rain to this parched land. When a cloudburst broke a long drought, water literally poured out of the sky like a shower bath. The parched soil soaked it up. People ran out of their homes fully clothed and laughing in the rain; they absorbed moisture through every pore. Children, drenched to the skin, splashed gleefully about. What a sense of relief we all felt! Nothing I had ever read about the desert had prepared me for the actual experience. I perceived again how handicapped we are in trying to understand a people's lifeway without first-hand experi-ence on the spot.

In Papagoland I was fascinated with the way human groups, as well as plants and animals, had adapted their biograms to the idiosyncratic rhythms and ecology of this particular region of the earth. Every organic species found here has developed special adaptations and defenses, genetic as well as behavioral, against drought. The giant cactus expands and con-tracts its fluted trunk like an accordion, it fattens when the rains come and slowly shrinks during the remainder of the year. Even the corn planted by these Indians matures during the two-month period before all the moisture from the July rains dries out of the flash-flooded areas.

I wondered what we would find if we studied human groups systematically not only from a cultural, but also a genetic viewpoint, since these Indians have lived and inbred in this isolated environment for millennia. Surely here was an ideal human genetic laboratory from which science had much to learn! But, of course, genetic studies were not included in our research plan. And besides, we could not ask for blood samples from this tribe, since the Papagos believed that the handling of blood brings bad luck.

We did learn, however, that the traditional Papago diet was based on beans and maize, supplemented with chili pepper, squash, wild edible plants, and game. Papago families who adhered to the old ways tended to be more adequately nourished than those who depended on wage work and bought much of their food at the trade store. But virtually all the Papago children in our sample who were medically examined suffered from malnutrition; the deficiencies especially in vitamin C, were most marked in those from the more acculturated eastern community.

In this connection it is interesting to note that formerly during the winter the Papagos lived in family groups in the mountains near a spring or well and hunted wild game. They moved to traditional valley village sites near their flood-water fields in summer. Thus this tribe adapted to its idiosyncratic ecological situation by creating a dual economy. The Indians adjusted work patterns and social structure to the natural tempo and vast spaces of the Lower Sonoran desert. Even Papago traditional religion manifested a duality. The youths pursued their vision quests alone in the hills. But the great wine ceremony, held in June when the giant cactus fruit was ripe, was an annual social event, when families gathered to harvest the fruit, brew, and drink great quantities of the foamy wine while singing songs to "pull down the clouds" (Underhill, 1938, 22).

PSYCHOLOGICAL TEST FINDINGS

In view of these ecological and cultural facts, we were nevertheless surprised to find, when the processed field data from the Papago study were analyzed, a similar dualism showing up in the personalities of our sample of Papago children. Dr. Joseph discovered an interesting type of psychological balance in the group averages. In contrast to the other tribes in the sample, the Papagos manifested a tendency to move back and forth between a clear-eyed practical approach toward "reality" on the one hand and what might today be called a "psychedelic orientation" (without benefit of drugs), on the other.

The tests and other field data revealed that the Papagos could and did face and cope with everyday problems as the need arose. But after the task was done, they almost automatically lapsed into a world of fantasy and dreams. Theirs was not the familiar world of the introvert escapist. It resembled more the psychological state of a medium or seer (Joseph, Spicer and Chesky, 1949, 219–220). This is the world where songs are born. And Papago songs, as "descriptions of desired events" are believed to have magical power to bring about the events described. The nature of this fantasy world is partially revealed by Ruth Underhill (1938). The Papagos believe that songs and dreams can phrase a wish in a way that will magically elicit its fulfillment.

This pendulumlike psychic dynamic apparently functions as a personality-balancing safety valve, affording immediate relief when the harsh conditions of everyday life generate stress and conflict beyond the limits of individual tolerance. It is associated with a tendency to avoid clear-cut commitments and the categorization of concepts.

Again, we found the following finding from the psychological tests a surprise. We had already observed that Papago children liked to "suck gas" from cars by removing the cover from the gasoline tank and inhaling the fumes, a trick they had learned at boarding school. The tests revealed that many of the boys at the age of seven or eight years had already started to drink bootleg liquor obtained across the border in Mexico. (It was against federal law to sell liquor to an Indian at the time.) We knew that drunkenness was a problem on the reservation, especially at fiestas. And we knew that the wine ceremony was the only large group ceremony still celebrated annually. We also knew that singing was the main medium of creative expression in this tribe.

But in those days we did not know enough to take behavior seriously —*all* behavior, even to the tiniest detail. I suppose we were still influenced to some extent by the "shreds and patches" theory of culture. We had not completely discarded the notion that, like the human body, culture carries a load of vestigial structures, useless except as concrete evidence to document some historical hypothesis. Perhaps the notion was borrowed from biology to bolster the unilinear evolutionary theory of culture. Indeed, many of us are still handicapped by incorrect and misleading analogies.

TINY DETAILS AS CLUES TO CULTURE STRUCTURE

The very special importance of recording and analyzing the observed behavior, even to the tiniest and most insignificant-appearing details, was continually impressed on me during the field work and analysis phases of the Indian Education Project. For example, one aspect of a culture in which the staff was especially interested was the rules of games and how they vary according to changing cultural emphases. The point is well illustrated by the following account of Papago children at play, taken from my pilot-study field notes.

After school eight little girls, about seven years old, were playing outside my office near the Sells day school. When I opened the door they approached with curiosity and interest. I asked them what their favorite game was, and after a pause, during which there was much giggling and wriggling, one replied, "Farmer in the Dell."

I asked if they wanted to play "Farmer in the Dell" and sat down on the school steps. After some whispering in Papago, they edged out of sight behind my office and returned in a few minutes. With the biggest child in the center, the girls formed a circle by holding hands. They moved clockwise while singing, "Farmer in the dell. . . ." During the game one little girl tripped another so that she fell down on the grass amid much laughter but without malice. Gradually each child was chosen and moved into the center of the circle until only the "cheese" was left out. The children laughed and jumped up and down. Several of them embraced the "cheese."

I asked another girl what her favorite game was. After a pause she replied, "London Bridge." So I asked the children to play this game. After a whispered conference the biggest, apparently the leader, and another good-sized girl left the group and talked in whispers. They decided that the leader would take "ice cream" as her lure, the other an "apple." The two girls then rejoined the group and, facing each other, began to clap their hands and sing, "London Bridge is falling down. . . ." The others, singing, simply passed between them in single file. (Note that the usual archlike stance was ignored. There were no bridges in Papagoland at the time.)

Each girl in turn chose "ice cream" rather than an "apple," so a line formed behind the leader. But as soon as the last girl had made her selection, three girls quickly left their places and cued up behind the girl representing "apple." This sudden maneuver equalized the number of players on each side. It happened so quickly that I could hardly believe my eyes. In the ensuing "tug of war," however, the "ice cream" side won, pushing the others down on the grass with much laughter.

As an observer I was impressed by the children's manipulation of the group structure in the London Bridge game, regardless of the traditional rules. In a wink they had altered it to a form in which, as Papagos, they felt comfortable. Inequalities resulting from free choice were erased, and a new balance was given the line before the "tug of war"—which, incidently they converted into a push. Ruth Underhill and Rosamond Spicer, who worked out the social anthropology of the eastern community, found a similiar type of balance and inward thrust in the Papago family structure. Such a balance may be detected also in Papago basketry designs and songs (Underhill, 1938, 108–110).

In both games I noted a tendency to minimize the scapegoat motif and, by actively showing affection and helpfulness, to alleviate the predicament of a "left-out" person or group. This observation reinforced the findings on child-training patterns among the Papagos reported by Jane Chesky (Joseph, Spicer, and Chesky, 1949, Part 2), who studied child development in the western community. A child is never allowed to feel isolated or rejected by the family group. Each individual is treated as a person in his own right and is given a rather wide scope for individual choices and musings. For example, when a teacher visited Papago homes in her district to find out how many children would attend school for the first time in the fall, a relative would call the child and ask him if he wanted to go to school. (At the time school attendance was not compulsory on Indian reservations.) If the child said "no," that was it: the child's decision was respected by the family. The child also decided whether he wanted medical aid when he was sick.

The game incident also revealed a tolerance for individual differences that was later documented by the test results. According to Dr. Joseph (Joseph, Spicer, and Chesky, 1949, 221), "although Papago children's personality patterns show structural simplicity, individual differences are quite marked." The low-keyed, almost whispered tones of Papago speech and the gentle laughter of the people (Underhill, 1938, 2), usually suppressed in front of strangers, are also evident in the behavior of the children, as is their deference to seniority and a marked preference for slow circular movement, for singing, and for making their own decisions.

Lessons from an interdisciplinary project

The Indian Education Project, later known as the Indian Personality and Administration Research, existed by contract for six years. The last three were sponsored by the Society for Applied Anthropology. During all this time the staff pushed and pulled the research on each of the five tribes in the final sample through several phases: field work, data processing and comparison, interpretation, application, and reporting. It took persistence, fortitude, and humor to survive the vicissitudes of team research involving, off and on, 150 workers (seventy-five in the field) with different kinds of training and interests, especially while the country was in a state of national emergency. It also required a complex holistic mental approach and the ability to suspend judgment before generalizing on the findings, until all the relevant data were available, a period that varied up to several years. And it needed deep concentration on the problem itself and a conviction that its elucidation was humanly important. Since completion and publication of at least one monograph on each tribe, a final report, and several major publications on the results of the psychological testing program were planned (a work program that extended several years beyond the formal termination of the project), a certain enthusiasm for the research did not come amiss.

In my opinion our cross-disciplinary search for adequate tools to evaluate Indian Service policy and program was rewarding on several levels. In concluding, I shall discuss some of these.

From the theoretical viewpoint our eclectic approach afforded the means by which we could proceed to the field stage of the research without undue delay. Such timing was a virtual necessity in a government-financed project that was expected to show tangible results quickly. Hence I feel that this approach was an expedient solution to a theoretical dilemma on whose horns many a cross-discipline project has hung itself. An early confrontation of basic theoretical alternatives probably would have prevented the project from getting off the ground. On the other hand, we paid a certain price for our refusal to face ideological controversy. The price might be measured in personal wear and tear on the part of theoretically oriented members of the staff, especially during the field and data-processing phases of the research. Sometimes I felt that my job required the "coordination" of basically incompatible approaches. The fact that ideological differences are often interpreted as personal incompatibilities, especially by pragmatic American academicians, did not help. A bonus emerged, however, in a certain tolerance that staff members developed toward one another as we learned to live with our differences and, by concentrating on solving a common problem over a long period of time, even gained perspective as a result of such differences.

Such growth was especially marked regarding the development and use of the psychological-test battery and the integration of findings from the field-testing program with those derived from other sources, such as ethnographic field work, medical examinations, ecological surveys, and historical documents. I believe that personality-development research of the type pioneered by the Indian Education Project, despite the difficulties involved, opens for inspection hitherto inaccessible aspects of the human phenomenon. It is difficult to convey the sense of excitement we experienced during the committee work, when the processed field findings from the several disciplines were presented, discussed, and analyzed. Some sixty-three seminars, each lasting at least three hours, were held for this purpose at the Committee on Human Development during the winter of 1942–1943. Supplying new dimensions of evidence regarding the culture of each sample community—evidence that stemmed even from the community's collective unconscious—the analysis helped our understanding of each culture to "jell." It especially afforded basic documentation for conclusions about a culture and its dynamics that moved intuitions and hunches to valid inferences and empirically based assumptions. For when many different kinds of evidence—ecological, social, cultural, and psychological—revealed a common structure, such as the balanced dualism of the Papago lifeway, we felt that we were on the right track. When we repeated the analytic process in regard to community after community with similarly convincing results, we gained confidence. We seemed to be acquiring an understanding of cultural dynamics in depth that might eventually reveal the secret of how to predict probable human group behavior within certain limitations.

THE PAY-OFF

A gratifying aspect of the project, to me at least, is the reinforcement of its findings by subsequent research using field methods, such as folk taxonomy and linguistic analysis, designed to investigate dimensions of culture that we did not attempt to probe. This has occurred regarding the Papago, Hopi, Navaho, and Sioux findings, so far as I am aware. Documentation of the point, however, is beyond the scope of this paper.

Thus we receive an unexpected bonus in carefully planned and executed multidisciplinary research. It stimulates the investigator to formulate a plausible hypothesis regarding the covert culture of a community. If valid, this hypothesis will hold up when tested against findings from subsequent research, even projects using operations from quite other disciplines. And we learn the value of probings in depth as a hedge against the pitfalls of ethnocentricity on the part of investigators, a handicap otherwise extremely difficult for a field worker to avoid or even to check.

The depth findings also provide a frame that may prove useful in interpreting, reinterpreting, and validating previously published research. For example, Papago hymns to the "glories of dizziness," collected by Underhill (1938, 40), take on deeper meaning in the light of our Papago culture and personality findings.

SOME SUCCESSES AND FAILURES

We found that every member of the team had to learn a great deal that was new to him. Especially was he required by the nature of the research design to assume new roles and act as he had never done before. In this connection I felt that one of our greatest deficiencies was a lack of sufficient supervisory personnel. And yet we could not provide more, and indeed could barely hold to the job, since the war effort required most of the country's manpower.

For me the coordinator's functions involved many new roles. In sharp contrast to that of an independent field worker concentrating on gaining rapport in a village, learning a new language, and winning the support of the inhabitants in a difficult descriptive task, I found that my main job involved interpersonal relations among Indians, field workers, and staff members. Despite the many duties which fell almost by default to the co-ordinator, my most constant and difficult role turned out to be that of morale builder. Multidisciplinary team research is not only more fun and more challenging, but perhaps also more difficult than any other type. At times its practitioners become discouraged. Hence someone has to keep up the morale of the group. Who is there for this job but the coordinator? I tried to handle this role as best I could in whatever way seemed appropriate: evaluating the individual's contribution to the whole, praising positive effort as well as good work, discussing problems and their possible solu-tions, laughing off mistakes, encouraging participation in the project at more subtle levels, placing events in a broad perspective, and especially trying to provide more personal contact and supervision.

Of course I made many mistakes. Misunderstandings occurred, and some of them were never fully resolved. I remember one particularly telling remark made by an irate "volunteer." "With all your psychology," she said, "you don't even know what I'm thinking!" "How right you are!" I thought, but what could I say? Probably the worst failure occurred when one of our field workers was requested by the council of one of our tribes, to leave the reservation. There was no way to convince her that the decision was made by the Indians themselves and in no way involved Project personnel. But I believe that my moments of greatest frustration came when our superiors on occasion failed to support our work or broke a promise to the field workers.

REWARDS OF TEAM WORK

At such times who was there to bolster the morale builder's morale? This question leads us to one of the most interesting aspects of team research. Concentrating together on a challenging real problem over a period of months and even years, we formed close friendships that encompassed an unusual bond. It was the comradeship that comes from worrying and laughing together, from working through psychological problems, and from defending our joint findings when they were questioned or attacked. It is the "togetherness" of a common endeavor, as when Alice Joseph and I worked out, day by day and point by point on the basis of Project findings, the integration of Hopi personality with Hopi culture, mythology, art, ceremonial, and world view in the context of the ecology and history.

We often experienced the thrill of mutual recognition when suddenly a long-sought resolution to a problem flashed into consciousness. So *The Hopi Way* (Thompson and Joseph, 1967) was forged. We had to buck many popular stereotypes regarding the Hopi tribe, as inevitably happens in multidisciplinary research.

The loneliness of the anthropologist working single-handed on a remote South Sea island is absent in team research, especially on Indian reservations where one is never really cut off from a fling in a nearby town or even a weekend visit by a friend from "outside." In times of discouragement as well as elation I looked to my friends and coworkers for understanding and support.

A WOMAN'S ANGLE

I recall there were those who said that nothing could come of a research project run by women. But it should be emphasized that substantial contributions at many levels were made to the Project by men, such as John Collier (1945), Clyde Kluckhohn (Kluckhohn and Leighton, 1946; Leighton and Kluckhohn, 1947), Robert J. Havighurst (Havighurst and Neugarten, 1955), Gordon Macgregor (1946), and William E. Henry (1947), to mention only a few. It was truly a cooperative endeavor.

As for me, I found in the Indian work what I was seeking and much more. The coordinator's role afforded a unique learning situation to me as an anthropologist. Especially did it provide an opportunity for me to orient myself to modern psychiatric theory and practice as they may be adapted to the needs of a policy project in applied anthropology. This occurred through day-by-day work with psychiatrists and psychologists in field and laboratory over a period of several years. Although I did not actually administer any of the tests myself, nor did I process the results, I participated in their selection and testing by means of the pilot study, their adaptation to the Indian field situation, designing the research as a whole, the training of field workers and supervisors, and the integration and reporting of the processed findings. Last but not least, the work gave me the opportunity to explore the cultural world of the American Indians, a unique and richly rewarding personal experience that no one who wishes to understand mankind's cultural heritage, especially no anthropologist, should miss.

If there were disadvantages in being a woman, I was not really aware of them. In fact, being a woman seemed to me in this and other field jobs to be a positive asset. The Indians, for example, found it appropriate that child-training patterns, school performance, work, and games should be investigated by women. The experience reinforced my preconception that anthropology is one profession in which women are indispensable. On the other hand, I was told that the Papagos, who confined their women to menstrual huts during menstruation and after childbirth, were uneasy when non-Papago women wandered freely about their reservation unless they had passed the menopause.

As an anthropologist, my greatest satisfaction from the Indian work perhaps came from an unexpected source many years after publication of our first tribal monograph, *The Hopi Way*. When the book appeared, I was amazed and amused when some of my colleagues decided quite seriously that I had invented the Hopi world view. A few days ago from the most conservative Hopi pueblo came the word that we are "the only ones who have told the truth about the Hopis." To an anthropologist, man or woman, such words are sweet music; they dim memories of effort and frustration and lure us, time and time again, back into the field.

BREAKING NEW GROUND

The most fascinating aspect of the work perhaps was its exploratory nature. It came at a historically significant point in time, which we now recognize marked the beginning of a new type of research in the sciences of man. A search for understanding human groups in depth necessitated a closer, more penetrating look at current theoretical developments in the social sciences and psychology. Despite the Project's genesis in practical issues, it called for clarification of a theoretical formulation congruent with the ever-growing stockpile of scientific findings about human group behavior. And it required psychological insight. At that time our multidisciplinary approach was unprecedented, regarding not only problem formulation, but also research organization, operation, and application. Indeed, although the Society for Applied Anthropology was founded that same year (1941), the form that the new discipline of applied anthropology would take and the problems it would illuminate were by no means clear.

Suddenly we found ourselves working at the very center of a basic enigma in applied anthropology. This enigma is now called "community development," and it is one of the most discussed issues in what is now known as "administrative anthropology." What is meant by "community development"? Development in what direction? Toward what goals? How can socio-cultural change be measured, controlled, and evaluated? In terms of industrialization and urbanization? On the basis of improved community welfare? In respect to personality balance and maturity?

Even today these questions are still being asked, and there is by no means general agreement regarding their answers. Or perhaps we may detect two quite different trends in the search to elucidate them. On the one hand, many people in our time assume that industrialization and urbanization stand for "progress," measured in terms of family income, standards of living, economic growth, public health, demography, and leisure time. According to this school of thought we have but to instigate, stimulate, and control socio-cultural change in a "progressive" direction and to evaluate it according to certain statistical indices, and our job as applied anthropologists will be done. Since "progress" is considered to be not only desirable but also inevitable, we use our skills to help it along or to accelerate the trend.

On the other hand, a growing minority questions this position as oversimplified and even fallacious. More detailed knowledge of the cultures of specific contemporary communities suggests the possibility that clinical standards of culture and personality change, using scientifically appropriate criteria, may be found. This possibility has sparked a deeper search for empirically derived standards and measurements to rate a community's health, sanity, and viability as a totality. Such criteria may eventually include indices of homeostatic cultural balance, resources conservation, and psychological maturity in relation to the problematic situation that every community, viewed situationally, has to resolve or perish as a whole living entity.

These two approaches toward the evaluation of community change were by no means clarified during discussions that preceded the construction of a design for the Indian Education Research. But I believe that the findings of the Project help to focus the second approach to community-development problems and indicate a direction for fruitful exploration.

A FINAL COMMENT

Returning finally to our research assignment: what pragmatic lessons do these findings teach? Do they illuminate the everyday quandaries of Indian Service personnel working on the reservations, in field offices, and at headquarters? Are they dated or can they be used by administrators of ethnic groups elsewhere, regardless of culture, personality type, and local situation? Do they throw light on the "democracy" versus "dictatorship" dilemma?

Most of the findings of the Indian Education Project have been published. (For details, see Leighton and Adair, 1966, v). I shall therefore make only one comment here. In the aggregate I believe that they reveal how the admonition "Respect the individual," so familiar to Americans, may have a more precise and subtle meaning than is generally accorded it. Without a well-documented knowledge of the hidden, tenacious ties between self, personality, and culture, we cannot even conceive of the repercussions that "respect" versus "nonrespect" types of behavior may have on the individual or the group to whom they are directed.

Our findings, it seems to me, move the concept of respect for the individual and his culture, for example, out of the realm of idealism, stereotyped patriotism, and ethics, and place it squarely in the realm of mental hygiene and community welfare. The alternatives are no longer vague. From the viewpoint of applied anthropology, if we would promote the mental health of an individual and the social welfare of a community, our findings indicate that we have no choice but to respect the individual's personality and the group's culture. Actively to aid a person or a community in distress or crisis, we need not only appropriate clinical indices, but also new knowledge in depth about personality and culture. Indeed, if we do not respect him and his culture, we may do him irretrievable harm. Personality and culture structures are deeply rooted and intertwined. They have been developed, according to a reciprocal feedback process, by the members of a community in their long-range persistent efforts to cope with and resolve real-life problems, as real and as serious to human group survival and welfare as the aridity of the Papago desert.

References

COLLIER, JOHN. 1945. "The United States Indian Administration as a Laboratory of Ethnic Relations," *Social Research*, 12, 265–303.

HAVIGHURST, ROBERT J., and BERNICE NEUGARTEN. 1955. *American Indian and White Children; A Sociopsychological Investigation.* Chicago: University of Chicago Press.

HENRY, WILLIAM E. 1947. "The Thematic Apperception Technique in the Study of Culture-Personality Relations," *Genetic Psychology Monographs*, 35.

JOSEPH, ALICE, ROSAMOND B. SPICER, and JANE CHESKY. 1949. *The Desert People: A Study of the Papago Indians.* Chicago: University of Chicago Press.

KELLY, WILLIAM H. 1954. "Applied Anthropology in the Southwest," *American Anthropologist*, 56, 709–719.

KLUCKHOHN, CLYDE, and DOROTHEA C. LEIGHTON. 1946. *The Navaho.* Cambridge, Mass.: Harvard University Press.

LEIGHTON, DOROTHEA C., and JOHN ADAIR. 1966. *People of the Middle Place: A Study of the Zuñi Indians.* New Haven, Conn.: Human Relations Area Files.

LEIGHTON, DOROTHEA C., and CLYDE KLUCKHOHN. 1947. *Children of the People.* Cambridge, Mass.: Harvard University Press.

MACGREGOR, GORDON. 1946. *Warriors Without Weapons.* Chicago: University of Chicago Press.

THOMPSON, LAURA, and ALICE JOSEPH. 1967. *The Hopi Way.* New York: Russell and Russell. First edition 1944.

UNDERHILL, RUTH. 1938. *Singing For Power. The Song Magic of the Papago Indians of Southern Arizona.* Berkeley: University of California Press.

MEXICO (GUERRERO)/NAHUA

Odyssey of Encounter

PEGGY GOLDE recently jointly edited the book CLINICAL ANTHRO-
POLOGY with Demitri Shimkin. This work defines the new subfield that
includes Golde's additional training as a psychotherapist. Before turning
her attention once again to the updating of her manuscript on the artistic
values of the Nahua Indians she studied in Mexico, she plans to publish a
book on the ordinary problems of living.

S eated sidesaddle, I had to cling to the saddle horn for balance as the mule
lurched up the narrow rocky path scratched into the mountainside. I
could look across the deep valley at distant purple graphs of mountains
outlined against the uniform blue of the sky while idly wondering, "What
am I doing here?" Despite my precarious perch, I felt strangely casual, even
bemused at my own calm despite the realization that only the mule's practiced step kept me from the precipitous edge. The feeling of suspension,
detachment, and unreality did not abate even when I noticed that the path
had turned into a roadway of hard-baked clayey earth, bordered by walls of
artfully fitted stones, and that thatched-roofed houses had begun to appear,
at first sporadically and then in more concentrated clusters. Reality must be
learned through small repeated doses, and that ride into the apparently
deserted village had the quality of slow motion through an empty movie set
or of a vaguely remembered dream. In a short time these feelings of unreality were to leave me. One day it would be hard for me to remember that I
had not always been part of the life of this isolated Indian village in Mexico.

To turn to the question I had asked myself as I admired the view of the
mountains of Guerrero from the back of a mule—what I was doing there
was both the end and the beginning of a detective story that had begun with
my interest in doing a study of art in its cultural context and with the
purchase of a painted pot, on a previous trip to Mexico in 1956, from the
museum of popular art in Mexico City (Museo Nacional de Artes e Indus-
trias Populares). The painted decoration, set off in cartoonlike panels bordered by geometric and floral forms, depicted a menacing leonine animal
ready to pounce on a bird, and a horse trampling a man wearing spurs.
Notably distinctive both in style and content in comparison to the simple
repetitive pottery painting I had seen in Chiapas, Oaxaca, and Michoacan,
this work so engaged me that I decided on the spot that I would someday
locate the village where it had been made and do my field work there. I
could make such a decision because the problem I wanted to study was the

67

nature of the development of art style, the meaning of both symbolic and formal features characteristic of the style, and the relation between style and aesthetic values. Since relatively little attention had been paid by anthropologists to problems in the study of art and culture, I had no clear idea of what aspects of the culture might be relevant to focus on; I knew how to study style itself, but I had no hypotheses about what style might be expressing. The hostility depicted in the pottery decoration pointed to a way to begin—to search for the sources of anger and aggression in the culture and the mode of its expression in other behaviors.

I returned to Mexico in the fall of 1959, buoyed by the euphoria of passing my last set of examinations and by the award of a Doherty Foundation[1] fellowship to support my field work. The director of the museum, Daniel Rubín de la Borbolla, told me that the Indians who sold the pottery to the museum identified its source as Tuliman, in the state of Guerrero. By chance, he was planning a trip to Guerrero to inspect a new museum in Chilpancingo, the state capital, and offered to take me along and personally introduce me to the governor with the explanation that my studies would further the national museum's goals to support indigenous arts and crafts. I was delighted by this possibility, for I had foreseen delays in gaining access to the governor; this offer was thus not only timely, but also afforded me the museum's institutional support and a meaningful rationale with which to persuade the governor of the value of my proposed study. This was to be only the first in a series of fortuitous happenings.

On the highway between the cities of Iguala and Chilpancingo, Borbolla called out suddenly to the driver to stop the car. Several Indian men were sitting at the side of the road amid large painted water jars and bulging burlap bags. Borbolla leaned out of the window and called their names. He and the Indians spoke together quietly, and I realized that they were men who sold pottery to the museum and that they were arranging for us to visit their village at that very moment. One of the men apologized that he had to remain behind with the others to wait for the bus to carry them to the city, but he softened his apparent rejection by offering to lend me his mule. Another, whom I shall call José, agreed to leave his pottery with some relatives living in the town by the road and to accompany us, on foot, for the two-and-a-half-hour trip up to the village.

While Borbolla mounted José's horse, José lengthened the stirrups on the mule's saddle to accommodate my greater height and helped make me comfortable in the unfamiliar side position, traditional for Indian women, with my right foot in one stirrup and the left foot dangling, one hand on the horn and the other holding the single rope rein. Entering the rocky riverbed

1. Henry L. and Grace Doherty Charitable Foundation, Inc.

that formed the perimeter of the roadside town, fortunately dry from the lack of recent rain, we followed its course through the gorge cut by the river, shaded by overhanging trees and vines. On reaching a massive ominous-looking cactus, we left the riverbed and abruptly began to climb the tortuous, twisting path up the mountainside. During that ride, while José strode easily beside me, I learned that Tuliman was not the true name of the village but was one of two pseudonyms used by the Indians to conceal the name and location of the village from outsiders in order to preserve its anonymity and isolation. Only because by chance we had seen the group by the road, and Borbolla had forced their hand by taking them up on a long-standing, but insincere, invitation to visit was the proverbial cat out of the bag.

Excitement and anxiety made José quite voluble—disconcertingly so, since he did not fit my preconception of the typical taciturn Indian. This first impression of his atypicality later proved to be accurate. When I told him I was looking for a place to live and study the language and customs of the people, he was extremely interested, not so much in the nature of my studies, but that I might actually settle for some time. He said that he—or, more correctly, his nephew—owned the only vacant house in the village and that I might borrow it, since the nephew lived in his house with him, his aged parents, his niece, and his wife and small daughter. I understood the alacrity of this invitation not only as a demonstration of hospitality, but also as the wish to impress me that he was a "man of the world" who had traveled much—unlike other villagers—that he knew the proper forms, and that he would therefore be an ideal host. His economic dependence on Borbolla undoubtedly operated as a factor in his extending this offer, which could be viewed as a means of personalizing their relationship and further ingratiating himself.

The journey ended at his house, where we rested briefly and were given warm bottled soft drinks while he gave orders to his retiring, unobtrusive wife to buy chickens for our lunch. He was in a great hurry for us to see the mayor to announce our presence and intentions, and as we made our way down to the center of the village (it is built on large terraces, the last of which plunges in a sheer escarpment of stone the color of seafoam), I remember a feeling of disappointment that people did not run from their houses to see us. I had seen too many Hollywood movies. When I asked why the streets were so empty, José explained that the people were off working in their *milpa* (corn plot). This information was not wholly true —I could detect some people peering between the woven stick walls of their houses to get a good, but safe, look at us as we passed.

The *comisaría* (town meeting hall), a white adobe one-story building with a red tile roof, faced a flat open area unadorned by trees or flowers, called the plaza. On the other side of the plaza was a good-sized stone church, an impressive structure in this small village of about 100 houses (total population: 637). As we entered the meeting hall, it took some moments for my eyes to adjust to the dark, cool interior after the glaring brightness outside. Several men were sitting around a table at one end of the long room otherwise unfurnished except for some low planks, placed like benches around the walls. All the men were drunk; the man in the center of the group had but one good eye, and this, added to his mustache and unkempt gray hair, gave him the look of a malevolent pirate. He was the *comisario* or *juez*, what I have referred to as "mayor." Borbolla introduced himself as the director of the museum in Mexico City that bought village pottery. He presented me as a student from a large and important university in the United States, who had come to find a village in which to live and learn about the people of Mexico. The mayor spoke excellent Spanish, despite his alcoholic slur, and welcomed us in grandiloquent phrases. As he talked, I not only lost my initial apprehension, but also made my decision to stay if it could be arranged. When Borbolla mentioned that we were on our way to see both the governor and the administrative head of the county, the mayor's attitude became a shade more respectful, if not obsequious, and it was clear that once I had obtained governmental sanctions, I would have no problem gaining the mayor's permission.

After lunching on savory chicken stewed in a broth flavored with local herbs, and corn tortillas about ten inches in diameter, we spent the remainder of the afternoon visiting another man and his family whom Borbolla had known for many years. They told us that the village schoolteacher was bilingual in Nahuatl (or Mexicano, as the Indians called it) and Spanish and could probably be prevailed upon to give me language lessons for a small fee. I was jubilant at this news, reassured that by hearing and speaking the language in daily conversation and taking systematic lessons from someone ostensibly trained in grammar, I quickly could master Mexicano. If I had foreseen the enormity of the problem of learning an Indian language through the medium of another language imperfectly understood by both parties, I would never have been so cocksure.

Two weeks later, I moved into the village. I had secured the necessary letters of introduction and had bought supplies of paper, medicines, books, soap, Kleenex, and toilet paper, as well as a small alcohol stove and a Coleman lamp. When I had questioned José about what else I would need, he told me I would have to buy a bed: two wooden sawhorses, which would support the long bamboo poles lashed together that would be my mattress, and a *petate* (woven mat) to place over the poles. (With my sleeping bag on top, the bed proved fairly comfortable, though if I turned too much in my sleep, the mat, the poles, and I slipped to the ground.) Sandwiched between these suggestions was his expression of surprise that I had not returned to the United States. This was my first intimation of the people's underlying lack of trust and their preparedness to believe the worst, to expect disappointment and loss. He also hinted that he'd had some difficulty with the villagers, who wanted to know how we happened to discover the location of the village and just why he had agreed to bring us. Much later, he was to tell me that for the first fifteen days of my stay, he did not leave his house, and though he wasn't specific, the meaning was clear that he was frightened of the people's animosity toward him for bringing a stranger to the village. At the time I had not noticed his anxiety or uneasiness, and it is a moot question as to whether any actual threat was present. However, he was expressing his assessment of the situation based on his knowledge of village reactions.

I went to his house twice a day for meals until my own kitchen was built by the side of my house. Though we had agreed that his niece, an unmarried girl about sixteen years old, would cook, do my washing, bring water, and sleep in the house, she was undependable and often surly. Initially I thought she was simply shy and somewhat overwhelmed by this enforced contact with me, the first outsider she had ever met. But with the passage of time and no diminution of tension, but rather an increase in her sullen silences and refusals to answer even harmless conventional questions, I had to accept the idea that, for whatever reasons, she couldn't tolerate being near me. Nothing explicit was ever said, she simply stopped appearing, and José's old mother assumed responsibility for me, with some inane excuse for her granddaughter that neither of us believed. I agreed to the old woman's demands for a monthly salary and fringe benefits of soap, gifts of cloth, and food (other women eventually told me this salary was far too generous by village standards, and she suffered the repercussions of their envy and anger in the form of gossip and sarcastic comments). Each morning she would rise, go back to her own house to feed her pigs, chickens, and turkeys, then return to my house to build a fire, grind corn, and slap out the tortillas that, with one egg, comprised my breakfast. She usually spent the day with her own family and returned again at twilight to cook and serve my dinner—she never wanted to eat with me—and to sleep when night fell. Sometimes her husband joined her at night.

Because he was my landlord, José also became my chief informant. I spent a good part of those early days watching him paint and talking to him about other painters and his evaluations of their ability, about how he had first started selling his work to the museum, and about the general history of pottery making and painting. When friends of his dropped by, they joined in the conversation and we were able to know each other in a casual informal way. With José as my pivot, I thus began to build a social network of friend-informants and gradually elaborated my mental directory of those individuals and families most actively involved in the pottery craft, whose friendship I would eventually have to cultivate.

My first public act was to present two very expensive, highly decorated candles to the larger-than-life-sized figure of the Virgin, the village "patron saint," that stood in a glass case over the altar of the church. Her large glass eyes, porcelain doll's skin, satin and lace robes, and gold crown and necklace gave her the appearance of a frozen Snow White, waiting to be brought to life by her prince. That day, many women had come to my house bringing bunches of freshly picked flowers for me to give to the Virgin along with the candles; then they joined me in a procession to the church accompanied by the village band, to make the offering. This gift caused little comment at the time, but the day I left the village the women reassured themselves and me that I would someday return because I had given candles to the Virgin.

This act of respect toward the Virgin may have acted to reduce some of the ambiguity about me, so that if there were any underlying anger, none of it was noticeable. The people were outwardly genial and more than a little curious. I had many callers in those early weeks: by day women would come with gifts of melons or ears of steamed corn; by night boys and men, attracted by the light of the Coleman lamp, came to play cards while I typed field notes. The typewriter was an object of much interest, and a succession of visiting children and adults would watch in silent fascination to see the words appear on the page. They came also to see my hammock, the table and shelves I'd had made, the books I'd brought, and a painted chest that held my clothing; they also inquired how much I had paid for each item. The children continued to be my most constant visitors even after their curiosity had worn off, waiting around in case I needed them to run small errands, for which I would pay in hard candy or chewing gum.

It wasn't ten days before I had my first request for medical aid. A wizened, toothless old woman, extremely agitated, brought her infant grandson wrapped like a cocoon in her *rebozo* (long, narrow shawl). He screamed in terror at the sight of me. Through gestures and an occasional Spanish word, I discovered that a dog had bitten him on his penis. Since I could see that the skin hadn't been broken, after debating with myself about the wisdom of acting as a nurse, I decided to take the risk and painted his little penis crimson with mercurochrome. The old woman left, highly contented with this flamboyant treatment, and after that my house became the village pharmacy and first-aid station. I was somewhat surprised at the Indians' assumption that I was competent to treat them medically. I discovered that in the past they had been given injections and medication by public-health nurses and schoolteachers; they therefore expected me, as an educated foreign woman, to do the same. Every morning there would be at least two or three people waiting in my yard until I awoke and could minister to their needs in my "nurse's" uniform of gaily striped men's pajamas, which they found laughable but not immodest. They always asked, "How much?" I began to charge an egg (even though they often managed to forget to pay), since I otherwise had trouble finding eggs to buy. I did what I could within the limits of my ability and of my supply of aspirin, Alka Seltzer, burn ointment, and Band-Aids, and when a difficult problem presented itself, I would send or accompany the people to the clinic in Iguala, which they had never used. As it turned out, acting as a nurse gave me access to many houses and legitimized my calling on people or their visiting me. Within a few months I knew and had helped a sufficient number of people that, when some villagers grew incensed over my taking photographs of the Virgin, even though I had been given the mayor's permission, and asked that I be expelled, those whom I had helped testified on my behalf. (I learned of this episode much after the fact.)

Though I had assumed this role with some reluctance and trepidation, I must admit that I found it deeply satisfying to be able to help people and to feel that my presence, in some cases, did make a life-and-death difference. However, the identity of "Great White Goddess" is an insidious one, and I had to guard against exaggerating my own importance, reminding myself that the village had managed to exist quite well before I came and would continue to do so after I left.

For a time I had lessons every day with the schoolteacher, a young man from another Mexicano-speaking town. In turn, I tried to teach him to type and play chords on the guitar, but he never learned. Unfortunately, the dialect he spoke was just different enough in pronunciation and vocabulary to be confusing, which I only discovered when the village woman who lived with him would correct mispronounced words or incorrect translations. I came to depend on her to check each exchange.

As I began to learn some rudimentary sentences, I began to visit in earnest. I was treated like a guest of honor with warmth, courtesy, deference, and gratitude, offered the only chair in the house or a gift of food in appreciation of my visit, and addressed always as Señorita. Conversations with those women who could speak Spanish had a ritualized quality, and when I learned Mexicano, the same series of questions was asked: "Do you like it here? How long are you going to stay? How much did you pay for your skirt? Why don't you get married here?" They might mention the name of one of the boys as a possible candidate, and I would respond with laughter at the idea of marrying anyone so much younger than myself. To forestall further discussions, I told them about a sweetheart I would marry when I returned to the States, showed them his picture, and explained that the letters I received were from him. However, from their point of view, since I was there and he was far away, they couldn't believe that my "engagement" was very real. I also showed them pictures of my family and justified taking their pictures by saying that my family was interested in seeing pictures of them and where I lived.

Taking pictures then became almost a business sideline, since I could obtain favors by promising photographs in return. At first the villagers were angry and demanding when I could not produce pictures on the spot, even though I carefully explained that I had to take them to the city to be developed. Their experience had been with itinerant photographers who used a box on a tripod, developing the film under a black cloth cover and producing instant photographs.

Because of my association with Borbolla, the villagers thought that I had come to the village to buy pottery for the museum. When this assumption was not borne out, they became suspicious that I wanted to learn their pottery-making secrets in order to set up a factory in competition with them. As long as I avoided questioning them too closely about pottery markets, prices, materials, and other touchy subjects I will mention later, and was willing to limit conversation to crops, my travels, Catholicism and the Pope, and other general topics, there were no problems in communication. Ultimately I was able to carry out my study of aesthetic values because the test I administered consisted of photographs of other Mexican pottery and of drawings I myself had made. The people's task was simply to choose which of two contrasting pictures they liked better or thought was prettier. They did not find this choice difficult or taxing; on the contrary, people would even ask to take the test, so that they could see the pictures in the hope of finding new design ideas. And because the test was nonthreatening and involved few direct inquiries for information, it elicited spontaneous reactions that provided insights into other than just aesthetic attitudes. For example, the men's approving laughter and strong preference for a drawing of a girl in Western clothing, as opposed to one in traditional Indian dress, was an indication of their growing acceptance of, and positive orientation to, life as it was lived outside the village.

When I started receiving mail regularly, and particularly when I got large manila envelopes, the local postmistress in the town by the highway started the rumor that I was living in the village only to identify the rich people and to pave the way for a gang of robbers in the city. Why else would I be receiving such large envelopes? The villagers were so eager to report this gossip to me, so vehement in their disclaimers of belief in my complicity, and so quick to denounce those who spread the rumor as being envious because I had chosen to live in the village instead of their town, that I discounted the apparent show of loyalty and alliance. Their suspiciousness seemed impermeable to anything I did or said to create trust. In fact, the more I attempted to help people, the worse it seemed to get. It was as if they were waiting, holding themselves in readiness to pounce on the real explanation of my presence when it finally appeared.

This attitude—the continuing resistance or bald-faced lies—in response to many of my questions, as well as the discomforts of life in the field, began to generate in me a sense of despair and hopelessness. I wrote in my field diary:

> The heat is so unbearable I don't even have the energy to walk around the village, much less to make the trip to the *milpas,* and they say it gets even hotter . . . my legs are covered with bites and I itch all the time . . . I can't get a whole night's sleep because I hear the rats running back and forth overhead as if they were couriers carrying important messages . . . I've taken only one genealogy and I can't map the village because I don't want to arouse more suspicions. Observing pottery making is haphazard because people won't or can't tell me when they are going to be working. . . . My old lady doesn't sweep or dust despite the fact she is getting paid . . . and keeps promising to do it and then doesn't . . . as is habitual here. When I ask about the meaning of something, the people reply, "es costumbre," it's the custom, and though at times they may not really know, I'm sure at other times they just don't want to tell me . . . everything is like fighting marsh-mallows. . . . And now the schoolteacher tells me he has asked for a transfer . . . how am I ever going to learn the language?

I would like to be able to report that this situation was only transitory and that with time the people came to love and trust me completely, helped me sympathetically when I needed it, and freely opened their hearts and minds; the truth is far from that rosy ideal. I carefully had to calculate a strategy for almost every piece of information I gleaned, and I bartered, cajoled, and wheedled or bluffed knowledge I didn't have in order to get more. At times I deliberately exaggerated or distorted facts, counting on the people's need to defend the village by correcting my impressions. Sometimes I was petulant, saying, "You say you want me to stay here, get married here, yet you won't even tell me what this means or why it is done."

I learned that situations in which I needed help that required no special hardship or extra exertion on the villagers' part—like finding someone to accompany me down the mountainside to the highway for my occasional trips to the city to replenish my medicines, to have photographs developed, or to take a hot shower—could seldom be successfully managed unless my trip was somehow crucial to their interest. Without making some implicit bargain, people would never reveal the truth about their plans. If I wanted to attend a fiesta at a nearby village, seldom would they openly admit that they were going, or if they did, at the last minute they might change their mind and stay home or leave without me. If I wanted something practical, money was the chief leverage at my command. Though I sometimes felt mortified that I had to pay for services, at the same time the very impersonality of the transactions was reassuring, since it precluded feelings of exploitation, guilt, or obligation on my part. The chief drawback of this situation was that even though money was a well-understood medium of exchange, it was not always sufficient to motivate the people. When the Indians were too busy or didn't need money at a given moment, they would not work. This was not only personally frustrating; it could also drastically affect my daily life and, consequently, my work.

For example, until my combination bathhouse-latrine was completed, I went to a sheltered grove five minutes from my house, which quickly became frequented by snorting, sharp-toothed sows, their noses angling the air for the scent of food, bristling with eagerness to devour my wastes. I had to arm myself ahead of time with a small pile of stones that I would fling at them to keep them at bay until I could make my escape.

I could not easily explain my need for the latrine, nor did José ever fully understand its use, and it took many weeks of nagging, mock anger, and even "blackmail" to get it done. Fortunately, he wanted to obtain a passport and needed to have letters written and application forms filled out. I finally made it clear to him that I wouldn't be able to help him if he didn't fulfill his promise to me. (In the case of drinking water, which had to be brought by burro from the spring located about twenty minutes outside the village, there was never any haggling or difficulty. The people needed no explanation to realize that without water I could not live.)

I found myself beginning to protect myself emotionally by never counting too much on anyone, in order to avoid both disappointment and anger. In many instances I never understood what motivated people to break faith, what minor incidents might have come up to distract them, what priorities, momentarily established, might have superseded other plans in a given situation. If at times it was important to find out, I knew I never could ask directly and expect an explanation. I had to wait, sometimes for months, for an explanation to appear in some unrelated context, in some unforeseen way. In the village direct confrontations and challenges are avoided, since these lead only to defensiveness and anger. Once such feelings are unleashed, there is no guarantee of controlling them or their repercussions, the aftermath in ill-will, that can be nursed in secret only to appear full-blown at some later time.

My feelings of bafflement and frustration lessened when I realized how much the people distrusted each other. No man would ever drink from a bottle if its cap had been removed, for fear that the contents had been poisoned by witchcraft; men resisted serving in village offices that involved handling money because they were sure they would become involved in accusations of theft; I was counseled not to be generous with money or medicines, since others would not help me if I were in need; I observed several occasions when villagers refused to lend someone medicines, money, paints, food stuffs—all scarce goods—claiming not to have any when they actually did and explaining their refusal to me with the cynical comment that the loan would never be repaid. More accurately, it was that repayment would necessitate a lengthy and troublesome process of requests and reminders, which could potentially lead to hard feelings. These examples may be trivial when compared to the latent suspicions of witchcraft that came bubbling to the surface whenever there was a serious misfortune, illness or death. Though there were a number of people who, by temperament or other signs, were thought to be witches, anyone who became involved in a dispute or altercation and had reason to be angry or resentful about the settlement might be suspected of engaging in witchcraft if any misfortune befell the other party.

I was learning that the village operated with the set of beliefs that no one could be trusted or believed, that it was dangerous to reveal specific information, that it was foolish to help others, and that the only sensible way to live was to look out for one's own interests, since no one else ever would. It was difficult for me to accept the picture I was forming, and there were moments when I questioned whether my interpretations of the Indians' behavior might not be distorted or exaggerated, when I doubted my perceptions and was unsure about how to validate them. Then I obtained Oscar Lewis' book that describes Tepoztlan, a peasant community in the State of Morelos, whose people were formerly Nahuatl speakers. He writes:

> There is a readiness to view people as potentially dangerous, and the most characteristic initial reaction to others is suspicion and mistrust . . . an individual who is obliging without cost to those who seek his aid is understood to have some yet unrevealed plan for capitalizing on his position. . . . The man who speaks little, keeps his affairs to himself and maintains some distance between himself and others has less chance of creating enemies or of being criticized or envied. A man does not generally discuss his plans to buy or sell or take a trip, except with persons who are directly concerned. . . . [Lewis, 1951, pp. 292, 297]

Though I did not consider this statement unequivocal confirmation, the similarities were nevertheless sufficient to make me feel that I wasn't simply projecting an image of my own creation. More importantly, I realized how much the process of field work would be enriched, and the psychological health of the field worker supported, by the opportunity of working in the field with another person who was undergoing parallel experiences. I would recommend that field work by solitary investigators of either sex be discouraged whenever possible. If the goal of research is unbiased understanding, two people working together, preferably one of each sex, would provide the balance, the necessary check of objectivity, and the control of sex-determined or personality factors that one person, however artful, cannot accomplish alone.

Once I was reassured that my observations had some basis in reality, I could begin to view these behaviors as modes of adaptation to a world perceived as capricious and to inner feelings that were potentially disruptive. If the culture's main technique for coping with the dangers associated with emotional eruption is to suppress the direct expression of feelings in the first place, this sanction against overt expression is buttressed by witchcraft beliefs, making those who are too aggressive, too quick to anger, immediately suspect of being witches. In addition, there are institutionalized roles of "go-betweens" or intermediaries to act as buffers for the involved parties.

This approximation of the dynamics of social interaction led me to reappraise the source of the differences I was experiencing. It wasn't that the nature of the people's underlying feelings was so dissimilar; rather, the difference seemed to lie in the limited alternatives available to them to handle, rationalize, channel, and cope with their feelings. If the people appeared to have less tolerance for real and imagined slights and were insecure about life in general, they had few means to strengthen themselves or enhance their opportunities—so why shouldn't they be defensive, self-protective and hypervigilant? They had grown up believing that the only sure prediction was unpredictability; why should I expect them suddenly to trust me or behave differently toward me than they did toward anyone else in their social environment?

I have gone into some length about this aspect of life in an attempt to recover the gradual process of understanding as it emerges from the daily encounters that comprise life in the field. If the achievement of understanding is the goal of field work, it is partially accomplished through the field worker's attempts to cope with her own feelings, misapprehensions, impotence, and, at times, sheer stupidity. Further, it seems essential to present this information as the backdrop against which to view the elements of the villagers' perception of me. Some of their attitudes are derived from the more general world view I have just described, while others seem more directly linked to my being female, light-skinned, unmarried, and American.

The people knew from comparisons with other villages and towns that their village was poor, lacking even the running water, electricity, and roads that could be found elsewhere. Their own self-deprecatory attitude made my choice of their village even more incomprehensible to them. The only sensible explanation had to involve some concealed motive on my part, and the most likely motive was money. I have written about their early suspicions that I would steal their pottery designs or techniques or that I was in league with a gang of robbers. Later they thought I might be taking photographs to sell for money, and nine months after I arrived, when I was pressed by government officials into helping with the decennial census, they were convinced I was a paid spy, seeking information about their wealth that would be relayed to the government.

But they were suspicious of all strangers: some textile interests had wanted to build houses in the village and set up looms, but the villagers refused to cooperate. Some independent teachers wanted to build a school in the village, but the people balked. When a young American couple once walked unannounced into the village, everyone was angry with me because they thought I had invited them. This attitude was explained to me as the result of the revolution, which the people remember as a time when they were in danger of their lives, when soldiers came and robbed them of chickens, pigs, cattle, and clothing. The villagers were still protecting themselves against a possible recurrence of this state of affairs by maintaining their isolation through secrecy about the village's existence and location. Indeed, one day when some uniformed soldiers came to the village inquiring about a thief who had been molesting people on the roads between villages, an old woman came running to my house wailing, "It's the revolution, it's the revolution." The fear was visibly present and real after more than fifty years. Obviously not all the villagers felt this anxiety to the same extent, but even the more acculturated among them subscribed to the rule of secrecy because it had become a norm that could be flouted only with the expectation of village reprisal in the form of anger.

Their mistrust of me as a stranger was counterbalanced by my being white and female. One man said he hoped that I would have a child in the village, whom I would leave behind when I returned to the States. It was his belief that such a child, having some of my blood, presumably would be fair, strong, and wise because of it. Fair skin was a highly prized attribute, and the girls who were considered most beautiful were all distinctly light-skinned. I also had curly hair, another much envied attribute, which symbolized white blood. And I was plump, a characteristic that further enhanced my desirability in their eyes. What was problematic was that I was unmarried and older than was reasonable for an unmarried girl to be, I was without the protection of my family, and I traveled alone, as an unmarried, virginal girl would never do. They found it hard to understand how I, so obviously attractive in their eyes, could still be single. The obvious remedy was to suggest that I marry in the village. They certainly recognized that I could not work in the fields, wash clothes, grind corn, make tortillas, or haul firewood, but they assured me that, if I did marry a village boy, my future mother or sister-in-law would do all that for me. In trying to persuade me, they would argue that I wasn't too old for the marriageable boys of fifteen, sixteen, or seventeen, since older women quite frequently married young boys. This was a patent untruth. Obviously, they discounted my real age, twenty-nine, since in comparison with village women of the same age who had borne five or six children and worked in the fields, I looked much younger. The important thing was to get me safely married so that I would cease being an anomaly.

Being an unmarried girl meant that I should not drink, smoke, go about alone at night, visit during the day without a real errand, speak of such topics as sex or pregnancy, entertain boys or men in my house except in the presence of older people, or ask too many questions of any kind. Initially I respected many of these restrictions, but eventually I disregarded all of them in the pursuit of my own work. I will speak more about the consequences of this later.

To minimize the difference between myself and the women, I wore skirts mid-calf length, blouses with sleeves, and earrings, and occasionally I combed my hair in braids. However, I did not go barefoot as they did, for fear of scorpions, nor did I wear a rebozo, but instead, on the infrequent cool nights, a sweater. I even had a blouse made similar to those worn by Indian women, in a misguided effort to express my approval of their ways. It was the precipitating factor in the first illicit proposal made to me by a married man: two days after I wore it, he told me how well I looked in it and that I truly appeared like a woman of the village, and he asked me to become his second "wife." I understood this event as a symbolic transformation; my wearing the blouse traditionally worn by women, not girls, conveyed the implicit message that I belonged to the category of "available village women." Previously I had been viewed as a potential sex partner and wife only for the unmarried adolescent males.

The men's knowledge of Americans was limited to those tourists who bought pottery from them as they sold their wares in the plazas of cities, on the beaches, or by the road. The men spoke positively of these brief encounters, usually ending their account with a description of gifts or money they had been given by the generous tourists. Those men who had worked as *braceros* seemed to have had little contact with Americans; such contact would, in any case, have been limited because of the lack of a common language. However, they did come back with an image of Americans as rich and clever and of the typical American husband as subservient to his wife, who was the actual "boss" of the household. Many times I was asked,

"Is it true that in America the wives give the orders in the house?" The people also associated radios (of which there were two in the village), television (which they saw in the cities), ships, airplanes, and the satellite with American know-how, and they often commented how smart Americans must be to have figured out how to make these things.

From the beginning I defined myself as having come to learn their language, and they never questioned why anyone would want to do that but took for granted that this was a worthwhile activity, perhaps because many urbanized Mexicans had expressed a similar interest in learning the language, though few ever made more than a desultory attempt. Their pride in me as I learned a few phrases and pronounced them correctly far outstripped my real ability, and when I traveled to fiestas in other places, one of the first things the people would say in introducing me was that I could speak their language. This pride also extended to my having chosen their village, however difficult it was initially for them to understand. And it pleased them inordinately when people from other villages would wheedlingly invite me to visit or to come live with them and I would reply firmly that I was happy where I was and didn't want to move.

Understanding the language was also a meaningful rationale for asking about aesthetic values, for I would say, "I want you to help me understand what the word 'pretty' means—when to use it, why one thing is prettier than another—for unless I know how to use words, I really don't know what they mean." But if language provided me the means I needed to learn the culture, its values and beliefs, language was also my chief problem. Since Spanish was not used in conversation in the village, except to talk to me, it was of signal importance that I learn Mexicano. Fluency in Spanish varied enormously, even among the men, and it was a problem to find someone who both knew enough Spanish to help me and also had time to devote to lessons. After the schoolteacher left, I went for instruction from individual to individual, but none persevered very long. Although I paid well, they all came to abhor the task, would complain that their head hurt after about half an hour's work, and would invent excuses to cut short or to postpone lessons. During the course of my fourteen-months stay, I worked off and on with eight different teachers.

The critical importance of the language and my own slow grasp of it made it the central focus of continuing anxieties. I had a recurring dream in which I found myself talking with some of the people, to suddenly discover they had learned to speak English. I hungrily began asking them a series of still unanswered questions, and they finally explained everything I wanted to know with startling clarity and precision. It would seem that I have my own overwhelming need to make sense and order out of the various realities through which I move.

If getting reliable information continued to be problematic, still, with the passage of time, there were sporadic cues that told me that I was becoming accepted by the community. I came to define one aspect of rapport as the extent to which I could take liberties without fear of others' reacting with sullen withdrawal or anger. I began to be able to push limits in a good-natured, humorous way, doing it, however, only when something was of great importance to me. For example, while visiting a painter friend and his wife, I asked if I could look at the plates he had already finished. In the course of doing so, I found a stylized painting of a figure with distended earlobes, long hair, and the unmistakable appearance of a Buddhist representation of a bodhisattva. When I questioned him about the source of the design, he claimed to have painted it from his own head, and I laughed and said, "Oh everyone here always says that, but you know that it isn't true this time." "Oh, no, Señorita, es puro sentido." In the past, when I had questioned men about the origin of their designs, it implied to them that I thought they had copied, and they would get testy and indignant. This time I sensed that my certainty that he had copied would be communicated to him, and I took the chance of pressing further: "How can it be purely your thought when I have seen such paintings many times in museums? Now come, show me where you copied it from." A few more rounds of banter, disbelief, and further challenges were necessary, but finally, with a mixture of sheepish laughter and the rueful admission that I was right, he rummaged through a pile of newspapers from Mexico City to sort out one with the original line drawing, accompanied, appropriately enough, by a few lines of poetry about the art of painting.

Another measure of rapport, or call it attachment, can be the small unpremeditated acts of thoughtfulness or concern that, like slips of the tongue, reveal an underlying identification. Like the time the itinerant photographer was posing the children of the family next door and asked me if I lived alone, how long I was staying, if I had a camera, and if I would show it to him. The eldest daughter, about twenty-two, warned me in admonishing tones not to show it to him, and in that moment, although she was exhibiting the usual mistrust of the stranger, I felt a warm sense of our being united together against a possibly treacherous outsider. Or the time when I was about to buy a chair from two traveling salesmen, and the people pointed out how badly it was made and wouldn't let me buy it. And the woman who told me she dreamed that I had left the village, and in her dream she had cried and cried, thinking, "Who will cure us now?" Then there was the day I accompanied the young girls in their climb up a steep, difficult hill as part of a religious ceremony to carry food offerings to the cross enshrined on its summit. Seeing me perspiring, short of breath, and violently red-faced from such exertion in the noonday sun, a young girl of about fourteen deliberately fell behind the others to give me her hand, to help me up treacherous places, and to inquire if I was all right. At the shrine, I found one of my village friends waiting with his horse in case I would be too tired to walk all the way back down.

The more usual way of thinking about rapport is the extent to which people give information without restraint and reveal their inner feelings. My experience in this village leads me to concur with Rosalie Wax, who states in her article, "Reciprocity as a Field Technique" (1952, p. 34), that an informant will talk because he and the field worker are making an exchange, are consciously or unconsciously giving each other something they both desire or need. What was borne in on me repeatedly was that *all* transactions in this village ultimately had to be reciprocal. Every offer or act of help carried the expectation of some return, either immediate or at some time in the future. Since I could not reciprocate by helping with the harvest, with food preparation for fiestas, with rounding up animals, or with housebuilding—the traditional exchanges—I repaid with money or food, gifts of cloth, knives, books, and most importantly, medical care. I paid dues to the pueblo like any villager, gave candles and incense to the church, bought a dictionary for the secretary of the pueblo, loaned stationery and stamps, changed money and even loaned it to good friends, and interceded with government officials on behalf of the people; in these ways I demonstrated not only my usefulness, worth, and importance, but also the fact that I could be counted on to keep up my end of the "bargain." When I would begin to resent the almost businesslike quality of my relationships, I would ask myself whether the people were really so different from those at home or whether village behavior only seemed a caricature because it was not camouflaged or disguised by lofty phrases and implicit fictions.

For a few individuals, the nature of the return was more psychological than material: the prestige of friendship with me; knowledge of the world they might gain; the feeling of security knowing me provided (as in the case of the man whose confiscated rifle I was able to retrieve from the authorities in Iguala by swearing it was mine); and in a few cases, the freedom some felt to say things without censure or criticism, expecting an understanding and sympathetic listener. If intense sharing was rare, I believe it was because the people were not inclined to introspection or accustomed to verbalizing feelings.

I cannot resist this opportunity to make a plea for the necessity of knowingly building some form of reciprocity into the field worker's role, both to enhance the process of rapport and to minimize concern about the asymmetrical quality of the field worker's relationships. To recognize that a "quid pro quo" relationship is more easily accepted, more stable, and more humanly defensible would reduce much of the researcher's conflict.

The closest approximation to friendship, as I conceived it, that I was able to create was with the members of the most acculturated family in the village. It was to them I turned for the kind of deeper emotional reward that accompanies being liked and valued for one's personal qualities rather than for possible material benefit. We could talk to each other in more truly human terms because they felt themselves to be outsiders by virtue of the mother's having been born in Mexico City, her experience and education. She, her husband, and the children could understand what I was feeling at confronting the newness of life in the village since she had once been a stranger too. I learned from them by seeing things from their perspective —being part of the life, yet removed enough to be objective about it—and in truth, they were the best teachers I could have had. Before I left, it was they alone who invited me to dine with them, seated at a table with a tablecloth on it as they knew was customary in the outside world; it was they who brought cigarettes and alcohol, the day I was leaving, for me to distribute to the people gathered in my yard and to the members of the band who had come to play; it was they who cried the hardest when they saw my tears.

Yet when I returned to the village to spend a month's vacation after an absence of three years, they were not as warmly glad to see me as I would have expected, nor were the other villagers. I had been led to believe, by the accounts of other anthropologists returning to their villages after some absence, that the very act of returning created a deepening of trust and regard. My experience was different; the people were outwardly friendly but somewhat distant. One villager even verbalized his feelings, surprisingly enough, in a mock-hostile yet revealing fashion: "Why did you come back if you are going to stay such a short time, if you are just going to leave again?" Perhaps it is a way of rationalizing my chagrin about the lack of enthusiastic reception, but I interpreted the tempered restraint of their response as one more manifestation of their defense against feeling too much, against the pain of disappointment, separation, and loss.

There were hazards as well as satisfactions in becoming close, and in one case I did not accurately assess the degree of involvement or its possible consequences. A widower, with whom I had worked translating a dictionary from Spanish to Mexicano, told me some unusual dreams in which I figured prominently. I made mental note, but I was not seriously alarmed. Then one night, long after the village was quiet in sleep, I was awakened by the sounds of someone shouting an obscene sexual endearment and rattling the stick walls of my house, trying to break in. I asked the old couple sleeping in the bed next to mine to go out and see what was happening. The old woman, obviously awake, finally roused herself and confronted the intruder, my erstwhile collaborator; she shouted at him to go home. The following day he came to say that friends told him that in his drunkenness he had come to my house, but he denied any recollection of his actions and wanted to know what he had said. He was ashamed and contrite and meekly submitted to a tongue-lashing by the old woman, ostensibly so angry because he had damaged the house in his endeavor to get in. This was the only untoward act of any kind, by him or anyone else in the village during my entire stay; it frightened me, not for my own safety, but for its implications of the wide discrepancy between controlled external behavior and inner wishes and needs. Though nothing was ever said to me about this incident, I can speculate that it only strengthened the villagers' belief that where there's smoke, there's fire. (Fortunately, the man did remarry while I was living in the village, and I like to think that his friendship with me gave him the self-confidence and prestige that enabled him to overcome his low self-esteem caused by his unattractive appearance and to woo and win a wife.)

If I had needed it, this event would also have served as a reminder of the inadvisability of intimate involvements on my part. Even if the professional and ethical norms of restraint hadn't been communicated to me as a graduate student, with the warning that intimate relations could result in the loss of the capacity for objectivity, and by presenting the ideal stance of the field worker as that of noninterference with the ongoing life of the community, my very inability to predict the short- and long-term repercussions of such relations, either for myself or for the people, would have acted to brake any impulses I might have had to move closer. (Of course this fact didn't prevent me from embroidering some fantasies of my own in those occasional cases when I found a man attractive.)

As I mentioned, early in my stay my house and yard would be filled at night with boys of all ages, marriageable young men, and occasionally some married men. That this was considered improper for a girl I discovered after they had stopped appearing; I subsequently learned indirectly that my protective landlord had, without my knowledge, asked them to stay away. I have come to believe that I lost the services of his niece because her presence in my house was making her position equivocal and exposing her to malicious gossip.

This enforced nightly isolation finally led me to seek out company despite my knowledge that it would be disapproved, and I began to walk about the village with my flashlight to watch the boys and men play tag games, go down to the plaza to talk, tell stories, ask questions, and drink beer with the men who might be there. If the first approach by a married man was the result of changing my image by wearing a "woman's" blouse, later proposals were probably due to these nightly sojourns and to the fact that I regularly began to attend the men's meetings held in the meeting hall,

where I became a familiar figure, interacted easily with the men, and participated freely as a resource person who interpreted government directives
written in legal phrases, wrote out birth forms, helped with arithmetic, or
generally acted as temporary secretary when the elected official was out of
town or drunk. No other woman was ever present at these meetings.

The men were always exaggeratedly respectful in their demeanor, but
even they would tease me about getting married in the village and question
me about whether I had a *novio* (sweetheart). But afterward, obviously
uneasy about taking this license in public, they would reaffirm that everyone held me in the highest esteem and would point out with pride that "no
one has ever said anything," by which they meant that no one had ever
insulted me or spoken disrespectfully.

Against this backdrop of carefully maintained public behavior, the fact
that a number of boys and men were able to approach me privately became
all the more salient because of the very contrast and because I knew that
many believed I might complain to the government and have them jailed if
they spoke to me. A man or boy might come to my house to ask for medicine or to have a letter typed, and we would chat. When he called a second
and third time without an ostensible purpose, I sensed what might eventually happen, but nonetheless I took advantage of his presence and willingness to talk until the moment when the covert would be made overt and I
would have to reject any proposals. Knowing how men felt in general about
rejection or humiliation, I was fearful of losing his good will and companionship. I was surprised however, that when the actual invitation was made,
it was often presented so tentatively, so indirectly, that I could pretend I
didn't understand and he could pretend he hadn't really said anything, and
both our feelings were saved. In those instances when the proposition was
unambiguous, it was done with so little expectation of success that I realized that for them the game was one of low risk–high gain. When they
noted that I didn't get angry, there was no fear that I would bring any
complaint against them; they therefore had little to lose by making the
attempt, and in the unlikely event that I might be convinced to marry, or at
least to have an affair, from their point of view they had a good deal to
gain. The difficulty was that it was expected of the female always to appear
unwilling initially, so that my lack of interest and my refusals were not
always taken at face value but were interpreted as typical female behavior.
I came to have no serious compunctions about playing the innocent or
prolonging the game, since there was no deep feeling involved and since
they were, in effect, trying to exploit me too. I will never know if some of
the young men were truly serious in their intentions, but of those who did
offer marriage, at least three of the five had other sweethearts at the same
time they were "asking" for me. Other proposals were from married men.

A whole segment of the culture was opened to me through these experiences, and I began to see how mistrust is built into the sweetheart relationship. The novia can never be sure she is the sole object of her sweetheart's affection, nor even of the nature of his intentions; she may therefore encourage the attentions of more than one suitor as a safeguard. He, in turn, uncertain of his acceptance, may attempt to court more than one girl. Objective evidence of the degree of strain intrinsic to these relationships is that during my stay seven boys were publicly accused of improper behavior with young girls, and though the boy paid a fine, there was always argument about which of a pair was actually culpable. Of these seven cases, only one ended in marriage.

The pervasiveness of suspicions centered around relations between the sexes, and the perception of me as a target of attention must have affected my ability to become friends with the unmarried girls, who, with some exceptions, were withdrawn and unreachable. As in the case of my landlord's niece, they might have been afraid that I would somehow taint them; in other cases they were actually hostile, perhaps seeing me as a potential competitor. Only in the process of writing this has it become clear that what I had assumed to be only reticence toward me, the stranger, on the part of young girls may have been complicated by these considerations.

Mistrust is also built into the marriage relation, since it is accepted as man's nature to be interested in other women. Conversely, men jealously guard their wives and are quick to believe that they might be susceptible to the blandishments of other men. One informant said, "Husbands and wives are very suspicious of each other, and some men beat their wives regularly." I commented, "Well, if a wife is going to be beaten anyway, she might think she might as well have a boy friend." He replied, "That's exactly the way it happens sometimes." He told me too that a man may test his wife by telling her he is going to another town when he really isn't, only to sneak back in an attempt to surprise her, or, "Men learn what their wives do from other women too—when a man sleeps with a girl friend, she will tell him what his wife is doing. She says, 'Come live with me, your wife goes with another man, so you'd better come live with me.' "

It seemed to me that courtship behavior, whether actual or vicarious, provided an important form of recreation in the village: it offered suspense, a challenge to the ingenuity, the deliberate creation of tension associated with the danger of exposure, and ultimately, with enough perseverance and cleverness, satisfaction and triumph. The intensity of interest in matters of sex, the fact that the villagers could not conceive that a man and woman could be platonic friends or have repeated conversations that were not preliminary to sex and that any woman or girl was open to testing to see if she might be willing to enter a liaison, all influenced their perception of me, as well as their behavior.

In trying to assess the impact of my gender on my relationships in the village, I would here like to add another overlay to what I have already written, to demonstrate how the densely woven complexity of reality always escapes attempts to neatly separate its threads. Even the perception of biological gender is not isolable but is intertwined with age, marital status, and other attributes already discussed; in addition, sex is symbolically affected by the move toward modernization that is occurring in the village. It is very likely that, somehow, I was an embodiment of that change —its simultaneously threatening and attractive aspects—so that I was not simply a female stranger, but also a representative of the greater world that was already making encroachments into the village in unexpected ways.

Women were, on the whole, far more conservative than men; few spoke Spanish, few had ever traveled further than Iguala, and few interacted with anyone, apart from tradesmen, from outside the village. Their inexperience coupled with their traditional role, which enjoined them to remain socially in the background, had left its mark. The women and I could exchange superficial pleasantries, but it was difficult for them to participate in a sustained conversational exchange unless it was about some universally compelling topic such as children, illness, or death. As the women aged, some were able to operate with more personal freedom and were less constricted by village norms. Some even smoked and drank alcohol occasionally and were more like men temperamentally and in their ability to talk with me. On the other hand, some old women represented the extreme of conservatism, suspiciousness, and inaccessibility; I was never able to break down these barriers enough to get any sense of them as fully dimensional individuals. Their role was to uphold standards of behavior, not to understand, condone, or be lenient about lapses from these standards. What they actually thought of me I will never know, but whatever it was couldn't have been very positive. And to the extent that they saw me as an example of what their own granddaughters might become some day, they could only be ambivalent about me as a tangible projection of the future. Their reaction to me, and my judgment of their inadequacy as informants, interacted to subtly propel me to seek out men as the best source of data.

Clearly men in this village were very different from women, and the divergences grow wider as an increasing number of men are exposed to the commercial world, other modes of life, other ideas. In regard to the heightened sexuality I observed in some of them, I cannot begin to conceive the effects on these men of seeing lady tourists in their bikinis on the beaches of Acapulco, movies of love and romance Mexican style, or television productions they might have observed in store windows or private homes in the cities. The more experienced men were the ones I got to know best because they were the painters and central to my study; probably I was able to establish fairly close relations with them just because they were painters, and consequently more sophisticated, more interested in me, and more "Westernized" in all their tastes.

These traveled men differed not only from the women, but also from those men who were totally involved in the traditional role of farmer. They were different in their spontaneity, humor, deeper awareness of the variety of human motivation, eagerness to learn, and willingness to take risks of all kinds. They were even visibly differentiated by the Western-style shirts and trousers they wore instead of the homemade white shirts and balloon-legged pants worn by the more traditional men.

There was other evidence that the village was in a state of transition: the breakdown of village institutions' ability to handle infringements of their own laws and increasing reliance on the government of the county to arbitrate conflicts, particularly those arising between novios; complaints about rising interest rates the people charged each other when loaning money; an increase in the number of young people of both sexes leaving the village to work in nearby towns and cities. Still other evidence of change was the variation in villagers' responses to a wide range of questions, from the duration of taboos on sex after childbirth to the meaning of traditional ceremonies. I would alternately suppose that the Indians didn't all know their own culture to the same degree, that they were lying, that they were ashamed to admit the truth, or that what I was seeing was the tattered version of a once seamless set of beliefs. All these suppositions may be true. Certainly there were many commonalities of belief and behavior— otherwise I couldn't have written the descriptive generalizations presented earlier; but what was equally true was that they were not a homogeneous group of people. The aesthetic-values test I administered also revealed this lack of homogeneity; the profiles of aesthetic preference varied according to sex, degree of exposure to the outside world, and amount of involvement with the activity of painting. The variety, discrepancies, and differences were also more salient than the commonalities because I experienced them as frustrations in gathering data and predicting responses, and because I saw them as the source of artistic creativity, hostility, and disputes, as well as the observable reflection of change that was occurring in the village.

To recapitulate, though the following do not qualify as established generalizations that would be equally applicable in all cultures, my own experience had led me to conclude that sex role operated as a determinant of the topics of information I could discuss with each sex, the abundance of information provided, the difficulty in using direct questioning (inappropriate for a girl) as a means to collect data, and most important, the quality of interaction with members of different age and sex groups in the culture. More succinctly, being a female influenced in some degree who could freely talk to me, what they said, where interaction could take place, and why they were motivated to behave as they did.

Obviously a male field worker would also have encountered sex-linked problems, but they would have been structured differently. He would not have been able to interview women or girls alone, and I suspect that he would have found even more lying, dissimulation, and suppression on the part of men because they would have a greater need to appear sophisticated in front of him. Were he to study the same problem I set myself, he would not have been able to administer the values test to women and get unbiased responses, and though he would have come to grasp more quickly the vision of the man's world—since he could drink with men, hear the stories they told only among themselves, and even brag with them—it would have taken longer for him to sense their tentativeness and anxiety in relation to females, the government, and the greater world. Though these effects may seem trivial or banal, to the extent that they operate they must be taken account of in interpreting interview material, test results, and observations —the basic data of the field worker.

In the early days I sometimes felt like a prisoner marooned on a desert island; the feeling of no escape or rescue was heightened by an acute, though intermittent, awareness of the narrow margin of life. I watched people who became ill quickly resign themselves to death, since no doctor ever had come to the village nor was it thinkable, in an emergency, to carry a suffering person down the mountain only to wait for a bus to carry him to a doctor in the city.

Before living in the village, I had never actually seen a person die, nor any dead bodies that had not been cosmetically transformed. In the course of fourteen months, I was present at enough deaths and funerals to empathize with the villagers' occasionally heartless joking references to death, their passive acceptance of its inevitability, and their anxiety about it despite or because of continuous psychological preparation for this extreme outcome in the case of any protracted illness, whatever the age of the patient.

Even though my apprehension about sudden illness diminished, the awareness of isolation continued as a feeling of oppression, of the village's closing in on me. Being surrounded by the same faces day after day, I sometimes felt a compelling need for variety; I longed to be anonymous, to be able to walk unobserved without having every action questioned, commented upon, or gossiped about. I remember a time when I went to the church solely in order to cry, knowing it to be the one place where I might be alone for a while, and knowing that if I should be discovered, my tears would not be remarked, since many women cry in church as they pray.

The things that made me laugh are more difficult to evoke. The way a child would squeal with delight—screwing up his face and crying "Ah, señorita," as I lifted and twirled him—isn't amusing unless it's experienced. A little boy playing at grinding corn on a makeshift stone, looking like a miniature replica of his mother as he reproduced the body movements and facial expressions that he probably didn't even know he had learned, made me giggle with recognition. Watching two drunks propping each other up as they weaved and stumbled along the street, totally engaged in what to them was obviously a deadly earnest, world-shakingly important conversation, reminded me of Charlie Chaplin at his best.

Toward the end I kept wishing that I could stay longer—so much was undone, and I was just getting to a point of fluency in the language. I knew, too, that it was the pressure of time that forced me at times to consciously manipulate people and situations in order to ferret out critical facts that would have appeared in the natural course of events, had there been time to observe and listen at more leisure. This manipulation creates guilt, as does the action of turning deeply felt emotional encounters into dispassionately dry field notes; as does the alchemy of transmuting the innocent testimony of unsuspecting witnesses into formulations they would not understand, or, if they understood them, would see as betrayal. I was split into parallel selves —a caring, participating, sympathetic listener; an interpreting, distant, re-moved observer; a guilty spy not always sure which side I was on. I hope this will not be read simply as an attitudinizing display of my personal conflicts in accepting the role of ethnographer, but rather as an attempt to provide emotional inoculation that may reduce the severity of reaction in other young people who are embarking on their first field experience.

Despite the frustrations, petty and great; despite the periods of depression, panic, loneliness, that were not infrequent; despite the irritations and my own irritability—I can still look back at this time in the village as the most fulfilling, most endlessly interesting, most vital and intense period of my life. Every day I felt that I had learned something of immediate importance. A belief, a word, a bit of information, a reaction were like colored chips to be placed in the mosaic of village life I was assembling.

If I romanticized my efforts by likening them to those of an explorer sailing unknown seas, charting unfamiliar territory, in truth I do appreciate the inexplicable thrill of having been there first. As well, to have perse-vered; to have dealt and coped effectively with a series of challenges; to have not simply endured, but found laughter, affection, and insight—all combine to make the experience of field work unique in its impact and in its result: an enlarged sense of self-confidence, a deeper realization of one's own identity, and a concrete intellectual accomplishment.

If I do an injustice to the people by having overemphasized the diffi-culties and frustrations I faced, I do none to the representation of the over-all quality of the experience as it came to me at the time. It was the negative aspects that had to be overcome if I were to isolate answers to the problem of artistic behavior from the diffuse and complex, sometimes chaotic, background. I could not have understood the art style of this culture if I hadn't known about witchcraft beliefs, sex roles and relations between the sexes, attitudes toward illness and health, the conception of work, the suppression of anger, and the pervasive insecurity that characterized the people's outlook on the world—all of which had shaped their aesthetic values and were embedded in the style. Neither could I have appreciated that artistic behavior provided the people a new means of strengthening themselves. Their pottery brought additional income, their success in selling created a new dimension of pride and self-esteem, and the painting itself was a channel for fantasies of sex, strength, power, and aggression.

I have only been able to suggest here the nature of the intellectual discoveries, but the chief motivation for field work, and a major reward, is intellectual in nature. But if this is not too narrowly defined, it can be said that the reward is at once broader and more subjective. I owe a debt of gratitude to the villagers, not simply for whatever scientific value there may be to what I found through their help, but for their role in furthering my development and widening my vision.

I now see, having done subsequent field work, that the first experience was qualitatively different in its meaning and implications from all later ones. Permeating this first encounter was the anxiety about my future as an anthropologist, which would be measured by my ability to successfully establish rapport; upon this rapport would depend the achievement of producing a "significant contribution to the discipline." I conceived field work as a trial by fire that would determine whether I deserved acceptance into the professional world.

If I were to write accounts of subsequent work, it is clear that they would not be as intense, as self-involved, as negatively toned, or perhaps as revealing. To convey more accurately the tension of that first encounter with a foreign culture, I have not modified the description by making use of the perspective of hindsight; the first time around, it is not possible to take things coolly; too much hangs in the balance. One is not only learning another culture but learning about one's current self, and one's capacities, in preparation for future journeys. If there was discomfort in discovering an arrogance in myself I hadn't fully seen before, it was a necessary discovery that would inform future behavior. Using oneself as an instrument of research, all feedback must be carefully considered because it can reveal the strengths and weaknesses of that self as a measuring device.

Though I have couched my account in what may seem highly personal terms, it is because the process of understanding another culture is the process of recognition; only by using the self as a filter is it possible to weigh and evaluate relative differences and similarities. If at times, I felt smug because of my education and training, habitual analytic reasoning, and ability to control my emotions, I also learned to accept an irrationality I shared with the people, to recognize my own susceptibility to social pressures and the need for the people's good will and affection to maintain my own feeling of security. Though I moved outside the system to a large extent, I was no less social a creature than any one of them, depending on the day-to-day gratifications of human interchange for my own emotional sustenance. I directly experienced the contagion of belief and feeling, since for me, to understand means to feel with, and in so doing to temporarily take inside a new set of reactions. To know the depth of someone's fear makes it impossible not to behave in terms of that fear; to know the people's definition of betrayal is to suffer in imagination their reaction to being betrayed. I cannot say whether this susceptibility is a particularly feminine trait. But if there is a difference between male and female anthropologists brought up in our culture, maybe it is that women are willing to a greater extent to screen experience through their own emotional net, to use their own feelings as a guide to understanding others, and to participate in a subjective way in whatever social setting they find themselves.

If in the end I didn't unqualifiedly like all my people, they are mine as my family is mine, because they are part of me and my personal history; they are mine, bound to me not by possessiveness or ownership, but by having lived common experiences, by having shared a common life.

References

Lewis, Oscar. 1951. *Life in a Mexican Village: Tepoztlan Restudied.* Urbana: University of Illinois Press.

Wax, Rosalie. 1952. "Reciprocity as a Field Technique." In R. N. Adams and J. Preiss, eds., In *Human organization research.* Homewood, Ill.: Dorsey Press.

MEXICO (OAXACA)/ZAPOTEC;
LEBANON/SHIA MOSLEMS

From Anguish to Exultation

LAURA NADER *has pursued the study of law and conflict behavior since receiving her doctorate in 1961. She has studied law among the Zapotec in Mexico and the Shias in Lebanon, as well as among consumers in the United States. She edited a special issue of the* AMERICAN ANTHROPOLOGIST *on the ethnography of law, and with her students at the University of California at Berkeley she published* THE DISPUTING PROCESS—LAW IN TEN SOCIETIES *(1978) and* NO ACCESS TO LAW *(1980). Her work is also found in two films,* TO MAKE A BALANCE *and* LITTLE INJUSTICES. *At present she is involved in energy research and in the study of professional cultures. She is currently a professor of anthropology at Berkeley.*

Clifford Geertz's review (1967) of *The Malinowski Diaries* and Hortense Powdermaker's critique of the review (1967) convinced me that this volume should be valuable in dispelling certain myths anthropologists have about themselves and their profession. It should also be useful in communicating to the noninitiates (those who have not done anthropological field work) a view of field work that is rarely—or not often enough—discussed in either oral or written form: the personal, managerial, and intellectual aspects of work in the field. In this essay I shall draw upon my field experiences in Mexico and in Lebanon as a way of commenting on the following themes: the profound ambivalence that characterizes most field experience, the problem of rapport, the specific effect of being a woman field worker, and the intellectual problems of anthropology as they affect the field anthropologist.

Mexico 1957

In the spring of 1957 I learned that I had received a Mexican government grant of approximately $1,200 to support nine months' field work in Mexico. I was in the midst of preparing for my general oral examinations at Harvard, and everyone—except Clyde Kluckhohn—advised me to postpone field work until afterward. Kluckhohn, who was my thesis advisor, told me that he thought I had been in the library too long and said, "Some people just have to do things ass-backwards." I accepted the grant. I had chosen to go to Mexico because during a year of undergraduate study there I had specialized in the history, culture, and language of Mexico and had traveled throughout the country. Moreover, during a visit to Oaxaca City I had

I am particularly indebted to Hortense Powdermaker, John Gumperz, and Claire Rosenfield for their critical comments on an earlier draft of this article.

97

taken a special interest in the Indian heritage of the country, and I wanted to pursue this further.

My project in 1957 was to study a region as yet unexplored by anthropologists, geographers, or historians and to focus on the question of settlement patterns. From the literature I knew that a variety of such patterns were to be found in Oaxaca, and I was intrigued by the possibility of comparing two Zapotec villages—one dispersed, one compact—in order to find out how settlement pattern affects forms of social organization. It was a fairly general problem, but my training had been general rather than specialized.

There was not much emphasis on methodological training at Harvard. However, Kluckhohn had often encouraged graduate students to experience psychoanalysis or psychotherapy as training in social anthropology. Because we wanted or needed it, I and a great many of my associates in graduate school sought such psychiatric experience. I have found it invaluable for learning how to elicit life histories. In general, some self-knowledge is indispensable in evaluating what must, indeed, always be selective reporting. "No matter how objective we may try to be, we must never forget the fact that we see with our own eyes," said Cardozo.

Before leaving Harvard I went to see Kluckhohn. In spite of the confidence I had gained from some of my training at Harvard, this last session left me frustrated. When I asked Kluckhohn if he had any advice, he told the story of a graduate student who had asked Kroeber the same question. In response, Kroeber was said to have taken the largest, fattest ethnography book off his shelf, handed it to the student, and said, "Go thou forth and do likewise." The story did not reassure me, but Kluckhohn went on to say, "Be sure to take a copy of my 'Personal Documents' paper with you, send back your notes regularly, and I hope to visit you some time while you are there."

I left his office wondering if he realized that I had never had so much as a minor field experience and that I had never conducted an interview or taken a genealogy. Preparations for the field swept the worries from my mind. I packed several good ethnographies, a copy of *Notes and Queries* (written for nonanthropologists), and a pack of medicines, and off I went. I was delayed for several weeks in Mexico City, where I had paused to make more or less official visits to several Mexican anthropologists. From them I received various introductory letters, but the manner in which they spoke to me suggested they had little faith that I would ever reach mountain Zapotec country and accomplish my task; few young women had done that sort of thing alone. One Mexican anthropologist, however, encouraged me and helped orient me to my task. I will be forever grateful to Professor Roberto Weitlaner for my several trips with him to Otomi country. He taught me by example what the usual anthropological techniques are, how to take a genealogy, how to take word lists, how to "make rapport," and how to interview. I left for Oaxaca buoyed by Weitlaner's encouragement and by a confidence gained through our trips to Otomi country. Brief though it was, it was the only specifically field-oriented experience I had had. In Oaxaca I learned of the work of the Papaloapan Commission, a Mexican version of the TVA, and of the work of that commission in the mountain Zapotec area. I spoke to the engineer in charge of road building and made arrangements for him to take me into the Rincón Zapotec area —a region that seemed ideal for comparative study of settlement patterns.

The engineer took me to the end of the road and left me. So began my first field work. As I walked down the path behind two Zapotec-speaking guides, I wondered what on earth had brought me to this remote place. Probably as good a reason as any was that no social scientist had ever before come to this part of Oaxaca to study the Rincón Zapotec. At least it was a dramatic enough reason to give me courage as I looked back at the disappearing Land Rover that had brought me into this uninhabited country of the Sierra Juarez. Walking along the mountain path, I was dimly aware of the settlements that were enfolded by the mountains in view. Here one may walk for hours without the settlements seeming any nearer, until suddenly there are houses everywhere. The Zapotec guides walked at a brisk pace, stopping only for water, and in three and a half hours we arrived at San Miguel Talea de Castro, the bilingual Zapotec town of 2,000 people that was to be my base for nine months during that year and for three months in the following year. Upon arrival I was taken to see friends of the engineer, a family that had tentatively agreed to house me. All was excitement, not because of my arrival, but rather because pilgrims were returning from the Sanctuario in Veracruz. Mole, memelas, otole—all foods for celebration—were combined in our supper. After eating, the head of the household began to interrogate me. Was I a Catholic, he asked. If so, I could remain in their house; if not, I was unwelcome, because Protestants were not wanted in town. I gasped at the righteousness in his voice and answered that I belonged to the original Catholic Church (Eastern Orthodox). He allowed me to stay.

Those first few days were paradise. The mountains are beautiful. Orchids bloom in abundance in May, before the rainy season begins. A vivid green constrasts with the brown houses, and the eye is impressed with coffee plants in bloom. Some distance below the village, sugar cane ripens for harvest. These pueblos have the charm and beauty that comes of harmony with the natural environment. The families of men who had worked in the United States as *braceros* during the second World War were especially friendly. I was very happy and secure in the reception given me and felt much less lonely and oppressed than I had felt before leaving Cambridge. But how wrong I was in my assessment of the situation!

When two weeks had passed, I was summoned to the priest's house, where I was accused of being a Protestant missionary. I felt very angry as the priest examined my letters of recommendation, which included a note from a well-known priest in Oaxaca. His only comment was that the signature looked faked. The family I lived with became much colder while the village priest wired the Oaxaca priest, explaining that I had been in danger of being accused. A return wire served to identify me as an anthropologist and a good Christian, and the Papaloapan Commission sent an engineer—as support and as a check on my safety. In spite of these assurances, the priest in Talea continued to wage his war on me both from the pulpit and in the streets and houses, throughout my stay. Missionaries had been to Talea before, arousing a conflict that ended with the Talean's burning homes of Protestants. For that action the town had been forced by state authorities to pay heavy fines. There is no doubt that this accusation hindered my work during the first months and most certainly limited the interaction I might have had with many people. Such behavior of Rinconeros is not directed at missionaries alone but extends to all outsiders, with the general exception of government agents.

The rosy beginning of those first two weeks was now marred by further accusations, and my anger mounted. People in Talea thought me lazy. After all, I did nothing but walk around asking questions. This was not considered a worthy activity, although it did create envy. I began to learn that industry is highly valued, and I found myself explaining the work of the anthropologist. All my explanations, however, only seemed to inspire the question, "What good will your work be to the Rincón?" I explained the work of the government development project, the Papaloapan Commission, and the need to provide it with information about the lives and customs of the people. Since the villagers were aware of the gap in communication between themselves and Mexican government officials, they were able to grasp part of my meaning. Nevertheless, I was asked this same question over and over, and over and over I explained, using examples that I came to know were important to them: the building of roads, the improvement of crops, the provision of musical instruments, health care (especially during epidemics of measles and whooping cough). But the Zapotec themselves are very persuasive and succeeded many times in putting me on the defensive. "What good are you to us? Why should we allow you to stay here [when you are not a 'functioning' member of society]? And just why, although you are very *simpatica* (likeable), should we answer your questions?" The Zapotec seemed never to care to give something unless he was sure of getting something in return—and preferably in kind. I found myself at times trying to be a member of their society on their terms. Although these activities did provide some data through observing behavior and listening to conversation, I realized that the process was interfering with my work. I remember saying to myself one night, "Laura, if you are going to be a nurse, go get trained and come back; if you're going to be a social worker, do the same; if you're going to become an anthropologist, you better get more single-minded about your daily routines."

Being an anthropologist twenty-four hours a day was a terrible strain on me, especially in a society where so many people, especially women, were strongly averse to answering direct personal questions; if they could see no direct practical relevance to a question they would avoid answering. I had been working among the dispersed villagers of San Juan Juquila and had been visiting a ranch family regularly for about three weeks before I dared to ask any questions. I then began making inquiries about godparenthood; after half an hour I asked, "How many godchildren do you have?" My potential informant, a woman, became very angry; she told me that she liked my visits but asked why I had to ask questions that were none of my business. I answered that Americans had a custom of being *pregontones* (big question askers), and as they say here, "Cada pueblo tiene su costumbre" (each town has its own customs).

Because the woman responded with laughter, I seized on this approach as a way to get the Zapotec to accept me on my own terms, as I wanted to be accepted in part because it relieved me of some strain and tension. I also realized that I had to become more skillful in indirect questioning because that eased the strain on the villagers. For example, in eliciting information about exchange at marriage, I would describe a stereotypic American wedding, noting who gives what to whom and when. When I became their informant, more symmetry of relationship could come about. Their comments on my information would reveal important disclosures on exhanges at marriage among Rinconeros. I used another technique in eliciting information about witchcraft cases, a subject that they were reticent in talking about at first. Fortunately I had secured the name of a *bruja* (witch), Juana, and I told a woman that I was thinking of consulting her about a personal problem. She immediately responded, "But why Juana? Maria is much better." And there began a discussion of the various brujos, men and women, and their respective specialities. Once I knew the names of the brujos, eliciting information was easier because I was now considered to be on the "inside." Although the attempt to ask questions in indirect and subtle ways was often tedious, it probably elicited more information than pat answers would have.

Field work is a series of trials and errors. When one makes a daring stab at building rapport and is successful, the experience is exhilarating.

Early in my Zapotec field work I went to a village neighboring Talea—San Juan Yaee—a village that enjoyed the reputation of being *cerrado* (closed). My trip was made on the occasion of a fiesta, and I went to the town accompanied by a twelve-year-old girl. The atmosphere was not only unfriendly, but also electrified. Since no one would talk with me, I began mapping the town. Finally a drunken Yaean came up to me and said, "How do you do?" in English. He had been a bracero in the United States in 1945, and now he invited me to his home. Drunk as he was, I went because he was the only person to have talked to me during what was a very long morning. When we arrived at his mud-brick house, the women scampered into a corner as he offered me some mescal. Suddenly a big blond-haired, blue-eyed man burst in upon us, also drunk, and began accusing me of being a Protestant, a bad woman, and a number of other rather compromising epithets. He had a large bottle of mescal in his hand and declared that I could not leave the house until I drank his bottle with him. At this moment my host slumped into a drunken heap on the floor. The women viewed me with fearful eyes from the corner. I knew no one in the village; my only friend had just passed out. I decided to take the visitor up on his challenge, since I had not had anything alcoholic to drink that day. We drank four shots one after the other, at which point he was so drunk that he could hardly keep his balance, let alone keep me a prisoner in the house. I coolly walked out the door, thought about complaining formally to the municipal authorities, but instead went to a nearby cantina where I began telling my story to all present (people who only an hour earlier would not speak to me). I must have been thoroughly unpleasant, which I imagine they would expect of any good young woman. I spoke frankly about the unpleasant welcome they had given me, and I told them they were impolite according to standards in my country (which I knew were not their standards). I told about the fellow who had forced me to drink with him and asked whether this was an appropriate way to treat a woman visiting so far from home. They became defensive and apologetic and explained that the man in question was even rude to his own father. In the time that passed until my second trip the social pressures had been so great on the culprit that he himself came and apologized.

In those first few months there were many problems, especially those having to do with my health and my sex role. I had been in the field only about six weeks when I came down with malaria and hepatitis. Apart from the obvious fact that such illnesses are physically debilitating, I would like to draw attention to the mental state they produce vis-à-vis field work and the people one is studying. When I first felt sick, I did not know what was wrong with me. Nor was there a doctor in the area. I thought I had the flu. I could not eat; I sweated a great deal; I lost my energy; and the bottle of cold pills I had with me did not help. Days passed. In the absence of "knowing," I began to consider the whole illness as psychosomatic. At the same time I became panicked because I was losing so many work days. I made myself go out to talk to people; I goaded myself to type up the materials I had collected; I tried to force myself to eat. Only after I had fainted one day while washing my hair in a public washing place did I begin to admit the possibilities of being sick. Fortunately, a medical doctor had been sent from Oaxaca to take care of an epidemic of measles. When he came to see me, he told me he thought I had malaria—a surprise, because this was not a malarial area. I had, however, visited a Zapotec village on the border of Chinantec territory, where I must have contracted the disease. I have often wondered what would have happened had the doctor not come along. I was in a completely depressed and debilitated condition, resenting these obstacles to my work. I couldn't stand being sick. I couldn't stand it (understand it) when an informant wouldn't "cooperate." I couldn't stand the Catholic priest and those self-righteous natives who encouraged his "persecution" of me.

What I had considered a paradise during my first two weeks became a hell. In the midst of all this, Kluckhohn had written me a warm and kindly letter to tell me that my field notes were not detailed enough, that a good day's field work ought to yield three times the amount of typewritten material I was sending. I felt guilty, but I had no energy. The doctor put me on a horse and made arrangements for me to go to Oaxaca City. I spent approximately two months recuperating, for the first three weeks living in a hotel. A recommended doctor had given me some Aralen pills, had told me to take them regularly and to get some rest. I had no choice. I continued to wake up every morning soaked in perspiration. The chambermaid would help me to wash; I would go next door to eat, and then I returned to bed. Various letters from home advised me to go to the American Embassy in Mexico City for a physician, but I could not even walk down the street. Slowly I began to feel better, except that I was terribly depressed. I thought that the depression must be related to my not working and made arrangements to return to the Sierra. When the Land Rover came early one morning, I could not get out of bed. That day I forced myself to walk five blocks to see an American nurse living in Oaxaca. I will always remember those five blocks and how shameless I felt; when I couldn't walk, I simply sat down on the edge of the sidewalk. When the nurse saw my state, she said, "Sick people can't know how to take care of themselves, I should know that." She put me in a taxi and sent me to a doctor. Upon entering his office, I burst into tears and said, "I don't care about being sick, but I want to know why I'm so depressed." It was he who told me I had hepatitis.

From that time on things went better. The nurse invited me into her home while I recuperated. With good food and daily liver and Aralen shots, I was ready to return to the Sierra by August. I was in good health although frantic from having lost so much time in the field, especially now, with Kluckhohn's letter ringing in my ears. I remained in the Sierra for several weeks, then returned to Oaxaca for a few days to talk with several anthropologists from Harvard. Those talks, brief as they were, had two functions: they relieved my anxiety about the amount of data one should collect in the field; and they served to focus what was entirely too broad a question by concentrating on fewer variables.

My real work began upon my return to the Sierra in September. I celebrated my good feeling by buying a barrel of mescal during the fiesta of the patron saint of Talea, San Miguel, and presenting it to the town officials. It was as if I had learned the magic words, for because I had *contributed* to the town, this gift was taken as a symbol of my becoming a citizen of the town. Now I knew what Julio de la Fuente meant when he advised me to remember that the Achilles' heel of the Zapotec was the gift. While I had always taken gifts of drink or tobacco when I visited the neighboring villages, never to have done the same in Talea was a great oversight on my part. Many public speeches followed the presentation, all saying in effect, "We were wrong to think Señorita Laura a Protestant. Now she has contributed; now she is one of us." As the Arab proverb says; "Empty hands are dirty hands." Henceforth I always gave substantial gifts to the town as a way of minimizing the necessity for giving individual gifts. (In the case of the Juquilan ranchers, I always gave gifts of food, since they refused to take money for feeding me.)

This, however, was public acceptance. I was a citizen, yes, but what manner of woman was I? They had never seen a woman with short hair; they had never seen a woman in button-down sport shirts wearing tennis shoes (all male features); they had never seen a woman taller than the men in the town. They were surprised that a woman would have the courage to walk between towns at night, alone or with only a young child, and they wondered why I was there at all, since it was not as comfortable a place as the city would be. Soon the myth grew that I had the power to turn myself into a man or woman at will. The women constantly badgered me to grow my hair, to change my clothes. By experimenting, I finally discovered that the best way to handle this attitude was to tell them that were they to visit my home town dressed in long dresses, without brassieres, and with such long pigtails, they would be ridiculed as the laughingstock of the town. Much merriment would result from such conversations, and I realized how lopsided some of our earlier conversations had been. I never tried to dress like them or to grow my hair. Rather, I capitalized on their indecision as to how to categorize me and gained the greatest freedom of movement among both men and women. Although I remained outside of their system, I did undertake certain social obligations, such as regular payment of pesos to the town treasury, which gave me some rights as a town resident. Knowing just when to step into the system and when to remain outside was a constant concern throughout my field work, whether or not I was consciously aware of this problem. It was mainly a problem because of the effect such steps would have on my work situation.

The Taleans for the most part were a warm and industrious people, but many of them suffered from the ambivalences of being bicultural and bilingual (Zapotec-Mexican). Writings about such "mestizo" situations often stress the between-two-worlds character of their everyday worlds. I was familiar with such a situation, having been reared in a New England town where over half the population was living between or in two disparate worlds. I myself had grown up in such a bilingual, bicultural household, but as an anthropologist I was now experiencing the "between two worlds" situation in a new way. It was happening to me again at the same time that I was studying people in a two-worlds state. I was reared to believe that only strength could or should result from such an experience. Yet observations in New England and in Zapotec country impressed upon me the negative effects of the situations when one culture—in this case Mexican—is seen as superior and, in fact, incompatible with the other, Zapotecan. Such a view was common to the family with whom I lived in Talea and, indeed, was shared by the majority of influential people in the town. My whole person railed against such an attitude, so that when Talea became too oppressive in this way, I would escape to my work on the dispersed ranches of San Juan Juquila—a monolingual, monocultural village characterized by an overwhelming sense of self-esteem and pride in being Juquilan. I was grateful to be able to escape from one field situation by going into another nearby, since the absence of easy transportation made it difficult to leave the Rincón frequently. My visits were a regular occurrence among the ranch people who simply made room for my sleeping bag to be placed between them on top of the *temascal* (sweat bath).

Assistants in Talea were not easy to acquire because I did not have enough money to hire an adult. Instead, after a time I located a seventeen-year-old girl, Virginia, who was an excellent interpreter and well liked by members of both towns. I was also greatly helped by the municipal secretary, who recorded under my directions a sample of court cases that he observed. On my second trip to the Rincón in 1959–1960 I hired an anthropology student from Mexico City, Jacobo Montes, originally from the Zapotec area around the Cajones. Although his spoken Zapotec was barely intelligible to the Rinconero it did help him in his work for although my knowledge of Spanish was fluent, I had only learned enough Rincón Zapotec to check formal interview sessions and to indicate general friendliness with monolingual Zapotecs.

I have returned to Zapotec country for shorter periods since 1957. My work there has become more focused, more related to particular problems of law and social control. Therefore, I have not had to experience the thrashing around and frustrations of that first year. The difficulties of that year, for the most part, stemmed from situations involving acceptance. But much more important, I was working in 1957 on the kind of problem to which everything seemed relevant: kinship and political organization, child rearing, life histories, law cases, division of labor, drinking habits, political participation, and the general network of communication. I have not since that first trip had difficulty with "rapport", in fact, "returning" has led me to value more than ever the anthropological possibilities of revisits. When an anthropologist who has been away from his field returns, he often finds that he has been placed on the "inside" because of the myths created about him in his absence and the knowledge people believe him to have already.

The people in the area remember me only in an idealized and exaggerated form. They remember me as speaking fluent Zapotec, as being more courageous than any man, with the ability to outwalk any native on a mountain path, as well as being able to get along with everyone without making distinctions of rank. They especially idealize this last talent and comment that I was able to work, without being resented, with the members of two villages who have long-standing feelings of mutual animosity. The Taleans in particular like to hold me up as a symbol to their own citizens living in urban areas because I dress and act simply when I return and because I always remember to "contribute" to the town. Any negative aspects tend to be forgotten or repressed. I have not, since 1957–1958, experienced among the Zapotec that Dostoevskian vacillation between anguish and exultation that Hortense Powdermaker speaks of in discussing the Malinowski *Diaries*. It was only a second field trip in another area of the world that allowed me to feel again that intense pain and pleasure that characterizes field work as an initiation rite.

Lebanon 1961

Again my choice of field station was determined by prior acquaintance with a language and a culture. I was reared in a bilingual and bicultural Arab-American household. In the summer of 1961 I went to Lebanon to begin research on Moslem village law. That relatively short experience was in many ways more complicated—and more intense—than my Zapotec experience. This situation was accentuated by self-imposed time pressures; in nine weeks of work time I was to find a village, "make rapport," and collect data to begin to compare with my Zapotec data on law and conflict resolution. I was attempting to do this in the summertime when it was hot and humid in Beirut, when the natives themselves think that anyone of right mind should be vacationing in the mountains, when the feelings between groups—in particular between Christians and Moslems—had not yet recovered from the 1958 political disturbances.

As I explored the question of how to find a good village, as I balanced whether it should be Shia or Sunni Moslem, I was deluged with warnings from Lebanese families and friends. I would get sick; if I worked in a Moslem village, there was no telling what they would do to me; I would not be safe, some told me, because Moslems "don't like Christians." Others said that this was nonsense, that the difference in perspective coincided with individuals' political positions. The long and many conversations and admonitions about the dangers of doing field work did not stop, what seemed like acute paranoia was undoubtedly related to the 1958 revolution. Certainly the fact that I was based in the Christian town of Zahle explained the reluctance of any driver to take me into the villages.

My interest in knowing to what degree formal Moslem law dominates village procedures for conflict settlement augmented my determination to work in a Moslem village. It took about two weeks of talking to people, taxiing to various villages, to realize that one of the most successful ways of locating an appropriate village in Lebanon was through politicians or lawyer-politicians or through engineers who work for development projects, rather than through social scientists, who do not concentrate their interest in the rural areas of Lebanon. Whereas in Oaxaca the link between the cosmopolitan centers and predominantly Zapotec villages was easily made through a development commission, in Lebanon the link is best made through politicians, who often function like ward heelers in the villages and who come to know the villages in the process of electioneering. The politicians and lawyer-politicians were the most knowledgeable, for my purposes at any rate, in dealing with the village scene in Lebanon. Since I had the unusual advantage of having family living in the country, a politician who was a relative finally helped me locate a Shia Moslem village. Unlike Mexico, where my frustrations were mainly connected with the place of actual field work, my difficulties in Lebanon stemmed from my inability to locate a university student who might have been able to assist me; from the ostensibly trivial problems of finding a car and driver; from the fact that there was a lawyers' strike and no court cases could be heard; and in particular from the problem of gathering any sort of "objective" information on a good village in which to work. All these difficulties may have been based in the local attitude that women's work, especially if it were in villages, need not be taken seriously. As I wrote in a letter to Professor von Grunebaum of UCLA:

> The summer was a most pressured one. I was so aware of the shortness of time, and there was much I wished to do. I began my work with a survey of several villages in the Bekka Valley, around Zahle. Lebanon was as tight as a drum. On the one hand we had fear of Nasser among Christians reaching a paranoic extreme, and on the other adoration of Nasser combined with hatred for the West—all of which made entry into a Moslem village, by a Christian, a bit difficult. I found the best entry into villages was through the local politicians, and this is where [previous] contacts were especially helpful. They helped me locate some villages, and I settled on a Shia Moslem village in the southern Bekka Valley, simply because I thought it was a place where I would get the most work done in a relatively short time. There was one important lineage in this town which was greatly indebted to my family because they had once made a *wasta* [remedy] for them.

The village, Libaya, is located near Marjayoun; it is not to be found on most maps of Lebanon because the road has only recently been completed. Its population is about 1,400. There are eight large families in the town and some 400 houses—a homogeneous population of Shia Moslems.

I trained as my assistant a village boy, who fortunately proved a good, conscientious helper. I had wasted much time earlier trying to locate a student at the American University of Beirut, but living in an out-of-the-way village in the summer did not appeal to the students recommended to me. My aide helped me to map the village, to take a census, and to collect case materials. I collected mainly cases of wasta making and histories of conflict cases. Unlike the Zapotec, the Shias readily admitted to conflict and were not at all hesitant to talk about the subject. Consequently, I felt that I was moving with the stream here rather than against it. Some of the cases I took down in longhand, some my assistant wrote in Arabic, and some I recorded on a tape recorder. Of the three techniques, the last was by far the best; the tapes are so much richer in contextual information. I collected case histories of conflict-strife in order to get at the *process* of settling conflicts. In such a short time I doubted whether I could get enough actual cases to constitute a large enough sample for statistical analysis. I became fascinated with the number and class of person with whom a Shia Moslem villager comes into contact when he is in trouble and has to look for a wasta. To whom he goes depends in part on the kind of trouble he is in and on the man who is to judge him in the civil court. Among the politico-elite of Lebanon there is a most incredible knowledge of interpersonal relations, so that it's a rather knowledgeable game they play—to see who can get to the best connections the fastest. Through my original contact in the village I was able to study the network that usually resulted from these wasta-making procedures. As a result, most often a conflict that started in a village led to the homes of the politico-elite of the country. This in itself was one of the greatest contrasts with Mexico, where the tendency was to settle conflict without ever leaving village boundaries.

Unlike my first experience among the Zapotec, the personal, managerial, and intellectual problems of field work were minimal once I got to the village. I did not have the hindrance of working with a bilingual interpreter, for I could understand spoken Arabic. The fear of being rejected because of my religion proved an empty one. I was at first asked by the family with whom I stayed about my religion; when I said I was a Christian, they advised me to say that I was Moslem if asked by the other villagers. I answered simply that I was not in the habit of lying. When that story circulated about the village, I was treated with an openness and respect that I had not expected. The villagers allowed, indeed invited, me to visit the mosque, to climb the minaret in order to see the view, to watch the men perform their ablutions before entering the mosque; they even inquired why I didn't take photographs. It was in my favor that I came from America, where some of them had relatives (both in the United States and in Brazil); it was in my favor—and caused much amusement—that I spoke Arabic with a Zahle accent; it was in my favor that I was interested in their lives. Since it was considered polite to ask questions, the villagers talked with the animation and eagerness one would expect in a society where the oral tradition is so valued.

In the village there were none of the irritations of dealing with the people of urbanized Lebanon. Some of those irritations I am sure had to do with the question of language, however; I wish I could have recorded what I myself was doing in the course of the experience. Perhaps I can verbally approximate the situation. I had learned Arabic at home in Connecticut, where the socio-cultural contexts of speaking this language were absent. Later in life I learned Spanish in the context of Mexican society and culture. When I went to Lebanon, I found myself speaking Arabic but substituting Mexican speech etiquette for the Arabic etiquette I did not know. The result was confusing to me and certainly must have irritated many people with whom I spoke, for I was using Mexican gestures and Mexican rules on when to speak, when to speak loudly or quietly or angrily, when to laugh, when to smile, and so on. The absence of Arabic speech etiquette meant that I was not always as persuasive as I might have been in handling bureaucratic and managerial situations. In field work, where I mainly listened, this handicap was inconspicuous, and my use of the language improved. At any rate, it didn't take much talking to elicit a conflict case. Moreover, at such times my questions were usually directed to the content of the case that was reported. Because I could speak and understand the language, because I was investigating a subject matter that these Shias themselves liked to talk about, I probably accomplished as much in those few weeks as I would have in Zapotec country in about four months. The ubiquitous use of proverbs in the Near East was often helpful in guiding the anthropologist to choose what values are important: "As you treat me so I will treat you" (usually referring to bad treatment); "As you are dressed so you are judged"; "One has to be flexible in life, or else you break"; "If you wish to move a man, send a woman after him, and if you wish to move a woman send a child after her"; "In my presence, face like a mirror, in my absence, like a shoe [base]." If I were advising young anthropologists preparing for field work in the Arab Middle East, I would strongly recommend that they become familiar with and memorize a selection of proverbs. The same advice would apply to other parts of the world as well. I collected during this summer many examples of proverbs as they are used in the context of conversation because I was interested in understanding the function of proverbs. One interesting pattern that emerges is the finalizing one. In an argument, for example, a proverb simply ends the discussion, unless an opposing view is expressed by a counter-proverb. I would guess, and many tales bear me out, that in serious situations the right proverb can save a situation or even a life.

The study of proverbs or any question dealing with socio-linguistics is a natural subject for study in the Arab world. Talking, particularly in groups, is highly valued. Never did a day pass when the guestroom of the house where I stayed was not full of guests. Some would have been there anyway, others were visiting principally out of curiosity about me. These visiting sessions were useful in acquainting me with the villagers and in acquainting them with me and my tape recorder. They provided some extraordinary tapes of spontaneous poetry recitations, songs, stories, and the like. But such a setting was virtually impossible for eliciting any kind of case material on conflict. The problem of the anthropologist's privacy is, I imagine, a problem for workers in most small communities, but I thought it more acute in the Middle East than in Zapotec country. At least, I complained in my notes about the never-ending number of family and friends that were dropping into the guestroom, about the fact that I was followed everywhere. At appropriate times I would withdraw with an informant (and I used only six carefully chosen informants that summer) to the bedroom. The first time I began taking down the information by hand, only to be asked why I didn't just turn on the tape recorder.

Whether being a woman field worker in Lebanon was a hindrance or an asset I perhaps cannot judge, but it never seemed to hamper me. I would agree with Professor Louise Sweet that the negative aspects of being a woman field worker in the Middle East have been highly exaggerated. I am, in fact, tempted to regard such statements as nonsense, considering how well people acted toward me, even given the tense political situation. It seems that in a Moslem village a foreign woman is in a better position to be "protected" than a man of foreign extraction. Much undoubtedly depends on the behavior of the individual woman anthropologist, her coloring, and innumerable other variables. I do not know to what extent, because of my background, the villagers were accepting me as one of them, although the family contact helped. In my short time in the village I felt no threats; none, certainly, associated with my being a woman. Perhaps this was because I lived with a family instead of separately; this residence made me a "daughter" of the village. Or perhaps it was because the Arabs have a category of woman called "sister of men"—a natural role that a woman anthropologist could walk into, should she wish. I did exactly that.

I am impatient with formulas for successful anthropological field work and feel that researchers should do what they are most comfortable doing —in choosing a problem, in building rapport, in deciding how to present their findings to the profession at large. Yet an attempt to generalize what is essentially an autobiographical statement seems in order. In these concluding remarks I return to the themes mentioned in my introduction.

The personal aspects of field work necessarily involve feelings of ambivalence—simultaneous feelings of attraction and repulsion. These feelings may be directed toward the people one is studying, toward oneself, and toward the state of the profession. I felt ambivalent on all three accounts, and would imagine this to be the "normal" rather than the deviant case. My ambivalent feelings both in Lebanon and Mexico would be the usual feelings between an anthropologist and the people he is studying and is a characteristic of any situation where "detachment and involvement," to use Hortense Powdermaker's phrase, is a necessary requirement of the relationship. What I felt in the field I often feel, albeit with less intensity, with regard to my students. A psychiatrist must experience the same with patients. Indeed, some degree of ambivalence characterizes all human relations. What intensifies ambivalent feelings in field work is the tension.

When Geertz spoke of Malinowski's having worked with enormous industry in one world and having lived with intense passion in another, I understood Malinowski's state so well. While I was in the field, the amount of nocturnal dreaming and the ability to remember dreams seems to have multiplied several times over my usual behavior. The content of those dreams dealt almost exclusively with my experiences as a child and young adult in that "other culture." Not only my dreams, but also my general emotional state appeared to be more related to pre-Zapotec experiences than anything else. I am not equipped professionally to analyze why my dreams and emotions were more directly related to experiences outside of the field situation, but it was not because I was emotionally neutral about the people I was studying. Returning from the field has its own features of confusion and ambivalence—that, however, is the subject for another volume.

There is a kind of confusion that in a larger sense is not common to the asymmetrical roles of teacher-student or psychiatrist-patient. I refer to the state of confusion caused by the attempt to experience or become to a limited degree a member of a second culture. The anthropologist in the field is learning a new culture and very often a new language. This is not peculiar to the social anthropologist; rather, the anthropologist in the field must share many of the same experiences of the immigrant who leaves a home country to settle elsewhere, who must learn a new language and culture. Since the level of sensitivity is necessarily heightened by the experience, the threshold of frustration must often be pushed to its maximum tolerance as well. There is a substantial literature on language learning—and on bilingualism in particular—that would be most relevant to any scientific (that is, orderly) understanding of the anthropologist in the field. There is also a large body of data on confronting and learning a new culture (in the social sciences, in fiction, and in nonfiction), on being "between two worlds," and such literature would be of some use to anxious young anthropologists prior to their first solo field experience.

The possibilities for serious research on the process of anthropological language and culture learning would indeed be fascinating if the anthropologist would be willing to use himself as an informant. And linguistics is full of stimulating ideas. Linguists speak, for example, of linguistic interference —referring to speech habits carried over from one language into another (see Briere, 1966, and Ervin-Tripp, 1967). Linguists have measured interference mainly on the basis of phonological or grammatical data. Interference also extends to rules of speech etiquette, for example when the speaker misjudges the nature of a social situation and the rules that govern relevant verbal behavior. As John Gumperz has said, the anthropologist needs something like an Emily Post for his culture. Surely all field workers have experienced linguistic interference, both in the technical sense of the word and in terms of speech etiquette. The use of Mexican speech etiquette in my Arabic speech behavior was such a form of interference. Probably, in a vague way, this is what all the essays in this book are about. Ervin-Tripp (1967) comments: "If the distinctions between different types of interference are correct, then the second kind of analysis, the analysis of the learner's system, is central to an understanding of the process of bilingual learning." Similarly we could say that the analysis of the learner's system is also central to an understanding of process of culture learning—or what the anthropologist is about when he does field work. And this relates back to an earlier note suggesting that a knowledge of self is prerequisite, if not to doing field work, to understanding the process of having done field work.

Rapport is a term frequently used by anthropologists in discussing field work, for rapport must be gained to overcome the barriers blocking entrance to a new cultural system. I always remember Professor Robin Fox's comment after his return from the Southwest one summer, which constitutes a kind of definition. "There were all the anthropologists, and there were all the tourists. The tourists were asking the Indians all the questions the anthropologists wanted to ask but didn't because they were afraid of ruining rapport." Rapport, pure and simple, consists of establishing lines of communication between the anthropologist and his informants in order for the former to collect data that then allows him to understand the culture under study. As Audrey Richards (1968, 189) illustrates, rapport may have nothing to do with being reasonable or pleasant in the field, or liking and admiring the people with whom one works, though Geertz (1967) seems to suggest that it does. Rapport refers to the ability to cope with a field situation in such a way that work is possible. My handling of the challenge to drink a bottle of mescal is an example of rapport building. As a result of my action, the lines of communication were opened for work purposes of a more formal nature. Both the rapport building and the eliciting that may result are sources of data for the anthropologist though quite different kinds of data may result.

Robin Fox's observation that anthropologists often hold back for fear of ruining rapport is important for us to think about. After visiting students in the field who were intending to collect materials on law and conflict, I commented to Beatrice Whiting upon the reluctance of these students, who had been in the field between three and seven months, to collect information on what they thought might be a touchy subject—conflict. Dr. Whiting told me that her experience with anthropologists involved in the study of child rearing was similar. Workers often leave what is presumably the focus of their interest until last because of a variety of fears. Sometimes we might be wise to wait or to change our research focus. But "nothing ventured, nothing gained."

The effects of being a woman field worker are difficult to generalize about. Relevant to the matter however, is the fact that anthropology, in comparison to the other social sciences, has attracted so many women who have been successful as members of that profession. Various explanations of this phenomenon suggest that women make a success of field work be-

cause women are more person-oriented; it is also said that participant observation is more consonant with the traditional role of women. Like many folk
explanations, there is perhaps some truth in the idea that women, at least in
Western culture, are better able to relate to people than men are. If this
assumption is valid, it is probably most relevant to the kind of material
women gather in the field rather than the quality of that material. Very few
women anthropologists are working in formal analysis, for example. The
role of gossip and child rearing on the other hand, were first illuminated as
subjects for study by women anthropologists.

I am tempted to generalize that it is easier for women to achieve good
rapport—at least working in Mexico or Lebanon. As I noted earlier, I
gained greater freedom from the Zapotec myth that I could turn myself into
a man or woman at will. Both in Mexico and in Lebanon I was respected as
a woman somehow different from their women. Consequently I had access
to both men's and women's culture. No man, even if he was considered
different from the local men, would have had access to women's culture
equal to mine to the men's culture. Of course it may be said that personality
makes for considerable variation; but I would still support the common
hypothesis that women anthropologists, if they want it, have access to a
wider range within a culture than men.

I originally wanted to subtitle this article "Field work—an Anthropological Initiation Rite," because so much about the culture of anthropology
indicates that the field experience is the principal initiation rite into the
anthropological profession. Indeed, it is sometimes a way of becoming
accepted as an anthropologist without professional academic training.
Anthropological rank is achieved through field work, and at times the
rougher the field situation, the greater the rank. Supposedly one grows
under stress, and the greater the stress, the more we grow. There may be
some truth in this view, although members of the "comfort school" of
social anthropology might question whether we become better anthropologists. Anthropologists do sometimes suffer needlessly and avoid the com-
forts of home in the field. Sleeping on a wooden bench is more anthropological than sleeping on a comfortable double bed in the hinterlands of Mexico
—the argument being that a comfortable bed would only accentuate the
differences between the anthropologist and the people he is living with. This
positive attitude toward roughing it (which we use as a way of distinguish-
ing ourselves from our social-science brethren) has until recently also
molded our philosophy of training anthropologists. The student is thrown
into the ethnographic ocean, and nature takes its course. If he is worth his
salt, he will return from the field an anthropologist.

It is difficult, and some would say impossible, to teach certain aspects
of field work, such as how to build rapport. At the same time many anthro-

pologists are concerned with showing students how to make the most of an opportunity to study the Booga Booga for a year or two. Leslie Spier once commented that the best preparation for field work would be a thorough knowledge of the most important theoretical and methodological issues in the field. Everyone would agree in theory.

On the other hand, there has been some interest lately in summer training in anthropological field techniques: census taking, interviewing, participant observation, and the like. Of eight students working with me on the Berkeley Comparative Village Law Project; seven had at least one summer of field work before their departure for a year and a half to two years in the field. Of these eight, only two students had a visit in the field from a faculty member, and such visits were brief. Real and practical reasons of distance and financing have made visits to students infrequent. Given the affluent situation of the last decade and the rapid advances in transportation technology, we will undoubtedly do more such visiting in the future. Whether the resultant field reports will be better as a result of summer training and, in general, more structured field training remains to be seen. This may simply turn out to be a response to problems of mass education. Summer training institutes may be educationally equivalent to what was taught to students in the Malinowski kitchen.

The formal teaching of anthropological techniques is intellectually related to the problem of focus. The argument is about whether one should select a problem prior to leaving for the field or uncover a focus by living in a particular society. This is not a question of cither-or. When an anthropologist is going into an unknown area, he should be flexible. If there is a literature about the place in which he plans to work, it would be more feasible to take a problem into the field. Traditionally our orientation has been that the anthropologist has the obligation to report in a general way about the culture—that is, to produce a general ethnography. This is especially true if he is working in an unreported area. Other traditions in ethnography may choose to explore a single topic, such as child rearing, kinship, law, or religion. What formerly would have been a mere chapter in the general ethnography now becomes the whole focus for an ethnography. Other traditions start with specific methodological issues or with a specific hypothesis. Whatever one chooses to do, a knowledge of the history of ideas in anthropology has value for refined and detailed data.

My first field experience taught me generally how to map forms of social organization. Perhaps only because of that exercise can I now focus in depth on particular questions of society and culture, but I question whether the two kinds of intellectual experiences could not have been combined. Personally I find myself less and less interested in what some have called intellectual vacuum cleaning. My satisfactions come from analyzing solid blocks of data—such as conflict cases, proverbs in natural conversation, coparent patterns—or from the exploration of specific "why" questions through which one can utilize those precious bits and pieces that come from astute observations. During my first field experience I did not work this way; I tried to gather all new information. In looking over my field notes, I discover that much of what I took down as field data has not been of much use to me; but this cannot be known at the time. After my second trip to the Rincón Zapotec I no longer collected everything. I focused on detailing blocks of data, the analysis of which was to take me again from anguish to exultation.

References

BRIERE, EUGENE J. 1966. "An investigation of phonological interference," *Language* 42(4), 768–796.

ERVIN-TRIPP, SUSAN M. 1967. "How and when do persons become bilingual?" Unpublished mimeo. Berkeley: University of California.

GEERTZ, CLIFFORD. 1967. "Under the mosquito net," *New York Review of Books*, Sept. 14.

POWDERMAKER, HORTENSE. 1966. *Stranger and friend*. New York: Norton.

POWDERMAKER, HORTENSE. 1967. "Letter to the Editors," *New York Review of Books*, November 9.

RICHARDS, AUDREY. 1968. "In darkest Malinowski," *The Cambridge Review*. January 19.

A Woman Anthropologist in Brazil

RUTH LANDES is the author of a number of books and articles stemming from her field work with the Ojibwa, Potawatomi, and Santee Dakota Indians. In CULTURE IN AMERICAN EDUCATION *she describes her work in training teachers and social workers in anthropological concepts relevant to minority groups. Her work since 1970 has included a book-length manuscript based on ten years of field work in four societies: Canada, Spain, Switzerland, and the Republic of South Africa. Each of these countries has two rival dominant languages. The work, called* TONGUES THAT DEFY THE STATE, *discusses culture, religion, history, and politics. Dr. Landes is a professor emerita at McMaster University, Hamilton, Ontario (Canada).*

In the United States, the 1930's was the epoch of "The New Negro," also the "Negro Renaissance," when black men's genius was acclaimed in the arts, sciences, and humanistic disciplines. A truly Renaissance man among them was Paul Robeson, singing and acting like a god not far from my New York undergraduate college. Another was Alain Locke, already then appointed professor of philosophy at New York's prestigious City College. W. E. B. DuBois, the great historian; James Weldon Johnson, the diplomat and poet; Walter White, brilliant writer and politician, all held the scene, the first two as retired heads of the National Association for the Advancement of Colored People (NAACP), the last as the incumbent head. There were many others, including the anthropological woman novelist, Zora Neale Hurston. I had met them all, originally through my family, and they directed my interests for life. The West Indian leader, Marcus Garvey, had just been jailed in Jamaica on British and American charges that concealed fears of his tremendous revolutionary impact on New World lower-class blacks; but his program lingered in New York's Harlem and elsewhere. The deep South's peasant blacks were streaming into northern cities, continuing a trend begun in the first World War, creating terrible ghettos, and substantially displacing the Jews in Harlem. They brought with them the folk cults then enshrined in so-called storefront churches. While at college, before ever thinking about anthropology (but studying psychology, sociology, biology, and history), I began a four-year field study of Negro Jews in Harlem (Landes, 1967b), composed of Garveyites and Southern migrants in "storefronts." The NAACP pursued civil rights issues, the Urban League pursued employment issues, but both voiced mistrust of Garveyites and "storefronts." This was the decade of the Great Depression; it saw the establishment of Nazi power and racism. I was in the avant-garde, with my parents' encouragement, of those who had social relations with Negro peers.

The study of Negro Jews led me to Franz Boas and Ruth Benedict, teaching anthropology at Columbia University, and so to the discipline that

119

has occupied me since. It could have been any other discipline, so far as my predilections went–from medicine to the arts. But Boas and Benedict, by their persons and intellectual commitments, decided me. Every other profession or gainful learned activity restricted women with a severity that, in our circle, we likened to the prevailing restrictions on blacks. These two scholars appeared to distinguish, not the sexes, but only ability. It was their overriding concern. Never before had I met it in a working situation, nor had I cared about being a Ph.D. bluestocking. But Ruth Benedict was beautiful and married. After a year of pondering their invitation to enter graduate anthropology and reflecting on the confines of my early marriage, I decided that their pursuit would be mine.

Because of my established interest in Negro-White relationships, they offered me, for my first field work, the choice of studying Negro life anywhere or examining the life of an American-Indian tribe. Though I hated the idea of a reservation, I chose the latter for the gross cultural variations I would meet. This decision resulted in trips to several reservations and the lapse of some years. Then we thought it was time for me to go to Brazil because we had heard–through the great sociologist Robert E. Park and others–that Brazil's large Negro population lived decently among the general population; and we wanted to examine the details.

I knew no Brazilian person and no Portuguese speech, and it was nearly impossible to encounter either in New York. However, I had studied intensively the literature about American Negroes, from the learned disciplines and the arts; I had read widely among the anthropological (including British colonial officers') studies of African cultures, even submitting these as an area for questioning by my doctoral examiners; and I read the new Brazilian materials generously made available to me by Professor Park and his student, Donald Pierson. More, at the joint invitation of Park and his great disciple in sociology, Charles S. Johnson of Fisk University, I went for a year to Fisk, in Tennessee, to teach and learn from this Negro campus something at first hand of American "racial etiquette," in Bertram W. Doyle's classic phrase. Only then did I embark on the 4,000-mile Atlantic journey.

I knew that Brazil in 1938 was governed by a severe dictatorship; that American pressure had barely forced Brazil's army to give up its Nazi-style ideology, called *integralismo;* that the so-called Axis powers, led by Germany, were prominent in Brazilian commerce; and that this was a land in the full plenitude of patriarchal authority. I was scared, with ample reason; but that was no reason not to go. I had been scared on my Indian field trips, also with reason–a girl anthropologist in the field had been killed by an Indian the year before I entered anthropology; a man anthropologist had been killed in the Pacific some years earlier, while doing field research. The pressure to go, despite such facts, was my own; and my father always said, "Come back whenever you want."

During that period Boas and Benedict also sent four men students to Brazil to study Indian groups in the great forests—Jules Henry, William Lipkind, Buell Quain, and Charles Wagley. My study of Negro life was to carry me, however, to the coast's capital cities of Rio de Janeiro and Bahia. On our first journeys, each of us worked alone, except for Mr. and Mrs. Lipkind. This solitariness rested chiefly on the factors of few students, limited funds, and resourceful temperaments.

The anthropologist's strong bent for field work begins, I suggest, before the individual ever dreams of the profession. I felt so when, despite police cautions, I entered Negro Harlem at the age of twenty. Field work serves an idiosyncrasy of perception that cannot separate the sensuousness of life from its abstractions, nor the researcher's personality from his experiences. The culture a field worker reports is the one he experiences, filtered through trained observations. Noted writers say that their craft cannot be taught, though it can be perfected. In the same sense, field work probably can only be perfected. The great founders of the discipline of anthropology were not taught specific field-work techniques; nor was our group of students at Columbia, who studied theory and research findings with Kroeber, Boas, Klineberg, Mead, and Benedict. Instead, we were taught to conjecture, to experiment, to use every tool we commanded, to venture. The last impressed me powerfully. I knew the great Arctic explorer, Vilhjalmur Stefansson, and pondered his injunction always to "live off the land," materially and in every other way. For a social anthropologist, this injunction meant entering deeply into the field culture, joining it twenty-four hours a day, each day, all the months or years of research. This could only be done superficially on an Indian woodlands or plains reservation, since the United States and Canada disapprove of "going native" in these Agency-supervised. harshly separated communities. It could be done in Brazil, for the newcomer (or visiting anthropologist) *must* conform to the rules of the host society.

No one told me, a young woman of conventional upbringing and advanced New York ideas, about the life sphere of my kind in a preindustrialized, postcolonial, natural resources economy, where the latifundium and the Catholic Church dominated, as they still do. Partly this was because no one of us had been there. Partly, there was this thing about overlooking sex differences, to prove a woman was a person, "as good as a man." Actually, my field work among American Indians, like my later field work in Brazil, made poor sense without explicit attention to women (hence the second book I wrote about Indians was entitled *The Ojibwa Woman*). I guessed, from materials Park and Pierson showed me at Fisk, that black women would figure importantly in Brazil, as they did in the West African Yoruba and Ibo regions, from where they mainly derived. But about white or upper-class women of the genteel rank, among whom I would belong in such a severely stratified society as Brazil's, not a word. My Ph.D. had unsexed me. The only contrary indication was my young husband's ultimatum about the marriage, because he raged at me for preferring scholarship to domesticity, for preferring its lonely exposed world and hazards to my private wifely place in our family undertaking.

In the end, I dreaded *not* going more than I feared to *go*. Perhaps this is a test of the field worker, that he feels restive when settled long or exclusively in familiar, especially his own, native routines. There is no question of not loving the familiar. (Someone asked Ruth Benedict how she felt about her own America after examining "culture patterns" of the world. She said, "I just love it the more.") But such a scholar must dip into earth's paintbox of cultures; he needs the changes they light up and ring on the familiar, the insights they release, the sharp awareness they bring him of his own self. The field worker finds this pursuit basic to his life, so emotionally dear that the field culture studied becomes "my culture." The poet Robert Graves was amused, he tells us, to hear two British women anthropologists, one his niece, talk of "my" African tribe. Thus do all field workers talk, for we have birthed the novel culture we experience and often show in print.

From our Columbia teachers we heard the view that field work was our discipline's rendering of the natural sciences' laboratory methods, for these were still the model of "objective" discoveries. But no scientist ever spent twenty-four hours daily in the laboratory for months on end, to become one with its complex whole, solely to understand the phenomena of interest. Field workers live this way, and there are no short cuts. One learns a culture by living it; the next best resort is to live *in* it.

It seems evident to me that the methods of an effective field worker are rooted in his personality, expressing some genetic potential evoked and shaped by the cultures he has lived in. Margaret Mead admired the "empathy" of certain field workers with the cultures they studied, as she told me. Obviously the field worker brings to his novel culture field a special, perhaps aberrant, personality; his mother culture's alien forces; his colossal ignorance of the new people; but a mighty, even zestful intention to yield himself to the field and ponder his and others' responses.

Boas used to say that a great liability of education is its injunctions about what to fear and avoid. He therefore told his students chiefly to *go out and get the material*. I recall that he would not waste time with a new student until after he had been in the field. Experience taught us, who were his disciples, that in the field anything worked, even large mistakes, short of being killed. Mistakes were, conceptually, evidences of cultures or culture bearers in conflict and, in that perspective, were instructive. This stoicism was shared by Park, also a great field worker. At Fisk University he explained to me the genius of certain Negroes in handling the offenses of American life, starting with his youthful observations as Booker T. Washington's secretary; and he advised me to emulate them—specifically, to note everything as "research data," never merely as personal shocks.

Field workers situated alone often feel private panic at being stranded in the oceanic vastness of a foreign people. One's concept of self disintegrates because the accustomed responses have disappeared; one seeks restoration through letters from home, addressed to the remembered personality. There are loneliness, uprooting, fears, true and marked physical hardships, diseases, lack of diversions to relieve tensions—all of these nurture melancholies and spiritual fatigue. I have known at least one person who toyed with the idea of suicide and another who actually committed it. Lucky breaks, the habit of living, and bull-headed obstinacy pull one through. (An American zoologist collecting for a museum once wrote to me in Brazil, while he was sailing along the great Xingú River of the Mato Grosso; he addressed the envelope to Mrs. R. Mallet-Head Landes.)

Probably in these grim stages the field worker discovers that the culture is "mine," for he or she has invested in it much emotion, self-regard, determination, and sheer physical reserve. That is, he or she invests the energies required for survival anywhere—but in the field the effort has heroic dimensions. The trials, the idealistic pursuit of knowledge, all touch poetry. Most jobs are paths to comfortable ends. But the solitary field work, whatever the eventual by-products in books and academic promotions, remains unique, stirring the researcher's optimum sense of himself as he tests himself continually against environing strangeness.

Some testings may be more severe or more startling when the worker is a woman. The woman anthropologist is a professional worker, which means that she is measured by standards attached to men, since the work is in a public sphere—the sphere controlled by men in our world. But her training as "a man" did not start until her anthropology did. So much is obvious. Even then, the training in "manhood" was spotty. For example, I carried my husband's name, was not supposed to "desert" marriage by taking a doctoral degree, and was supposed to lean on a man's financial and social support. This was standard; all departures were considered temporary, incidental, and guilt-arousing. I recall discussing these one summer with Ruth Benedict, who was also troubled. (Despite the many years between us, we agreed that the "ideal" husband would be Chekhov! Because he understood everything, with a warm humanness.) One knew, no matter how young, from one's own husband, that one had not been brought up as a man. The importance here is that, though the woman field worker might be considered an honorific man by title, she was appraised and censured as a *private* woman-person by the patriarchal culture she studied as well as by most of her men colleagues. My own experiences in Brazil exposed this fact amply, even for decades after I had left the country. But every woman scholar has had her share. In part it is in the nature of human competitiveness to attack the rival at his or her most vulnerable point. A competing male Negro, Latin, Oriental is attacked for his scorned minority rank; a male Jew, Catholic, or Jehovah's Witness is belittled for his low-ranked or embattled religion; until recently male homosexuality constituted egregious vulnerability for a professional person, regardless of the truth of the allegation. With a woman for a rival, many men and women have no need to seek her secondary traits of race, religion, or national origin; her sex alone suffices. When I mentioned this circumstance years ago to a British colleague, a man much my senior, who was interested in the UN's Commission on the Status of Women, he told me, "Don't say that! It doesn't sound nice." I had thought that he was my friend and would understand; perhaps he did, but he would not pursue the matter.

Because tradition assigns women to specific private or domestic status —places in our world's societies governed by men, occasional literary efforts to represent daring—anthropological characters have focused on women. These efforts cast the women's ways in an unfavorable light, making them appear ludicrous, suggesting they are also astray socially. I have noticed this inclination in at least one or two Broadway musicals, a 1967 film, novels, and journalistic accounts, the last including a spine-chilling King Features piece about my stay in Brazil. The characters were shown as inherently farcical or weird; and the works fell flat. Also, there is a general impression, even among academic folk, that "most" anthropologists are women. Colleagues in sister disciplines are astounded at the actually minuscule number, when they start counting on their fingers, compared with men. The mere presence of women is riveting and disrupting.

To enter Brazil was to find a world, then and now, where women are situated in one social domain and men in another, such that women are ranked below and men above. I struggled to follow Park's philosophy: it's all research data, okay. Others did not do the same, obviously, unaware of Park's culture or subculture. Many years later, my second husband, a Latin-American of another country, told me that it was a great matter to be a man, the best; and it was another great matter to be a woman, it was "even beautiful," but vulnerable. The qualification may have occurred to him because he was educated (or "shaped," as Spanish puts it) at the University of California. Though not an anthropologist, he had heard of my Brazilian happenings years before we met; rather, he had heard about a woman stumbling into men's affairs.

In the field—Brazil, 1938–1939—emotions surge, habits struggle, for the researcher is captive to the reflex or second nature of usual practices. Can he control the pupil's dilation in the dark? Suppose the woman wants to take a walk—in Rio de Janeiro, let alone Bahia? Or attend the movies alone? Perhaps leave the hotel or house after sunset alone? Buy an item and carry it home? Pay the bill herself? Visit a restaurant, a theater, any place, alone? Journey to a friend by public transport alone? Pay the physician's bill herself? Get a decent job? Interview a male colleague, possibly alone? The woman cannot commit these acts without incurring reprisals. These lessons were knocked into me so profoundly over a period of fourteen months that, when I returned to Brazil after twenty-seven years, the memories enchained my movements as agoraphobia did those of William Ellery Leonard (see his *The Locomotive God*). Writing now, a year later and over 4,000 miles away, the anthropologist in me would not alter one detail, for all these constitute tradition's drama. But to do field work under the traditional conditions meant rising each day and tossing each night to the hardest doubts of oneself, privately, and of the struggle, professionally.

How does the "field" perceive the woman researcher from foreign parts? One can only infer, and only after the event. For example, two and a half decades after my first departure, I was confronted with evidence in public print, documented by events of the intervening twenty-five years, that 1938–1939 had left me one bitter enemy and one enduring friend, both reacting to my field work and my publications. I was the same ethnoprofessional specimen to both—or wasn't I? Did their individual temperaments and vested social interests, which differed somewhat, find support in their common Brazilian heritage? The self-proclaimed enemy, the late Dr. Artur Ramos, was a good dozen years older than the proven friend, Dr. Edison Carneiro, who was about my age; the men were senior and junior colleagues, famous in the great realm of Negro-Brazilian, or Afro-Brazilian, studies; the former was white, the latter a "man of color" (*homem de côr*) in a class society that ranked this trait low by implication. Since similar phenomena occur in our own society, often to the bewilderment or even amusement of onlookers, one might discard the whole matter on the assumption that "these things happen," as the Latins say (*acontece assim,* in Brazil). On the other hand, they do affect the field worker's job and life; in my case, the consequences were drastic, as I have told elsewhere (Landes, 1947) and as I describe in the following pages.

From the start, the "field" had its views of my status. I did not trouble to accommodate to some of them, considering that to do so would nullify my goals and wipe out my finances. For example, in May 1938, soon after reaching Rio de Janeiro (then an exquisitely lovely and grand city), I left my costly tourists' hotel for a charming, reasonably priced Brazilian one, on

the Praça José de Alencar, called the "Foreigners' Hotel" (Hôtel dos Es-
trangeiros). Through a mutual acquaintance in Washington, I had met
Brazil's Minister of Foreign Affairs; later I told him of my move to a place
where I could hear Portuguese conversation and eat national foods. This
worldly man answered that he was "ashamed" to have me in a "national"
hotel, that he had planned for his daughters to call on me, but now. . . .
In short, the visit was never paid. At the time I supposed that he wanted me
to fulfill the stereotype of the wealthy, daring American girl; there were
such in Europe who wrote and painted; indeed, he said I looked like an
"artist." Years later, a Brazilian woman friend told me that I wasn't all
wrong and that men of his class kept paramours in the rich hotels. But now
I think the underlying reason for his rejection was that with my move I had
gate-crashed the traditional world, where a female needed patrons or "protectors" through her family or a male connection outside; the move raised
basic issues of propriety and morality that were irrelevant to the tourists'
strip of no-man's-land. I thought only that I was behaving efficiently and
that the Minister behaved snobbishly. So I blundered upon the "field's"
crucial conventions without comprehending.

Occasionally, I went to the movies in Rio's *cinelândia,* where I ampli-
fied my Portuguese by hearing the actors' American talk and comparing it
with the Portuguese subtitles. My clothes and bearing were often recognized as American, from the films; the title of a current song was *Ameri-
cana, quero teu amor* ("American girl, I love you"), which children would
yell at me in the street. Once I was standing in line for a movie ticket, and a
young man joked about me with his friend, in slang, "I wonder who runs
that [American] garage?" It was a legitimate issue, for a Brazilian of my
sort would not have been alone. The Americanness of my presence introduced an amusing dimension for ridicule.

In Bahia, where I went after three months in Rio for my principal field
work, most people did not recognize an American by his traits, and I was
never taken for one. Instead I was thought to be German, because Hitler's
representatives were omnipresent and I seemed to resemble them; besides, I
spoke Portuguese, albeit with a "gringo" manner, whereas Americans and
British were known to avoid Portuguese speech and most of Brazilian life.
(In 1966 I was no longer taken for American in Rio either. Over a long
period a host people's confusion of one's culturo-national identity becomes
as exasperating as any other rejection of bona fides. They—taxi drivers,
servants, maîtres-d'hotel, shopkeepers—thought that I came from any of
half-a-dozen European countries, because of how I spoke Portuguese and
because I did not dress "showily.") In Bahia, literate but generally uneducated black folk told me, when I asked, that the United States was "somewhere in Europe." This blur was consistent with a general belittlement of

American accomplishments in all humanistic arts, balanced by a worship of France's achievements and an admiration of Germany's efficiency.

Nearly every step I made or that was attributed to me, as it advanced my special goals of field work, *pari passu* drew upon me the threatening notice of army and police. But I did not know this until the crisis that obliged me to depart after eight months of rich work in Bahia (Landes, 1947). I'll give details in later pages. Others did know of my difficulties, gathering hints as everyone does from the atmosphere of one's world. However, it was not my world and not my language. When a Negro cult priestess, of my age, treated me with herbal recipes and formulas against mysterious persons' "envy," I recorded these on the simple-minded assumption that she was merely revealing cult practices and amiableness. She was telling me, rather, what any *Bahiano* would have understood. But I was a New Yorker, immeasurably alien, lacking the instinct that keeps most women everywhere functioning in the place assigned them by tradition.

Brazil is a vast stretch of land, physically larger than the continental United States, excluding Alaska. In the 1930's, as now, most of the population clung to the Atlantic coast. Rio de Janeiro, then the capital of Brazil, and Bahia, once capital of the brief Empire of Brazil and Portugal, were and are centers of a brilliant culture that includes a marvelous folk culture led by Brazilians of African and slave origins. Bahia's folk culture is the more celebrated; the city was dubbed the "Negro Rome" by a nationally renowned black woman, the cult priestess Aninha. The huge folk world in Bahia and Rio had organized itself around many separate temples of religious and mutual-aid nature, drawing upon African, Latin Catholic, and Brazilian slave elements. The followers were not wholly black, but the leaders were Negroes; and the greatest cult leaders in Bahia were Negro women. I describe this Bahia world in *The City of Women*. (Carmen Miranda sang of it in New York and in Hollywood films, as well as in Rio.) The cults were a fashion among the intellectual and artistic elite, but they were also dangerous, because the police were persecuting them on the excuse that they harbored criminals and "Communists" in addition to practicing black magic. Secretly persons from the highest social levels patronized them. In this setting I had to study "race relationships."

My most pertinent introductions came from Park and Pierson. One was to the highly esteemed American missionary Dr. Tucker, whose residence in the country had begun in the last century and in the reign of the last monarch, Don Pedro II. Beloved and enlightened, D. Pedro had received the missionary as a friend. Rio's first great *favela*—a slum climbing a rocky hillside where the poor, chiefly blacks, took squatters' hold on unclaimed terrain—was patronized by Dr. Tucker's mission. In 1966 it was a sort of showplace, for postwar Rio, like postwar São Paulo, had spawned acres of menacing favelas. Dr. Tucker, originally from Tennessee, had seen both slavery and the abolition of slavery in Brazil, and he was not impressed by my "race relationships" concern; but, aged and kind, he said little. From the noted school attached to his mission he sent me my teacher of Portuguese, a cheery, tightly scheduled young woman with a physicist husband and two sons; promptly at eight each morning Dona Dina arrived to give me my lesson.

Another vital introduction was to Dr. Artur Ramos, also living in Rio. He had been a *medico-legista* (the official practitioner of forensic medicine) of the State of Bahia, where his duties had brought him in contact with the black cult folk. He had written books of repute about them, following the interests uncovered by Brazil's great initiator of cult studies, Dr. Nina Rodrigues. He and his wife eventually gave me letters of introduction to people in Bahia and agreed that this was the place for me to settle down. Their key introduction, as events developed, was to Dr. Edison Carneiro, a junior colleague.

Never in the history of field work, I am confident, has anyone been more fortunate than I in the association with Edison. Apart from Edison's repute as a scholar and writer, and apart from his high talents and character, the fact was that I could not have stirred a step in Bahia without his, a man's, "protection." I saw this each day that I tried to move about on my own, when I became a vulnerable minor and a potential sexual target. My *City of Women* shows my great esteem for Edison and our friendship, as do my articles (Landes, 1940a, 1940b, 1947, 1953). Of course, Ramos learned of our joint labors, especially after Edison and I arranged to meet his ship in Bahia, where it stopped briefly en route to elsewhere from Rio. It did not occur to either of us that he would resent our enterprise; on the contrary, as our respected elder and the recognized scholar in the Afro-Brazilian "vineyard" we had also chosen, we thought he would be pleased. Subsequently my Latin husband assured me that Ramos saw, rather, that I had switched allegiance from him to Edison and so was guilty of a client's treachery. In that highly personalized world of factions, as in our American Old South, one must not act solely on his private initiative but only as the leader directs. In view of later recorded events (Carneiro, 1964), it seemed that Ramos expected "gratitude" of a far-reaching order for his kindnesses; his slanderous retaliations (bald statements that I used sexual lures to get informants—that professionally I was untrained and unreliable) followed me to the United States, the United Kingdom, and Africa. Also, he found an American ally (now deceased)[1] and late in 1939 the two wrote a voluminous letter about me to Gunnar Myrdal, for whom I was working in New York on his American Negro study, and he showed me the letter while

1. Melville Herskovits

ridiculing its fixation on my alleged eroticism and incompetent scholarship. Those aspects, indeed, Ramos reiterated over the years in "vulgar, vindictive" articles and in lectures to university students (as three students told me). I had heard verbal reports of all this in the 1940s and 1950s from colleagues residing in São Paulo, London, and Kampala in Uganda. To anticipate one of Ramos' actions by several years, the time came when his written language about me obliged São Paulo's leading social-science journal to refuse one of his articles, despite his established reputation; so the editor told me in New York and so Edison reports (Carneiro, 1964, p. 227). After Ramos' death a woman colleague in Europe sent word to me that, because of him, it was said I had "run a brothel" in Brazil.

The gossip also conveys the idea that my presence mattered in Bahia and that it was to be tested relentlessly. Edison, who must have known the risks, was my sole shield. He introduced me to nearly everyone I worked with, and I know that the blacks admitted me because he vouched for me. The absoluteness of his patriarchlike responsibility is inconceivable to the average American, brought up to let women (or any individual) look after themselves, the devil taking the hindmost. The condition of respect for a woman in Bahia was the word of a worthy man. Often I recalled, as I do now, young Dona Dina's incredulous laugh at my plan to move to Bahia: it's a fine place, she would quote from a popular song, but leave it there and leave me here. I thought she meant because Bahia was so near the equator, and 900 miles north of Rio.

I had sailed for Bahia on a Nazi boat, where portraits of Hitler covered the walls, where officers saluted with "Heil Hitler," where dozens of large German families from the Brazilian state of Santa Catarina were passengers heading for the "Leader Schools" (*Führerschulen*) of Greater Germany, where the purser pitied me for having to stop in "black" Bahia. I took a room in Bahia's best hotel because there was no other accommodation for a single female. I heard from the United States consul that I might be thought a "Communist spy," and I heard from the annoyed German hotel manager that the colonel in command of the army of the northeast, also a hotel guest, thought I might be a fancy prostitute from the south. The body reacts to such blows, at least when it is American. My inflamed sinuses bugged my eyes so far out of my head that I lay for hours each day with icepacks, on medical order. I developed bleeding intestines that were incurable until long after my return to the United States. A year of diarrhea left me gaunt and yellow; the consul's secretary said that I seemed to lose weight as he looked at me. The resulting anemia took four years to handle. I thought of suicide, though I never really planned it. When I mentioned this to a friend in Rio, before my departure, she said coolly, "Why? One can always be dead."

There was an American colony in Bahia, 200 strong. Except for one unhappy young matron, they wanted nothing of the place, the people, the life. As the consul said, "I live for the age of forty, when I'll retire." They thought my enterprise was very amusing and wanted to hear about cult "orgies." They constituted a living death—far worse, I thought, than the threats in Bahian life. So I turned entirely to Edison and the cult life that absorbed us.

We had implicitly agreed to pool our work resources, I contributing taxi money and Edison nearly everything else. As he says in his article (Carneiro, 1964, p. 225), he escorted me everywhere all the months of my stay so that (my translation), "Never, absolutely never, has any scholar, Brazilian or other, had so much intimacy [as R. L.] with the candomblé [a cult tradition outranking all others] of Bahia." He reported cult events for the daily newspaper that employed him; and he assembled materials for his later books and articles. He bought me a library of volumes that no one else had ever suggested and that was a foundation for all my understandings of Brazil. He listened to my observations, examined them, discussed them. Never was there time off, and he too got sick. We visited people day and night, ate in their homes, chatted long afternoons and evenings with them in the forests, in the city, out on islands, passed days and weeks at tedious parties and rites, took pictures that still live.

Edison's university friends joined us occasionally and, whether poets or medical men, concentrated on the fabulous cults. The zest and color of the folk life somehow fed the university as well; the great class gap was bridged and yet maintained by the mutual interest. We, young ones of the upper class were inspired by the cult people and their acts. Years later, I thought, "There is a joy of life in Bahia, tangible as the young palm trees" (Landes, 1947, p. 15). The life had elegance, content, ideals, and injustices, it was centered on people, for good or ill, everyone mattered, there were great concerns about honor, sacrifice, brutalities, inequities, and they were all worth fighting and dying for. It was exhausting and satisfying, and it fostered what the Brazilian lovingly calls *saudades* ("nostalgias").

The threat of being labeled a Communist was real; this was an official tactic for destroying any political opposition. A well-known scholar of northern Brazil, despite the social qualifications of his excellent family, was labeled "Communist" and thrown into jail, as the American press reported and as I heard upon reaching Bahia. The official explanation was that he had studied at Teachers College, Columbia University; and the University was presented as a hotbed of Soviet interests. The actual reason for his imprisonment was that he and his family supported an opposing political faction. Now here was I, also from Columbia; and under suspicion even though the predeparture New York police certification of me, routinely required, had been approved. The dictator's former army comrade, Luis

Prestes, led the Brazilian Communist opposition when he was not in jail. Students and university personnel, as everywhere in the Latin-American world, were suspected of political deviation. During my Bahia stay there was a round-up of such "Communists," who were put in jail for about a week; among the gentlemen, as they were by class, was Edison. And I was inseparable from Edison. Both of us were inseparable from the cult leaders, who, suspected of harboring "criminals," were also believed to shelter political suspects (as was not unlikely). Looking back, it seems that Latin women rarely were placed in this political category, either in 1938 or in 1966; women were absent from this eminently male domain throughout Brazil, though occasionally a woman's voice was lifted in Spanish-speaking lands. Largely because of my uncorrupted political innocence, I did not imagine jail for myself; but I suffered anxiety increasingly, a realistic enough mood at the time. Often I told myself that this enterprise was a case of (female) fools rushing in where the well-known angels would fear to tread. Edison was the only person I trusted, and I leaned on him entirely. He never objected, nor even made me aware of the burden I put on him. Against this rich friendship, Ramos' later published protests about my neglect (meaning that I did not write him and use his letters of introduction to Bahia's officials) seem irrational, apart from their extraordinary language. Having never done field work, as everyone told me and as his books show, he perhaps did not realize that parlor courtesies flourish only in protected soil; he was a "gentleman" office scholar, not a "working" field one, like myself and like Edison. Indeed, he had counseled me not to take pictures; not to talk with the disaffected lower class, who felt the general great inflation; not to ask questions. I was to be a "lady" and read.

The "prostitute" threat was real also, and it employed against me the "evidence" of my location in the central hotel. It seemed that there was an annual trek north from São Paulo of such well-groomed ladies and that the good hotels were their headquarters. Eventually the colonel who lived in my hotel abandoned the notion, but his vanity, wounded by my indifference to him and preference for Edison, engendered notions similar to those of Ramos and moved him to suggest to the authorities (who leaked the news) that I must be conniving politically with the cults. The light broke for me when, puzzled, I showed Edison a book (Zweig's new novel, *Maria Stuart*, about the Scots Queen) sent to me, through the head porter, by a hotel guest (who ran a car agency), asking me to "teach him English." It seems that this was a known Brazilian ploy. Edison went wild—without raising his voice—and ordered me to return the book, even taking it from me. He saw, where an American could not, that it was a smirking gesture to my literacy, which made me not any less an available woman. It had not escaped me that the men occupying the lobby, all business or military men, eyed the slight young intellectual "of color" who waited daily among them to escort me out. Indeed, the next year in Rio I was to hear, for the first time in my life, an American call me "nigger lover"; he sent me the epithet via his Brazilian wife, who added that hereafter she would have to meet me secretly. (We learned also that Edison, solely because of his physical appearance, and despite his obvious social quality, would not be admitted to Rio's Urca night club, where Carmen Miranda was singing.) All she understood was that "nigger lover" and "prostitute" were the same, which confused and shocked her; yet, on her own, she respected Edison.

Before I had met Edison, who soon ordered me never to leave the hotel alone after five in the afternoon, I had tried to walk in the fascinating streets at night, after the equatorial heat had eased. I naturally wanted to see what was happening. People ordinarily crowded their windows and balconies to see life. I knew that I was conspicuous with my fair coloring and rather tailored American dresses, but it was my shoes that proved crucial. For walking I had a handsome pair of shoes of laced black leather and suede, called "ghillies." About eleven one night a young woman approached me from an opposite direction, on the prowl in a trailing evening gown. Catching sight of me, she stopped, stared, then shrieked. I fled. The following day I learned that she was a properly licensed streetwalker, who knew that I was none but resented my competition on her beat—because my ghillies resembled shoes of the profession!

It was a problem, being a woman out of doors. Until Edison could include me in his schedule, I had traveled the city occasionally with the American consul's Bahian secretary, Jorge, at the consul's suggestion. Though meagerly schooled, Jorge spoke fine English, looked like a red-haired Englishman (but he had small use for any foreigners), wore immaculate white linen suits, and was fragrant with toilet water. He was of the modest middle class and all but penniless. Believing in aristocracy, he criticized me for using my hands, besides my feet—I was not to *carry* anything, not even writing pads. When he met me with my mail bundle, he would say that he felt "ashamed" at the sight. It was the gallant sentiment, but he also meant it. On a tour among some of Bahia's 365 churches it was impossible to avoid slums and here too he felt "disgraced"—not by the indecent, hopeless poverty, but that I, a lady, rich beyond his dreams, was walking there. "Dona Ruth, my fianceé would never walk there. Any Brazilian lady would be ashamed to." He decided that I was showing American courage, but thereafter I had to engage taxis, which he loved. Once we blundered into a better prostitutes' quarter, where a woman yelled to Jorge, "Is that your wife?" He knew she meant to insult him and, outraged, he declared, "Of course not!"

If I had lived as he saw fit, the police would have ignored me and would

not have set up the twenty-four-hour daily watch that terminated my stay in Bahia. But I should then have learned nothing about the blacks and their cults, which Jorge feared and detested: "They murder! The candomblé is black magic! It's superstition! They hypnotize people! They're not civilized. No, forgive me, but never can I accompany you there. Please do not ask." Nor did he trust church priests, he said, and he forbade his fiancée to make confession; but such was a man's right in his world.

Years later, in California, my Latin husband understood poor Jorge. I should have been accompanied by some staging of womanliness; for this, even a small boy-child would have served to "protect" me, symbolizing my mother status of dependence on a patriarch. No one trusts females except under lock and key, my husband believed; and trusts the American least of all—"why should they?" As to the "Communist" smear that finally reached me—he thought that was a flattering admission of my human or intellectual quality. Flattering? Attending the movies in Rio during 1939, I was handed a program featuring an article headed (my translation), "Can education help a girl to be a good mother?" The ferocious argument of "No" rested on such points as the need of good lactating mammary glands and of tenderness, which could only be ruined by education, certainly not bettered; besides, men do not want educated women and do not marry them. The last point was difficult to deny, as one met educated women who were beautiful, of good families, and financially sound but not married; there were rare exceptions, like the poetess Cecilia Meireles. On the whole, there was no place for an undomestic woman in respectable Bahia or Rio, though these were societies of high sophistication. Still in my twenties, a married woman but without my husband or child, with a doctoral degree that lacked true significance there, I had been sent to a world without a place for me.

One cannot believe this quite, partly because the "field" is not one's real life. It is like the riskiest gaming, rather, from which one can pull out if necessary. Hence the police angered me, as did Ramos' outrageous actions; but I also thought them ludicrous. To Edison, on the contrary, the "field" was his life as well; and so he wrote the " 'Falseta' de Artur Ramos' " even as late as 1964. When Ramos and his American colleague wrote to Myrdal, the "field" did merge briefly with my real life. Field work can be so taxing to physical and emotional states that it would seem well to maintain a large distance between it and one's private world. Yet an anthropologist may pursue his or her interests as his chief way of life, marrying from the "field" or bringing the spouse into it, sometimes with children. The last possibility, which I have never tested, may cushion the intruding field worker against personal shocks and may add to information, but it may also reduce exposure to the alien culture as emotional dependence is reduced. We behavioral scientists are not in the position of novelists, who say they are free to write

about states they have never experienced but can imagine through empathy. We are supposed to have gone through the ice and the fire we describe. Are we supposed to shatter ourselves? It is easy to say no, certainly not. But some have done so, leaving work as a monument—notably William Jones and Buell Quain. I have a small inkling of the emotional loneliness, boredom, and exhaustion Quain suffered in Brazil because he wrote me about these in 1939 shortly before he died there.

Edison used to ridicule my bookish Portuguese; through him I realized how extraordinarily idiomatic the present language is. He and fellow-craftsmen, like the Bahian novelist Jorge Amado, listened to the black folk and others, then handled the ornate and complex language with some such liberties as, in the 1960's, the Beatles were to take with popular commercial music. I listened to Edison and to the cult people and polished my speech. Edison's article (Carneiro, 1964, p. 227) remarks about me that I "spared no energy to understand [the cult people's] religious manifestations in Bahia"; for this I had to speak and understand in the folk modes. Happily, the cult people spoke well, and the chief ones also wrote little things for me. When I returned to Rio in 1939, and again in 1966, people noticed my Bahian accent, not an American one! It was like an American's noting a "Southern" accent. A Rio friend who was bilingual said to me in 1939 that my "personality changed" when I switched languages; years after, in Lisbon, my Portuguese labeled me a Brazilian (and a colonial). By comparison with French and German, I thought Portuguese very difficult, and Brazilians agreed; besides, certain sounds are uncouth by general English and European standards, so that it took determination to achieve them. And they clung. After twenty-seven years' absence, and despite my second husband's typically Spanish-speaking distaste for any other language, Edison told me in 1966, "One really couldn't place you by your Portuguese pronunciation"—meaning that it was not offensively foreign. So had the cult world clung to me. Taxi drivers and servants, even in 1966 Rio, assumed from my speech that I was Argentinian, French, or anything else Latin from elsewhere, or that I had lived years in Brazil.

In 1938–1939 Edison and I were endlessly available to the cult folk, endlessly patient and cheerful, always alert, mindful to take notes and snapshots. We never used a tape recorder or a comparable instrument. Edison rarely took detailed notes, but he had a highly sensitized memory. He produced feature stories for his newspaper about cult doings; he wrote books; he wrote memos for me, which I still keep. One saw all of him as an instrument for sopping up impressions. From him I learned to listen—a technique that cannot be matched for garnering insights. Watching me in the field years later, my husband said that I gathered information the way a busy stream runs underground through woods; I must have modeled my technique after Edison's way.

Finally, toward mid-1939, the end was imposed on my work. I was apprised by these incidents: one day as we awaited a tram into the forest, or *mato,* for our cult-temple destination, Edison muttered to me in labored English, "There's a spy following us—he wants you, I think. Speak English." As this was our code for anything serious, I believed he sensed instant trouble. But how could he know? He replied that "every Brazilian" gets acquainted with the police! But why me? Because of him; and the blacks. How could he recognize *this* spy? Well: "Look at him, he's not flirting! Spies are the only men in all Brazil who are forbidden to flirt. He's black but he's wearing a dark [gentleman's] suit. What black wears a dark suit in this climate?" We deduced that the suspect had been directed to dress up to my, or our, social class. Alarmed and fascinated, I glanced toward him some yards off. (The direct gaze especially between the sexes is improper and can be dangerous, as Edison had told me more than once.) Called then *jogo de olhos* ("the game of eyes"), it could signal titillating love information and settle rendezvous. In an open streetcar I would watch some individual, then find myself cracked down by Edison's scorn: "What is this? Are you hunting trouble?" Nor did the full gaze ever convey the American suggestions of honesty and courage, honored proverbially among us. On the contrary, there it was impertinent, vulgar, an invitation to reprimand. In a Rio bus during 1966, I happened to glance at an arresting young *mulata* forgetting the *jogo* rule (prohibiting direct eye contact); she hurled herself into a fit of abusive words. When I reported this to an American diplomat there, he answered feelingly, "I too have met lots of crazy people in the buses."

In 1939 the police spy we suspected did indeed look away, sullenly. He would not flirt. "Take care," Edison said, as I examined the laborer's build and the tough leathery face. When the tram halted for us, Edison decided on the last row of seats, where the "spy" could not breathe down our necks. But we studied him easily after he had seated himself a couple of rows ahead. Nearly an hour later we reached our stop in the woods, got off, and picked up the faint trail to the secluded cult ground. Where was the suspect? We found the building, where a birthday party was in force and the people were dancing *fox.* Girls fluttered to Edison, but he refused to dance with them because this would have left me open to invitations from the men— class rules and those separating the sexes forbade me to be available for dancing here. True, the musicians and the dancers lumbered frightfully, I thought. But the study required me to join them, I protested to Edison. No, he replied with Chinese calm, I'll explain everything. He proceeded to psychoanalyze the dance holds with devilish point when—"What?"—I thought I heard him say in English, as startling to sense as a typesetter's errors, "There's your man."

Across the floor he stood, looking uncomfortable, his dark garb and face like soot among the others' dress pastels, his glance carefully absent. "Can't flirt," Edison chuckled. "No man. Just a spy." Damn all, I decided, I'll let him know I'm an American! I trotted around, tapped the black, and said gently in my careful Portuguese, "Do you want me? Or did you come to dance?" His eyes rolled white, like those of a frightened horse, and he ran. I was shaking when I got back to Edison. He said I had been foolish; he meant, I thought, that it was beneath my station to have recognized the fellow. And he said, "In this land that God forgot, we all come to know the police."

Later, when we reached the home of a young priestess I knew well and I told her the story in astonishment, she answered quietly, *"Minha Senhora,* we've known this a long time. We didn't tell you because we didn't want to frighten you."

The next spy trailing us in the open was younger, was light-skinned, wore starched whites and almost a smile, and generally was more polished. He entered the temple ground after us and did not run when I addressed him. "Do you like these people, Senhora?" he responded. Now the spy assignments were stepped up to eight-hour shifts around the clock, watching the hotel's doorways, placing anonymous phone calls. It was crazily nerve-wracking, but it roused my fighting will and took me out of the long-standing depression bred by the strains of perpetual humid heat, poor food, social isolation, insults to status and ego, want of light diversion, want of the barest social approval, my acute sense of responsibility for the research, my acute sense of obligation to Edison, my dislike of the German employees who showed arrogance and pruriency, my resentment of the army officers who watched and watched from their dining-room tables and lobby armchairs. And during this time Edison had his week in jail.

When he was free again, he agreed to accompany me to the police for an explanation, a reason for the espionage. They denied that spies had been set on me. There was no explanation, only feeble words about an alleged passport irregularity. "But I have a letter from the President's office!" Aha! Soon there came an order of expulsion, with a firm date for me to be on the high seas. Later, in Rio, I learned that the governor of the state, though appointed by Vargas, was a political enemy; that Bahia would have liked to rebel against the federal administration; that a ministry head in this governor's administration was one of those to whom Ramos had given me a letter, which I had not used (fearing to expose myself to the politicians).

A woman friend was visiting me from Rio, the anthropologist Maria Julia Pourchet; now she assured me that we would escape safely, not out of Brazil, but into the capital and her home. I asked the American consul's aid in finding ship bookings before the date of my ultimatum, for the carnival season was at hand. Quaking with fear, he refused, saying that I might well be a spy, for all he knew. The British consul ridiculed the intimidation and helped me amply. But I had to move secretly because, for mysterious reasons, the police wanted my notebooks, my many snapshots, the wonderful priestess dolls made for me by cult women, anything coming from the field study. Between Edison's family and Maria Julia, however, we smuggled everything safely aboard ship. In Rio the federal police chief turned out to be a Bahian. But his politics were Vargas', and he assured me that now I was safe. Two Columbia fellow students met me at the boat, and I felt I was back among the sane. We could laugh at the nightmare happenings in the field—well, sort of. Edison was still there. Rio was calm only under the clamp of the dictator's *estado forte* ("strong state"); actually, soon after my 1938 arrival army rebels had tried to assassinate Vargas in his residence, down the street from my hotel.

Certainly each culture fleshes out its own nightmares. I was the American she-bull in Brazil's china closet. But there is no she-bull in nature, and there was no accustomed place for a woman field anthropologist in Brazil. If I had been Brazilian-reared, I would have known what to avoid—perhaps, indeed, I would have known to avoid the whole enterprise. My luck in meeting Edison and having his escort produced a miraculous approximation to Brazil's model for female conduct. If "spy" means "nosy, alien intruder," the Brazilians were right, symbolically, in so classifying me within their social scheme. They could not have believed this literally, as they could not have believed the prostitute stereotype. But the notions lingered, becoming handy formulas for levering me out, which Bahia finally did. Edison tells of liberties taken with truth by a Rio reporter to whom I refused an interview upon first arriving in 1938 because I did not command Portuguese. The reporter's stereotype-weighted fancy led him to publish, as Edison quotes (Carneiro, 1964, p. 224, my translation), that I would "sweep across Brazil's highlands and jungles . . . [to study] Indians . . . [hence I needed] vigorous men" for my baggage. The leering nudge of sex given the reader here was to appear much more crudely in Ramos' writing; on the same page Edison quotes Ramos' printed equivocal assertion that I had come to study "the sexual life of Negroes"; and Edison observes (p. 227, my translation) that he and another colleague expressed outrage over Ramos' "vulgar insinuations" about my work.

One may ask why my field presence did not disturb Edison. Of course it did, as I have illustrated repeatedly, but clearly it did not threaten his self-concept. My Macmillan editor observed that he came through well in my account in *City of Women*; I and others always saw him free of pettiness. He hated "American imperialism" but could not hate a woman for being that special bearer of the culture. A young Turk of an intellectual, his slingshots were aimed at abusive systems and their political representatives.

Partly this was why he studied the cults and defended them. A writing craftsman of quality and national repute, he applied a craftsman's standards to his significant acts. He never dreamed of playing me down as a woman, as an American, as a colleague, however hard others tried to do this, as I indicated earlier, where the culture let them. He notes (p. 227, my translation) that Ramos' "injustice" to me, his "indelicate and vengeful pages" about my work, "flow[ed] solely from [his] pride and vanity." False and shaky pride was never Edison's.

Through field work at the pleasure of the host culture one learns one's place there and that it is one's only vantage point for penetrating the culture. Mistakes and mishaps in the field are great lamps of illumination if one survives; friendships there are the only greater source, besides being a divine comfort. One gets to love the culture if one meets friends among its bearers; through friends' love, the foreign tradition becomes "mine." Brazil brought this fruit to me in huge measure. In August 1967, when the Brazilian version of my book and articles about the 1938–1939 field work first appeared, it was not just a foreign-language edition—it was a coming home. So field work permits one to live further, beyond the ordered arrangements of one's origins, in a personality and a society with other borders. Briefly one lives two or three additional lives. How much does this cost the psyche? A great deal, I think, if the heart sinks roots, as it does when the mind is stirred. I have worked intensively in six or more cultures beside Brazil's, have absorbed some of each, and left pieces of me with them. My mind balks at the thought of taking on still another, partly because I do not want to lose those I have taken unto myself.

But does one lose? Or is it rather that one knows so much about the hardships of field work? However, the addicted field worker does not really care for ease any more than does the competitive athlete. The lure of another culture can never be discounted, for it is the lure of self, dressed otherwise. Moving among the world's peoples, one sees that personalities here may resemble personalities there, underneath and despite the culture differences. So one comes home, again and again, to friends and kinsmen. Underneath culture's variations we are not all the same, but we are recognizable. When the field worker recognizes personalities this way in the alien culture, he discovers his own. This gives the human depth to information he gathers and will interpret for scholars and others. Back at home he sees his own people afresh, himself among them. The stance of field work becomes a private philosophy of living. What counts in the field and after is that one glimpses, over and over, humanity creating.

References

CARNEIRO, EDISON. 1964. *Ladinos E Crioulos. Estudos Sobre o Negro no Brasil.* Rio de Janeiro: Civilização Brasileira. (This volume contains the article, "Uma 'Falseta' de Artur Ramos," pp. 223-227.)

LANDES, RUTH. 1940a. "A Cult Matriarchate and Male Homosexuality," *Journal of Abnormal and Social Psychology,* 35, 386–397.

———. 1940b. "Fetish Worship in Brazil," *Journal of American Folklore,* 53, 261–270.

———. 1947. *The City of Women.* New York: Macmillan.

———. 1953. "Negro Slavery and Female Status," *Les Afro-Américains-Mémoires de l'Institut Français d'Afrique Noire* (Dakar), 27, 265–268.

———. 1967a. *A Cidade das Mulheres.* Rio de Janeiro: Civilização Brasileira. (This is a translation into Portuguese of all the Landes titles above.)

———. 1967b. "Negro Jews in Harlem," *Jewish Journal of Sociology* (London, World Jewish Congress) December.

Field Work in Rwanda, 1959–1960

HELEN CODERE is a professor emerita of anthropology at Brandeis University and a past member of the executive board of the American Anthropological Association. Her field experience includes work among the Salish and Kwakiutl of British Columbia, about whom she has written monographs and articles that have been published in the professional literature. She retired in the spring of 1982.

M y field work in Rwanda, then Ruanda, dated from the beginning of July 1950 to mid-July of the following year. During that period Rwanda underwent violent internal political upheaval, and, although I had no confidence during the first half of my stay that I would be able to remain the year through, my best Christmas present to myself—the wine was a fiasco and certain other anticipated flourishes no better—was the realization that I was getting good data in quantity and could continue to do so. Since then I have regarded myself as fortunate to have been an observer at a turning point in the history of a people and to have been able to record the views of many Rwanda as part of a firsthand chronicle of change.

Most of the year's field work revolved around the opportunities and problems of the Rwanda political situation, and this account of it will have the same emphasis. However, an essential first task is some briefing on field work and on Rwanda.

Anthropological field work

Anthropological field work is a total experience. The only qualifications to such a statement are that the usual conditions for field work hold: Some significant length of time should be involved, and a period of just a few months is probably not sufficient; something like genuine cultural displacement is probably also necessary, for it is difficult to see how field work could be a total experience if it comprised easy and long-standing famili-

The field work was supported by a Fellowship of the John Simon Guggenheim Foundation and a Vassar College Faculty Fellowship. IRSAC (l'Institut pour la recherche scientifique en Afrique centrale) furnished the base of operations in Africa, and IRSAC specialists, especially Andre Coupez, Marcel d'Hertefelt, and Jan Vansina gave invaluable practical and scientific aid, for which I express my gratitude.

arity with the language, ecology, culture, history, and a number of given individuals who are old acquaintances and friends. Field work, therefore, is a total human experience, involving on an hour-by-hour basis our private physical and psychic well-being, the minutiae of daily living, everything we know of our own culture and of our science, and all of these in relation to new problems that demand solution or fresh contexts that provoke reaction and thought without letup.

Physical energy and well-being are necessary for good work. While sickness is often accidental, in the sense that its existence is beyond the control of the individual, the field worker can make an enormous contribution to his own physical well-being by an intelligent, consistent, and imaginative use of rudimentary medical knowledge and simple hygiene. Failure to recognize or solve such problems as those of usable water and clean food handling means trouble—malaise, hypochondriasis, dsyfunctioning, and time lost from work or the lowering of the quality of attention brought to the work.

The demands of daily living usually go far beyond those of the physical world into the social and intellectual worlds, for the hungers, fatigues, and disquiets of social and intellectual life can become mighty and isolating preoccupations, much more difficult to deal with than merely physical demands.

I have generalized in these remarks from the particulars of my experience. In discussions of field work with others who have experienced it there seems very general agreement about the totality of field work. It is a human, cultural, and scientific welter, at one and the same time the most stimulating and exasperating of human situations, not only to exist in but also to work in—perhaps I should say to create in, since finding order and knowledge in such a welter goes beyond mere work. I have, of course, thought, in that way in which we all seem bound to be most sympathetic and appreciative of our own particular experience, that the lot of the single female field worker is a particularly hard one. Single women lack some of the freedom and mobility of single men; they are objects of even greater curiosity and scrutiny in a world in which going two by two is projected even for all of Noah's birds and beasts; and they are expected to be masters of housekeeping in any land, whatever its pests, produce, and proprieties happen to be. I have thought that the ideal situation in the field would be that of the married couple, since with a team practical matters could be more easily subsumed to management by dividing them up and social and intellectual isolation would be automatically avoided. Friends have convinced me, however, that teams have had many of the same problems as the single woman, as well as a problem peculiar to a marriage—that the frustrations and anxieties of the total field situation have all too handy a target and can threaten the marriage itself.

THE CHOICE OF RWANDA

My choice of area, East Central Africa, and culture, Rwanda, was in general the belated choice of the kind of place I wanted for my field work when I first joined anthropology in part, at least, to see the world. The second World War effectively limited American anthropologists of my generation to the New World, and the enthusiasm I had long had for the Kwakiutl of Vancouver Island determined where I first worked as well as a necessary specialization on culture history and change. But the Kwakiutl of recent years, as I saw them in 1951 and in 1954–1955, were neither numerous nor different enough to satisfy the earlier personal and scientific craving to live and work in a large, relatively unacculturated, and, to me, exotic population.

Narrowing the choice to an area of Africa in which English was not the mediating language again involved a mixture of personal and scientific reasons. Some of these were, if not impeccable, at least objective and arguable, such as the desire to work where the anthropological tradition had not been set up by British social anthropology, much of which seems to produce beautiful entomological accounts of various human hives. I also needed to go somewhere where basic ethnography had been done over time, so that something might be accomplished in a period limited to one year.

Some of my reasons, if not disreputable, were highly subjective. My first confession along these lines is that I thought I would function best where it was not too hot much of the time. Rwanda, though near the equator, had an elevation that guaranteed a temperate climate, which did favor work. Though I did, in fact, get bored with its eternal temperateness and felt sharp nostalgia at a *New York Times* photograph of cars stalled in snowdrifts, still, neither the nostalgia nor the climate itself ever interfered with work.

My next confession is of a sort I suspect many anthropologists might make, although I have known only one to admit, as I shall do, that place and tribal names have an irresistible appeal. In my case they have had since I first heard of "Timbuctoo" or of the "Onandaga" or the other five tribes of the Iroquois League. On this score, "Rwanda or Ruanda" could hardly miss, with its twin kingdom of "Urundi" (now "Burundi" which is just as good), its access via "Usumbura," its capital of "Nyanza," and its populace divided among the "Tutsi" ("Batutsi"), "Hutu" ("Bahutu"), and "Twa" ("Batwa") castes. For a nomenclature gourmet, these were but staples in a feast of names, every one of which was a delight. Reading and map study before I left for the field made me a devotée of Rwanda names, and it is a less trivial basis of attraction to an area and culture than might be supposed, when the addition of marvelous new names can be an almost daily pleasure. After all, pleasures of any kind can be rather meagerly laid on in the field, and one that contributes to learning personal and place names and the language, offers no major distractions, and produces no hangovers is not to be despised.

PURPOSE OF THE FIELD WORK IN RWANDA

The general purpose of the Rwanda field research was to study change, and a number of specific designs for doing so were drawn up—mostly as a demonstration that I knew how to plan in detail, since the decision about exact procedures had to wait on the possibilities and options of the first-hand situation.

As it turned out for the proposals that were originally drawn up—and there were four of them for as many foundations—nothing except the initial language learning and survey part of the general plan was carried out. Everything had to be subordinated to the practical and scientific exigencies of the political situation. At least in my case this was true, because I could not think of any research on change in Rwanda as worthwhile that did not relate closely to the revolution. It seemed like a once-in-a-lifetime opportunity, which could not have been planned for but which had to be utilized. No visa would have been granted me had the political violence been anticipated. I could not have obtained a grant if I could not guarantee access to the area and the certainty that I could carry out work. Yet once I was there, with some hope of staying and working, there is nothing I would rather have done than engage in trying to understand the events that were occurring by getting at their antecedents, recording the opinions that were shaping them, and doing every other relevant job within my power to imagine or carry out in the time I had.

Rwanda

Rwanda, located on the Nile-Congo crest in East Central Africa, is at the great divide of the continent. It is bounded on the West by the Congo, some of whose forests still cover small areas of the crest; on the north by Uganda; on the east by Tanzania; and on the south by Burundi. Rwanda's elevation is some 10,000 feet at the crest in the west of the country; its large central plateau does not go below about 4,000 feet. These altitudes produce a temperate climate in spite of the equatorial latitude of from one to three degrees south.

In Rwanda's 10,000 square miles—an area about the size of the State of Vermont—there lived in 1959 a population of almost three million, figures yielding a population density of about 300 persons per square mile, the highest in sub-Saharan Africa and one of the highest in the world.

The population was divided most disproportionately between the Hutu at over 83 per cent, the Tutsi at 16 per cent, and the Twa at less than 1 per cent of the total. There were hardly any aliens in 1959—merely a few hundred Belgian administrators, churchmen, schoolmen, businessmen, and specialists; a small group of Greek, "Swahili," and other storekeepers and coffee traders; and a few visitors. There were almost no colonists, since the Belgian administration had discouraged settlement even in the few spots that might have been economically attractive to Europeans.

The three native groups were physically distinct and endogamous. The Tutsi were tall and willowy—Nilotic in racial affiliation; the Twa were Pygmoid; the Hutu, Negroid and of a stature that placed them between the averages of the two other groups, about ten centimeters shorter than the Tutsi and taller than the Twa. So little intermixture had occurred that it was possible much of the time to make accurate assignments of individuals to their respective groups—with, of course, the frequent help of such additional indicators as wealth, activity, and role. The three groups had been occupationally specialized: the Tutsi were pastoralists and rulers; the Hutu, horticulturists; and the Twa, hunters, potters, and specialists of other sorts, ranging from musicians to spies. Acculturation had not blurred these occupational specializations as far as the majority of the population was concerned.

The visual drama of Rwanda is unmatched in its interplay of natural setting and human occupation. The land is laid out in hundreds of steep-sided hills separated from one another by flat, marshy valleys. The hills demarcate natural population and political units and are thickly dotted with homesteads, each with its enclosure and a few acres, at best, of banana grove and millet and corn patches. These, and the sweet-potato beds in the uninhabitable marshes often far below, provide the livelihood of the Hutu horticulturists. In a few places in the west and north it is still possible to see the forest being cut back by the land-hungry population; but in most of the country the deforestation is so complete that it is difficult to imagine that the land was once all tree-covered.

Small herds of Egyptian cattle are pastured, according to the sequence of wet and dry seasons, on the slopes that are too bare and poor for cultivation or around the homesteads, in harvested fields, and at the edges of the marshes. Even a lone cow will be watched over by a herdsboy, and the proportion of herders to herd is always so high that this circumstance alone could bring about the ultradomesticated mildness of the cattle's dispositions, although the general fussing over them and bringing them into the household enclosure for the night contributes to the same end result. Though surrounded by the big-game section of East Africa, the only sizable beasts are cows as biddable as house pets and sheep whose potential yield of meat is refused out of prejudice and who yield no wool. The swamps still hold some wild life—wildcats and otters—but the people avoid the mosquitoes, other pests, and snakes by living up on the hillsides.

The significant feature of Rwanda's settlement pattern is the absence of towns, in spite of evident density. Before the Europeans came, the largest center in the country was that of the peripatetic residence and court of the Mwami, or king. Next in size were the administrative centers of some eight great chiefs of provinces, the residence of the Queen Mother, and those of an impressive number—perhaps three score—of royal wives. These political residences and centers descended in size to those of the subchiefs on each "hill," but not even the largest of the lot were towns in the sense of possessing townsmen whose lives and occupations were peculiar to towns, and the centers the Belgians were to build later were towns only for them and a handful of other aliens, not for the native population as a whole. It was as though Rwanda had become suburban without reference to an accepted necessary condition of concentrations and focii of population with all their varieties of community and specialty. I grew to see this—or, for that matter, to hear it in the noisy rising, going to bed and local night partying of the densely inhabited countryside—as a major product of Rwanda's politicized historical development. The dispersal of the people and the absence of any community center that could form any group interest or facilitate communication and organization against the ruling minority fit the old situation perfectly.

The Tutsi minority of 16 percent ruled Rwanda—which is to say they ruled the Hutu majority of over 83 per cent—until 1959. It is impossible here to set forth enough detail to describe old-time Rwanda political and social organization, the complex influences of the German and especially the Belgian administration beginning after the first World War, and the antecedents and events of Rwanda's revolutionary year. A brief summary and chronology will have to do, and the reader must be forewarned not only about oversimplification, but also about the provisional nature of my interpretation in many respects.

Before 1959 there had been virtually no foreshadowing of the troubles that began in July following the unexpected death of the Mwami Mutara III. In retrospect the *Hutu Manifesto* of 1957 seems of vital importance. It recorded the lack of Hutu voice and participation in government and enjoined brotherly cooperation and sharing, in line with the ancient myth of the origin of the three caste groups in Rwanda. It was answered with contempt and hostility by the Tutsi *Letter of the Twelve Great Servitors of the Court*. The Tutsi nobles indicated that the Manifesto was an impertinence, disclaimed the notion of any brotherly kinship whatever with the Hutu, noted that the Tutsi sanction for rule was that the Tutsi were the conquerors and natural superiors of the Hutu, and made a de facto threat against any dissenting Hutu by ending with a lengthy list of all the Hutu chieftains who had been killed in the early days of the establishment of Tutsi rule and whose genitals adorned Karinga, the royal drum and the symbol of Rwanda. In spite of such an exchange, which was well publicized, the Mwami Mutara was to tell Hutu leaders in a hearing before the High Council in 1958 that no Tutsi-Hutu problem existed; and somewhat later in the same year the Belgian governor of Rwanda came up with what might be considered the diplomatic compromise of declaring that a Tutsi-Hutu problem existed, but only as an economic problem.

The revolution and its consequences can be seen as a conflict in which each side pushed the other to ever greater extremes of action. Neither the United Nations nor the Belgian policy or presence accomplished much more than a little policing and a little moderating of the pace and force of events. A brief chronology may be the best way of summarizing these as the setting for the field work.

POLITICAL EVENTS: RWANDA, JULY 1959–JUNE 1960 [1]

July 25	Death of Mwami Mutara
July 28	Tutsi coup in the graveside announcement of Kigeri V as Mutara's successor.
September 3	L'UNAR (L'Union Nationale Ruandaise) formed as a political party of Tutsi interests. Active membership drive and rallies during the month. The meeting at Astrida unsuccessful, since some 2,000–3,000 Hutu onlookers made fun of the proceedings and made so much noise the speakers could not be heard. From September to November many incidents, though nothing serious. They arise out of such rumors as that the Belgians poisoned Mutara or mounting tensions from, for example, the Tutsi allegations that only L'UNAR is loyal to the Mwami and has his blessing.

1. This chronology merely gives an indication of some of the most important events of the period, along with some detail on events in the Astrida area that particularly affected field work there. By April 1960 the United Nations Visiting Mission Report listed 22,000 Tutsi refugees, and the Belgians reported 200 dead. The number of refugees was to swell through 1961 to many more thousands, although the number of deaths remained very low.

November 1–15	Serious disturbances begin in the north. Three Tutsi sub-chiefs are killed. Others are treated according to their popularity or relative lack of it. Many Tutsi are burned out and driven away, fleeing to towns and missions.
November 11	Crowds and armed bands close to Astrida. The Belgians bring some 300 paratroopers into Rwanda.
December 8–15	Assassination of several Hutu political leaders in the south and in Astrida district. Tutsi groups attack Save, a solid Hutu area near Astrida, and the residence of Gitera, the Hutu's most vigorous spokesman. Belgian patrols disperse the groups, but they reassemble. Save under continual attack. There is incendiarism, looting, and many casualties, Tutsi and Hutu. Many arrests.
December 22–Feb.	Trials in Astrida growing out of the earlier events.
March	A UN Visiting Mission tours Rwanda, hears many depositions and sees many demonstrations.
April and May	Incidents continue, and more and more Tutsi are chased from their residences among the Hutu population. There is, however, little violence against persons.

The field work: problems sustained or solved after a fashion

As anyone who has read *Return to Laughter* will appreciate, a true narrative of field work requires many printed pages to unfold and not only the literary skill, but also, perhaps, the same freedom, the use of a pseudonym, and the form of the novel gained for that account. A true narrative of any field work might also have the same theme as her account—that of the change in character that comes about in so total and intense a learning experience. However, the purpose of the present chapter is to be a case study that will add whatever it can to the subject of "women in the field," and, although I have had a great deal of trouble with that title—how foolish "men in the field" would sound—I shall do my best with it. I shall organize my account according to a series of problems, in each of which being a woman seems to me to have played some helpful or hindering part. Perhaps at the end it can be seen whether it counted for more or less than any of the other role criteria, or qualities, or knowledge, or whatever, which each of us brings to every situation.

THE PROBLEM OF THE AMERICAN IN AFRICA: AMERICAN-WOMAN VERSION

As in all colonial situations, the American embarrassment over having and over needing to have personal servants exists in Africa, and for the American liberal it probably exists there in its most exacerbated form. Black skins, impoverishment, and miserable life chances exist on the one hand, and their opposites on the other, with the evident and reasonable expectation that as much as possible of the white man's wealth get into African hands. From the first to the last time that I heard "Boy!" in Africa, I winced, and I cringed at much of the behavior of the "haves" toward the "have-nots"; I cringed especially when floundering in the false positions that seemed to be unavoidable. The problem of being a source of income to Africans without appearing to buy social superiority had many facets, and I shall take in order those of relationships within the household, the office, and at large.

My quarters were a two-room apartment with kitchen and bath. I lived first in the lower and then in the upper such apartment of a small house on the grounds of IRSAC [2] in Astrida. A two-burner gas plate, electricity, refrigerator and electric water heater added up to luxury but—far more important for my purposes—made it possible to reduce the business of living to a minimum and thereby to gain time for work.

At first communications difficulties stood in the way of hiring the house servant the entire situation required. I refused to use Swahili, with its dandy phrase books specifying how the master orders the servant for any household purpose, because in Rwanda it was wholly the language of superordinate-subordinate relationships except for its use in stores. Making myself understood in Kinyarwanda and French, and understanding the available French and Kinyarwanda addressed to me by applicants for the house job, was a problem of major proportions. The French-speaking "évolués" were generally in other and better jobs than that of house servant. The problem was, however, solved, although to this day I have never figured out how Sekamaana, the Rwanda Tutsi who became my domestic and I did communicate for the first few months. We were, to be sure, good at charades, but complex matters got communicated also. Although thoughts about the changes in household schedule required by an impending political crisis could not be transmitted like thoughts of an impending beer shortage by pointing at any object, the fact that we were able to understand each other not only maintained my faith in verbal communication in general, but deepened my sense of awe at the entire process.

2. "Institut pour la recherche scientifique en Afrique Centrale."

Once life settled down, I did my own cooking, my household buying, and my personal laundry, as the American euphemism has it. It had taken a while for me both to find a house servant and to arrange a division of labor and a daily schedule that was workable. What was finally arrived at was hardly any outpost of civilized homemaking by either Belgian or American standards. My housewifery, and my dress, were neat, clean, workable, and appropriate to my sex, but even with the help of Sekamaana, who kept me in spotless blouses and skirts and kept my rooms at a constant spring-cleaning shine, I and my house and cuisine were so far from the elegance and style achieved by the Belgian women in the area that I felt as I imagined that the English of an earlier colonial day must have felt if they did not dress for dinner in the bush—that they were considered to be lowering the tone of the entire Western enterprise in Africa and letting civilization down. I can recall one moment of giddy private hilarity when two of Belgium's finest, most modish, most carefully coifed, most high-heeled women in Africa came slurping through the mud in a downpour to a local garage. Their car had broken down a mile outside the village, and they were mad as wet hens and far worse looking since their fall had been from such soignée and impractical heights. However, if the moments I felt vindicated were few, the moments spent brooding or being bothered about my appearance were equally infrequent. I grew to think my plain "American" dress was a good fit to my question-asking and listening role, since it signaled separation from precisely that sheltered and segregated European-woman role that would have been impossibly confining and crippling to anthropological work.

PROBLEMS AND PROGRESS OF THE WORK

I had to spend more time in my house and with matters of housekeeping than I should have liked. My work was done in an office at IRSAC. Even before I left for Africa, I had been unenthusiatic about the institutional connection forced on me. In the early days of my stay I felt that an office was ludicrous, accommodating to its civil-service time schedule was extremely frustrating, and other bureaucratic procedures—such as paying informants—were intolerable. The contrast with the independent, open, free initiative of most American Indian work, such as I had done among the Kwakiutl, was about as sharp as the opposition between being a poor anthropologist with an academic income less than most Kwakiutl and being a rich one in Africa. While I never overcame, but only became used to, my discomfort over the differential between my income and Rwanda poverty, I did make my peace with IRSAC, in part through substituting my own procedures, and in an even more important part, which I most gratefully acknowledge, in utilizing IRSAC's facilities to the fullest in ways and kinds of work I had never anticipated that were nonetheless appropriate to investigating Rwanda's revolutionary year. This story takes a bit of telling, however; it is thoroughly bound up with not only my gradually increasing knowledge of Rwanda, but also with what for me were extraordinary problems of revising my concepts and methods of work. I had to undergo my own private revolution of cherished anthropological doctrine in order to function effectively. As far as I can see, my being a female rather than a male anthropologist had nothing to do with this at all, although I believe it entered the practical picture from time to time.

My first assistant was selected for me by IRSAC personnel on the basis of principles that I acknowledged to be both sound and promising. Gahenda was elderly for a Rwanda and had been witness to much of the old-time life of the country and to the changes it had undergone. His career had been typically Tutsi—he had once been a subchief, for example; and he was literate in French and Kinyarwanda. There seemed to be no question then about the possibility of his being a steady and well-qualified helper and teacher of the language and the ways of the land. The situation proceeded quite otherwise. Almost immediately we developed the kind of enmity that usually comes only with years of opposition on every imaginable question and of mutually irritating association. Our empathy seems to me to have been nearly perfect, and nearly perfectly hostile.

He despised women—for him even Tutsi women were a lower order of life, as various of his depositions made clear—and working for me was so impossible for him that he must have set a record for absenteeism and contemptuously improbable excuses. I think my being both a woman and a "European" had something to do with his attitudes, although there will always be a question when one of these almost once-in-a-lifetime personal antipathies is at work. It was politicking, of course, that demanded his presence elsewhere, and he was so full of extremist Tutsi politics and racist attitudes that I learned all about them at first hand right off. The perfect incompatibility of his views with everything I believed as an anthropologist and a democrat got our association off on its flying start to dissolution. I should like to go into more detail about the times he did work with me— he was, for example, an excellent antiteacher of language, in the sense of being able to thwart learning and muddy up and diminish what had been learned. The point, however, is to give Gahenda his place in an account of the "field work," which is not as impersonal or even horticultural as it sounds, but which generally consisted of instructive personal relationships. During the first couple of months of my stay in Rwanda I was not only learning much from Gahenda—in spite of him, to be sure—but I also began to help the first of a number of young Rwanda men with their English. I started this practice because I couldn't refuse their very polite and serious requests, and for me the lessons proved a godsend. The tutorial sessions were not only an educational welter of languages and glosses, but also a mine of information and a source of great pleasure in the discovery of thoroughly likable Rwanda.

It took more than two months, but at the end of that time the initial difficulties of the field work were over. My household was a going concern; I finally got a car (a good secondhand VW); Gahenda was fired; I knew there were Rwanda I liked and could get along with; I had learned quite a lot and, though still green—or, as the Belgian French would have it, "blue" —nowhere near as bright a green as before. All of this, however, added up to little more than having a certain optimism and resiliency with which to confront the real problem of doing some worthwhile field work in a country in which there was increasing political tension and unrest.

Tutsi-Hutu violence and the beginning of the revolution did not break out until November 1. By about that date I knew what I was doing, what I could do, and how to proceed. The month and a half or two months before then was a period of furious and disorganized activity on my part and an equally furious internal revolution in my anthropological thinking. My anthropological problem could be reduced to one of drastic simplicity: I had come to study social and cultural change, and there was too damned much of it. It was too vast, too widespread, too fast, too violent, too much of a mass phenomenon for me or any anthropologist to deal with according to the book. The political question was the focus of cumulative changes in every facet of Rwanda life; I do not believe I am applying wisdom after the fact, to think that most Rwanda and most Belgians felt change and points of no return to be in the very air, as I did. It was this change I wanted to understand, but all I had prepared for was the peaceable and detailed investigation of matters like entrepreneurship and the repercussions of increasing cash income on family and social life. My task, then, was to discover some method to study change in the entire social and political order of Rwanda.

Anthropological doctrine would have the researcher get to know some few people in some local situation very well and to settle down with them and work most intensively on the general structure of their social lives and on such particular focii of their activities and thoughts as the anthropologist considers significant and capable of detailed investigation, given the field worker's background, interests, talents, and often temperament and even physique. Surveys were always permitted in order to get an over-all picture and context and to settle upon some representative or optimum or particularly interesting community within it, but "living with the people" is of the essence, and that is a pretty localized and small-group affair. Not very many anthropologists in Africa had ever lived with the people to the degree that anthropologists working with American Indians or various Oceanians had done, but whether or not they were in African households, they worked at the same close-order type of inquiry, with every bit of information acquired through talk or observation assignable to individuals of known genealogical relationship and social roles in what became, at least eventually, a completely known network that was supposedly a microcosm of the larger society, even if its context was a larger society.

The sanctions for the anthropological doctrine of participant observation were severe. Those who failed to understand and apply it in their procedures were considered doomed to useless labors yielding only superficial or invalid results. They would never get the real stuff; and given the vigor and relentlessness of their peers as critics, they would do well never to publish any of the results of their field work.

The over-all scientific resolution of the problem of finding appropriate methods of investigation did not come clear for some time, but it gradually emerged as I confronted a welter of specific situations; I felt like a rat running a maze, either bumping against barriers or finding an opening.

I did run as actively as a good maze rat. For a while I thought I would center on studying markets, or *centres de négoces,* as they were called by the Belgians who had established them. Were these nonindigenous market centers at all important as centers of change in the economic life and expectations of the people or as centers for the development of entrepreneurship and market attitudes? While I continued throughout my entire stay to collect information from any kind of vendor or artisan-vendor to find out what kind of an entrepreneur, if any, he was, my marketing project was soon scotched as such, since the Belgians closed the centres de négoces as they frequently forbade gatherings of any sort and anything except local circulation of the population.

With IRSAC's help I looked first at two possible places to settle, which would be in the countryside away from Astrida and would permit me to work with the local community. I did not like and discarded the idea of using the Belgian administration rest houses offered me as being too connected with officialdom. I worked away at finding a place myself and was pleased at the hospitable offer of Chief Mbanda. I was prepared in my mind for settling there and being a "good" anthropologist working according to the book, but I delayed my move because of the uncertainties of the political situation. Mbanda's deep involvement, soon thereafter, in the brutal assassination of two Hutu political leaders and his consequent trial and imprisonment scotched that plan, although by then it did not matter because I was taken up with plans that were working out.

In the meantime I had been acquiring assistants and becoming ex-

tremely busy with their training and with unexpected responsibilities. After
Gahenda, I determined to find my own assistant, without IRSAC's intervention. Nelson Rwagasore was my first and chief assistant. He was a Tutsi,
twenty-eight years old, of very lively intelligence; he turned out to have a
capacity of being interested in learning what Hutu were thinking in spite of
his own Tutsi political affiliations, activities, and sympathies. Rwagasore was
the only assistant I acquired on my own initiative; the others presented
themselves to me. By the last months of my stay I had an astonishing
number of them; even more to my astonishment, I was also administering a
complex and many-faceted enterprise.

After Nelson Rwagasore, there was Léocadie Mukamusoni, a young
Tutsi woman of twenty who was certainly the first Rwanda woman ever to
hold a quasi-professional type of position. I think that she made her greatest contribution to the work as a woman, and by that I mean simply her
presence as a woman. When I went about with her and usually Rwagasore,
our quality as a group seemed to me one that everyone—Twa, Hutu, or
Tutsi, old or young, male or female—found interesting without experiencing
as threatening. While Léocadie had neither Rwagasore's education nor his
capacity for objectivity, she had the shy, courteous manners appropriate to
her caste, sex, and unmarried state. Whether that contributed much I do not
know, but I have always been convinced that attitudes get communicated
somehow through any screen of manners and forms. The main thing, I think,
was that two women—and maybe especially the combination of a shy quiet
one and a necessarily aggressive anthropological field worker—made contacts seem easy and harmless and consequently people were responsive and
unguarded.

The last member of the first team was Jean Gakwaya, who was nineteen
years old and also a Tutsi. He proved to have extraordinary talents, energy
and sense.

It was with this group I worked out and did the major share of the three
systematically collected blocks of data that I regard as the chief production
of the field work. Toward the end of my stay, when it was quite clear how
additional assistants could add to some established job and how their work
could be assessed and controlled by comparing it with the work already
done, I added several others.

To complete this story of a veritable field work corporation that got
established to my astonishment, I must tell about my reporters and notebook writers. Again, it all started tentatively on a trial basis when the teen-
aged Freddy came around. He wanted a job in an office—a white-collar
job. He was perky and brash, and his round gold-rimmed glasses completed his appearance of a skinny adolescent owl some years away from
wisdom. Confronted by Freddy, I recalled that Carl Withers had had the

young keep notebooks for him in his Plainville work. I thought, why not try it, and appointed Freddy a "reporter," explaining that he should write down what he had seen and knew about. I furnished him with a Bic pen and a notebook—the first of what would prove to be dozens he and other reporters were to use up. It was only work as such that I paid for after the early period when I still went along with IRSAC practice in this matter, and it was, of course, very uneven. I promised to be at IRSAC at certain times to buy back the notebooks, so to speak, and to furnish new ones if the ones turned in were all right. Over a dozen mostly young men and women contributed to a mass of material, about half of which is not only chaff, but even repetitious chaff, as one might expect. Some notebook writers shamelessly exploited the opportunity and never got to do a second book. The most curious of these was a local prostitute, who added to her income by having her waiting clientele fill notebook pages for her on sundry topics. However, some of the notebook material is not only fine and detailed, but it is on topics about which neither I nor my assistants could have obtained much material, or would have given high priority to obtaining that year. The good notebook material does give a picture of the activities and preoccupations of the young Rwanda that year, of their mobility, and of their version of what they saw around them and how they reflected the political ideas of their elders.

This description of the notebook project, as well as of its personnel, moves ahead to the story of the work itself of which the notebooks were one of the least important parts. Getting back again to the initial period of the real work, that of the third and fourth months, I can report that I was doing a number of things that "good"—in the sense of well-behaved—anthropologists do, some things of a doubtful character, and some things I should never have imagined I would catch myself doing.

Among the acceptable anthropological jobs was that of going about meeting and talking to people and getting a constantly expanding and expandable acquaintanceship. Note pages became filled with general information, impressions, and background material. A daily log was kept, and fairly ordered and systematic files were begun on a number of standard ethnographic topics, as well as the overriding topic of political developments, on which a day-by-day record of every conversation, rumor, and event was kept and to which every document I could get my hands on, from clippings to air-drop leaflets, was added. In all candor, the standard ethnographic data was often the least interesting to me. Not only was there plenty of it already in publication, but few of the additions I was making to it were very momentous. Léocadie and I kept working away at the subject of girls and women and their lives, and that was all right, as were the household inventories and price lists for native and European goods in the countryside that I worked on with Jean Gakwaya. I thought some of my accumulating files

—such as my list of every Rwanda personal name, with its meaning—were nice and potentially useful, but none of all of this was at the heart of the excitement and action of the period that began with the death of the Mwami Mutara, took a definite and revolutionary direction with the outbreak of Hutu violence against Tutsi in the north in November, and affected the Astrida area, where I worked, continuously, even through the incendiarism and violence there were never great.

I cannot say when I began to become stubbornly resolved to get through to Rwanda men and women of every caste, age, occupational group, and educational level, but that began to seem a pre-eminent concern in a society in turmoil. It was also quite clear that all the data that had been collected in the past had not included this concern and had an overwhelming Tutsi bias, since it had been collected through and from Tutsi. I had been appalled by a work of J. J. Maquet that was based on the rationalized assumption that this "Tutsification" of the data was even an advantage, since the rulers were the competent authorities on the system by which they ruled; by inference the masses of the people, the Hutu, had nothing to contribute to a structural, dynamic, or human picture of the situation. I quote from the translation that has since been made of Maquet's 1954 work: "As might have been expected, the more competent persons on political organization were Tutsi and in fact more than ninety percent of our informants were Tutsi. Since the number of Hutu and Twa was too small to be of any significance [there was, in fact, only one Twa!] their interviews were not taken into account in the computation of results. (Maquet, 1961, p. 3)."

I could not see how *The Premise of Inequality in Ruanda*—the title given Maquet's work in translation—could be established by the Tutsi alone in a Tutsi version when the Tutsi constituted a mere 16 per cent minority of the population.

My determination to get to Hutu and every kind of person in Rwanda in order to understand what was going on became a driving force. I first tried something most uncongenial and, to me, most unanthropological: a questionnaire. If instead of close-order local inquiry I wanted to range over a district wide enough to include individuals of every possible category that might prove to have special views and a special role in Rwanda at the time, I had to allow for an element that could be held constant and systematic, and asking the same questions of everyone was such a device. After trying various approaches on my assistants, English students, and a number of other IRSAC employees—and after getting suggestions for questionnaire statements from the same group and winnowing out what seemed to me such overprovocative ones as "The Tutsi should be given the atom bomb to stop these troubles"—I drafted a questionnaire and piloted it in the time-honored way, with two captive school groups, one made up of the young men who were students at the École d'Administration, the other with a group of younger girls at a religious school emphasizing domestic science. The final draft was then prepared in Kinyarwanda and French, though it was the native language, "Ibibazo," that was used over 90 per cent of the time. The form contained forty statements, all having something to do with change, with the old and the new: towns, native medicine, European medicine, money, schools, women, chiefs, agriculture, Tutsi and Hutu, cows, Europeans, other foreigners, vassalage. It was responded to not only with the built-in nuancing of Kinyarwanda, which could have been made especially for questionnaires, but also with what proved to be the real bonus—volunteered commentary explaining why the response was "Yee ("yes") or "cyane" ("emphatically yes)," "Oya" ("no") or "ashwi" ("emphatically no"). Not that, except in a very few cases, individuals commented on each of the forty statements, giving reasons for their responses, but there were always enough comments to expose and test understanding and meaning. I administered many of these with Rwagasore. The record questioning took three hours, but most took about an hour or slightly more. In the course of the examination it not only became clear that Hutu liked answering and liked having their opinions taken down, but also that their responses were Hutu responses. Rwagasore, for reasons other than mine, became an objective and interested listener. This response broke through the Tutsi screen through which my information had had to pass because my assistants were Tutsis. Of the more than 350 questionnaires finally administered, over half rejected the opinions of Hutu; over a third, women; almost a fifth, individuals who either saw the questionnaire given or heard it and asked to take it too. The final statistical study of these results is only now being run through the computer, but even the tallies and percentages done to date show the different and particular responses of the various groupings of Rwanda's population and contribute to an explanation of what was happening and has since become final.

Sometime in the course of this project, which continued up to the end of my Rwanda stay, it occurred to me that I wanted to get a measure of the importance of caste (Tutsi, Hutu, or Twa) in the minds of the people by some indirect device, one which would, so to speak, allow them to read caste into their responses, if they chose to do so, quite uninfluenced by any verbal cues mentioning the caste names or any matter that was closely related to caste, such as cows, chiefs, marriage, or troubles. I went through scores of IRSAC photographs and finally chose a number that I tested out on my assistants, reporters, and so on. All I wanted was photos that would be responded to, and I found interestingly enough in this pilot phase that photographs that did not show people were useless. I settled on six, three of which were scenes of traditional Rwanda—a Twa smoking hemp (marijuana), a Hutu mother giving beer to her child, a Tutsi diviner receiving Hutu clients in his compound—and three of which were scenes showing

something quite modern and untraditional—a Tutsi chief absorbed in looking at glass laboratory apparatus, a storefront with a miscellany of people
gathered in front of it, and an évolué reading a book. I thus had a mixture
of castes in old and new situations, so that in half the cases there was a
certain amount of distraction and ambiguity because of the modern scene,
and in two of the traditional scenes there would be some uncertainty based
upon the relative unlikelihood of the respondent's having seen an old-time
diviner or the usually secretive smoking of hemp.

The experiment worked out beautifully. Over 250 individuals, a quarter
of whom were children between eleven and fifteen, gave their opinions and
comments on the six photos. Again individuals drawn from each caste, both
sexes, every age, all occupational and educational groups made caste specifications in an overwhelming number of cases, but with differences in both
the number and accuracy of their specifications, according to their own
caste, sex, age, and other grouping. The commentary material, the preju-
dices that were detailed, the stories people saw in the photos, the opinions
they expressed on everything from the evil of hemp smoking to the beauty
of motherhood and the advantages and uses of literacy—these were the
additional bonus of this substudy, which cannot help being a favorite of
mine for having worked so smoothly from its design to its results.

My last large project was quite unanticipated. I wanted very much to
get Tutsi, Hutu, and Twa life histories, hopefully both a man's and a woman's
in each caste group. I had very little confidence that this project would be
realizable, since, as it has become perfectly clear in the description of the
work up to this point, though I had numerous contacts with very many
Rwanda individuals, they were not intensive except those with my assistants
whom I grew to know very well indeed but whom I never treated as captive
informants in my employ by asking any questions or pushing any inquiry to
the point of invading privacy. To cut a long story very short, we finally
ended up with forty-six depositions in which, again, every kind of Rwanda
individual—excepting, unfortunately, a Twa woman—told what he or she
saw fit to tell of a life story, with no other direction except that we expressed and maintained interest in whatever was said and wrote it down as
it was told. This project expanded to its extraordinary size for two reasons.
The first can only be described as that of the Rwanda's articulateness and
willingness to talk. Since the material is so unlike anything in any of the
large bibliography for Rwanda, I can only conclude that the year that saw
so much coming to the surface and being expressed in political talk and
action was also one in which individuals were busy rethinking their whole
lives and hopes and were eager to talk about themselves. The second reason
was that of my constant fight against the "Tutsification" of my material. It
was always the case that for my Tutsi assistants it was somehow much

easier to turn up other Tutsi who were ready and willing to tell about their lives. To counteract this, I finally reconciled my dogged insistence on getting Hutu with what seemed their parallel drive to get Tutsi, by simply obtaining as many life accounts as possible. In the end the proportion did not turn out too badly—twenty-four Tutsi as against twenty-two Hutu accounts and two Twa accounts. While the sum was not a proportional sample of the Rwanda population in respect to caste, it was a good sample as regards sex, age, and so on, and since it was drawn from the Astrida district of Central Rwanda, the life stories and political situation—vassalage, for example—is seen from the point of view of many vassals as well as from that of their overlords.

Considering the outcome of the revolution, which went against the Tutsi to the point of no return to their old position in Rwanda or to the possibility of the relevance of their attitudes to the new Rwanda, I am now very glad for historical reasons that they are so well represented in numbers, ages, and types of past role and experience.

PERSONAL NOTES

If my account of field work in Rwanda has been almost wholly taken up with a discussion of the work itself, it is because the drama of Rwanda held the center of the stage, and that and the work were the sources of the major pleasures, interests, and rewards of my stay.

Some personal notes, however, may be relevant to this account. I had left a situation in which I had had a most delightful social life. Good talk and drink with a number of friends and colleagues were its main components, and from this point of view Africa was a desert. I do not mean by this to imply to any of the friends and acquaintances I made in Africa that I was unappreciative of their kindness and hospitality; rather, the reason for my deprivation was a love affair with my own language that went quite unrequited for twelve months. Not to control a language well enough to make play with it was an intolerable frustration, for I had no such control of French, to say nothing of Kinyarwanda. Nor was there any compensation in hearing any of the English that I occasionally did hear, for it bore no resemblance to the kind of talk that I missed. Loneliness I could manage, mostly by reading every moment of the day I was not working, but that only compensated in part for my loss of my spoken language.

There were reasons and matters of information that made me feel that I had to work and live in Rwanda with the greatest discretion and inconspicuousness of which I was capable. My visa required renewal in six months, but even after that point had passed successfully, the Belgians could have quite understandably sent me out of the country had I gotten into any trouble or looked as though I might. Rwanda in 1959 and 1960 was a land of tensions, rumours, and troubles, and it was this Rwanda—the one having to do with all the sensitive issues—that I wanted to learn about. Here being a woman, playing dumb, and being inconspicuous all played their parts. There were only a couple of Europeans with whom I was ever remotely myself, and I became bone-weary of my harmless, quiet, flabby role with the other Europeans. With Rwanda and none but Rwanda it was different —the disciplines I had to impose on myself came naturally; but creating and maintaining the other role—that of the woman who was inconsequential and who caused no trouble or inconvenience—was a constant irritation. I can recall a moment of sharp anger when I learned that every European but me in or near Astrida had been invited to a reception for the United Nations Visiting Commission investigating the troubles in the country. Since I certainly did not think that I was being kept from the proceedings because of my views, my anger was at what seemed a slighting oversight. It disappeared when I had to admit that being overlooked had been just what I wanted and was proof of success, however irritating it was to a fundamentally un-Milquetoast type of person.

A personal note is also required on the question of actual and imagined physical danger during much of the year. There were several occasions when the possibility of physical harm was an actuality—all in crowd situations—but their most frightening aspect was my discovery that I was quite fatalistic, an attitude I never held and still do not hold in ordinary circumstances. But the actual situations were practically nothing compared to the never-ending stream of rumors, advice and activities that were extremely difficult to assess moment by moment. I feel and felt, even before I left Rwanda, that the Belgian role in Rwanda was a mitigating, positive, and honorable one. However, that does not alter the facts that the Belgians were not in control of the situation and that the more the Tutsis lost out and were driven from their residences among the Hutu, the more desperate and the more anti-European they became; and that civil order throughout central Rwanda was everywhere so fragile as to be shattered by even minor incidents. What the Belgians presented to me—and to themselves, as far as that goes—was the conflict between, on the one hand, their assurance that everything could be controlled and that everything was rather comic-opera in character anyway; and, on the other hand, the considerable precautions they took to defend themselves and their households. There were some good features, if not comic ones, about the way the revolution was fought, for it may turn out to have been the last such conflict in history conducted without the use of firearms. I have to confess my amusement even at the time, when we learned that the IRSAC Museum storerooms had been extensively drawn on for spears, but what was happening in general was not funny at all; in retrospect, I think one of its worst aspects for everyone was the extraordinary pressure and tension created by rumors and hearsay reports. It was all too human, of course, for Belgians and Rwanda alike to have circulated these in excited and dramatized terms. The only ones to have a personal reference concerned Gahenda, my one-time assistant and antagonist. Various Rwanda told me various versions of how he had killed a Hutu child, or children, with a spear—this in a nearby area. I responded to that news with the thought that I should have expected as much. Then there were later stories, again from Rwanda, of how Gahenda had fled to Uganda and returned, of how he was in hiding here and there, the last of which did scare me—he was hiding very near Astrida and had been making various charges against me to the effect that I had not paid him what was due him, and so forth. In any event I had no confrontation with Gahenda, and no more reason to worry about him than about other impersonal reports. Here I am trying to give an account of the tension and pressure to which I overresponded at some points, although never to the point of acquiring or having any weapon in my house, in my car, or on my person.

Conclusions

The year in Rwanda was a hard one physically and emotionally, and I was sick for over a month when I got home: physical fatigue, virus pneumonia, and mental fatigue. It all took some mending and time.

The strongest pressure of all in this venture—or any such venture—can perhaps be inferred from this account. It is quite simply a matter of discharging the professional and scientific commitment to learn something to bring back, something worthwhile, from a period of field work. While the pressure of such a commitment can be harsh and nagging, it can also hold things together and keep them going when nothing else can. I am still under this pressure as I work at my Rwanda data, since the obligation will not be discharged until there are full published results. Any value or interest this chapter may have will only be decided at some future point on the basis of whether the results of the field work are considered to be of any worth.

Being a woman clearly played some part in the enterprise, but in fact every anthropologist, like every Rwanda, is a combination of role factors, to say nothing of personality factors, and, along with sex, there are age, education, nationality, economic level, and social group affiliations, all determining action and response. Had my investigations in Rwanda been directed to the topics of sex, women, childbearing, and so on, the factor of my sex would have been of far greater importance; but for the topics I was attempting to investigate—those relating to the political and social changes that were taking place—neither my sex nor the sex of any Rwanda individual was a central role factor determining attitude and action. The computer results of the big questionnaire, for example, show the factor of sex to have produced few valid or definite correlations of responses according to sex, whereas caste, age, and education show pervasive influences.

My final and speculative note is one that has just now crossed my mind in trying to think of everything possible to do with the subject. The women of Rwanda whose views and qualities I found most moving and with whom I grew to be most sympathetic were the poor, uneducated Hutu women leading their traditional lives of labor in their fields. They came through as people of transcendent common sense and humanity. The Tutsi women were quite otherwise for the most part. The worst were arrogant and inhumane, but even the best did not have the quality of the Hutu, and though I sympathized with them for the sad reversals in their lives, they never moved me as did the Hutu women. I wonder now whether a male anthropologist would have troubled to seek out and deal with Hutu women because, from the point of view of their physical appearance, they could not compare with the attractiveness of Tutsi women who were not only often exotically beautiful but who were not grubby, muscular, and calloused from their work with the earth. Clearly European men made liaisons and were attracted to Tutsi, but never to Hutu, women; the very extensive (male) anthropological literature on Rwanda had given the Hutu no special labeled place or quality. But had such a bias operated to distract a male anthropologist from dealing with Hutu women, that year, at least, he would have missed some of the most interesting and expressive and important views to be discovered among the Rwanda.

References

BOWEN, ELENORE SMITH. 1954. *Return to Laughter.* New York: Harper & Row.

CODERE, HELEN. 1962. "Power in Rwanda," *Anthropologica*, 4, pp. 45–85.

MAQUET, J. J. 1961. *The Premise of Inequality in Ruanda.* London: Oxford University Press. Translated from *Le systeme des relations sociales de l'ancien Rwanda.* Academie royale des sciences morales et politiques. Memoires—Collection in-8. Sciences de l'Homme. Ethnologie Vol. 1. Tervuren, 1954.

UNITED NATIONS TRUSTEESHIP COUNCIL T/1538. 1960. *Visiting Mission to Trust Territories in East Africa,* 1960, Report on Ruanda-Urundi.

In a World of Women: Field Work in a Yoruba Community

NIARA SUDARKASA received her doctorate from Columbia University in 1964. Currently she is associate vice president for academic affairs and professor of anthropology at the University of Michigan in Ann Arbor. She also holds appointments in the Center for Research on Economic Development and the Center for Afro-American and African Studies. In addition to conducting the research on which this article was based, she has studied Yoruba traders in Ghana and the role of women entrepreneurs in the People's Republic of Benin. Her publications include the monograph WHERE WOMEN WORK *and articles on women, trade, and family organization in West Africa as well as on the African antecedents of Black American family structure.*

When I accepted the invitation to contribute to this volume, I was en route to Ghana, where I am presently studying the Yoruba community in Kumasi. Left in Ann Arbor were the notes and documents that I collected, the diaries that I kept, and the copies of letters that I wrote during the fifteen months I spent studying Yoruba women in Nigeria. A copy of my dissertation (Marshall, 1964) and a few photographs—highly selective embodiments of my "field experience"—are the only recorded data utilized in this re-creation of my stay in Nigeria.

What follows, therefore, might best be described as remembrances of, and reflections upon, my efforts as an anthropologist in the making. These are the encounters, the evaluations, the episodes that are chiseled in memory. As such, they can only begin to represent the totality of my experience in Nigeria. This shortcoming is at least partly redressed by the fact that here is a measure of the experiences that left their personal and professional marks, and that, hopefully, will therefore interest others in the field.

Getting to Nigeria

Ask any anthropologist equipped with camera, tape recorder, typewriter (and spare ribbons), note pads, ball-point pens (a year's supply), *Notes and Queries,* "sensible shoes", and a veritable pharmacy whence he is headed, and his probable response will be: "I'm going into the field."

Toward the end of May 1961 I set out, via ship, from Liverpool bound for Lagos. Although an American linguist in New York on leave from the University of Ibadan had assured me that virtually anything I would need in Nigeria could be bought in Ibadan or Lagos, my baggage included many

The Ford Foundation, through its Foreign Area Training Fellowship Program, provided the financial support which enabled me to carry out the research discussed herein.

167

items that I would later have been embarrassed to admit had been brought from the States. I hasten to say, however, that these did not include sun helmet, bush jacket, sleeping bags, and many other items listed in one reputable handbook as essential field equipment for Nigeria, to be purchased, if possible, *before* arrival in the country.

My traveling companions in the cabin class were mainly secretaries, lawyers, physicians, young businessmen returning from "U.K. training courses," and students of various vintages. In the first class were government ministers, chiefs, financiers, and first ladies. Nearly all the passengers were West Africans making their way back to their homelands.

At night we danced the "high-life"; during the day we played table tennis and engaged in our favorite pastime—serious and mock debate. In such a setting I had the air of a student on holiday. Were it not for the fact that I kept a diary—a task intended to sharpen my powers of observation and recall—I would have forgotten that I was "headed for the field."

We stopped first at Las Palmas. My companions and I were tourists of the first order: buying this and photographing that. In the evening, back aboard ship, with Las Palmas and Europe behind us, we settled down to await our first sighting of the West African coast.

Such was the magnificence of the coastline of Freetown, our first African port of call, that I could hardly wait to see the city. I was to be shown the city by an American Negro family (the designation "black American" was not in vogue at the time) employed by the American government. It was in the heart of Freetown that I saw my first West African market and there that I glimpsed life as it is lived in West Africa. Before I could assimilate the experience, however, we were off to lunch in a typical "Europeanized" section of town.

When we arrived at Takoradi, I prepared to disembark for what I thought would be my first real tour of a West African city. To my surprise, I was met on board ship by an old college friend who was in Ghana to prepare the way for the arrival of the first contingent of Peace Corps volunteers. We drove through the town on our way to lunch with an official of one of the shipping companies in Ghana. Soon Takoradi was no more than an enchanting villa overlooking the Atlantic.

When the MV *Aureol* finally pulled into Apapa wharf at Lagos, the anticipation of a genuine encounter with an African city gave way to anxiety that, black or not, with the dispersal of my traveling companions and without the presence of old friends, I would be overwhelmed by a foreign land. Mine were the eyes of a stranger as they looked out on a crowd of women, mostly dressed in subtly varying shades of blue, whose movements and shouts of welcome gave them the appearance of a vast evangelical choir.

For me the pier at Apapa was singular confusion. People were greeting each other with laughter and tears: the women kneeling and bowing; the men shaking hands and prostrating before elders; and everyone embracing. For a moment in the commotion my ability to understand Nigerian English seemed to vanish, and I was in a sea of foreign sounds. I pulled myself together and started to respond to directives that, to my relief, began to come through as sounds that were only variants of those in my mother tongue. After a while I could even be amused and disappointed that, despite nearly six months of study in London, I could not understand a single complete sentence of the Yoruba that was being spoken around me.

I had expected to be met at Apapa by a Canadian couple who had flown ahead to Ibadan and whose trunks I had brought by sea. They were not there, and I had no idea how I could get their luggage through customs. Before I could become too distressed by the situation, however, several of my shipmates came to offer assistance with my luggage, transportation to Lagos, and accommodation until I departed for Ibadan.

My cabin mate advised me to clear my suitcases with the customs, and to leave the trunks, including my own, until I had made contact with Ibadan. I was invited to stay at her cousin's home in Yaba, a Lagos suburb, until I could arrange to go to Ibadan. She herself would be staying there for about a week before proceeding to Eastern Nigeria. I gratefully accepted the invitation and, together with my hostesses, set off by car for Yaba.

I do not know precisely what we anthropologists refer to when we speak of "culture shock"; nor am I certain at what point in one's travels it is to be experienced. However, if the concept refers to something more than an initial strangeness in a foreign land—or in one's own after an extended absence—then, intuitively, it does not seem an appropriate phrase to describe the impact that the first days in Lagos had upon me. What struck me most was the familiarity of much of what I saw.

Physically Lagos was reminiscent of many towns I had known in southern Florida. Here were bougainvilleas, crotons, mangoes, poinsettias, hibiscus, papaya, and many other types of flora I had known from childhood. Parts of Lagos reminded me of the crowded shanties that were the heart of the ghettos in many southern cities well-known to me. Tin roofs, pastel-painted buildings stained ugly from the rains, dilapidated houses—these were not strange to me. Nor was the architecture and the elegance of the split-level and ranch-type homes in Ikoyi. The Lagos Marina might have been one of a dozen tree-lined boulevards along the Florida coast. Even the frightening rainstorm that greeted me on my first night in Yaba brought back the thrill and terror of a tropical hurricane.

When I walked out in Lagos on the day following the rain, my first thought was that the muddy red clay, which I had found so irksome in northern Florida towns, would ruin my far-from-sensible shoes.

The field work in perspective

My interest in Yoruba society developed when, as an undergraduate at
Oberlin College, I took a seminar with Professor George E. Simpson on
Africa and the Caribbean. The researches of M. J. Herskovits, Simpson,
and others on "retentions and reinterpretations" of Africanisms in the New
World took on a special relevance when I realized that the esus[1] formed by
my grandparents and other Bahamians in the southern Florida town where
I grew up were institutions brought to the New World by slaves of Yoruba
origin. From that time on, my interest in West African peoples centered on
the Yoruba and Dahomey, and when I decided to do graduate work in anthropology rather than in English, it was with the intention of eventually
studying the extent to which Bahamian religious beliefs and practices and
patterns of social organization could be traced to these two societies.

When I communicated my interest in Africanisms in the New World to
Elliott P. Skinner at Columbia University, he suggested that I might begin
to pursue the problem by writing a master's essay on the historical influences of African and European mutual-aid associations on the structure
and function of benefit societies in the West Indies (Marshall, 1959). It
was my close association with Professor Skinner, whose research interests
had turned to West Africa after a period of field work in the West Indies,
that led to my decision to conduct predoctoral field work in Africa rather
than in the Bahamas. As a logical development of my earlier interests, I
thought of field work in Western Nigeria, and it was Professor Skinner who
suggested that I study Yoruba market women.

In consultation with Professors Skinner, J. H. Greenberg, and C. M.
Arensberg, I conceived of a study that would focus on the ways in which
women's economic activities affected, and were affected by, the other activities entailed in their various roles, particularly their roles as wives and
mothers. The specific problems to be studied included: (1) the point in
their developmental cycle at which women began their trade activities; (2)
the ways in which women combined the management of business activities
with domestic responsibilities toward their husbands, children, and other
kinsmen; (3) the extent to which women depended on their husbands and
relatives for financial and other assistance in their trade activities; (4) the
extent to which the geographical range of a woman's trade activities, the
commodity lines in which she dealt, and the financial scale of her operations depended upon her position and responsibilities within the family and
community; (5) the ways in which women's economic independence

1. My knowledge of the origin of *esu* (an elision of *esusu*) came through the writings
of M. J. Herskovits. It was later that I read Bascom (1952).

affected patterns of authority within their immediate families and other kin and domestic groups; and (6) the relationship between a woman's success as a trader and her socio-political status in the community.

In preparation for my field trip, I spent nearly six months doing research in various libraries in London and learning the rudiments of the Yoruba language at the School of Oriental and African Studies. In retrospect, the period of language training in London always appeared much less useful than a comparable period of study at the University of Ibadan would have been. However, this was compensated for by the fact that the formulation of my research plans greatly benefitted from discussions with various scholars in London.[2]

My first base in Nigeria was the University of Ibadan, where I spent the summer of 1961 getting acquainted with Yoruba towns, markets, and market women. Fortunately my initial ventures "into the field" were guided by scholars whose own researches provided essential background for my own. My first on-the-ground introduction to the morphology of Yoruba towns was provided by Peter Lloyd, well-known for his ethnographic and theoretical writings on Yoruba society. I was introduced to the world of the rural market by B. W. Hodder, who had begun to publish the results of his research on the location, periodicity, and function of Yoruba markets; and I was introduced to markets in Ibadan by S. Edokpayi of the Western Regional Ministry of Economic Planning. My appreciation of the implications of my research for the over-all study of Yoruba settlements and social organization was enhanced as a consequence of my acquaintance with the work of A. L. Mabogunje.

One of the complaints often voiced by anthropologists against "the field situation" concerns their isolation from scholars with whom they can discuss their research. Conducting field work some thirty-five miles from Ibadan was tantamount to doing research as a member of an on-going seminar. The university's faculty and libraries were available for consultation, as were many informed and interested people based in governmental departments. Moreover, on numerous occasions I was visited "in the field" by academicians who wanted to discuss problems of mutual interest to us. It is difficult to imagine how I would have fared in this first research endeavor had I not been able to draw on the expertise and experience of the many scholars and governmental officials I met in the course of my field work.

2. Professor Raymond Firth and Dr. Alice Dewey were particularly helpful on the question of studying markets and economic behavior, and Dr. William Shack, who had recently returned from field work in Ethiopia, gave me much valuable advice on field-work techniques.

A place in the scheme of things

When I left New York, I had not chosen a town in which to carry out my research. I had read in manuscript one of Hodder's papers on Yoruba markets (Hodder, 1962) and had decided that I wanted to be based in a locality that would enable me to study women who traded in both rural and urban markets. The work of Mintz (especially 1955) and Katzin (1959) in the Caribbean also suggested that a base outside a major city would give me a broader picture of the overall range of movement of women traders than would a base in the city itself.

While in London I had met Isaac Akinjogbin, who was then a graduate student in history and who directed me to various sources of historical information on Yoruba society. In the course of a conversation about my proposed research, I asked if he could suggest a small town near Ibadan or Oyo in which I might conduct the study. He mentioned Awe as an old and important Yoruba town, described its location, told me something of its history, and recommended that I visit the place when I got to Nigeria.

Soon after I arrived in Ibadan, I drove to Awe, a town of about 5,000 inhabitants, situated thirty-three miles north of Ibadan, thirty-six miles south of Ogbomosho, twenty miles northwest of Iwo, and a mile and a half east of Oyo. The main street through the town is a major road linking Oyo and Iwo.

The view from "Main Street" left the impression that not very much was going on in the town. My picture of small Yoruba towns had been formed by acquaintance with those between Ibadan and Oyo, where one sees many women selling foodstuffs by the roadside and gets the impression of lively commercial activity. By contrast, Awe seemed dull indeed. I would later learn that being situated astride a less trafficked route than the Ibadan-Oyo road, Awe's commercial and social activity is evidenced in the morning and evening; in midafternoon, when I first saw the place, the town, as it were, takes a siesta.

Although I was disappointed by the quietness of the town, I decided to see more of it before I considered choosing a different town, perhaps one of those on the Ibadan-Oyo road, as my home base. At the University of Ibadan I was introduced to Ojetunji Aboyade, an economist from Awe, who encouraged my interest in the town by telling me something about the economic activities of its women.

I finally decided that I would move to Awe, and through Dr. Aboyade I gained an introduction to the town. One Sunday a few of Awe's "sons" in Ibadan took me to the town and introduced me to the *Balę* (literally, Baba ilę, or "father of the land" or lineage) and other chiefs, the leaders of the churches and their congregations, the Imam, and some of the town's older women traders. So gracious and friendly was my reception by the townspeople that I was pleased to have given up the notion of living somewhere else.

Like most anthropologists going into the field, my idea was to station myself in the heart of town and "live like the people." My friends from Awe soon convinced me of the impracticality of such a plan—pointing out, among other things, that the compounds in the heart of Awe contained no "apartments," but rather were divided into small rooms that would probably be too ill-lighted, even by day, for me to be able to do any serious reading or paper work; and that, in any case I should find it most inconvenient trying "to live like the people."

Just where I would live in Awe was decided by coincidence. Near completion on the western edge of town was a bungalow belonging to an Awe businessman resident in Ibadan. In keeping with the practice of prosperous Yorubas "abroad"—that is, outside their hometowns—my landlord-to-be was building the house in Awe as a tribute to his success. He had planned to use it as a weekend retreat or to rent it to the high school, located across the street. Dr. Aboyade suggested that I might live there, and the owner of the house was contacted about the possibility of my renting it.

I was delighted when I saw the house, and without giving serious consideration to the few alternatives which had been proposed, I agreed to rent it as soon as it was completed. Everyone in the town regarded it as a stroke of good fortune that the house was virtually waiting for me to move in.

My landlord's housewarming, held in late August 1961, was the first social occasion on which I met a large gathering of Awe citizens. I came from Ibadan in the company of the men who first introduced me to the town. We arrived to find the chiefs and other town officials seated under a canopy erected for the occasion. Hundreds of men, women, and children from the town and many Awe people resident in Lagos, Ibadan, and Ogbomosho were present to celebrate the opening of the new house. The clothes were elegant; the food and drink abundant; the drumming and dancing continuous.

The drummers came to greet us as we got out of the car. They beat out the praise-names associated with the lineages to which my companions belonged, and the men, in gestures of appreciation, placed coins and pound notes on the foreheads of the musicians.

I was outfitted Yoruba-style for the occasion, and many people expressed surprise and pleasure at my "being able to wear" their national dress. The women were particularly impressed with the way I had tied the *gele* (the long head scarf); some of the elderly ones danced before me, spreading the hems of their skirts in a playful sign of deference. They addressed me as "Adukenke," an affectionate diminutive of Aduke, a pet name for women. I thought this an auspicious social introduction to the town, and I returned to Ibadan in anticipation of my move to Awe.

When I returned from Ibadan, I found myself cast in the role of the town's guest. In Yoruba society a stranger, whether from another town or another country, is always a guest. A community, a household, an individual, all make a special effort to be generous and considerate toward strangers. The people of Awe, who seemed to feel a special sense of responsibility for my well-being, made me feel like an unusually pampered and privileged guest. I attributed this to the fact that I was a young unmarried woman who happened also to be black.

I was informed upon my arrival in Awe by the Chairman of the Town Council that the Council considered it unsafe for me to live alone in a house at the edge of town. Although the Council realized that I would have an interpreter in the house with me, and a steward living in the quarters behind the bungalow, they had decided to hire a nightwatchman for me. He was engaged, at the Council's expense, for the duration of my stay in Awe.

I had been in Awe about a week when the captain of the Awe soccer team informed me that the team would play a match in my honor against a team from the neighboring town of Akinmorin. The match was held at the Awe high-school stadium and was attended by hundreds of people from the rival towns. As guest of honor, I was asked to make a speech, to kick out the first ball, and to present the trophy to the winning team. A professional photographer was on hand to take pictures, copies of which were later presented to me. My friends from Ibadan, whom I had invited for the occasion, were as surprised as I was that the young men of Awe had thought of welcoming me in this fashion.

During the first month or so of my stay in Awe—and, to a lesser extent, throughout the year I lived there—many people brought or sent me presents—yams, corn, okra, tomatoes, bananas, oranges, and the like—and sent their children to perform various chores or run errands for me.

My landlord took a special interest in my welfare. Although the house was furnished when I moved in, certain items, including a large oil cooker and a kerosene refrigerator, were added, I was told, especially for me. It was my landlord's custom to visit his relatives in Awe every few weeks, and each time he came, he brought me bread or other provisions from Ibadan.

Not long after I moved to Awe, I went to Ibadan for a few days. On my return, one of the women told me that people had missed seeing me in the town and that she had sent her daughter to see if I was all right. When I told her that I had been to Ibadan, she replied that I should have let them know that I intended to travel. After that, as a matter of routine, I informed certain people in the town whenever I planned to be away for more than a day.

Being "looked after" by the town did not always work to my advantage. Before I moved to Awe, I had told some of the townspeople of my intention to hire a young woman to act as my translator and assistant. On one of my visits to the town, a young woman, born in Awe but resident in Lagos, was introduced to me as someone who "would be suitable" for my purposes. I was told that her father had agreed to let her live with me in Ibadan so that she might begin to learn what would be expected of her. Although my misgivings about her suitability developed during our first conversation, in my desire not to offend the townspeople, I agreed to take her on. The young woman had not been working with me for more than a week when I felt certain that she was not the person I wanted as an interpreter and assistant. Her comprehension of English did not enable her to give accurate translations of my speech nor to accurately convey what was being said to me. Although I tried to train her as a translator, it was obvious that she could not cope, and my impatience became apparent.

Soon after we moved to Awe, the pastor of one of the churches accompanied us on a survey of some of the compounds in the town, during which time I was able to appreciate just how inefficient an interpreter the girl would make. The pastor had to correct most of her translations into Yoruba and to elaborate on those rendered in English. By this time I was near the point of total exasperation, and I resolved to get a new translator. The young woman stayed with me for another few weeks, during which time our relationship became very strained, and both of us wanted it to end. Finally she asked for and received my permission to visit her father in Lagos. Shortly afterward her father came to say that she could not continue to work for me without a raise in salary; I said that I could not afford the raise, we both expressed perfunctory feelings of regret that his daughter could not continue to work for me, and that was that. When I informed the pastor and a few others that my translator had left, they assured me that no one would be offended; when I brought a new interpreter from Ibadan, the people of Awe welcomed her as if she were one of their own townspeople.

Before I went to Awe, the only Americans known to most of the townspeople were white Southern Baptist missionaries. Although some of the old people eventually related to me stories they had heard from their parents concerning the slave trade, even some of these old people did not know that there were blacks in America. (This was in the days before Muhammad Ali and "soul music" became household words in every West African village.)

People were very interested in learning about blacks in America. They wanted to know how we lived, whether we spoke any language other than English, whether we ever planned to return to Africa to live, and so on. As regards myself, they especially wanted to know if I could trace my genealogy to any particular part of West Africa. When I said that I could not, they invariably claimed that I was undoubtedly a Yoruba (in Ghana, the Ashantis I meet say I must be an Ashanti), and added, jokingly, that my forefathers probably came from Awe.

My having grown up in a predominantly Bahamian environment seemed to add credibility to the belief that I was "truly an *omowale*" ("a child who has come home"). People were fascinated to hear that I had known about *esu* from my childhood. They were surprised that I could plait my interpreter's hair in styles similar to those worn by Yorubas. When people referred to markets held at eight-day intervals as markets that met "every ninth day," I sometimes told them of my exasperation when, as a child, my grandmother insisted that "from Sunday to Sunday is eight days." Now, I would tell my listeners, I can appreciate that she was using your system of reckoning: one in which the calculation of intervals includes both the first and the last day.

Being regarded as an *omowale* was one factor that contributed to the transformation of my status from that of a privileged guest to that of an adopted "*omo* Awe" (literally, "child or descendant of Awe"). The second, and perhaps more important, factor was my conscious adjustment of some aspects of my behavior to conform to that which I observed around me.

Months before I even saw Awe, I had come to realize that by calling attention to seniority as a determinant of status in Yoruba society, Bascom (1942) had singled out the most important regulator of interpersonal behavior.[3] Age, sex, office, and what might be termed "priority of claim" are the variables that interact to determine seniority. Degree of formal education is not a determinant of seniority: however, because it enters into the assessment of status, it can affect the patterns of deference displayed in particular situations. In some circumstances the determination of seniority can be a delicate and complex affair, and ambiguity may be a necessary attribute of both the display and the interpretation of deferential behavior. Generally speaking, however, men outrank women, and greater age confers seniority. In appropriate circumstances, however, both age and sex may be overriden by office and "priority of claim" as determinants of seniority.

The senior man in a compound is he who holds the position of *Bale* (literally, *Baba ile,* "father of the house or lineage").[4] He is usually, but not necessarily, the oldest man in the compound. The ranking of wives according to the order in which they enter—that is, marry into—a compound illustrates that priority of claim may override age as a determinant of seniority.

3. My use of the term "seniority" differs from Bascom's usage—he limits the meaning of the term to what I call "priority of claim." Bascom juxtaposes seniority to age and sex as a determinant of status. I am suggesting that age, sex, and "priority of claim" are determinants of seniority.

4. In the Yoruba alphabet, the letters e and ẹ represent the sounds *ay* and *eh,* respectively. The word *ile* (house) is not to be confused with *ilẹ* (land).

Some of the signs of deference toward seniors are obvious: men prostrate, genuflect, or bow before their seniors; women kneel, curtsy, or bow before theirs. Normally the plural form of the second person pronoun is used in addressing a senior, and the plural form of the third person pronoun is used in referring to one. These signs of deference may also be used to show mutual respect or social distance between two individuals. Other signs of deference, particularly verbal ones, are more subtle. For example, a subordinate does not normally take the initiative in conversations with his seniors, as is evidenced even in the exchange of greetings. It is the senior who inquires, "How are you?" ("*se alafia ni?*"), who asks most of the questions about the health of family members, and so on.

One of the first decisions I had to make in Awe was whether I would make an attempt to act in accordance with the general rules governing subordinate/superordinate relationships or whether, as an outsider, I would for the most part ignore them. This is not to say that *I* considered that I had a choice in the matter. However, the people of Awe, by their expressions of surprise and approval at the fact that I was beginning to "behave like a Yoruba," indicated that I could have chosen otherwise.

In my speech and in other aspects of my public behavior I conducted myself more or less like a Yoruba because, consciously or not, in greeting situations, people behaved toward me as if I were one. In such circumstances the fact that I was black seemed more important than my nationality in determining their responses to me. Young women and men—who undoubtedly would have greeted a white woman by shaking hands—knelt, curtsied, or bowed when greeting me. When children did not greet me in the Yoruba fashion, the parents told them to do so. Old men and women talked to me the same way as they talked to other young women in the town. It seemed that the only thing to do was to adjust my verbal and nonverbal behavior accordingly.

I made many embarrassing, and some hilarious, mistakes in my efforts to speak Yoruba, a tonal language in which, to my ear, too many words sounded alike (I usually asked women about their hoes when I meant their husbands). However, I never made the mistake, as European-speakers of Yoruba often did, of using the familiar mode of address when speaking to adults. My respondents could choose to reciprocate the deferential or respectful mode of address, or, if they considered it appropriate, they could use the familiar mode. When speaking with people older than myself, I followed the Yoruba practice of interspersing my conversation with "Sir" or "Madam."

In a community where most people, even educated ones, spoke Yoruba most of the time, and where they used all the other signs of deference and respect, it seemed to me highly inappropriate that I should try to speak the language and refrain from behaving with respect toward my seniors. Therefore I curtsied, bowed, and sometimes knelt, as I did before the *Balẹ,* as a sign of deference. Yorubas are very fond of discussing people's "characters." I was often told that the townspeople approved of my character; that despite my education and my having grown up in "the European's country," I displayed the humility and respect they so greatly admired.

In retrospect, it seems that one event that also contributed to my becoming a member of the Awe community, rather than its guest, was the fact that after the incident of the ill-chosen interpreter, I made a point of being candid in my dealings with the people of Awe and less cautious about the "image" I presented to the town. At the same time that I was adopting some of the behavioral attributes of the people around me, I also began to show them more of "myself."

It was a custom in Awe, as it is in many small towns and in most of West Africa, for people to pay visits without notice. I let it be known that the townspeople were welcome to "drop in" on me whenever they chose. However, if people came when I was very busy or had prior commitments, I would apologize for the fact that the visit must be brief and would ask them to come again. After a while people got to know that in the mornings and early afternoons I was usually occupied with some aspect of the research, and they visited me in the late afternoons, or on Sundays, the days when I did not normally attend markets. This habit allowed me plenty of time to visit compounds in the town, to write up my field notes, and to rest.

As soon as I had the opportunity, I began to let people in Awe know what my food preferences were. Since I had been introduced to Yoruba cooking in London and in Ibadan, by the time I moved to Awe, I knew which of the standard dishes I liked and which I did not like. No one expected me to be able to eat stews as peppery as those preferred by most of the townspeople, but in fact it was much easier for me to increase my tolerance for pepper (many West Indian dishes are highly spiced) than it was for me to learn to eat some of the starchy dishes. When I was offered something which I did not like, I simply said, as a Yoruba would, "I don't know how to eat that." My taste in Yoruba food often surprised people in Awe. They could not understand, for example, how anyone could prefer *eba* (a cooked form of cassava meal) to *iyan* (pounded yam) or *amala* (made from yam flour). All the same, when people knew that I would be present for a meal, they prepared what I liked.

My candor about food was reciprocated by those who visited my house. If they came around mealtime and I invited them to eat, they would ask, "What could we eat?" and go on to say, "we can't eat European food." It was only when I cooked Bahamian-style that a few of my friends would join me in a meal. Even so, the Bahamian version of okra stew was sufficiently different from that prepared by the Yoruba for one of my guests to remark that West Indians must be Yorubas who had lost their culinary skills.

I served orange squash (orange concentrate mixed with water) to two old women who called on me about two weeks after I moved to the town. Both women gingerly took sips from their glasses and made such frowns as they did so that I burst out laughing. They too laughed and asked if that was the sort of thing I always drank. When I said it was one of the drinks I liked, the women shook their heads. Then I inquired what drinks the women of the town liked, and was told that they "could drink" krola, a soft drink that I loathed. Thereafter I kept a supply of krola in the house.

To most people in Awe I was known only in the role of researcher. They saw me in the markets, at funerals, weddings, and other celebrations, and on the streets of the town. Such people often referred to me, particularly when we met in markets outside the town, as *"arabinrin wa"* ("our townswoman" or "our female relative"), and they addressed me by the nondescript, though kinship-derived, terms "Sisi" or "Aunti." However, my relationship with them never extended beyond an exchange of greetings or an interview situation.

A relatively small group of women, ranging in age from about twenty-five to forty, became my friends. We used the term *"Ore"* (literally, "friend") as one would use a personal name. Each of them referred to me, and addressed me, by that name, and I used the same name for each of them. When I wanted to distinguish among them, I spoke of *Ore* from such-and-such a compound. This was the group of women with whom I often exchanged visits and presents, for whom I did special favors (such as driving them to distant towns or lending them money), with whom I gossiped, to whom I went for advice, and who gave me all kinds of assistance and information relating to my research.

About a dozen old women and a few old men in Awe "adopted" me as their daughter. They called me *"Aduke"* or *"Anke"* (both pet names) or addressed me as *"omo mi"* ("my child"). It was generally known in the town that I was particularly close to three of the women and one of the men. They, and one of the women whom I called *"Ore,"* were the ones to whom I reported most of my movements, and whenever I was away from the town, it was from them that people made inquiries about my whereabouts.

These four old people and my special *ore* were the only ones in town who regularly called me aside to give me advice on personal matters. One might say: "You know, Yorubas are difficult. I don't think you should do too much for So-and-So because other people might be jealous." Or: "You know that little boy who has been visiting you every day—I think his parents might be planning to ask you to take him on as a ward. If you are not prepared to do so, you can just thank him for coming, tell him that you have nothing for him to do, give him sixpence, and send him home."

If I wanted straightforward information on anything going on in the town, I went to one of my four "parents" or to my special friend. Whenever anything happened about which they thought I had not heard, they would send someone to inform me. If someone died, if a ceremony was being planned, if a dispute or a fight broke out, and the like, these people were usually the first to notify me.

My private social life was quite distinct from my life in Awe. There was almost no social event in the town that I did not attend, but most of the social activities in which I participated took place outside Awe. I was very friendly with a number of people in Oyo, and in the evenings I often went to play cards or drink beer at one of the clubs there. On a Friday or Saturday night I might go to a nightclub in Ibadan.

No doubt one reason why I did not become a part of the social group formed by some of the teachers at the high school was that to a great extent my circle of personal friends was formed before I left Ibadan. My closest friend in Oyo, for example, was an old classmate of a friend of mine who lived in Ibadan, and it was through this classmate that I met most of the people I knew in Oyo.

My regular escort during the time I was in Nigeria was well-known to the people of Awe: he accompanied me to various convivial and ceremonial events in the town, and he sometimes joined me on visits to my friends. Unmarried women in Awe did not "date" various men, as American women do. Young men and women of marriageable age had ample opportunity to meet and get acquainted through friends and relatives, at ceremonies, in the churches, in the evening market, and so on. When a young woman started "moving with" a particular man, it was understood that he would become her husband. A female anthropologist of marriageable age who was usually seen in the company of the same man was regarded as behaving in a normal and appropriate fashion; one who "dated" various men would have been suspected of being loose or licentious.

Americans who visited me in Awe often remarked that I had "become a Yoruba." The people of Awe would not have made that statement. I often dressed like a Yoruba; when my hair grew long enough, I sometimes had it plaited like a Yoruba; I took on some of the Yoruba mannerisms. I knew how to greet people in Yoruba, and, to an American listener, my simple Yoruba sentences made it appear that I could speak the language. To the people of Awe I was a foreigner, albeit one for whom they had an affinity, who had acquired some of the manifestations of what is entailed in "being a Yoruba." But to the people of Awe there was no mistaking the difference.

Field Work in Awe

In Awe I was immediately struck by the separateness of the world of women and the world of men.

At all major ceremonies in the town, women "did their part"; men theirs. At the feasting that accompanied all celebrations—naming ceremonies, weddings, funerals, and the like—the men ate in one place, the women in another. In the churches, no less than in the mosques, women were grouped apart from men. Women usually sat on the lefthand side of the churches, men on the right. The center section was usually occupied by young people, but here too men normally sat in groups, apart from the women. In the compounds men relaxed in their parlors; women sat around on the verandas. Husbands and wives managed their business affairs separately, kept separate purses, and contributed separately, though in cooperation, to the maintenance of the household (see Marshall, 1964).

Everyone was aware that my main purpose in coming to Awe was to study the activities of women, and it was taken for granted that, like other women, I would have relatively little to do with the world of men. It was known that I wanted to interview men about their trade and farm activities, but it always seemed to come as a surprise that I wanted to find out some things about men that could not be directly related to Awe history or indirectly to the world of women. This was particularly evident when I made inquiries into the details of men's political activities in the town and when I tried to find out about men's associations and their leisure-time activities.

I was never expected to enter into, and never did see, certain aspects of the life of men in the town. I never witnessed any ceremonies that were barred to women. Whenever I visited compounds, I sat with the women while the men gathered in the parlors or in front of the compounds. At such times, if there was something I wanted to know from the men, I would go to them or they would be called to speak to me, and afterward they went back to their own business. I never entered any of the places where men sat around to drink beer or palm wine and to chat.

Whenever I attended a ceremony, I could observe and record what women were doing, but I often had to rely on the men's report of what they did. There were many times when I wished I had a husband or a male co-worker in the field, to study the life of men while I studied the women. On some occasions, I asked a friend of mine from Ibadan to come to Awe in order to take notes on the male side of something going on in the town. At other times I received similar assistance from the son of one of my "mothers" in the town.

I once kept detailed records of the forty-day funeral ceremonies for an old woman who had died in the town. These records included accounts of the expenditures of the woman's daughters and of several of her female relatives who were "doing their part" of the obsequies. I recorded the amount of food distributed, the persons to whom it was distributed, the amount of money paid to drummers who performed for various festivities, the amount of the contributions received by the celebrants, and so on. Although I thought I knew all that was going on in connection with the funeral, it was not until late in the period of mourning that I learned of several celebrations that had been held by male relatives of the deceased. For example, one of the grandsons had celebrated the funeral by providing food and drinks for his age mates. Although this young man knew that I was keeping a record of the funeral expenses, he thought I was only concerned with what his mother and the other women were doing. It had not occurred to him to ask me to witness, or to give me information about, his own part in the funeral rites.

I attended almost all of the weddings held while I lived in Awe, and I kept a detailed record of that of a daughter of the old man who was my special "father" in the town. I observed the preparations (of food, dress, and the like) made by the daughters and wives of the bride's and the groom's compounds, and I noted their roles in the wedding ceremony itself. I had to rely on my "father," however, to supply me with the details of the activities of the men at the various states of the engagement and marriage.

Being a woman, I was naturally able to see aspects of the marriage ceremony that men do not witness. I followed the bride through every step of the marriage ceremony, including her brief seclusion in the room where she changed her dress just before entering her husband's house. There women from her father's house advised her to take care of her husband, to avoid disputes with, and to show respect toward, him and the other members of his compound, and so forth. It was a time of weeping: the tears were an expression of the genuine sadness with which the women parted and an indication of the joy they felt as the bride prepared to assume her role as a fully adult woman.

It was much easier for me to learn about men's activities from elderly men, who regarded me more or less as a daughter to whom they could explain things, than it was for me to get information from men who were about my own age. I could and did interview some of them concerning their trade and other occupations, but I never felt free to talk to them about "men in general" or to query them too closely about their personal lives. They always seemed a bit uneasy in the presence of the woman whose status put her "out of their class" but whose age made her their peer. It was only from a few young men that I collected detailed information on their domestic affairs, whereas I collected such information from almost all the women I interviewed. The result was that most of my information about men came from old men and from women.

Being in a field work situation as I write this essay, I am aware that my relative insulation from the world of Yoruba men in Awe resulted partly from the way I presented my research interests to the town. In Kumasi as in Awe, the world of Yoruba women is in many ways distinct from the world of men. However, I made it clear from the time I arrived here that I came to study the Yoruba community and to learn as much as possible about the history of Yorubas in Ghana. In Kumasi I have been moving relatively freely in the world of men: I attend their meetings, interview them on various subjects, and receive their fullest cooperation in the research. In many cases I have had to make a point of telling them that I also want to be introduced to, and to interview, the women. Being keenly aware of the contrast between my field experience in Awe and that in Kumasi, I have tried to pinpoint the factors, other than my presentation of the research problem, that contributed to the difference between the two situations. The most important seems to be the fact that here all my assistants are men.

I usually interviewed Awe women in their shops and other places of work and in their compounds. Rarely did I conduct interviews in my own house: I regarded people's visits to my house primarily as social occasions, rather than as "research situations." I always tried to be at the places where women worked when I interviewed them about their occupations, and I seldom queried them about domestic matters when they were at these places of business. Women at work, particularly traders, were always impatient with questions that distracted them from the business at hand. It was in their homes that they were prepared to discuss marital histories, genealogical trees, relations with their husbands and relatives, child-rearing practices, and so on.

The fact that I was unmarried did not seem to affect my ability to elicit any type of information from the townswomen. Details of practices surrounding conception, contraception, birth, and the like, were freely discussed with me. I never witnessed a birth in Awe, but that was because I was not around at an opportune time.

On the days when I did not attend markets outside the town, I usually spent the mornings interviewing traders and other people in the town or collecting information at the sites where women made pottery, palm oil (*epo pupa*), palm-kernel oil (*adin*), or soap. At these work sites I sometimes joined the women in some of their tasks. Although women were always amused at my ineptness at handling the long heavy stick that served as a pestle, I was particularly fond of "helping" them with their pounding operations. On one occasion, after watching me struggle with a pestle for about ten minutes, one of the women said: "*Ore*, please sit down. You are pounding the *ekuro* [palm kernels] as if you were handling a pencil."

In general I was much more of an observer of, rather than a participant in, the life of women in Awe. My participation in activities in the town was usually confined to ceremonial occasions. I never joined the women in the work of preparing food for a ceremony, but I made financial contributions toward the expenses, and sometimes I bought and wore the *aso* ebi ("family dress") chosen for the occasion. I was a particularly enthusiastic participant in the dancing at such celebrations. After I had attended a few ceremonies in Awe, the town drummers "composed" a special set of rhythms that was my summons to dance. The townspeople expressed surprise that I was so quick to learn many of the Yoruba body movements, and they were always amused by the Afro-American variations I introduced into my imitation of their dances.

What surprised me most about field work in Awe was the scarcity of topics that people seemed unwilling to talk to me about or, excepting events barred to women, to have me witness. There were a number of aspects of people's personal lives about which I did not choose to ask, and there were some things, such as religious cults, that were so peripheral to my research problem that I did not try to study them. In general, however, by the end of my stay in Awe I felt that I knew as much about what I had come to study as could possibly be known after only a year of research.

In the course of field work one always learns that some questions are likely to be answered honestly, whereas some are not. Early in my stay in Awe I gave up asking straightforward questions about the number of children people had, about how long a woman had been pregnant, and about the amount of a man's contribution to the routine expenses of his household. Answers to these and a few other questions had to be obtained through interrogational subterfuge.

As a matter of course some types of information are kept from any stranger in a Yoruba community. Once I was thoroughly frightened as a result of my ignorance of something that was known to everyone else in the town. One day one of the women with whom I often chatted, and whom I had recently interviewed, confronted me on the street, eyes blazing, and started shouting threats and abuses at me. She accused me of having killed her children, and she vowed to take revenge. My first reaction was to ask what had happened to her children, but before I could finish the question, she lunged at me and had to be restrained by people in the crowd that had quickly gathered. I was shaking with fear. Within minutes I was being sent home in the company of some of my friends. After that day no one ever mentioned the woman or the incident. When I inquired about what had happened to her, I was told that she had been sent to the farm. The emotionally or mentally disturbed were not exposed to outsiders; in many cases they were hidden from everyone outside the family.

The world of the market

By 6 A.M. my assistant and I would be preparing for our trip to the market. About this time an old woman who sold firewood usually passed my house, her load on her head, en route to Oyo. She always called out in a humorous, almost mocking, tone: *"Oyinbo dudu, Oyinbo dudu, e k'aro o!"* ("Black European, Black European, good morning, o!") I would exchange greetings with her from my bedroom window or from the front porch. The day began.

After breakfast we drove to the center of town, where Awe's morning market at Bode was in full swing. Here was a consumer's market: pepper, okra, onions, and tomatoes were displayed in small piles; beans, *gari* (cassava meal), and maize were sold by the panful; smoked and dried fish occupied one section of the unshedded marketplace, canned and packaged provisions (groceries) occupied another. The sellers of cooked foods (most of which were made from beans or maize) carried on a brisk business with men, women, and children who were buying their breakfasts before going to the farms, to other markets, or to school. The nonconsumer items sold in the market were leaves, which traders used for wrapping various foods, and firewood, which was bought mainly by women who manufactured soap and oils in various parts of the town.

The town had awakened long before we arrived, and if we lingered at Bode until 8:00 or 8:30 A.M., we would see the beginning of the dispersal of the morning market in Awe. On most days, however, we did not stop long at Bode but proceeded to one of the rural markets in which most Awe women traded.

The rural markets we attended were held at intervals of four days or eight days, and most of them were within twenty miles of the town. Occasionally we might drive to a more distant market that had been described to us by Awe women or that was frequented by "informants" from other towns, whom we had met in rural markets near Awe itself.

During the dry season getting to the markets was not a problem. During the rains, however, it might take as long as forty-five minutes to make our way over gutted laterite roads to a market no more than twelve miles from the town. Our aim was always to reach the market by 7:00 or 7:30 A.M. If we slept late, if the roads were particularly bad, or if we stopped to give someone a lift to a nearby place, we might not arrive until 8:00 or 8:30.

Town met countryside in the rural markets. Some traders from the towns came to buy foodstuffs for resale in the urban markets; others came to sell to the rural population. Men and women from the farms brought yams, maize, *gari, lafun* (dried pieces of cassava), *elubo* (dried yam slices), pepper, plantain, bananas, oranges, green vegetables, and so on, for sale to the buyers who came by lorry and by foot from the towns. The sellers from the towns brought canned and packaged provisions, hardware, ready-made clothing, imported and locally manufactured cloth, patent medicines, cosmetics, and so forth. Alongside the traders in the market were barbers, tailors, hairdressers, tattooers, and men who repaired bicycles and other machines.

From about 7 to 10 A.M. the market was a mass in motion, the pace being set by the women from towns such as Awe, Oyo, and Ibadan who came to buy foodstuffs from the farmers and their wives. These foodstuff buyers were never stationary: they were busy locating their "customers" (those from whom they bought goods), concluding purchases, and finding new sources of supply.

A farmer spotted along the road with a basket on his head would be met by three, four, five such women, each imploring him to sell to her. Unperturbed, the farmer would move into the market, unload his goods, and state his price. Then began the bargaining, the pleading, the calling of others to witness that a fair price had been offered. Through scores of similar encounters the town-based buyers collected whatever they could afford to buy that day.

There was no possibility of interviewing foodstuff buyers and sellers during the peak hours of the morning. If my assistant and I were in a market that we regularly attended, we would make our routine tour: counting sellers; noting items offered for sale; comparing prices with those collected at other times; looking for our "key informants" (those women whose activities we regularly recorded) and noting their purchases for the day; interviewing market officials; noting the number of trucks in attendance, their capacities, the towns from which they had come, the number of trips they had made; stopping to take notes on the bargaining for this or the gossip about that.

By approximately 10:30 A.M. my assistant and I could begin to approach traders for the individual interviews. Sometimes the interviews could begin earlier—as, for example, when we were interviewing relatively stationary traders such as those dealing in dried fish, hardware, or provisions, who could talk to us in between waiting on their customers.

We interviewed both people from Awe and traders from other towns and villages. The Awe traders whom we interviewed in these rural markets were usually those who sold there. Our notes on the Awe women who came to buy in the rural markets were usually restricted to records of the quantity, variety, and cost of the foodstuffs they purchased. When we returned to Awe, we would interview them regarding the over-all patterns of their trade (see Marshall, 1963). Though most of the foodstuffs buyers from Awe were interviewed only once, there were about ten women (our "key informants") whose activities we followed throughout the year I stayed in Awe.

At least once a week we questioned these women about their current trading activities.

Traders from towns other than Awe were interviewed in order to provide the broadest possible picture of the commercial traffic between rural and urban areas. Interviews with these traders provided supplementary and comparative data on the variations in the scale of traders' activities, the levels at which they entered the distributive network, the geographical range of their activities, the sources of supply and destination of their goods, and the array of personnel and facilities utilized in financial and operational aspects of their trade.

I did not interview non-Awe traders at random. My aim was to interview at least two or three traders for each major commodity. If I found that the patterns of trade were highly variable among people dealing in the same goods, I sought out individuals whose activities were representative of the various trade patterns.

It was sometimes very difficult to get non-Awe traders to permit me to interview them. This was especially the case in markets where there were no well-known Awe women or men to make the necessary introductions. People were suspicious of the woman with the notebook, the more so because she did not look like the American student she claimed to be. When I tried to interview people whom I had not met before, I often found that my first task was to convince them that I was not a Yoruba collecting information for the government.

Within the first month of my move to Awe, I discovered that Western-style dresses were very inconvenient for the type of positions I had to assume when conducting interviews in the town and in the markets: I often had to sit on stools about a foot high. Given that my field work predated the era of the miniskirt, it is understandable that both I and my respondents were embarrassed when, thus seated, my legs were more exposed than covered. I opted for the long wrap-around skirts worn by most young women in Nigeria. The result was that although I did not look like a market woman—most of them wore the more traditional type of Yoruba attire—I did look suspiciously like most young Yoruba women seen in the towns.

The fact that I was accompanied by an interpreter was not sufficient to allay suspicions. If people heard me utter a few Yoruba greetings or ask the price of something in the market (the only instances when my Yoruba could possibly be mistaken for that of a native speaker of the language), they became convinced that the use of an interpreter was merely a ploy to throw them off guard. At one market some women sent a group of children to follow me around to see whether or not I understood Yoruba. The children made a number of rude remarks about me, and I had to pretend that I did not understand a word they said.

I was so often "accused" of being a Yoruba that when I went to a market in which I was not certain I would find a friend to identify me, I made a point of speaking only American-sounding English (for the benefit of the English speakers there) and of dressing "like an American." On my first trip to such a market, I even abandoned my sandals in favor of moderately high heels and put on make-up, including lipstick. After the market elders got to know me, and after the "regulars" among the traders had seen me in the market a few times, I would then appear in the more convenient and comfortable long wrap-around skirt and blouse (an outfit referred to as an "up and down").

Even after I became known in a market, I seldom found non-Awe traders who were willing to answer the full range of questions I asked, but at least I could not blame their reluctance on the fact that they thought I was a Nigerian.

Once I had made sure that there were some people whom I could call, when necessary, to introduce me to anyone I wanted to interview, I often found it quite convenient to "pass for a Yoruba" in the market. If I hid my notebook, I was wholly inconspicuous in a crowd. I could listen in on conversations, disputes, and the like, without people's being conscious of a strange presence in their midst. I often went around bargaining for those items on whose price fluctuations we kept check. I would then compare the prices quoted me with those given me by other retail buyers. In this way I got an idea of the mark-up that almost inevitably resulted when a seller confronted an *akowe* (literally, "clerk"; colloquially, any educated person) rather than a trader or a woman from the farms.

Although I concentrated on the activities of women traders, I also interviewed men, and I was constantly amazed at the differences in the responses of men and women toward me and my questions. To interview a strange woman was a most difficult task, and the closer she was to my own age, the more reluctant she was to talk. Old women were more expansive, more willing to enlighten me concerning the ways of the market, but even they were often not as cooperative as the male traders. I was queried less frequently by men than by women concerning the purposes to which I would put the information I collected. Men were less reticent about disclosing the details of their financial operations and about discussing their domestic affairs. Many times I had to rely on male traders in the market to convince their female counterparts that they should cooperate with me. Whereas in Awe, where I was known, I had better rapport with the women than with the men, in the markets where I was not known, the situation was completely reversed.

I think this situation reflects the fact that, generally speaking, men "take the lead" in dealing with the public, including dealing with strangers. Anyone who has lived in a Yoruba town knows that when it comes to matters affecting their interests, women will not take a back seat to, or allow themselves to be bullied by, their men. All the same, it is normally the men who are called upon to act as spokesmen for their families, their compounds, and their communities. It was my impression that women in the markets often felt that if there was any information to be given concerning trade activities, it was the men who should give it.

Conclusion

Who can ever say all there is to be said about a first "venture into the field"? Here I have tried to convey something of the atmosphere within which my field work was conducted; to provide a glimpse of those dimensions of the field situation that would not appear in my technical descriptions and analyses of the results of fifteen months of research in Western Nigeria. Each of the experiences I have related reminded me of scores of others left untold. Some of these occurred in Awe; others in Oyo, Ibadan, and the other cities, towns, and villages in which some of my data were collected. Many of these experiences were similar to those recounted by various anthropologists, male and female alike.

There were tragic and comic events to which I could not remain emotionally indifferent. A well-known and highly regarded Awe chief died unexpectedly, and I mourned with the rest of the town. An old man told me about a woman who was so ugly that after the death of her husband not one of the men in his compound was prepared to inherit the widow; the description of the woman was so funny that I laughed, with tears streaming down my face, for almost half an hour.

People I met by chance became great friends or went out of their way to assist me with my research. At the end of a meeting I attended shortly after my arrival in Ibadan in 1961, a stately old woman came up to tell me that an uncle of hers, one Oluigbo, had been sold into slavery and to ask if I had ever heard of a family in America bearing that name. This innocent and touching inquiry led to my friendship with the woman, now deceased, who was the *Otun Iyalode* (second-ranking female chief) of Ibadan. Her subsequent assistance with my research in Ibadan was truly invaluable. More important, however, was the fact that she became my first and most beloved "mother" in Nigeria. Her kindness and affection made me realize that I would actually cherish some of the relationships I would form in the course of my excursion into the world of Yoruba women.

There were incidents and conversations that, like meteors, cast unexpected light on a particular research problem or suddenly revealed new directions the research should take. On one of my strolls around Awe I stopped at *Ile Eleyiele* (the "House of the Keepers of Birds") to admire a magnificent bird cage that one of the men had made. In the course of our conversation about birds and bird cages, the man remarked that Awe's *Balẹ* was an *"omo Ile Eleiyele"* (a descendant of their house). When I expressed surprise that the *Balẹ* was not a member of the lineage associated with the *Balẹ's* compound, I was told that the chief had established a right of claim to the title through his mother, who was a daughter of the *Balẹ's* house. It was this conversation that led me to re-examine some of the generally accepted statements about compound and lineage membership and about the role of women in the inheritance of lineage properties in the patrilineal Yoruba areas (see Marshall, 1964, Chapter II).

The practical difficulties that came up in the process of collecting and recording data were also similar to those reported by many anthropologists. One example will give an indication of the nature of these problems. Acting on the advice of some social scientists in Ibadan, I did not use a mimeographed questionnaire in the collection of data on trade and markets. The questions were written in a small notebook, and the responses were recorded on a pad the size of that used by stenographers. I never found this a satisfactory procedure. It was not always possible to ask questions in the order they appeared in my notebook, and without a questionnaire, I could not quickly discern gaps in the information given by a particular respondent. Often it was only after I had typed and reorganized an interview that I realized that some of the important questions had been left unanswered. I could easily collect supplementary information from residents of Awe, but it was often difficult to hold second interviews with people I met in markets outside the town. As a consequence, I found that the amount of quantifiable data on market trade was disappointingly small.

By omitting a full-scale discussion of the technical problems that confronted me in the course of my research, I have neglected some of the most trying aspects of my field experience. However, it is precisely because these problems are those likely to be encountered by any social scientist in the field that I have left them out of this essay. I have tried to present a measure of the experiences and problems that derived primarily from the fact of my being a black female anthropologist working in Africa.

My experiences in this regard were not the stereotyped ones that usually find their way into discussions of the black American's encounter with Africa. No doubt my training as an anthropologist partly accounted for the enthusiasm with which I tried to understand, to accept, and to adjust to life in Yoruba society. There is also no question that my response to the life around me was a factor in determining the nature of my reception by the people I met and those with whom I lived. Nevertheless, throughout my stay in Nigeria I was made to feel that the relative ease with which I moved among the Yoruba was due in large part to their interest in, and their eagerness to welcome and to help, a "relation from across the seas."

References

BASCOM, W. R. 1942. "The Principle of Seniority in the Social Structure of the Yoruba," *American Anthropologist,* 44(1), 37–46.
————.1952. "The Esusu: A Credit Institution of the Yoruba," *Journal of the Royal Anthropological Institute,* 82, 63–69.
HODDER, B. W. 1962. "The Yoruba Rural Market." In P. Bohannon and G. Dalton, eds., *Markets in Africa.* Evanston, Ill.: Northwestern University Press, pp. 103–117.
KATZIN, MARGARET. 1959. "The Jamaican Country Higgler," *Social and Economic Studies,* 8 (4) 421–440.
MARSHALL, GLORIA A. 1959. "Benefit Societies in the British West Indies: The Formative Years: 1793 to 1846." New York: Columbia University, unpublished master's thesis.
————. 1963. "The Marketing of Farm Produce: Some Patterns of Trade Among Women of Western Nigeria," *Proceedings of the 1962 NISER Conference* (Ibadan).
————. 1964. "Woman, Trade and the Yoruba Family." New York: Columbia University, unpublished Ph.D. dissertation.
MINTZ, S. W. 1955. "The Jamaican Internal Marketing Pattern," *Social and Economic Studies,* 4 (1), 95–103.

Field Work in a Greek Village

ERNESTINE FRIEDL is a former president of the American Anthropological Association (1974) and has worked among the Pomo and Chippewa Indians. For the past ten years she has devoted most of her attention to studies in Greece, with the results published in her book VASILIKA, A VILLAGE IN MODERN GREECE. In 1975 she published WOMEN AND MEN: AN ANTHROPOLOGIST'S VIEW. She is the James B. Duke Professor of Anthropology at Duke University in Durham, North Carolina.

Since field-work roles, regardless of whether the anthropologist is a man or a woman, are inextricably tied to the nature of the problem the investigator sets himself and the methods of data collection he chooses to utilize, it seems best in this essay to begin with a statement of my aims and methods for the field work in a small Greek village.

I had four main objectives. First, I was interested in doing a study of a rural community in what appeared to be a peasant situation. I assumed that, because of its peasant quality, the community would have some significant connections with the nation and that the discovery and analysis of the relationships would be part of the investigation. Second, I was attracted to the analysis of change in underdeveloped countries. It therefore seemed best to choose a village that was situated near some main arteries of communication and whose inhabitants engaged in some commercial agriculture. Third, there was so little information published on Greek rural communities in 1955 that the basic work of learning the categories of the culture and social structure as seen by the participants in the society still needed to be done. This circumstance suited my intellectual conviction that good anthropology can result from following where the informants lead and my personal preference for such an approach. Finally, I wanted to add to my previous experience on American Indian reservations by doing field work in a setting where it was essential to learn the local language and where the culture and social structure of the society were not dominated by problems of acculturation in an American setting.

Greece was chosen as the locale for achieving these aims both because so little was known about its villages and because my husband is a classicist. We wanted a year together; his knowledge of ancient Greek language and culture would be useful for giving a certain kind of historical depth and contrast, and his secondary interests in foreign-language teaching methods would be helpful in our learning of modern Greek. From his point of view, a year in Greece would provide him with a living supplement to his knowledge and understanding of ancient literature and society. We agreed at the outset that my husband would help with the field work whenever and in whatever ways seemed appropriate.

Since the formation of a model of the culture and social structure of rural Greek communities was the aim of our research, and since even the main outlines of that model were not clear, it seemed best to choose a village small enough to minimize all sampling problems. Since we made up the equivalent of one and a half field workers, we looked for a community of no more than 300 people (a figure originally suggested to me by Margaret Mead). Vasilika actually had a population of 216; we got to know every inhabitant by name and visited all of the fifty-odd households at least once. We were also fortunate enough to be accepted as tenants in the upper story of a house whose lower floor was occupied by the family of the owners. This living arrangement made it possible for us to function as participants in at least some diffuse primary group roles, such as kin and neighbor. Given my research goals and what turned out to be the nature of the cultural and social structure of the village, the chance to assume kin roles in relation to the family in whose house we lived was extraordinarily fruitful. Had we not had the simulated rank—which is what participant observation always involves—of family member, the cognitive and emotional meaning of human relationships would have been harder to observe and harder to analyze and interpret.

The kind of participant-observation field work that predominated during our stay in the village contrasts most strongly with survey-interview techniques, in which topics of discussion are focused and in which participation by the field worker in his informant's society is minimal. It is different also from the methods of field workers who, although they operate in natural settings as participant observers or observer participants (Pearsall, 1965, p. 38), do so in bureaucratic settings, so that their simulated ranks are quite specific and involve only secondary relationships. Finally, the kind of anthropological field work that is possible in societies and cultures that have been well studied was not practicable until about the last third of our field stay. Once we knew something of the main outlines of the culture, I began a series of depth interviews and focused interviews with especially selected informants in order to test some hypotheses and to complete information on particular subjects. My assumption is that in societies where much of the culture has been studied, more narrowly focused problem-solving studies are possible and need not involve the degree of participant observation necessary for a basic community study.

That it is at all possible to do the kind of basic field work we undertook in Vasilika, and that anthropologists have been doing all over the world, constitutes a significant demonstration of the accuracy of generalizations about the nature of man, culture, and society that we enunciate in our writings and in our classrooms (see Casagrande, 1966, p. 281). Although such a statement appears obvious, I do not think it is unimportant. The characteristics of Homo sapiens that include a capacity to learn new languages, the universality of some system of cognitive classifications, and the existence of universally ascribed roles are necessary prerequisites for field work in cultures alien to an investigator. They make communication, however imperfect, a possibility, and they provide a basis for mutual empathy. Our equally common generalization that cultural forms vary from one society to another, and that culturally patterned relationships to other human beings and to local objects and physical surroundings involve both conscious and unconscious psychological structures, is clearly demonstrated by the reciprocal anxiety generated between investigator and investigated during the first months of life in an alien community. The function of predictability we assign to the existence of cultural forms and the function of security we assign to familiar situations are tested in the negative by these anxieties. The uncertainty about the cultural meaning of any of one's own words, gestures, movements, or other actions on the one hand, and the impact of unfamiliar and sometimes shocking sights, sounds, foods, and the like on the other (see Williams, 1967) create some emotional tensions in all field workers, although the degree and intensity may vary with the personalities of the anthropologists. Culture lodges in the viscera as well as in the minds and muscles of its participants; minds, muscles, and viscera all react to strangeness.

The experience of field work affirms, therefore, within the persons of the anthropologist and his informants the polar and historically cyclical concerns of the profession: human universals and human varieties.

From this point of view a volume on "Men in the Field" is a necessary companion to one on "Women in the Field," because the universal ascription of different roles for the sexes and the varieties of expectations as to how these roles are to be played influence the type of field work possible for men as well as for women. A systematic examination of the contrasts and similarities could add to our information on the nature of sex roles in human societies, both those to which the investigators and those to which the investigated belong.

To return to the Greek village, I shall give a basically chronological account of our introduction to Greece and to the village and its inhabitants. As the recipient of a Fulbright research grant, I had an official status in Greece in that I was formally associated with the University of Athens and had entrée to Greek government services through the United States Educational Foundation. My husband, who was then a professor of classics at

Hunter College, had no formal connections, though he did, indeed, receive from both Greeks and Americans the courtesies normally accorded a university professor.

At the outset, then, from the standpoint of special problems of women in the field, I was involved in a formally and publicly wife-dominated enterprise in a society that was husband-centered to a degree even greater than is customary in Western Europe and America. Half deliberately and half as a matter of natural development we pragmatically compensated for this anomaly. My husband became the spokesman for the two of us in Athens and in the village. He would give the first explanation and description of our research aims and methods. This occurred partially because he is more articulate than I am in any language, but also because he is a better language student and his modern Greek usage progressed considerably faster than mine.

My grant had been awarded in my maiden name, but the Greek personnel at the Fulbright office found it excessively awkward to introduce Professor Levy's wife as Dr. Friedl; they dubbed me Mrs. Friedl-Levy, a formal designation I still use whenever we are in Greece. A hyphenated name (perhaps after the French fashion) is often adopted in Athens by married women who also have professional careers.

Our first problem, of course, was to choose a village for study. From the standpoint of our research interests, the range of choice was very wide; there was no need to search for a "typical" village, and if there had been, Greece would not have been the proper place to do so. The kind of information necessary to establish systematic criteria for typicality was lacking. Nevertheless, a specific spot had to be found, and we began by asking friends at the American School of Classical Studies for suggestions. The archeological work of the school requires travel around Greece, and our acquaintances knew local conditions at first hand. Professor Caskey, who was then director of the school, suggested the Boeotian plain as an area that fulfilled the criteria we had established. We next visited the librarian at the Gennadeion. (The collections there are devoted to Byzantine and early Modern Greek studies and are based on the donations of John Gennadius, once Greek ambassador to Britain. He gave these to the American School of Classical Studies; they are housed in a building provided by the Carnegie Foundation.) Professor Peter Topping, a historian, was the librarian; his wife is a classicist; both are of Greek descent. They not only concurred on Boeotia as one hypothetically reasonable alternative for our study, but they were also able to contribute a practical advantage: Mrs. Topping's cousin was then the Nomarch (provincial governor) of Boeotia, and she kindly offered to provide us with an introduction to him. In the meantime I had consulted the Geographical Handbook on Greece compiled between 1939 and 1945 by British Naval Intelligence for official use. It had just been declassified, and a copy was available in the Gennadeion. A three-volume work of much wider scope than its title implies, it is an excellent source for basic information on Greek government, political administration, economics, and history. Nothing I read indicated that any other region of Greece was significantly more suitable for our purposes than Boeotia, and the possibility of a personal and unofficial introduction to the government officer whose advice and sponsorship could be helpful weighed heavily in favor of starting our search for a village in that province.

After about two weeks of these discussions and visits with professors at the university and others who had done extensive work in Greek folklore, we felt ready to set off for Boeotia in the new Ford we had brought with us from the United States.

Although what I have described up to this point is a brief summary of what I hope was a basically rational procedure—and the events did, in fact, take place—the history is incomplete without some indication of the emotional quality of the experience. First there were the intellectual uncertainties. Might it be better to try to search through whatever little statistical and other information was available, in order to try for typicality? Was the decision not to take the time to do this the right one? Should we have gone to government ministries immediately for information and advice, instead of waiting until we ourselves had made a preliminary survey? We knew that a personal introduction to the Nomarch would be helpful in meeting him, but what was the villagers' attitude to such an official? Would his sponsorship be an asset or a liability? Was it wrong to use the fortuitous circumstance of a kinship connection as a pivot on which to rest the choice of a village? And how would we discover alternatives to this pivot without spending too much time at it? Was our Greek adequate for making arrangements and for living in the village? Was our decision to work without interpreters the right one? We knew that Greeks who had a sufficient knowledge of English would probably be urban, and we did not know whether they would have the kind of a respect for villagers that we thought both morally and scientifically necessary. We decided not to take the chance, but we were also aware of our own reluctance to add to the strains that the constant association with and adjustment to the villagers would put on our relationships to each other: a third person in our household would have been a serious additional complication. Were we, then, pampering ourselves at the expense of the success of the field trip? Was my judgment about the need for respect for the villagers a real issue, or was it just an excuse for not complicating our personal lives?

And there was always the pressure of time! We arrived in Athens at the end of September; the Fulbright grant expired at the end of June; it was already the middle of October, and we hadn't yet talked to a single Greek farmer.

These intellectual uncertainties connected with the substance of our research were compounded by anxiety about money. Our dollar obligations at home left us with no funds for the year in Greece except the drachmas provided by the Fulbright grant. We had already had to borrow money to buy and transport the car; we were trying to live cheaply in Athens by staying at an inexpensive hotel, where the room turned out to be cheerless and dispiriting. Moreover, the more time we spent in Athens or on the road living in hotels and eating in restaurants, the faster our funds would run out. Here, too, the question was the extent to which personal considerations were intruding on scientific ones. Was the decision not to try to ferret out information in Athens too strongly influenced by my fear of increased debt?

Finally, there were the uncertainties engendered by the encounter with a different culture. During those first weeks in Athens these manifested themselves largely in touristlike problems and reactions. Questions arose about appropriate prices for hotel rooms, taxis, and tips; the pleasures and the disappointments in sampling Ouzo, squid, octopus, sheep's-head soup, goat cheeses, and vegetable and meat stews cooked with liberal additions of olive oil and served lukewarm; living entirely without ordinary American-style coffee, to which I am practically addicted; fumbling until we learned how to answer direct questions from waiters and taxi drivers about exactly why we had no children of our own and what our income was.

In addition to these minor and expectable discomforts in another culture, we were frequently tired from the strain of including some formal study of modern Greek in each day's schedule and from the constant effort to talk Greek and to try to comprehend as we encouraged those whom we encountered to speak Greek to us. We also tried to acclimate ourselves to Greek rhythms of daily life. In the cities this means a substantial midday meal around two in the afternoon and a second substantial meal after nine in the evening. A nap, or at least a rest, after the midday meal is virtually obligatory because shops and offices are closed for several hours after two and no business can be conducted. I found this daily rhythm particularly frustrating and debilitating. The heavy midday meal, usually accompanied by beer or wine, made me sleepy, so that if I tried to work, I could do little that was constructive; but if I went to sleep, I'd wake up with a headache that lasted the rest of the day.

The tension we were living under engendered by real self-doubt with respect to our ability to complete the study, on the one hand, and a series of accumulating minor discomforts and inconveniences, on the other, made the relief from these pressures all the more vivid and exciting. Our association in Athens with the other Fulbright teachers and scholars whom we had first met on the ship coming over, and whom we saw frequently in the first weeks, was one form of true recreation. Many of the friendships established then as we explored our common miseries, were deep and are still enduring.

On our third night in Athens we went to a performance of Sophocles' *Oedipus the King*, done by the Greek National Theater at the Odeum of Herodes Atticus. We sat in a tier of seats near the top; if we turned around, we could see above us the edge of the Parthenon shining in the moonlight; down below, the actors were presenting, in modern Greek, to an audience that could understand and respond, a magnificent tragedy not far from the spot where Sophocles actually wrote it. The situation was dramatic and romantic, particularly for a classical scholar who had never before set foot in any part of Europe; the vividness with which it is remembered was undoubtedly a result of our emotional state. Our first trip to the Acropolis and to the Temple of Poseidon at Sunion partook of this special quality of sharpness, boldness, and clarity.

The total situation contributed the kind of heightened perception to all that was going on, and an ability to remember a great deal, that is certainly an advantage for field work. We both felt as sensitive as peeled eggs, and I believe that this made our observations more acute than they might otherwise have been.

I kept a journal from the first day we arrived in Athens, listing the day's events, books read, people seen, letters written and received, and similar information. In addition I wrote notes on my observations of life in Athens. My assumption was that, even though I expected to work in a rural village, the culture of the population of Greece was homogeneous enough to make what I learned in Athens of some value in understanding the villagers. I did, in fact, make the first notes on diglossia, and on what I later called lagging emulation with respect to speech forms, from conversations with elevator boys, waiters, and maids in the city. It was when my husband remarked to the elevator man that he had forgotten something in his room—using the demotic word for "I have forgotten," *ksékhasa*—and the elevator operator chided him by saying that as a professor he should have used *lizmónisa*, the Katharevousa or formal version, that we had the first intimation of how the sociolinguistic phenomenon of diglossia actually functioned in Greece. The first appearance of a pattern of discrepancy between formal statements and actual events came when we were packing to move out of a hotel because the price listed on the back of the room door was much too high. When we were about to check out, the concierge asked bluntly and directly why we were leaving. We said because the price was too high and because we wanted to be in a more convenient neighborhood. Thereupon the concierge and the bellboys had a heated discussion which we only slightly understood; then he turned to us and told us that the actual price was only half that listed, and anyway, we really didn't want to go to another neighborhood, theirs was much better. We stayed. This same incident was the first example of what later became so familiar—the effort on the part of Greeks, whether one knew them well or not, to give vehement advice as to what one should do.

In this early sensitive period these manifestations of public manners different from those we as Americans were accustomed to were jarring. We frequently had to argue with waiters to get what we wanted to eat, and often we did not succeed because their way of telling us they didn't have the item— though it was listed on the menu—was phrased as advice to order something else. It was all the more bewildering because sometimes they did have the item and were really just giving advice. But having to put up an argument in a foreign language to get food you wanted in a restaurant when what you craved was a peaceful, restful meal made the behavior of waiters all the more noticeable and provided indicators for a later analysis of cultural patterns. When we were back in Athens some four months later, even after so brief a period of acculturation, it required a conscious effort to notice and record the kind of behavior that filled my notebooks during the first few weeks.

I can now continue the narrative of our survey trip. The main road to Levadhia, which was our first stop, went through the olive groves of Attica; the tortuous, narrow passes of the Parnis range; through to Thebes; the plain of what was once Lake Copais; and finally the foothills of Mount Parnassus. The scenery was magnificent. The twisting, narrow mountain road without railings was frightening, particularly because, as the main communication link between northern Greece and Athens at that time, it was traveled extensively by trucks that loomed unexpectedly as we went around curves. The weather was changeable; the rainy winter season was just beginning. The best hotel in Levadhia, a town of 12,000 inhabitants, was clean and adequate except for the water closets. Since the rural population of the surrounding region and many urban and town dwellers as well were accustomed to Turkish-style toilets—which consist of openings in the floor without seating of any kind—they neither knew exactly how to use nor were they comfortable with the standard water closet. Although the hotel maids cleaned up the resulting messes rather frequently, my husband, who is less squeamish than I, was good enough to scout the place for me each time before I tried to use the facilities. I mention this matter because the first encounter with the problem came on that first afternoon in Levadhia and was only the beginning of a long day of misery. The hotel room was bare, with the usual very hard, small pillows on the beds; it had rained and the walls smelled of wet plaster, the room was damply chilly; the narrow streets of the town were muddy; the best restaurant had no available food except the lukewarm oily stews which at that period we had not yet learned to like. The carcasses of sheep and cattle hanging in the butcher shops, unrefrigerated and covered with flies; the array of other shops, with their strange wares displayed on the streets; the hustle and bustle of the crowds, whose conversation was mostly unintelligible—all combined to create an atmosphere of strangeness that struck me forcibly that first night. The thought that we would have to work in this alien environment for a whole year was almost too depressing to bear.

The following day we paid our visit to the Nomarch, who was most cordial and understood just the kind of small village we wanted. He called his staff in and explained that we were looking for a village that we could hold in our hands—"like this," and he held out his hands, with the worry beads he had been playing with nestled in his palms. With his staff we went over the characteristics of the smaller villages in the neighborhood, ruling out some for one reason or another until we had narrowed the choice down to four. One of our considerations was that the village not be too poor. We had what turned out to be a mistaken notion that we would be living off the village in some ways, and we did not want to impose hardships on the population. (We actually bought most of our food in Levadhia.) We were assured that the four were about average for the area. The Nomarch and several of his staff members drove out with us to visit the villages.

Vasilika, twelve miles from Levadhia, is visible from the main road. When we caught our first glimpse of it, we were struck by the trees that were profuse enough to hide some of the buildings, an unusual feature for this vicinity. As we drove into the agora of the village, we passed what were obviously the cemetery and the church, and the Nomarch pointed out the school building. In the agora, at one of the coffee houses, we found several men sitting at the outdoor tables. They rose to greet us, welcomed the Nomarch whom they apparently knew, and invited us—including me—to sit with them. One older man ordered Turkish coffee for us, and as the conversation progressed, he bought some grapes and later chestnuts from itinerant vendors who were coming through and offered them to us. This was our first encounter with the hospitality pattern in which the host does not eat with his guests; we weren't sure whether we were meant to eat the grapes then and there, since only the visitors had been offered any, and the normal expectation that you can learn how to behave in such situations by watching your host obviously was not relevant. We watched our fellow stranger, the Nomarch, instead.

The president of the village council was sent for; when he joined us, the Nomarch explained that we were American university professors (colleges in the American style don't exist in Greece and "college professor" would have had no meaning to the villagers, yet we had to be distinguished from gymnasium instructors, who are also called "professors" in Greece) who wanted to study the way of life of the village by living in it and asking a lot of questions. He added that if we came to live there, we'd expect to be told when events of importance were scheduled, and that the villagers should help us by answering our questions. When it became apparent that Vasilika had a resident priest and a functioning school and was technically a *kinótis* (a governmentally designated community, even though it had fewer than the 300 inhabitants required by law for this minimal political unit), we asked about the possible living arrangements. There were no empty houses. The school building had a second room that was not being used, but when we all trooped over to look at it, we saw that it was obviously too small. One family had an extra room, which was kept for a frequently visiting relative, and it was suggested that perhaps we could use that. It was also small but was at least possible, and we left the village with the understanding that we would return in about a week to see if the family could give us the spare room or if any other accommodation could be found.

The pattern was the same in the other villages we visited that day; housing was going to be the real problem.

We then spent a week traveling north through Thessaly as far as Larissa, stopping at random in villages without any introduction, and found it possible to strike up conversations in the coffee houses. There were many one-crop villages in the area; we did not want these, and by the end of the week, we had decided that Boeotia was adequate for our purposes. Again, we did not want to waste more time traveling around. We stopped in Vasilika on our way back, and this time, with the aid of the school teacher, we discovered that another family had expressed willingness to have us use the upper story of their house. When we looked at this apartment, we found it very good for our purposes. It was at the edge of the agora, on the main street of the village, with a veranda that overlooked the tables of one of the coffee houses. Although we could not see anyone who stopped off in the village before reaching the agora, we were as close to the center of activity as we were likely to get in any of the villages we had visited. Moreover, we understood that we were being offered the entire upper floor furnished. It consisted of three rooms; a very large *salóni*, or parlor, a small winter room with a fireplace, and a minuscule "kitchen." The salóni was furnished with a bed, a center table, several chairs, and trousseau trunks. The winter room held a cot and the hand-driven sewing machine of the daughter of the house. The kitchen was empty. The family, consisting of a husband and wife, their nineteen-year-old daughter and their seventeen-year-old son, would presumably live in the lower floor of the house, which we did not at that time see. The exclusive use of the upper floor would give us the privacy we felt we needed; the family's occupancy of the lower floor would give us a better opportunity to observe daily routines than we would have had in a separate house. Fortunately also, the house compound included a combined storehouse and barn at one end of which there was a Turkish-style latrine. Reasoning that we were not likely to do better, we accepted the offer and left saying we would get from the Nomarch some indication of the appropriate rent. When we asked the landlord how much he wanted, he said, "Whatever you wish"—a characteristic answer, we later learned, and one we also learned not to take literally. Whenever we asked such questions as, "What time do you want to come?" or "What day would be best for a trip?" the first response would be, "Whenever you wish." We would then state precisely what we "wished," only to find that there was always some reason why that wasn't suitable, until by giving several alternatives, we hit upon the time or place or idea that, we finally realized, our informant had had in mind all along. This sort of twenty-questions game on what to us seemed insignificant matters often led to our irritably muttering to each other, "Why can't they ever come out and just say they want to go on Saturday?" Nevertheless, irritating conversations such as these were the first clue to what is apparently a pattern of unwillingness to give any information to anybody if it can possibly be avoided. Also involved are certain patterns of deferential behavior.

We returned to Athens very much relieved to have found a village and eager to return to it as soon as possible. We still had to consult the relevant government ministries, and we thought it best to do this before moving into the village. Through the Fulbright office we had an introduction to an appropriate official. In the course of a two-hour interview, he told us in no uncertain terms that we were all wrong to go to Boeotia; that the proper place for us was on the Island of Cephalonia, where there had recently been a devastating earthquake and where we could assist with rehabilitation; that, in any case, we should spend at least three or four months traveling around Greece before we made a choice; that he would be glad to arrange a trip, on which he or members of his staff could accompany us. We tried to explain that we wanted to do a community study first, without reference to ultimately possible applications of our knowledge and without immediate social-work objectives. He scarcely heard us.

We left his office thoroughly shaken. All the earlier anxieties about how best to go about choosing a village returned, and to these were added the fear that we had antagonized a government official who might be in a position to prevent us from doing our work. We agonized for two days until, in the course of describing our woes to some American scholar friends, one of whom had been born and raised in Greece, we discovered that the government official was our Greek friend's cousin. Not only that, but as we sat talking with these friends in the park, the official's wife came strolling by with her baby. Our friends undertook to explain to her that our mission was not social work or applied anthropology but was purely scientific; that for our purposes, excessively poor or recently disrupted communities would not be suitable. They requested her to explain all this to her husband. We, in turn, apologized profusely for not wanting to do as her husband had suggested and asked her to express our apologies to him. She told us not to worry about the matter further.

Fearing that the Greek Fates, who must have engineered so amazing a set of coincidences, might easily arrange some less favorable ones, we left Athens. For the rest of that year we confined our contact with government officials to those with functionaries stationed in the provinces. As it turned out, the way the central agencies actually operated out of Levadhia and Amphiklea, the two provincial centers in whose jurisdiction Vasilika finds itself, was more directly relevant to our study than the formal descriptions of government organization we would have gotten in Athens.

We returned to the hotel in Levadhia, asked the Nomarch's staff to write up a rent contract for our landlord to sign, and, armed with this, went to the village. We found the upstairs part of the house empty of all furniture except the salóni table, which was too big to get out the door. Where were the bed and the chairs? The family needed them downstairs. Protest seemed futile; obviously we couldn't sleep in the house without at least a bed, so we sent back to the hotel in Levadhia and spent the next two days looking for furniture. We finally accumulated a simple bed, four rush-bottomed chairs, two canvas folding arm chairs, two folding tables, a wardrobe, and a small old-fashioned icebox. The furniture we couldn't fit into our car was loaded onto a 1932 Chevrolet sedan—the elderly driver being the only man we could find who would take the stuff—and we entered the village in caravan on October 26, St. Demetrius Day. The children rushed down to the agora to see the sight, the men sitting there stared, but as is customary once we reached the house, only the members of the family stood around to watch. Anyone else had to do so covertly.

Two days later the twenty pieces of assorted luggage and boxes we had stored in Piraeus arrived. The advice from the Fulbright office had been that we bring enough of essential toilet articles, nylon hose, and clothes of all sorts to last the entire year because such items were either not available or very expensive in Greece. By the end of 1955 that was no longer true, but Greece was changing so rapidly that the Fulbright office quite reasonably couldn't change its directives fast enough. In any case, I had pondered long over just how many tubes of toothpaste we normally use in the course of a year, how many boxes of bath powder, how many jars of hand cream, and similar serious questions. Besides such items, clothing, and a few pots and pans, I had also carted along enough paper and notebooks to last out the year (ten years would have been more like it) and a collection of monographs and other reference books. As we started unpacking, the wife of the household and her son and daughter took turns watching us and asking what the various items were. We became progressively more embarrassed, not only because strangers were watching us unpack all our belongings, intimate and personal ones as well as books and papers, but also because the place began to look like a general store. Then the daughter of the house asked me if she could have a pair of nylon hose, since I had so many. I was startled by the direct request and uncertain as to what to do. In Dorothy Lee's (1953) discussion of Greek culture and in novels and other sources I had read before coming, there were many references to the Greek contempt for people who are easily duped. The family we were going to live with had already emptied the place of furniture that we thought they had agreed to leave for us, and we had not protested. Now they were asking us to give away some of our belongings. Would they lose all respect for us if I said "Yes," or would they be pleased? Would a single pair be enough, or would the girl want more? The decision had to be made immediately. I did what was most comfortable by my own standards; I gave her a pair, since I would have felt like a fool not to when I had two dozen pairs at hand. I hedged against what I thought were the hazards of Greek culture by saying that I needed to keep the rest because they had to last through the entire year.

The storage problem was severe; there were no closets of any kind except for the wardrobe we had bought; we lived out of boxes and suitcases all the time we were there. Moreover, their arrangement was the cause of a silent tug-of-war between the daughter of the house and me. I wanted them arranged for convenience of access, which meant having two or three piles, the top cases being reserved for frequently used articles. She apparently disliked the appearance of these piles (rightly so) in a room that, though we were renting it, she still considered very much her own. Every other week, when she came up to do what she considered a proper cleaning, she arranged our impedimenta in one pile and put one of her white homespun embroidered cloths over it. I would then take her neat pile apart and go back to my system.

This little struggle was a petty exemplification of far more serious ones that were constant during a large part of our stay. The first night we slept in the house, the mother brought her son upstairs and suggested that he sleep on a pallet in the winter room. Such an arrangement was in clear violation of our agreement. My husband decided we just had to take the risks involved in protesting this one, and he rejected the suggestion flatly. When the family was not disposed to accept his decision, he felt that the issue was important enough to get the priest to mediate. The priest did so, and the boy slept downstairs.

Our next problem was that of housekeeping. We knew we would need someone to help me with the housework and cooking. We had two kerosene burners, which we had bought to cook on (the family used the fireplace downstairs for cooking), and the rainy weather meant that mud and dirt were easily tramped into the house. In dry weather the dust was considerable. Moreover, all water had to be carried from the uncovered well. Because little attention was paid to the admonitions of agricultural extension agents against watering the animals right at the wells, there was grave danger that the water might be contaminated. There was also the possibility of pollution from household wastes. All these circumstances made it necessary to boil water, including that used for washing the dishes—a tremendous task with our primitive heating apparatus.

Obviously we needed some domestic help. Anthropologists in the field always have some such need, but for a woman anthropologist running a household, such help is utterly indispensable. Had I had to do the housework under these primitive conditions, I would have had time for nothing else.

Consequently, again using the village priest as intermediary (we were mindful of what Dorothy Lee [1953] had written about the functions of priests), we told him first that we would be happy to have the daughter of the household work for us. The priest explained that the girl had had training as a seamstress in Levadhia and that domestic service was really inappropriate for her; he promised to find someone else for us. Some days after our original conversations he recommended a fourteen-year-old girl in the neighborhood whose father was willing to have her help us. When we hired her, we also acquired the sister next in age as a frequent household visitor, her older sister as a laundress, and her three-year-old brother as another appendage. She herself was a beautiful and intelligent girl who was an excellent informant for whatever matters were within her ken. We are in her debt for what we learned directly from her and also from the opportunity to observe her relationships with various members of her family.

Nevertheless problems arose from this situation. When the daughter of the household in which we lived had refused to work for us, neither she nor her family had fully realized that the refusal would mean that another villager, and a neighbor at that, would have access to what our family regarded as its own house from cellar to roof, with all its contents. Eventually, when we ourselves began to acquire prestige value, it also meant that they had to share some of the prestige with the neighboring family.

A specific incident can illustrate something of the quality of the struggles that went on. I wanted some clothes hung up, but not enough clothespins were to be found. Since I knew there were always some on the wire line on the veranda, I assumed that the daughter of the house had borrowed them for her line downstairs or, if not, that she might remember where they were. By American standards, what could be more natural or reasonable! I asked our fourteen-year-old helper to go downstairs and see if anyone knew where the clothespins were. My husband overheard and told me immediately that I had made a serious mistake. He was right. The little girl called down in triumphant tones, "Mrs. Ernestine says you took the clothespins." The answer from below was that no one had ever seen or heard of our clothespins; they did not have any of our clothespins and never had had any of our clothespins. Several hours later the mother and daughter came upstairs and explained that they were honorable people; that we had insulted their integrity by suggesting that they had stolen clothespins from us; that it was a disgrace to their family; and so on. It took literally an hour of the most diplomatic assurances and protestations from both of us before they felt sufficiently relieved to go back downstairs. This interchange happened during the first month of our stay; it exhausted us, but it also sensitized me to the quality of relationships among village families, especially those not bound by kinship ties. Later events and observations made it possible to understand, if I am right, that the incident had little to do with us. Rather, it was part of the rivalry between the two village families. By sending the girl down with the question, I had unwittingly given her dominance over our own family that their *philótimo* (amour-propre) would not permit them to accept. In terms of village values, each of the girls had acted appropriately; I had been the foolish one.

Another of the lessons learned from the war of the clothespins was that in situations where several families are involved, things don't ever get mislaid, they must be stolen. Several weeks later it was my husband who fell into that trap; he had mislaid a pair of scissors and asked the son of the house if he had seen them. A scene similar to the earlier one, but with male actors, ensued.

In those first months, each time we went on an excursion to a neighboring village or town, we tried to take our helper with us. From our point of view, she was young enough to be a daughter, certainly not old enough to be a maid, and she had before our coming never even been as far out of the village as Levadhia. But some of the excursions also involved members of our landlord's family, because, as our principal informants, they were gradually becoming more willing to involve us in the events of their lives. Never once did they say that they did not want us to take the younger girl; but each time they contrived some reason, often at the last minute, to try to keep her from coming. My husband and I took to planning trips with great care and thought up reasons in advance for our taking the girl along, but in spite of the considerable emotional energy we spent on the problem, we did not always manage to keep her with us. We gradually learned that this, too, made sense in terms of the separateness of village families, and that it was not as painful for our helper as it was for us.

When working in a field situation, particularly within a limited time, an ethnographer always has a kind of double vision. He must act to keep himself functioning and to maintain a relationship in the community in which he lives; but he constantly also has to observe himself and his own reactions as he works. He is not a tabula rasa but a creature of his culture on the one hand and an idiosyncratic personality on the other. The incidents that bruise him have to be analyzed to try to discover how much of the bruising is a result of cultural differences and, if so, what particular differences, and how much is a result of his individual psychological peculiarities, or in what combination these occur.

I chose to use in this paper the incidents I have just reported—the deliberate removal of the furniture, the lack of privacy in unpacking, the direct request for a specific gift, the effort to keep the son upstairs, the mutual stubbornness over furniture arrangements, the war of the clothespins and the scissors, and the use of our young helper as a silent pawn in the effort to maintain the integrity and separateness of each family of contestants—because it was by thinking about why these events irritated us so much that I began to learn something of the culture and social structure of the community. I also became sensitized to a general problem in the study of European rural societies. As I have briefly stated elsewhere (Friedl, 1962, p. 5), Greek society and culture are closely related historically to American society and culture; both belong to Western civilization with Judeo-Christian religious traditions. The Greek villagers share Western technological culture; they are literate and part of a long-standing nation-state. Moreover, their recent compatriots form one component of the variegated American ethnic population and therefore have connections with the social structure of the United States. In outward appearance much of the clothing and other material culture of the community is familiar. In Vasilika we were fairly sure that there were no lineages as corporate groups; households often consisted only of nuclear families. Therefore, when such familiar, ordinary people act in ways that are at first incomprehensible, I believe the irritation, if not the shock, is likely to be greater than in less familiar societies, and the irritation then serves the excellent purpose of providing one kind of clue to differences.

None of the incidents I have just reported had to do with male-female relationships or with any problems arising from Greek attitudes toward the position of women, except minimally, or from my role as a woman field worker in relation to the villagers. One reason for this may be that, from my reading of the literature, I was prepared to find a strongly male-oriented culture. Here was one anticipated difference that I knew would be a subject for study and to which I would have to adjust.

In the field the situation produced no shocks, nor did I find the role in the community that the villagers and I gradually evolved personally uncomfortable for me. That of the village women had its own integrity, and I was not distressed by observing the limitations placed on their activities (Friedl, 1967).

The sex role that did create some problems was the relationship between my husband and me. We were in a setting in which I was directing our activities, and in spite of discomforts of all kinds, I constantly had the excitement and satisfaction of discovery. However tediously detailed an interview might be, I knew its purpose and was eager for the results. My husband was not working at his profession in any direct way, and neither he nor I was accustomed to having him in the role of assistant to me. For him a tedious interview remained only that; he was always having to learn more then he cared to know. He was also oppressed by the notion that my constant questions and picture taking and poking about were an imposition on the villagers and that we gave insufficient return for all they did for us. The matter troubled me too, but as an anthropologist I was convinced that our actions were in a serious cause and that, by exercising great care, we could avoid hurting the villagers. The tensions created by our unaccustomed roles in relation to each other and by our different motivation remained with us throughout the field work. One of the consequences was that we needed to get away from the village for a change of pace more often than we might have otherwise. (We took three- or four-day breaks in Athens about every three weeks.)

As I have said, our roles in relation to the villagers were more simply, if not less interestingly, developed. There were several reasons for this. First, Vasilika is a peasant community in Arensberg's sense. The inhabitants are aware of national statuses and roles and class differences, including those not functioning in the village itself. They also have some knowledge of the behavior that accompanies those roles. The villagers' reaction to us was compounded of their perception of us, not only in terms of the universally ascribed positions based on age, sex, kinship, and the stranger, but also on their awareness of what a professor is and that such creatures as women professors can exist.

Let us consider these in turn. My husband was forty-eight and I was thirty-five when we reached Vasilika. We looked much younger than villagers of the same age do, but my husband had some gray hair and could be assimilated as an elder. I was more difficult to categorize because they quickly learned that I had no children of my own and that my husband's children were from his first marriage. Looking young, especially by the women's standards (they kept commenting on how smooth my hands were), and having no children seemed to overweigh the fact that I was married, so that in the household with which we lived, the family gradually dropped the Mrs. part of the "Mrs. Ernestine" term of address. I would half seriously call the mother "little mother," and the daughter and I often ad-dressed each other as "little sister." With the family of our helper and with several other women I got to know well, I was also on reciprocal first-name terms.

Another reason for this development was that I chose deliberately not to play the role of the urban professional woman or of the urban middle-class or upper-class woman vis-à-vis rural villagers. Behavior in these roles was known by the villagers, and in the first days they made clear to me what it was. The term of address for such a woman is "Madame," pronounced in the French way; she is permitted to sit in the coffee house, as the village women never do; she is treated with the forms of deference customarily accorded the old or the important, such as being seated at all times and having others do all fetching and carrying. If I had been working alone, I would have had to take on the urban woman's role, at least at the start, because access to men's conversation in the coffee house would have been otherwise impracticable. I would have had to stress my professional status and observe the dignities expected by the villagers in order to be taken seriously by the men. But my husband's generous willingness to work with me obviated that necessity because he could sit in the coffee house and report on what was happening. Since he was the man of the family, his age and professorial status gave us all the prestige and solemnity we needed. This situation left me free to simulate more aspects of the village woman's role. Since in my own person as an American I did not smoke and never wore shorts or slacks, these requirements of the village woman's role caused no hardship. Moderate amounts of wine drinking were permissible with meals, but when we returned to the village after my two-and-a-half-month bout with hepatitis, I was not allowed to have any alcohol anyway. I dislike being waited on and expect to help with cooking and cleaning up after meals in all but the most formal settings. For the field work situation, by not having to stress the high status guest role with all families, I was able to keep my eye on women's activities and to listen to many of their conver-sations. Women know about fewer subjects than men in Greek villages, but they are less reticent about those they do talk about.

My husband's role in relation to the family we lived with, and with all but one or two men, remained more formal. Several men had had a gymnasium education, and they quickly recognized his competence in ancient Greek and spread the word. They also admired his correct spelling of modern Greek and his knowledge of ancient Greek mythology and history, of which they knew something from their schooling. The village men also enjoyed my husband's sense of humor and his considerable ability, even in Greek, as a raconteur. They discussed politics with him, talked about crops and farmers' problems, and even occasionally teased him, but very gently. He made the greatest stride toward acceptance on the day the Nomarch and some of his staff came to see how we were getting along. We invited the village president, the priest, and our landlord to talk with the Nomarch. He asked about the crops, whereupon my husband delivered an impassioned speech about the poor lot of the farmer, repeating all the complaints he was continually hearing from the men. The following day, as we took our daily walk out to the fields, one man after another told us he had heard how Mr. Harry had taken the farmers' side and how well he had presented their case to the Nomarch. On that occasion my husband's reaction had been wholly spontaneous (so much of what is done in the field has to be calculated that this is worth saying), and it started the best discussion we ever heard in the village on agricultural economics.

We were aware of the formal role the villagers assigned to my husband partly by their disapproval of his first attempts to wear American country-style clothing. We had assumed that Greek countryside customs were like American ones, and we took along lumberjacks, heavy woolen trousers, plaid wool shirts, and heavy boots and shoes for my husband to wear. On the first cold, wet day, when he appeared in some parts of this outfit, they asked where his tie was and told him it wasn't hunting season yet. He wore a white shirt and tie from that time on and went around with cold, wet feet like the rest of the men. Neither was my husband allowed to wash our car; our family insisted that such work was not proper for him. Professors dress formally and do not do physical labor in Greece; the villagers' pride depended on their having knowledge of this distinction, and they made clear that they did know it.

Their deference was also apparent from their unwillingness to tell any jokes about sex or to discuss sexual subjects with my husband or to use vile language in his presence.

His role as an older professor, therefore, limited his access to certain kinds of information that were also unavailable to me. We know less than we want to about the attitudes, values, and general behavior of young unmarried men. We have limited knowledge also of adult men's sex attitudes and behavior. In addition, we had difficulty getting information on disputes among the villagers, including family quarrels. I attribute this partly to pride before strangers, but also to an unwillingness to talk about what the villagers consider immoral subjects with a man of my husband's high status. To test the degree of inadequacy of our knowledge (a few men did discuss these subjects on direct questioning near the end of our stay), we would have had to check court records, which we never had time to do.

Interestingly enough, I was allowed more freedom to dress in warm boots and heavy jackets, on the assumption that I was a delicate urban woman and needed more protection. But they drew the line at letting me wear a standard village woman's kerchief to guard against the sun, because that was clearly a symbol of the rural woman who works in the fields and I was allowed only partially to simulate the position of village women.

The villagers, with the possible exception of our helper and her family and perhaps one other man, never overtly accepted the fact that I was the anthropologist writing a book and that my husband was helping. He often came with me on interviews with men on specific subjects, and on these occasions I would tell him in English what questions to ask and he would help me to follow the Greek if it was beyond my abilities. I sat with a notebook and wrote down questions and answers. Although, when we collected genealogies, my husband did the writing because it required Greek script and spelling, we overheard one village man explaining to visitors from outside that Mr. Harry was writing a book and that Mrs. Ernestine was acting as his secretary. The reversal of role in which a wife publicly directed the activities of a husband was beyond their ability to comprehend. Indeed, it was also almost beyond ours.

The degree of acceptance in the roles I have described developed gradually from a bad start. Village ethics require formal politeness and hospitable treatment of strangers. If strangers have high social status, it is especially necessary for the villagers to show that they know how to behave properly, and in such instances the forms are even more scrupulously maintained. When we were taking census data—which was our second task, after we had made a rough diagram of the village's buildings and numbered them for convenience of reference—we were invited into each house for sweet preserve and a glass of water. The villagers were also curious about these strange Americans, and it relieved the monotony of their lives to look at them and to talk with them.

But underneath the public surface deference, there was considerable suspicion of our motives; the villagers thought we were spies, and our overtly stated intentions were incomprehensible. Since we arrived at the time of a Cyprus crisis, when the American position was not clear, there was some conversation to sound us out about that.

Some of the suspicion was overtly stated during a conversation in the coffee house by a man who accused us of asking questions and taking pictures so that we could put it all in a book for Americans to laugh at. My husband ran home in great alarm, collected several well-printed and handsomely bound monographs I had brought along, and got the son of the house to help take about ten of them down to the coffee house. One of the books was on a Bulgarian village and included a photograph of a Greek Orthodox priest, the mayor, and other officials. My husband explained eloquently that these books all cost a great deal of money and that American publishers wouldn't waste such sums just to make Americans laugh. The men became interested in the Bulgarian book and correctly deduced which photograph was that of the rich man in the village. That particular crisis was over.

We were aware of the suspicions long before that day, however, because the women especially kept asking me the same questions about our activities in different contexts. Whose money were we using? How much were we getting? Why did we buy all the furniture? Where were we going now? What were we going to talk about? Why? The women would be excellent designers of sociological questionnaires; indeed, Greek culture incorporates the principle that information must be acquired obliquely and checked repeatedly to assure its accuracy. The one advantage of this habit of questioning was that it made me less self-conscious about using the same techniques to check *their* accuracy.

We tried to gain the villagers' trust by being as scrupulously honest as possible in any human situation. We did not tell them the actual amount of money involved in the Fulbright grant because by village standards it was so large that they would have assumed it appropriate to get some from us just as the girl had asked for the stockings. We said what was true, in spirit—that the grant was allotted to cover expenses, that we billed the Foundation for what we spent, and that the Foundation knew the true prices of goods.

In another kind of situation we found that since ours was the only automobile in the village, people asked us to drive them to the towns or on other excursions. Since we had no principle by which we could accede to one household's request and not to that of another, we soon discovered that, unless we found some way of refusing, we would be on the road all the time and not get any work done. We began telling those who asked for rides that we had limited time to study the village, that our project was to learn about Vasilika, and that we were not free to go elsewhere. In consequence, we could never take a drive ourselves as a respite from the pressures of village life. We scrupulously used the car only for marketing in Levadhia or for other well-publicized errands, and we had to take long walks as a means of getting out of the village occasionally. One other rule we established was that the car was available in any emergency, and if anyone was ill or needed a doctor, we were there to help. There were several occasions of that kind during the year.

My description has emphasized stresses and strains because during the field work they seemed to dominate over the satisfactions. I am normally not subject to colds and virus infections, but that year, in addition to hepatitis, I had three separate bouts with mysterious fevers. I believe they were partially a consequence of tension. The difficulties as I felt them are important to this narrative because they account in part for the interest I developed in the genesis of the agonistic quality of human relations in the village.

In spite of the stresses and strains, however, there were two significant sources of satisfaction in the field. The first of these was the sense of mastery produced by the successful use of field techniques. By using the skills I had aquired in my professional training, I was gaining a steadily increasing knowledge about and understanding of the village. This fact was an important source of stability as well as of gratification. (I have not, except incidentally, described these techniques. They are described in the literature. For two recent examples see Powdermaker, 1966, and Williams, 1967.) The routines of field work also produced new foci of interest, such as the dowry, hospital care, and the urban quality of the village. The discovery of these was genuinely exciting.

The second source of pleasure was the process whereby the villagers and we, by mutual accommodation, traveled at least part of the path that leads from stranger to friend.

References

CASAGRANDE, JOSEPH B. 1966. "Language Universals in Anthropological Perspective." In Joseph H. Greenberg, ed., *Universals of Language*. Cambridge, Mass.: MIT Press.

PEARSALL, MARION. 1965. "Participant Observation as Role and Method in Behavioral Research," *Human Organization* 14, 37–42.

LEE, DOROTHY D. 1953.—"Greece." In Margaret Mead, ed. *Cultural patterns and technical change*. Unesco.

POWDERMAKER, HORTENSE. 1966.—*Stranger and friend. The way of an anthropologist*. New York: Norton.

WILLIAMS, THOMAS RHYS. 1967.—*Field Methods in the Study of Culture*. New York: Holt.

Publications based on the field work in Vasilika

FRIEDL, ERNESTINE. 1958. "Hospital Care in Provincial Greece," *Human Organization*, 16, 24–27.

————. 1959a. "Dowry and inheritance in modern Greece," *Transactions of the New York Academy of Sciences*, 22, 49–54.

————. 1959b. "The Role of Kinship in the Transmission of National Culture to Rural Villages in Mainland Greece," *American Anthropologist*, 61, 30–38.

————. 1962. *Vasilika, a Village in Modern Greece*. New York: Holt.

————. 1963. "Some Aspects of Dowry and Inheritance in Modern Greece. In Julian Pitt-Rivers, ed., *Mediterranean Countrymen*. The Hague: Mouton. pp. 113–136.

————. 1964. "Lagging Emulation in Post-Peasant Society," *American Anthropologist*, 66, 569–586.

————. 1967. "The Position of Women: Appearance and Reality," *Anthropological Quarterly*, 40, 97–108.

LEVY, HARRY L. 1956. "Property Distribution by Lot in Present-Day Greece," *Transactions of the American Philological Association*, 87, 42–46.

————. 1963. Inheritance and Dowry in Classical Athens. In Julian Pitt-Rivers, ed. *Mediterranean Countrymen*. The Hague: Mouton, pp. 137–143.

INDIA (ORISSA)

Studies in an Indian Town

CORA DU BOIS was president of the American Anthropological Association and Zemurray Professor, Harvard University. Well known for her classic study PEOPLE OF ALOR *and for* SOCIAL FORCES OF SOUTHEAST ASIA, *in 1961 she received the American Association of University Women achievement award. Over the years she has taught at Sarah Lawrence, the University of California at Berkeley, the Washington School of Psychiatry, and the University of Hawaii. She has also served in the Department of State as chief of the Southeast Asia Branch in the Division of Research for the Far East.*

I am writing in the State Guest House of Bhubaneswar. It is a very comfortable hostel, and the various rooms I have occupied here intermittently for six years have been large and airy. There is electric light, an overhead fan, modern plumbing, and excellent service. I realize how vastly different from other field experiences this has been. It has little relation to my first field jaunts in the early 1930's among the Indians of California. There I was tied to a dilapidated car and stayed in roadside cabins on a minimal living and travel allowance. My task was largely salvage ethnography, and I never really left my own culture except by an act of imagination. Nor has this sojourn in India any relation to the eighteen months I spent in Alor, an Indonesian island, during the late 1930's. There a largely untouched and very primitive people provided the isolated environment among the "savages" that my generation considered both adventurous and romantic. My quarters, of which I was inordinately proud, were comfortable simply by dint of considerable ingenuity; they consisted of a spacious thatched house and a bamboo water conduit.

Short of furnishing the data for an intellectual history, which can be of no possible interest to anyone but myself, these three field trips seem utterly disparate in their purpose, in their human relationships, and in their "managerial" requirements. I shall not attempt a comparison.

However, it is not possible to speak of these six years of research in India without describing briefly the town and the task on which I have been working intermittently since 1961.

Even a brief sketch of the town of Bhubaneswar will emphasize that work here can have no relationship to archival ethnology among the American Indians or an isolated hill people of Indonesia. Additionally, what I say about this enterprise will make obvious the very special and not to be generalized nature of the field work. Nor are my responses to this endlessly intricate challenge of the Indian scene those of the many anthropologists who have done field research in India. It is trite to say that the

221

only generalization that can be made about India is that one cannot generalize.

The core settlement of Bhubaneswar is an ancient religious center whose archeology is traceable to approximately 300 B.C. and whose legendary founding is attributed to Shiva. Despite at least two periods of great florescence, this sacred precinct was in 1947 a small community of some 4,000 people. In that year a new capital city for the state of Orissa was established in a scrub jungle area some two to three miles north of the temple center. When I first began work in Bhubaneswar in 1961, the municipal area of approximately eleven square miles had a census population of about 40,000. It included not only the old congested temple town, but also the new capital, a dispersed and planned center of administration. And I say "a census population" because I am convinced that in most national censuses the count underestimates by from 10 to 25 per cent. Our project community censuses confirm this as, more importantly, do the malaria-control counts.

In any case, the most traditional and the most modern aspects of Orissa are dramatically juxtaposed to provide within a relatively small area and small population the situation I sought—the confrontation of modern and traditional ways of life in contemporary India. The municipal area also embraced several villages of very different composition, which are slowly being "urbanized." By "urbanized" I am using a term popular in American city development; it has only marginal relevance to the influence of the new capital on the adjacent villages.

From the beginning my intent was to seek the assistance of a small group of American Ph.D. candidates from several disciplines and to work with local Oriya graduate students. The individual studies so far pursued range over surveys of five villages, a new slum area, and a new middle-class community; inquiries into modern and traditional types of leadership, including the elections of 1967; changes in the major temple and in the local Hindu monasteries and retreats; the nature of the educational system; comparisons in child-rearing patterns among different social groups; the responses of an outcaste group to new occupational opportunities; the execution of the planning process and associated decision-making; and a values interview administered to fifteen social groupings. From the many Indians and Americans involved I expect nine Ph.D. theses to be written—three by Indian colleagues and six by Americans. The incoherence of these theses is as great as the incoherence of the situation itself. To try to make order out of variety is the task I have set myself. I hope I shall not do injustice to its rich and all too human diversity.

Our common responsibility has been to deposit current carbons of field notes in a master file, which now runs to some eight file drawers. The arrival of field notes while I am in the United States, as well as the guidance provided for the theses and individual papers, has not only kept me abreast of my colleagues' work, but has further broadened and deepened my knowledge of the community far beyond anything I could have done alone. The American students have access, by way of preparatory briefing, to the master files. As an incidental bonus, both undergraduate and graduate students have written term papers from field data in the files. Clearly the enterprise has emphasized training, although research has been its primary intent.

This, then, is the context from which the following remarks stem. The differences in my present field enterprise and previous ones reflect changes in the world situation, in anthropology's new role in the social sciences and its concern with high cultures, and also in myself over a period of forty years. Anthropology has altered greatly in its problems, relevant subject matter, and methodology. I, too, have changed with the intervening four decades from a descriptive and historical ethnologist to a somewhat critical and cautious "social scientist." And certainly my pleasure in complexity has grown steadily with age. Readily resolved exercises in methodology, considered impeccable in the rhetoric of persuasion now fashionable in some of the social sciences, seem to me scientifically admissible but intellectually boring. Similarly, to me, the abstractions of deductive theory building, however interesting, seem either irrelevant or, when translated into ordinary English, trite. There are fashions in intellectual matters and their rhetoric as pronounced as styles in clothes. In both realms it is neither necessary to resist nor fully to espouse the extremes. It has always been obvious that description without explicit intent is often irrelevantly archival. But I still firmly believe that without a broadly based contact with personally perceived realities, the investigation of "problems" runs the risk of being merely a projection of the preoccupations of Western social science, which can be as ethnocentric as was Freudian psychology. In context such problems may be useful, but they are narrowing and even misleading cross-culturally.

My Indian experience has confirmed my impression that questionnaires and even guided interviews are subject to gross errors that statistics and computers only accentuate. This is not to say that if one is concerned with the differences between theory and practice in any society, quantification is undesirable. It is simply that the distinction between theory and practice must be explicit, that quantification must be cautious, and that the problems posed must not be prematurely culture-bound.

The need for caution becomes all the more marked as anthropologists have turned from relatively small homogeneous social groups to large and complex national units. In India, at least, I feel myself on the verge of questioning once again the analytic value of the concept of culture. Dismissing such questions for the time being, I believe that the social diversity and cultural complexity of my own culture seem trivial by comparison to those of India and that facile projections from our social sciences can seduce and mislead the culturally unsophisticated investigator.

The salient differences, then, are those of changes in anthropological problems and techniques, my forty years of varied experiences within and outside my own culture, and finally the attempt by anthropologists to perceive social and cultural regularities in such highly heterogeneous national entities as India. I am also aware that the study of a limited community in such an entity is as artificial and as false as too great a preoccupation with preconceived problems or techniques of investigation.

In a more practical context other matters bearing on field work in complex societies are professionally less important but nonetheless must seriously to be reckoned with. Prime among these is the development of national sentiments and swollen bureaucracies. The shrinkage of space that the speed of transportation has provided is, paradoxically, countered by institutional barriers. The lavish post-second World War financing of research in the United States entails months of planning and paper work. Further, permission to do field research in new nations, if allowed at all, involves elaborate procedures and clearances. More than ever good briefing and tact are professional obligations. Today, in India at least, no anthropologist can hope to do field research without a reasonable knowledge of its bureaucratic regulations and, best of all, influential and helpful acquaintances in the government and universities. There have been cases of long-laid plans and potentially productive research unrealized because of inadequate or unreliable contacts. India is not unique in having its power structure based on a bureaucracy that works from the top downward on the basis of complicated and ill-understood regulations. On the whole, it is a good idea to follow the flow of authority in establishing one's bona fides. Fortunately I have found in India many understanding and helpful officials, some of whom I dare now to consider cherished friends.

In India, as elsewhere in the world, the question of one's integrity as a scholar may come under suspicion. The ineptitude of our Central Intelligence Agency, as well as the Chinese and Pakistan hostilities, have accentuated—fortunately only in a minor way—what I have come to consider the normal suspicions that I or my American colleagues are spies. Even after six years such rumors are current. Certainly I consider it desirable to leave my notes freely accessible to any intelligence officer who may wish to examine them during my absence from my room. Such is his duty, and I feel that I should make no attempt to outwit him. I also believe that my policy of making my presence and objectives known to the highest officials has reduced gossip on this score. I have pursued a policy of making my arrivals and departures known by brief visits or letters, beginning with the state governor and working downward. Further, when gossip of spying has reached me, stemming from persons of some status, I have made a point of tracing it to its source, of expressing my concern, and of asking for evidence—with assurances that, if any evidence exists, the culprit would be dismissed immediately. I consider covert "intelligence work" in any case disreputable, but to pursue it under cover of academic research is an unpardonable betrayal of professional ethics.

There is another attitude that I have met occasionally in India. It is a feeling that we foreign academicians come to India to exploit local scholars and go home to advance our careers at their expense. I am aware that exploitation of this sort is not unknown in the United States, where professional ethics are rarely explicitly insisted upon. In India junior professionals have even more reason to suspect exploitation. Despite this, some Indians evince an almost excessive generosity in contributing to the foreign scholar's enterprise. I have had to resist attempts to put me under obligations that could never be met. All this had to do, I suspect, with role conflicts between the traditional guru-chela relationship in the past and the more contemporary "arrivism" of academic life. Another and more encouraging version of resistance to outside research personnel is: "Why aren't our own scholars doing this kind of research?"

I know of no single way of dealing constructively with this recurrent aspect of a legitimate national pride, on the one hand, and, on the other, the personal variations that range from excessive generosity to excessive fears of exploitation. The explanation lies somewhere in the nature of contractual relationships as they are perceived in both cultures, and it is by the quality and expectations of these relationships that I am most frequently baffled. I sense either that the element of mutual trust is lower in the Indian professional scene or that, as a stranger in the land, I am more distrustful. I should add that the not uncommon generalization that India operates on status relationships and the West on contractual relationships is a very poor dichotomy indeed. Just as both shame and guilt can operate simultaneously in any society or individual, so also do status and contractual relationships.

For various reasons I found formal institutional affiliations undesirable. I went to Bhubaneswar in 1961 with rather grandiose American notions of setting up a local executive officer, renting an office-cum-residence, and establishing an advisory committee. After six months I drew up such a proposal to which was attached a list of possible personnel and a budget. I circulated this proposal to appropriate academic and government persons. The response convinced me that the special interests of the individuals consulted would serve only to disperse the intent of the project and that administrative costs in both time and money would far exceed those spent on research. I settled for a looser and more independent enterprise, even though it increased my supervisory burdens.

But let me repeat that foreign research personnel can be a heavy burden to responsible and overworked teachers and officials. When phasing in my younger American colleagues over the six-year period, it has seemed both considerate and conciliatory to have never more than two graduate students in the community at one time and to have these students addressing themselves to different segments of the town's small but highly diversified population.

Other considerations have also entered. As I have indicated, one cannot, and should not morally, work in a community on whose good will one depends without rendering some services in return. The employment of local personnel is not only a research necessity, it is also a training potential. Seven Americans have worked in Bhubaneswar over a period of six years. Three Oriya M.A.'s, employed steadily during these years, have been trained to the point of writing their doctoral theses; at least twenty-five local persons have been given some training in interviewing and systematic data collection; several typists and translators have been employed for varying lengths of time. I am not sure just how much money and encouragement the seven Americans have dispensed in these various enterprises, but I am sure that I have spent a disproportionate amount of time training Oriya students to collect data systematically, to analyze and present material cogently, and to note the implications of such material. I can only hope that the training and the financial support have been some small return for the assistance they and many other members of the community so generously contributed.

There are, of course, the innumerable small favors sought of strangers —aid in securing publications, advice in applying for fellowships, talks to various groups, and, as far as it is legally permissible, meeting the apparently insatiable demand for gadgets, ranging from ball-point pens through typewriters, watches, and binoculars, whose possession frequently has been valued more for display than for use. I have met on an ad hoc basic, as have my American colleagues, the legitimate and sometimes less legitimate requests for financial aid in hardship cases, ranging from dowries to illness or to the education of children. I know of no rule of thumb for judging how and where assistance should be provided in a society where poverty is pervasive. I find that I have met such requests not so much in terms of real need as in terms of relationships I have had with either the requester or with the go-between who approaches me.

I have spent a disproportionate amount of space in discussing these more commonplace aspects of relationships that have consumed a great deal of time and thought at the expense of more purposeful research. I do not begrudge such demands, since they add greatly to my understanding of the Indian scene.

On a more personal level the rewards have been even greater. Although my experience with Indians suggests that they are as hospitable and friendly as Americans, they appear to have a far greater capacity for forming genuinely intimate and supportive friendships than do Americans. It is this capacity among at least a few Indians whom I have encountered that gives me the warmth and concern I feel not only for them but for the nation they represent.

I also believe that such success as I have achieved in personal relationships—and it has not always been smooth sailing—is facilitated as much by my age and status as by any sensitivity or trained insights on my part. That I am a professor at a highly esteemed university and in a grandmother generation has countered the liabilities of being not only a woman but, worse yet, an unmarried one. I believe also that a certain modesty of demeanor, combined with self-assurance, is also persuasive. An eagerness to learn, as well as the conviction that what one is learning is important, has a way of communicating itself even when, or perhaps just because, it is not explicitly stated. Discreet, objective, but genuine interest in other people seems everywhere to overcome a host of other barriers to communication.

Both I and my American colleagues have been, I believe, discreet. None of us are experienced "India wallas." We are, in varying degrees, amateurs (in both senses of the word) of the culture. In a society where open and perceptive discussion of almost any topic exceeds in quantity and quality that to which I am accustomed, even in America, one learns much simply by listening and reading. The excellence of the press, at least the English-language press, is a remarkable resource, and most of us have fallen into the habit of selective newspaper clipping. One learns rapidly to sort out the sometimes paranoid suspicions and destructive gossip from facts and interpretations. Fortunately my colleagues are, on the whole, good listeners rather than eager-beaver interrogators. They have waited to pose questions; they have conversed rather than interrogated. Methodologically, such an attitude may be considered in some quarters an old-fashioned ethnographic approach compared to systematic interviewing. Although all of us have also used systematic interviews and even questionnaires, I still retain the impression that in this highly articulate country, listening is the single most instructive approach.

In the same vein, since I am concerned primarily with the encounter in India between modern and traditional values and their supporting institutions, and since the freedom and variety of comment by Indians on their own society is so penetratingly debated at almost all levels of society, I have toyed with the idea of presenting the terminal report I plan to write in terms of what Indians themselves have to say on their traditional and modern institutions and the changes they observe. I shall probably not carry out such a tour de force, but it is fun to contemplate.

It is now perhaps time to be more specific about my own part in this collaborative multidisciplinary research enterprise. What I have to say is largely a confession of inadequacy. My area training falls far short of the standards we require of students now being prepared for anthropological research in India. Although I had been in India during the war in 1944 and 1945, and again in 1950, I was not then engaged in Indian studies. I am, in sum, not a trained Indologist, and I command no Indian language. Here in Orissa I have spent an amount of time quite out of proportion to the results in trying to learn Oriya. I do not wish to make excuses, but the reasons for my failure are many. I have always been linguistically untalented, and age is no asset in acquiring a new language. Also, I live in the comfort of the State Guest House, where English is widely spoken by both guests and staff. Systematic, spoken language training in Oriya was not available until 1965, when Dr. Pattanayak and Mr. Gagan Das were persuaded to quickly develop such a training text; from them, two of the American students acquired spoken fluency in Oriya. Lastly, my other research and training obligations are heavy. Both spoken Oriya and its script are still largely blank areas to me. This fact has cut me off from close relationships with Oriyas who do not speak English, and particularly from such relationships with Oriya women.

Orissa is a conservative state, which means that even its upper-class women, who may be traditionally highly educated, rarely have modern schooling. I know many schooled Oriya men, and I can relate to them easily, but not so easily to their wives. I am rarely invited to the homes of middle-class Oriya families, and when I have been, I am primarily the guest of the husband rather than of the wife. I should immediately enter here a distinction. The non-Oriya English-speaking and progressive couples whom I have met are unstintingly hospitable, and I have formed friendships in India more readily and, I believe, more deeply than I have formed in the United States over a comparable period. It is traditionalism among Oriya women, combined with my linguistic ineptitude, that has created such barriers as exist. The village and lower-caste women seem, on the whole, more open and free in their approach than do middle- and upper-class Oriya women.

Returning to my relationship with Oriya men, many frequently drop in to chat with me on the neutral ground provided by the Guest House. Their conversations range widely and outspokenly. It is, after all, a commonplace in all societies that the sympathetic stranger is the repository of confidences that are encouraged by discretion and distance. I sense that my age, in India at least, facilitates rather than inhibits confidences. Grandmothers in India are, stereotypically, loving and indulgent figures. Indian men speak frankly to me of matters they would hesitate to discuss with their families, their peer groups, or their working colleagues.

But age and the role of a detached stranger are by no means the only assets I have discovered. The desire to travel and even to emigrate is widespread among many persons in India today. Although the popular cliché of the brain drain seems to me somewhat exaggerated, the educated and ambitious Indian today is as curious and as searching as are his counterparts in other countries. Since travel outside of India is severely restricted by difficulties of foreign exchange, the visiting foreigner—if he is accessible at all—is a substitute. I remember meeting the same attitude in Spain in 1950 and in Russia in 1960. It is a little like being a lion in the zoo. Unexpected Indian visitors drop in, usually in pairs, as if facing a stranger alone is too embarrassing. Such calls are often touching in the fantasies they reveal. Americans are perceived as endlessly rich and powerful benefactors, of whom the most improbable demands can be made—from arranging admission and funds for study at Harvard to providing birth-control information, getting jobs, or using influence to hurry the settlement of a pension. My visits to the villages or outcaste wards invariably are associated with the most courteous of receptions, but almost always they also entail special pleas to help right wrongs. If assigned status is high in a rigidly hierarchized society, then by the same token, influence is presumed to be extensive. In some cases help can be given. I, for one, have at times to remind myself that social work is not my chief purpose and that to interfere in what is often the none too admirable administration of municipal affairs would jeopardize my official relationships. I also learned early that the statement of difficulties is not only incomplete but is frequently a case of special pleading. It is difficult, if not impossible, without the most painstaking inquiry to get at the root of these prolonged and tangled requests. I recall one young man who visited me repeatedly seeking advice and assistance in being admitted to an American university. It was only after several visits that he revealed that he had already been accepted, if not subsidized, by three such institutions. Negotiating a favor seems a very complicated and delicate procedure.

There are also rewarding contacts with Western-educated men more nearly my own age. I am keenly aware of what the changes that have taken place in the first half of the twentieth century mean to me as an American. Much that strikes my younger colleagues as traditional Indian is simply the persistence of nineteenth-century customs and technology. The changes experienced by the older Western-educated Indians are, in some respects, even more vital and varied than mine. These men came of age and into positions of responsibility during the heyday of Indian westernization. In the twenty years since independence there has been in many respects a

reassertion of Indian values and modes of expression that leaves these older
men stranded between two worlds to neither of which they can bring un-
divided loyalties. Many have remarkable memories and have kept careful
records. From such distinguished men I have learned a great deal about
socio-cultural change, much as I did in the same way from elderly informants among the American Indians when I began my field work in
California about forty years earlier. But the human, historical, and socio-
cultural wealth of experience my Indian friends bring to our discussions
epitomizes for me the pleasure and value of dealing with complex cultures
as one grows older.

I am quite aware, I hope, of the implications contained in these last
paragraphs. My personal view, if not my knowledge, of India derives
primarily from my contacts with men who are to varying degrees westernized. Although I sense that I know a good deal about Indian culture in
transition, I do not profess any more than a limited competence in the
inwardness of its social and personal variations.

Some hint of this comes from the young Oriyas whose research I have
guided and to whom I am deeply indebted. Let me begin by saying that we
have had very different expectations of each other. I have treated them as I
would American graduate students; I have expected motivation, competence, and initiative. They, however, see me as a professor. This position
still carries in India some of the aura of a guru, to whom one docilely
surrenders one's self, in return for which one expects to be molded through
minute guidance to successful accomplishment. I suspect it is not unusual in
some universities of India for professors practically to write their students'
Ph.D. theses. In addition, they also see me as that ever-loving, permissive
ideal, if not actual, grandmother who overlooks every lapse and indulges
every whim. I was not prepared for, nor am I temperamentally capable of,
playing either role, and certainly not the combination of both. During the
first year I found myself frustrated and angry by the way my young Oriya
colleagues depended slavishly on my instructions, by their low level of
motivation and competence, and above all by their long and unpredictable
disappearances into thin air. I have come only slowly to understand and to
clarify our legitimate and nonlegitimate expectations of each other.

Among other factors I had to learn in my first year was the importance
of physical stamina. For some of the young Indians (and, incidentally,
Americans) the psychological and physical resources required to sustain
steady and stressful field work are too high for their reservoir of energies,
their associated attention span, and their spasmodic habits of work. These
young Indians are probably all more or less anemic; certainly some are
infested with a variety of intestinal parasites and, therefore, subject to every
passing infection. When I suggested to one young man that he go to
Calcutta at my expense for a thorough treatment, he replied, "Respected

madam, what is the use? I shall only be reinfected when I come back." Or when I asked another young man, early in my stay and before I learned better, what his professional aspirations were, he looked at me blankly and answered, "How can I say? I shall take any position open to me." When I offered to subsidize another youth to a more adequate diet, including vitamin pills, he made it clear that he liked only the food he was eating and that Ayurvedic medicine served his purposes. These young men were all M.A.'s from the local university.

It took some time to adjust myself to all these realities as well as to the educational standards. Although the young men's college and graduate studies have been in English, it is clear that their command of the language is elementary, their knowledge of the discipline slight, and their comprehension of research rudimentary. None has adequate access to professional literature. Some are still reading slowly, with lip motions. Let me say immediately that I am not making a generalization about Indian graduate students but speaking about my particular, and in some respects, excellent, colleagues. Schooling and intelligence are clearly not equivalents. Much of the time I have spent with these young colleagues is to be equated in part with the time one spends interviewing highly competent informants. The rest of the time has been spent teaching the rudiments of written English, organizing data, and perceiving the implications in data. The combination of these expectations and lack of competences produces a level of noise in our communications that at times approaches cacophony. This lack of communication, I believe, would never have occurred had I been working with illiterate tribal people, simply because mutual expectations would have been so different. I still regret the time it has taken me to understand what was happening, and I regret my frequent outbursts of bad temper. Now, at least, I hope we have reached a compromise in our expectations of each other. I suspect that only those Oriya students who could cope emotionally with the strain of such misunderstandings have finally settled down to complete their Ph.D.'s. One of my young friends delights me by evidences of initiative and self-reliance that at times reflect a certain lack of traditional courtesy toward a professor and a grandmother. He may lack frankness, but he shows considerable aptitude for dealing with his situation in his own culture. In India, perhaps more than any other place in which I have done field work, I have had to remind myself, as well as my American colleagues, that we will eventually leave but that our Indian friends will have to go on living their own lives in their own society. However task-oriented we may be in our own terms, our ultimate responsibility is to leave our colleagues, not only with no onus for their collaboration with us, but also with some very real advantages in terms of their own life situations.

Having talked for some time about what the intrusive academician faces in relating to Indians, I would like to flip the coin over and contemplate what the Indian scene connotes to some visiting American field workers. All field workers seem to proceed through the stages of anticipation, arrival, and adjustments to the task. These stages have been reasonably well described in the literature on foreign students. Fears and anxieties, particularly those of anticipation, seem part of all ventures into the unknown. Yet I remember no fears and very little "anxiety" associated with my first field work in California—nor was there cause for them. Similarly, I approached India with no hesitancies, but perhaps with fewer good reasons. In California I was not leaving my own culture in any real sense of the word. The field work in Alor was a different story, and I recognized some of the responses E. S. Bowen aescribes in *Return to Laughter*. India belongs to the Old World of which we are heirs, and I had traveled there twice before. Also, I was a good deal older and more experienced. Nevertheless, I acknowledge that India has swamped me.

It has been my observation that not only most young anthropologists, but also technical-aid personnel and students setting out for their first trips to genuinely unknown cultures, entertain qualms in various degrees that seem to me as normal as the stress associated with all true learning. Different personalities fasten on different ways of expressing such uncertainties. Some, and I am one of these, cope with uncertainties by almost obsessional advance planning and an attempt to foresee imaginatively, and often erroneously, every contingency. With me it has taken the form of interminable lists, a superfluous number of letters of introduction, an unnecessary number of predeparture conversations with those acquainted with the area, and, of course, as much advance reading as possible. These preparations can be seen as a gestation period. I am sure the symptoms differ with personalities. I have known some who set out with little more than a vast and often unfocused enthusiasm and a knapsack, while others set out with a thousand mental reservations and tons of luggage. I have no reason to believe that in the long run one field worker is more competent than the other.

Once in the field, I, at least, have always experienced a burst of euphoria and vitality. It invariably wears off in time as the new becomes familiar and as the tedium of everyday life anywhere in the world sets in, particularly when associated with long and regular hours of work. I have always regretted that my obsessional character kept me tied to the job at the expense of diverting and refreshing side trips. For me these opportunities have been irrevocably lost; I have warned my younger colleagues against similar errors. Side trips help to clear the mind and clean the eye, so that one returns with renewed zest and balanced perspectives. I am speaking here, of course, of field trips that last not just a summer but a year and a half or longer. In the case of my present work in India, the staleness that comes from my overzealous task-orientation has been partly limited by the time I have had free from teaching to return to the field. In the past six years I have been able to make five trips to Bhubaneswar varying in length from two to eleven months and totaling about two and a half years in all. Each return has provided new insights into some aspect of Indian life and culture that I feel sure would have escaped me had I spent those two and a half years in continuous residence. On the other hand, there have been discontinuities and forgetting, which needed to be mended on each return.

My American colleagues have varied greatly in their need for change and diversion. Some, like me, rarely leave their work. Others have found occasional periods of protracted sight-seeing a respite. Still others, more urban in their tastes, have found frequent weekends in Calcutta the kind of change they require. To my shame I must confess that I have been more than once openly disapproving of what seemed to me a rather light-hearted amount of vacationing. I believe that part of my disapproval harks back to my early professional experience, when the opportunity and funds for field work, and even an education, were a privilege to be earned and not a right to be assumed. I belong to a generation for which earnings and savings, rather than credit cards, provided the opportunities for travel and study.

Looking back, I see very little difference in the actual accomplishments among my young colleagues. Whatever their position and attitudes, each has creditably completed his field work. Two or three well exceeded their preconceived goals. The greatest gratification is to see young professionals gain in assurance and maturity through that experience. Field work has always been the crucial educational experience and the determining polish of professionalism in anthropology.

Returning now to some of the questions faced by myself and my American colleagues in coming to terms with the Indian scene, there have been the usual and quite commonplace but nonetheless trying adjustments that range from feelings of frustration to the fears associated with health and the adaptations of accompanying families.

Frustrations in performing the most ordinary tasks associated with travel, housing, appointments, and interviews are largely a matter of misplaced expectations and ignorance of procedures. I suffered acutely from such frustrations at the beginning; I tried to forewarn outbound Americans; my Indian friends and colleagues in residence were generous in their help to newcomers. Nevertheless, for whatever reasons, no newcomer was spared periods of frustration and a sense of harassment. At first the grousing is monumental. The longer we stayed, the more we accustomed ourselves to the procedures and pace. Grousing subsided and tempers flared more rarely. This sort of experience is common, I believe, to most strangers in a new country. I often wonder what irritations and frustrations our Indian guests feel when they first arrive in the United States. They are usually too cour-

teous to evince them as openly as Americans do in India. To my sorrow, I
and some of my colleagues have had lower levels of restraint and courtesy
on this score. None of us has been really happy in the field until we had
learned what to expect and how to cope. These are such ordinary experiences, even for tourists, that they hardly need to be emphasized. They
range from the irritations involved in spending an hour registering a letter in
the post office or cashing a check in a bank to the more painful observations
of abject poverty and persistent begging.

There are always, of course, the fears, either real or projected, that
center on health. Except for my usual bronchial infections and a certain
lassitude as I readjust to heat and dietary changes, India agrees mightily
with me, and I feel better here than in the, to me, wretched climate of New
England and the incessant and disparate demands on my time. The climatic
difficulties of which some Americans make so much and of which some
pseudo-westernized Indians make even more, are not really a problem, at
least in Bhubaneswar. Of course it rains during the monsoons, but getting
wet is not lethal. The cool winters are what American tourists look for in
the Caribbean. The heat, from March through early June, requires simply a
different daily schedule: up at four thirty or five, like most Indians; retreat
and siesta from two to five; and then another period of activity. These are
the simplest of adjustments.

Unfortunately, the simplicity of such adjustments to climate is not
always apparent to resident Americans. Further, even among my colleagues
there has been great variation in the way they have envisaged real or
imagined health hazards. Some have flourished in the new environment.
Others have run the gamut from hepatitis to amebic and baccilic dysen-
taries, intestinal worms, appendicitis, and even a rabies scare. Though these
are all maladies that might afflict one almost anywhere, the absence of
reliable medical care in Bhubaneswar and in nearby Cuttack has reinforced
reasons for concern. The trip to Calcutta, where medical facilities are good
if one can pay for them, is either an all-night trip by train or, more recently,
an hour or two by the daily plane. It is a commonplace that there are many
hidden stresses associated with cultural transitions in which health often
has a projective expression. The hazards that are real enough require
caution. In coastal Orissa filaria, cholera, and leprosy are endemic. Inadequate sanitation by our standards and the abject misery everywhere
apparent in India shock most middle-class Americans. I would guess that
responses to this encounter range from illness through fear and anger and, in
some of the more extreme cases, to contempt and withdrawal. Fortunately
contempt and withdrawal have not been manifest in any of my American
colleagues; they have been only marginally evident, and then only briefly,
among their families. Most of us soon learn where our inadaptabilities lie in
the face of the unaccustomed circumstances. Misery and squalor, which

exist in our own society but less evidently, are the first lesson. It is hard to learn—but, as the Indians do, one accepts one's helplessness and lives with it without denying it. The pervasiveness of misery and one's helplessness in the face of it carries, of course, the risk of callous dehumanization. This is a very great risk anywhere in the world to which we affluent and privileged research workers are transplanted by all too easily available research funds.

I have mentioned families in the context of field work in India. Of the seven Americans who have worked in Bhubaneswar, two men and I were unmarried and therefore without such responsibilities and solaces. Three were newly married but childless, and one had two children. None of the three wives and one husband was professionally involved. To my regret, there has been no case of a professional husband-wife team.

For many years and in varied situations I have either observed or listened to discussions about study abroad. Clearly many variables are involved. The most significant ones seem to be the nature of the task and the degree of unfamiliarity with the society and culture, combined with the individual's expectations of himself and his host society. I suspect that persons engaged in macro-social problems experience realistically the least strain, even when they are highly task-oriented. Research that requires formalized quantitative materials and that can be pursued through access to the most westernized and usually urbanized levels of an unfamiliar society entails relatively light personal stress. Research inquiries demanding close and personal relationship to people in an unfamiliar context are the more taxing as the culture is strange and the research worker is task-oriented. Limiting my remarks to India, and given these very bland generalizations, the question of whether one is working as a young person, male or female, alone or with a family, acquires varying colorations. Let me attempt a series of dicta that certainly need study. A young unmarried male may find himself shut out from certain relationships in India where free roving bachelors can be suspected of less than honorable intentions. A young unmarried woman, *pari pasu,* may be suspect but, with skills that include language, I believe she is more easily able than a single man to acquire a wide range of intimate relationships. The young unmarried woman can rely on her status as an educated person, her privileged role as a foreigner, her helplessness, and her access to women. In my own experience I have never ceased to be astonished by the allowances and protective kindnesses extended to me.

A childless married couple in India seems to have particular advantages. In Orissa the wife who is content to serve her husband's domestic and professional interests rather than pursuing an independent course is likely to be the more admired. I do not generalize this statement beyond Orissa. In general, whether one or both of the couple are professionals, I suspect that all field situations strain recent or unequilibrated marriages.

In India when a married couple has children the assets and liabilities are multiplied. Very real conflicts arise between doing a research job and caring for the health and education of the children. But there is also no doubt that children may be a great help in establishing contacts. Whether children are assets or liabilities may depend on the nature of the research and how relaxed both parents are about the "new" environment. There seem to be no rules of thumb about families in the field. On the one hand, they may provide intimacy and mutual support that drain off the stress of adjustment. On the other hand, this mutual reinforcement may delay coming to grips with a new community, and domesticity may assume a disproportionate emphasis. In this experience—new to me—of dealing with a group of delightfully diverse colleagues in a joint enterprise, I was at first of the persuasion that a nonprofessional spouse should be encouraged to undertake a special and independent inquiry. In such an effort I have failed egregiously in three cases out of four. This does not for a moment imply that the three cases of failures to enlist spouses in adjunct inquiries have been failures in adjustment. All three couples, after the usual backing and filling, have made admirable adaptations to each other and to the community. I am now willing to concede that I was wrong in the first place and that an independent inquiry may simply have represented an additional stress.

I realize, as I review what I have written here, that my comments have been heavily weighted on the side of personal adjustments and human relationships. I have asked myself whether this is because, as I wrote, I merely got stuck in a groove or whether they are indeed one of the salient aspects of field work in India—at least as I have seen it. I believe the latter is the case. I believe the reasons for my preoccupation are that Indian society is so greatly diversified and Indians themselves are often the most subtly complex individuals it has ever been my pleasure to encounter. Patterns are not easily and quickly perceived. A research worker or a practitioner who does not exercise the greatest caution, reinforced by a sensitivity and an omnivorous curiosity about people, is likely to find exactly what he is looking for to begin with. To do anthropological field work in India requires a continuing willingness to immerse oneself in an infinitely varied series of life ways and not just to perpetrate a research project.

The longer I live the greater is my pleasure in, and my perception of, complexity; by the same token, the more acute has become my distrust of facile socio-cultural generalizations. I am indebted to my Indian friends and acquaintances for gratifying this bent. As I look back, I realize that inadvertently I have been directed to this personal and professional position by the sequences of my field experiences: the archival nature of ethnography in California, the vital but exotic primitive society of Alor, and finally this experience with the complex high culture of India.

On Ambivalence
and the Field

HAZEL HITSON WEIDMAN is professor of social anthropology and director of the Office of Transcultural Education and Research, Department of Psychiatry, at the University of Miami School of Medicine. Working at the interface of community and a variety of clinical settings, she has sought to transform unicultural approaches and perspectives to transcultural ones, thus improving the delivery of health services in a multiethnic environment. Her current activities include custom-designed cross-cultural training programs for agencies and corporations that are involved in international health.

In August 1958, as I was recuperating from serious illness in the field, Professor Cora Du Bois wrote to me in Burma as follows: "It does seem to be that you have had your share, and a bit more, of the traditional trial-by-ordeal, field experience. . . . I am sure you are discouraged, the bugs alone would assure that. The situations you have had to encounter would also depress one. I can think of no immediate way to cheer you although I am sure, as sure as one can be of anything, that the long-run satisfactions will be irreplaceable." She was right, of course. The long-run satisfactions of field work have been irreplaceable. I would not exchange this experience for any other in my life. Yet I have known for some time that this chapter must be written, and I have procrastinated. I have refused to come to terms with it until now, when time is growing short and a deadline for publication nears. I do not really know all the explanations for my delay, but I suspect that I know of one very basic reason: I believe it is because I am deeply ambivalent about Burma and my experience there. If this is so, then it would seem to be most important to communicate something about the sources of that ambivalence.

It does not begin with all the difficulties in the field, of course, but at the personal, emotional level. No matter how intellectual and objective we try to be; no matter how we try to rationalize our interest in studying other peoples in other places—our motivations for becoming professional anthropologists are not solely to contribute to a growing body of knowledge of man. They are, primarily, I am sure, to contribute to a growing knowledge of ourselves in a particular social context. True, we are genuinely curious. True, we are concerned about people and mankind as an abstraction. True, we must find an acceptable professional place in our own society. But true, also, participant observation in a setting very different from our own allows us in a sense to escape our own social system and the values that bind us. But we can never escape completely, for what we are and what we strive to

239

be is most meaningful in terms of the social system from which we emerged as human creatures with particular personalities. Many of us do not fully realize this fact, however, as we undertake our first field study in a distant land.

In my own case the particular dimensions of freedom that were problematical do not seem highly differentiated along the lines of religion or sex or aggression or authority, although my research did focus upon the direction in which aggression is expressed. For the most part the problem was a global one—which means, of course, alienation, estrangement, or, if you will, a problem of identity, as seems epitomized by my early fantasies about field work. I originally intended to work with one of the Baluch tribes in Southern Iran. The Baluch are a nomadic, herding people, whose men at one time wore long beards, dyed red, which, in my thoughts, always flowed with the wind as they galloped on horseback across that rugged, arid region called Baluchistan. Interestingly, in the predominant image I carried there were no dwellings, no groups of men, no women, no children. There was, in fact, a single rider; there was space; there was difficult terrain; and there was movement. I am sure this vision symbolized a freedom for which my own spirit was struggling. I had not yet discovered fully the ways in which one has freedom within his own cultural system. At that time, I suppose, freedom for me was against or in spite of a particular cultural tradition.

I did not go to Baluchistan. I was female and single. In such a highly sex-differentiated society my role would be restricted by gender primarily to the female sphere and restricted further by my unmarried status. I went to Burma, instead, a choice narrowed from a broader range of possibilities by a number of rather fortuitous circumstances but with a conscious consideration of greater flexibility in the female role in that country.

One of the factors in selecting Burma was related to the excellent Southeast Asian coverage in the graduate program at Harvard. From all the culture areas that might have met the requirement for geographical specialization, I chose Southeast Asia. Another factor in selection was the requirement of my research topic. It was necessary to study families in a country with a high homicide rate. Burma, which has one of the highest rates in the world, met this requirement nicely. Happily, Burma was located in Southeast Asia.

Another very personal factor in this choice was my close friendship with a number of Burmese students in the Boston area, and a rather special association with one in particular. We shared much together, and our relationship was probably deepened by common problems and pressures in the same graduate department, although our disciplines were not the same. The fact that each could throw a different light on areas of mutual interest undoubtedly enhanced even more the mutuality we experienced for a good two years prior to our respective departures for Burma, his several weeks before mine.

I think we both expected to share, as colleagues engaged in research in Burma, the kind of experiences we had shared during our graduate years. Even though we discussed the ways in which the social context would inevitably alter the character of our interpersonal exchange, we were not prepared for the depth and impact of the alterations that did occur. This must be included now as one of the sources of ambivalence about my field experience.

Other sources of ambivalence lay in different directions. My field work was not simply the fulfillment of a requirement for the doctorate in anthropology. It was not solely a means of escape or a way of learning more about the self. It was not just a convenient way of continuing a most important relationship that grew out of my graduate years. Most importantly, it represented one of the last hurdles to professional status. It required the consolidation of a body of knowledge and the utilization of the key method of a discipline in a creative way. It meant becoming an anthropologist—and anthropology, itself, represented the crystallization of an approach that, for me, provided the kind of meaning and significance that religion does for others. Becoming an anthropologist represented the culmination of many years of synthesizing and integrating cognitive and emotional elements into a unified psychological system that allowed me as a person to relate most meaningfully to others while being at ease with myself. In essence, anthropology helped me to establish an identity.

What I am trying to convey here is the extent of my involvement with anthropology and the nature of its origins in my past. As a child I had had some exposure to the concept of culture without realizing it. My father had great respect for other belief systems and ways of doing things. He talked from time to time of American Indians, the differences among various tribal groups, their religious beliefs and ways of life. In so doing he allowed me to understand something of the meaning of culture without ever using the term. Whether or not this talk fell on especially receptive ears I don't know. Perhaps my concerns were those of any adolescent. Somehow, however, I came to see beliefs as linked in certain ways and as related to the ways people behave. When I observed discrepancies between what people said they believed and what they actually did, I was puzzled and angry. I was especially outraged by the Christian teaching of the brotherhood of man in a community that prided itself on not allowing a Negro to remain overnight.

Later I was bitter about religion, not just because the discrepancies I observed were related to the prescriptions and proscriptions of Christianity. I was angry and disappointed, primarily, I believe, because religious explanations of the ultimate concerns of man and the nature of society did not satisfy me. Religion also failed to explain for me the pervasive pattern of disjuncture between belief and action that I seemed to observe in myself and in so many areas of life about me.

It was in my freshman year at Northwestern University that I discovered a more meaningful conceptual system for viewing the ways of man. Here were the intellectual tools that would allow me to make sense out of much that had troubled me before. I did not understand the process of enlightment in just these terms, of course; when I discovered anthropology in that first course with Professor Francis L. K. Hsu, my response was an incredulous realization that here was a whole discipline that "thought" as I did. The path was set. I changed my major from philosophy to anthropology and continued on this route through three degrees.

Field work was the final obstacle to the third one, the degree that would legitimize a basic orientation held from childhood and would professionalize an approach that I would have had difficulty avoiding under any circumstances. This was what lay behind my field experience, and this undoubtedly, is what sustained me through the most stressful periods of that endeavor.

With so much vested in it, I must have assumed, consciously or unconsciously, that field work would be fairly immediately and rather continuously gratifying on many different levels—cognitively, emotionally, personally, and professionally. Given such assumptions, my expectation must have been that field work would be experienced with a marvelous sense of mastery and professional growth. Actually, the promise held by field work was fulfilled, but not in the way I imagined. It was a struggle from beginning to end. Very little came off as planned, and the constant awareness of a great lack of control over my own research effort weighed heavily upon me.

I arrived in Burma in July 1957 and tried not to allow myself to be shocked by its impact upon me. Burma frequently had been described in the early literature as "The Golden Land," "The Happy Land," and "The Land of Laughter," and the Burmese I knew reflected such characteristics. But in 1957 Burma was neither golden nor happy. At that time Burma was in great distress and bordered on anarchy. Her independence from Britain was gained in 1948, and the years since had been turbulent ones. For almost a decade the dominant political party had been fighting Communists and struggling to suppress powerful insurgent forces. Banditry was rife. Refugees had flooded the urban centers. At one point rebels had gained control of the entire country except the capital city of Rangoon.

By the time I arrived, the principal political party and the Burmese army had gained the upper hand. They were still plagued, however, by myriad pockets of Communists, rebels, and bandits called "dacoits." Buses were frequently held up and their passengers robbed. The water main to Rangoon was dynamited for the eighteenth time during this period. Railroad tracks were periodically destroyed, and no night trains dared make their runs. In a population of twenty million people the crime rate was a staggering five murders a day and twelve kidnapings a week.

I tried to be objective in my appraisal of the situation as I wrote to family, friends, and mentors in the United States, but I found it very difficult to force myself to write at all. In my early letters I deliberately tried not to communicate some of the disillusionment I was experiencing; it was of such magnitude that I could not come to grips with it. In time, however, I was able to sort out some of my mixed feelings and to verbalize a marked ambivalence about the physical setting, general appearances, and Burmese behavior.

In September 1957, for example, I wrote to Dr. Daniel Funkenstein, of the Department of Psychiatry at the Harvard Medical School, as follows:

I think before the war [Rangoon] must have been one of the loveliest cities in Southeast Asia . . . for there are many hills, winding roads, and, in the middle of the monsoons, the most luxuriant vegetation I have seen yet. The foliage of the rain forests seems to be making a quiet but determined effort to remove every sign of urbanization from the delta of the Irrawaddy. Mildew from the dampness has darkened large areas of many handsome big buildings, office and residential. Paths are overgrown and moss forms in every shaded spot.

By the same token the village population in Burma seems to be making a more vociferous and more successful attempt to remove every trace of Westernization from the delta of the Irrawaddy. [Literally] thousands of villagers have moved into the city for protection from dacoits and insurgents, so that makeshift bamboo huts, shops, and bazaars line almost every street. To add the evidence of damage from the war [destroyed buildings and sidewalks in horrible repair] to the array of hutments and the throngs of merchants and food sellers with their merchandise spread out along every busy street, is to present the depressing picture of what needs to be done. And yet, golden pagodas rise from numerous lovely green hills in Rangoon and out across the countryside. Women wear brightly colored, flowered longyis [ankle-length skirts], with sweet-smelling flowers in their clean, well-cared-for hair, and men wear handsome checked and plaid longyis, many of which are handloomed and made from beautiful mercerized cotton that looks like silk. Every rickety old bus, with hard wooden seats and no springs at all, holds a vase within, filled with some lovely plant or flowering branch. And the ponies that literally prance along, pulling the ubiquitous, covered-wagon-type pony-cart taxis, are fitted out with bronze trappings and sweet-sounding bronze bells, which convey a lightheartedness to match the ready smiles of the Burmese, men, women, and children alike.

To Dr. Funkenstein and to others I commented further:

There is much here, you see, to learn about, and I have chafed under the lack of freedom to experience it as I would like. I say "lack of freedom" advisedly, for we literally cannot come and go or travel about as we please without thinking of all the dangers involved. Everywhere windows and doors are protected by iron grill-work, which is kept locked at all times, whether we are in or out, and though ours is not, fences are frequently topped with barbed wire. At first I had the feeling I was living in a state of siege, and while I still dislike living behind bars and locks, I now take it a bit more for granted.

Later I spoke more directly in a letter to Dr. William Caudill at the National Institute of Mental Health:

[Rangoon and Burma] are so full of contrasts and seeming contradictions that one ends up being ambivalent about the town and the country generally. Rangoon itself is a very dirty city, and yet it is well laid out in a lovely locale, with lakes and hills and many, many wonderful trees. People appear everywhere to be sitting by the hours, doing nothing, and on foot they move with slowness and lethargy, almost, but in automobiles everything in the road ahead is an obstacle and a challenge that must be met and overcome. The people themselves seem warm and wonderful, but many of their values are diametrically opposed to ours —and in the areas which hurt most when one hasn't a lifetime to spend here.

I do not remember what was troubling me at the moment of writing, but I suspect that it was the prolonged frustration I was experiencing in trying to locate a village in which to do my field work.

My research plans called for two major efforts: to study families of mental patients falling within depressive categories of illness on the one hand and within paranoid categories on the other; and to study family patterns and child-rearing practices generally in a village setting. The problem with which I was concerned was the direction in which aggression is habitually expressed, either inward upon the self or outward toward others.

There was no difficulty whatsoever in arranging for the hospital research. My Burmese friend from Harvard knew the superintendent, introduced me, and secured proper sanction for me to proceed. He also introduced me to numerous key officials at the university and in the ministries of health and social welfare by way of seeking entrée for me into an acceptable village in which to work. But here the response was quite different indeed. I was greatly puzzled, because everyone to whom I spoke appeared to be solicitous of my welfare; yet no one really did anything about helping me to move into a village. All seemed to be in a position to do so, but I was passed from person to person. Everyone was charming. Everyone said, "Yes, yes, of course we'll help you. Come back next week and meet So-and-so"—and nothing happened. Later I understood why, of course.

Single women simply did not live alone within the city, let alone outside of Rangoon, in a poor little farming village. Such behavior did not fit my role as a woman; it was not appropriate to my social status. As a friend of educators at the university, I was to be protected more than ever. I was sure to be kidnapped and held for ransom; taken as the wife of some rebel leader; even killed because I was a foreigner and supposedly a wealthy one, at that. It was only by overhearing a conversation in English that I discovered what I believe to be another very salient reason for the polite run-around I was getting. "Who is going to be responsible for her safety?" Who, indeed? No one was willing to take positive action. By doing so he would be blamed if something should happen to me, and everyone assumed that something would happen.

These most hospitable people were genuinely solicitous of my welfare, for they respected our mutual friend. His request for assistance, however, placed them in a most untenable position. How could they possibly accommodate him by helping me when that very help might jeopardize their own position if I should meet with disaster? By the same token, how could they show their concern for me by helping me into a situation that they perceived to be most dangerous? They were immobilized on these grounds alone. They were further inhibited by political and economic threats to their own well-being in the event I should fall victim to one or another of the possible dangers. What would be the consequences for them if they had been responsible for my entrance into the village? It is not surprising that I made no headway whatever on the village study. I had no alternative but to forego this part of the research plan for a while. Between various appointments with kindly but unhelpful people, I began working at the mental hospital. After some time I wrote to friends:

As for my work, I can't even say that it has gone slowly and surely. Rather, it has gone in fits and starts. . . . I . . . have concentrated on the part of the study having to do with families of mental patients and physiological measures of mental patients to gather information that is to be compared with some we obtained in the States on patients in different diagnostic categories. The hospital here is about ten miles out of Rangoon and, though terribly crowded, is in a nice setting. The British had released all the patients when the Japanese occupied Burma, and the Japanese used it as a headquarters of some sort. As a result about half the buildings were bombed out and haven't been rebuilt as yet. There are approximately 200 female patients on one side and 400 male patients on the other with no mixed or open wards. There are two women M.D.'s on one side, two men M.D.'s on the other, and two administrative M.D.'s. Not one has been trained in psychology, and there is no psychiatrist on the staff, although there are two being trained in England, and a World Health Organization psychiatrist is coming in June. Care is, of necessity, custodial, and the patients are kept in good physical condition in surroundings as clean as the crowded conditions allow. The doctors have been most kind to me and helpful to the extent they are able, so that I more or less have free run of the hospital. My greatest difficulty has been with diagnosis, because the diagnostic categories employed are not those of the international system developed after the war. Because of this I don't really know whether or not the patients with whom I am working are strictly comparable to those in the States and along the dimensions we are especially concerned about. I have spent a great deal of time at the hospital interviewing, through an interpreter, patients and members of families who have brought them for admission or who have come to visit, and, finally, we have taken physiological measures on one series. We shall have another ready by the first of January, I hope, and after that I shall be moving into a village for more intensive work on child-training practices—something that is absolutely necessary, danger or no.

I was beginning to feel quite desperate about locating a village. It was essential to my research design, and as my determination increased, so, I suspect, did my impatience with Burmese ways. This may well have been one of the contributing factors to a growing sense of alienation from my university companion. Because the disintegration of this relationship represents a significant degree of emotional trauma during field work, it might be well to discuss it briefly.

First, I think it important to stress that our expectations for mutuality and collaboration in Burma were most unrealistic. Although marriage was not a consideration, we did expect to operate at some midpoint between our respective cultural systems. While the social structures that might have allowed this relationship did exist, we were not part of them. My friend was attached to the university and all that this implies about a way of life in the Burmese social system. I was an independent researcher with few linkages into Burmese culture other than through Burmese friends and acquaintances. His future lay before him in Burma; mine lay elsewhere.

Whatever the forces in operation, the emotional support we provided each other in Cambridge gradually disappeared in Burma. The process of being involved in a dissolving relationship undoubtedly contributed to our respective "stress loads" but in different ways. Our reactions varied as well. I attempted to discuss the changing nature of our relationship. He countered with dismissal or efforts at reassurance. Knowing the Burmese as I do now, it would seem that my companion probably felt very *anadeh* toward me during this period. *Anadeh,* a Burmese term that cannot be translated into English, is applied in a situation in which one wishes to behave in a certain way or to say something but is prevented from doing so for one reason or another. Often the reasons involve knowing that the other person will be hurt or angry or embarrassed or disappointed by what would be said. Usually one feels *anadeh* toward someone for whom he cares and to whom he feels close. It is difficult for Westerners to understand such behavior, but it plays a central role in the Burmese patterning of interpersonal relationships.

It was during the middle period of this growing estrangement that I began to relate to a much greater degree to other Americans and Westerners, generally. When I arrived in Rangoon, I had made a conscious effort to reduce my contacts with non-Burmese; I was determined to become involved in Burmese life through Burmese people. I am sure this intention reflects, among other elements, the degree to which I felt secure in my Burmese contacts. Originally I had no doubts about smooth entrée into the Burmese system at whatever advantageous points were required for the purposes of my research. Only gradually did I become disillusioned in this respect. As my disillusionment increased, I began to enter more and more into the life of the community of technical advisors to Burma. I now consider it my greatest mistake upon arrival in Rangoon not to have done this sooner.

The community of foreign specialists with their national counterparts constitutes an intermediate social organization that can serve as a bridge between separate cultural systems. Useem has described this as the "third culture" (Useem, et al., 1963). Whatever one's attitude, it is much more efficient to work within a structure that already exists than to try to establish new linkages, which is essentially what I had been attempting without the sanction of a supporting authority structure.

I began to accept invitations that I had disregarded earlier. Casually one evening over cocktails with friends I mentioned my problem to the United Nations resident representative in Burma. He was from India, in a position extremely important to Burma. He had authority, and he was not afraid to use it. Suddenly doors opened. He introduced me to the district health officer as well as to the director of the government's demonstration health center twenty miles or so outside Rangoon. He talked with them about possible villages in which I might live. He personally accompanied me on visits to several of them. Transportation and an interpreter were provided when he was not free, and eventually our reconnaissance trips led us to the right village. I was introduced to the headman by people whom the villagers knew and trusted.

The village felt exactly right the moment I walked into it. It was all-Burmese, all-Buddhist. Typically, rice agriculture and vegetable gardening provided the economic base. It was within commuting distance of Rangoon, had about 100 houses and approximately 450 people—it was a size I could handle. It even had a house available for rental in the center of the village. It was well-constructed and had belonged to a former village headman. What more could I ask?

Actually there was a great deal more I could have asked. I had a village in which to work and permission from all the proper authorities to live there. I had rented a house, but in order to work efficiently I also needed a cook and an interpreter. This was something less than easy to accomplish. In order to simply chronicle the difficulties I had in this regard, let me briefly sketch some details of this dimension of field work.

It was asking a lot of the Burmese in such a time of turmoil to see me as anything but "odd" for wanting to live in a strange village without family or friends in the immediate vicinity. This view was no asset in finding appropriate help, but through an increasingly close relationship with an Anglo-Burmese woman of remarkable strength and ability, I did manage to recruit a little Burmese woman about sixty-five years old who was willing to cook for me. The elderly in Burma have considerable status, and presumably she felt she would be shown sufficient respect to go without fear of harm. She was a widow, spoke no English, and perhaps welcomed the opportunity to escape the closeness of living with relatives.

An interpreter was something else. It would have to be a well-educated woman: well-educated because such a person would speak English fluently; a woman because we would be living in the same one-room house—our only privacy during the day would be found behind a blanket hung from the rafters to separate us from all outdoors. Because Burma is an age-graded society, it had to be someone mature enough to be respected, yet someone whose age or status would not inhibit rapport by calling forth too much respect and distance from the villagers.

Many disappointing interviews taught me that it is precisely the well-educated who are most afraid of villages—they are the most vulnerable to robbery or kidnapping. It is above all the well-educated single woman who should be protected and kept close within the family. My task was almost impossible.

I decided to move into the village anyway. I would spend weekdays observing what I could, letting the villagers get used to my presence by observing me. Weekends would be devoted to the hospital and the disheartening search for an interpreter. There is nothing I could have done to have established rapport more quickly. I spoke very little Burmese, and only the schoolteacher in the village spoke a few words of English. I was literally placing myself in Burmese hands. By doing so, I let the villagers know that I trusted them, and they responded.

I was alone in the village for a month. I wore Burmese dress and ate Burmese food. I worked hard to learn the language and to communicate with those who chose to visit me. I let the villagers take the initiative. Soon I was going with them to outdoor plays across the fields in bullock carts, attending weddings in the neighboring villages, visiting pagodas on special Buddhist holidays. I was invited here and there about the village to see young women weaving at their looms, small children at play in the evening, food being prepared for special ceremonies, and anything else the villagers wanted me to know about their way of life. All the while I was wondering how much I was understanding correctly. How accurate were my interpretations of the kaleidoscopic impressions through which I moved?

With a feeling of urgency about the need for an interpreter, I decided to try the one girl I had found who wanted to gain such experience. She was a Karen, one of Burma's most antagonistic minority groups, and she was a Christian—both handicaps. She was too young, and her English was not good enough—greater handicaps. Had there been any other prospect, I would never have considered her. Under the circumstances, however, I thought that anyone would be better than no one. I could not have been more mistaken.

Though she was born and reared in Burma, she was so unaware of Burmese customs and beliefs that she offended the villagers in many ways. She promptly committed the greatest affront by pointing her feet toward the altar while sitting. This is simply not done. To the Burmese the feet are dirty, the head sacred, and nothing is more revered than the image of the Buddha seated upon every household altar. She was so involved with Christianity that she was reluctant to translate my questions about Buddhism. Instead, she took every opportunity to teach the villagers her beliefs. In many ways she indicated that she felt superior. She bragged about her house in town and spoke of what a hardship it was for me to live the way I was living in their village. In no time at all the villagers began to bridle. Fortunately they dissociated her behavior from mine, but the arrangement proved impossible. I knew I would have to let her go at the end of the week we had agreed upon as a trial period.

This unpleasant task was taken from my hands. Since I had an interview scheduled at the hospital one morning, we went into Rangoon the night before. When we returned the following day, the whole village was in a state of fear and shock: during the night the village headman had been kidnapped and carried off to be held for ransom; the defense guns had been taken; the village was without protection.

The police arrived at about the same time we did. They promptly ordered us back to Rangoon, thus providing me with a ready excuse to dismiss the interpreter. Several days later the headman escaped his captors and fled to a much larger, police-protected village. But it took a month before I could obtain clearance to return, and then only after signing a statement to the effect that no one was responsible for my safety; I returned at my own risk. The villagers were delighted, but my spirits sagged as I realized that my chances of finding an interpreter were greatly reduced by this unfortunate incident.

However, the impossible happened as a result of a chance meeting in the home of my very good Anglo-Burmese friend. She introduced me to a Chinese girl who represented the solution to my problem. She was Buddhist, twenty-six years old, born and reared in Burma, an English teacher at Rangoon Boys State High School, on vacation for the summer, and bored with nothing to do. She was eager to come and would be available for what at this point seemed a very long time. She would be with me for two months.

My few initial doubts about the villagers' acceptance of a Chinese person were soon dispelled. She was an excellent interpreter, quick and sure. She was intelligent, sensitive, and very well liked by everyone. We worked tirelessly for a month, into the hot dry season, when the heat became almost unbearable. Most of us in the village were covered with heat rash. Toward the end of the month the interpreter felt that she could not go on. Ringworm had appeared on her arm, and she felt ill. She reluctantly resigned, but when after a week I had had no success in locating another person, she volunteered to return. The rains would be coming soon. It would be cooler, and she thought she could better cope with village conditions then.

The rains did come. Except for pathways the village was one huge mud puddle. Two weeks later my interpreter had developed a profuse rash on her forehead, scabies on her legs, and an infected foot that suggested blood poisoning. We rushed her to the doctor in Rangoon, and that really was the end of her stay in the village.

Another two weeks were spent in relentless pursuit of every possible lead to "someone who might be interested." One of these possibilities was a fifty-three-year-old Sino-Burmese woman, formerly a Christian but at that time a Buddhist. I was in the process of trying her as an interpreter when I discovered that my cook was having bloody diarrhea. A trip to the demonstration health center for examination disclosed a chronic case of amebic dysentery. Since the organism is transmitted through food, it would not have been wise for her to continue in the capacity of cook until the long-term treatment had been successfully completed. There was no alternative but to return her to her family and to arrange for her treatment at home. My search began again, this time for another cook.

At the end of a two-week quest the British embassy referred an experienced cook of about fifty, and we returned to full-time work in the village. We had worked exactly one week when in the middle of the night I became acutely ill. By morning it was clear that I would have to be hospitalized. In some still hazy fashion the cook, the interpreter, and the villagers managed my removal. I was away an entire month, during which time at my request the still new interpreter tried to carry on by recording folk tales for me.

Within a week's time after my return I had to reprove her on several different occasions. She was, I discovered, a rather hysterical type, difficult to direct. She was impatient and even rude to guests at times. She was not translating everything that was said. After hearing and recording many tales about supernatural spirits and bewitchings, she had grown more fearful. She had begun to wear a charmed ring made from elephant's tail to ward off evil. She was terribly frightened of leeches and snakes, and our bare-legged trips through mud and water into the paddy fields were becoming too much for her. On our next trip to Rangoon for supplies, she refused to return.

The political crisis was reaching its peak at this time; the party in power had split into two factions, the struggle had become a struggle for power between the two opposed leaders. These alignments cut down through the entire social system to the village level. Loyal supporters of each were rallying around. People in every walk of life chose sides. Feeling ran high, and loyalties were so intense that the nation was setting itself up for civil war. Dock workers were rioting and attacking each other. Political assassinations increased markedly. Firing occurred frequently in the area surrounding the village. At one point all public transportation was stopped. The army formed a cordon around the city. All cars entering or leaving were searched for smuggled weapons and ammunition. The situation, in fact, became so explosive that the army, under General Ne Win, took over the administration of the country in October 1958.

We were reaching the crest of this political surge when I embarked once again upon my seemingly endless struggle to find the means whereby I might carry on the village research. Coincidentally, it was at this time that the wife of the superintendent of the mental hospital was kidnapped and brutally murdered in an area not too distant from our village. Women simply were not leaving their homes within the city limits. To move into a relatively isolated, completely unprotected village in rebel-infested territory was unthinkable.

This combination of events was almost disastrous to the village study.

To compound the problem, the new cook was growing more and more aggressive in her relationships with the villagers. She was roaming far and wide in a high-handed approach to procuring the best of everything to prepare for me. Her meals were excellent, but she was alienating the villagers in the process. Without an interpreter I was having trouble keeping her in line.

This time it took five long, desperate weeks to find that one person who was willing, despite the circumstances, to come along with us to the village. She was Burmese and Buddhist, thirty-five years old, divorced, with two children. She was trained as a government nutritionist and was experienced in working with country people. She had status in her own right, but she related easily to the villagers. There were no problems here. We worked hard and well together for the remainder of the study, despite the rifle-fire that sounded plainly in the distance almost nightly.

This chronicle of events indicates something about the kinds of problems an anthropologist is likely to face in many areas of the world today. They are related to the disorganization that comes with nationhood in the wake of colonial status. They reflect the underlying disorder and fear that accompany the loosening of social controls under certain kinds of disruptive social change. They suggest the kinds of expectations about field work that our new generation of anthropologists must have for a realistic appraisal of what field work entails.

This chronicle does not, however, convey anything of the sheer effort involved in maintaining the research endeavor under the conditions of my particular field experience. When good results depend to a large degree upon others (cook and interpreter in the village; physiologist, psychiatrist, and interpreter in the hospital study), a different kind of tension is involved from that experienced when anxieties focus upon questions of personal ability in the field. One is kept on edge, in a sense, trying to anticipate what the next interference with good, steady work might be. I was constantly aware that my project was perched precariously upon many unstable foundations and that it might topple at any moment. Great energy was expended in keeping the various components working well enough to produce results, but the feeling remained that I was rather like an inept juggler who wanted very much to juggle well without the wherewithal, either financial or emotional, to do it.

Insufficient funds coupled with the burden of personal loss from the distintegration of a significant relationship reduced my flexibility and maneuverability considerably. Until supplementary funds became available late in the field session, I had no margin of safety to cover exigencies, and exigencies marked the entire field experience. I managed for a while by sharing a house in Rangoon with a most congenial Fulbright teacher from Ohio and by selling a number of personal items, but my expenses were much higher than anticipated, and this was a constant source of worry and a great inconvenience to me. I was unable, for example, to have a car regularly at my disposal. Instead, I had to rent one on those days when others who were assisting me in the hospital study needed to be picked up and returned to their homes or offices. A cumbersome process at best, it was particularly so in the face of the public transportation facilities available into Rangoon and back again to the village—a portion of the trip on occasion being made by pony cart.

Emotional resources that under ordinary circumstances would have been accessible to meet the problems at hand were being dissipated in an effort to maintain sufficient stability to function at something approaching a normal, if not optimal level. To this day I do not know how such factors affected my observations. I was studying the expression of aggression. Since I was feeling hurt and angry and considerably put-upon by a situation that was not easily mastered, I suspect that my awareness of feeling tones was considerably heightened. This may have been fine for the major focus of the study, but in terms of balance and proportion and significance in the functioning of the total cultural configuration, there may have been lack of clarity or even distortion. All I can say is that I was acutely aware of the strength of my emotions in all of this and made a conscious effort to look for contradictory, exceptional, or opposite patterns from those I thought were operating generally. I feel that whatever I have described from my field experience accurately reflects patterns that I observed. Another investigator, with a different cognitive and perceptual organization, would undoubtedly be able to describe other facets of Burmese life more fully. This would not necessarily make either view inaccurate or unacceptable, however.

Of one thing I am certain. When I was in the village, with sufficient freedom from problems to be effective, work progressed nicely. Not only did I have little difficulty establishing rapport, I also had no trouble establishing a suitable role. I fell into one accidentally my first night in the village.

I had been invited by the village schoolteacher to come to his house at 7 P.M. for tea. I put on Burmese dress for the occasion and made a point of always wearing it in the village thereafter. I wore a long, flowered print longyi, Burmese thong slippers, a cotton bodice, and a nylon blouse with high collar, cap sleeves, and buttons down one side. This pleased everyone, as did my attempts to speak Burmese. There was much laughter as I put into use the few words that I knew well and tried to add others that were not yet entirely familiar to me. This was my only means of communication, for I was without an interpreter during the first month in the village.

Several women were waiting on the veranda of the teacher's house when he, a government-trained midwife, and I arrived. They urged me to sit on the mat placed for us, and there was a feeling of gaiety and excitement as I did so. We chatted as well as we could, the schoolteacher's few words of English now being added to provide a better basis upon which to build some common understandings.

At one point someone asked my name, and I replied, "Ma Hay zeh," the closest approximation I could make to the Burmese pronunciation of "Hazel." The Ma, of course, is an honorific title meaning "sister." When asked my Burmese name, I replied in Burmese that I had none. It was promptly decided that I should have one, since I was wearing Burmese dress, was learning to speak Burmese and was now a daughter of Burma. Some names were suggested, but not understanding at that moment that anything was expected of me, I said nothing. Later, during the conversation, someone said, "Shwe Mi," and silence followed. More to fill in than anything else, I remarked in Burmese, "Good, Good," and the members of the gathering hooted with delight. My name was fixed with the approval of all. From that moment I became Ma Shwe Mi, which means something like Golden Girl. What I did not realize at the time was that there is in Burma a very popular folk song about Ma Shwe Mi, who is unmarried, loves everyone equally well, and is a village benefactress.

I do not recall when I fully realized the appropriateness of this name for my role in the village. I know that I did not make any particular associations along this line during the early part of my stay. It was, in fact, the villagers who pointed out to me one night that there was such a song; so I am sure the association existed in their minds. One of the young men who had a pleasant voice was asked to sing it for me. Because he was too shy to do so in my presence, he went off into the darkness of the night and sang for me there. Even so I did not see my role in the village as being very closely connected with that of the Ma Shwe Mi in the song. Apparently I was still too much the "researcher" tied to a different reference group. I included this incident in my field notes but made no special comment about it. In retrospect, I think it was highly significant and helped to establish my village identity as benefactress.

My behavior certainly fell into line with this image. My house was constantly open to guests. Refreshments were always served. I let people stay to talk as long as they wished. I offered medications and vitamins when I saw their need. I frequently brought gifts of food to different families upon my return from trips into Rangoon. I was willing to speak to government officials on the villagers' behalf, and they often commented upon my lack of fear. Most importantly, I was interested. I wanted to know about them, and I expressed genuine concern for their welfare. After initial census data the questions I asked were appropriate to such a role. It seems only natural that

a benefactress would be interested in families and children and interpersonal relationships and village harmony and that she should be unafraid.

It took a while for such a role to be unquestioningly established, however, and it was not until my departure was imminent that I learned there
had been a competing one available for me at first. Prior to my departure, it
seems that I had truly become an adopted daughter of the village. My
presence was being explained in religious terms. I was told, for example,
that I had been Burmese in a previous existence. I had been well loved, and
that is why I came back to Burma in this existence. Furthermore, because
we got along so well together in this existence, we would all be together
again another time.

Because this was now the most meaningful explanation for my presence
in the village, some of my closest friends could tell me how I had been
perceived originally. I was a spy, of course, only they were unable to tell
whether I was a spy for the Burmese or the American government. They
finally decided that it must be for the Burmese government, but when, time
after time, my questions indicated that I was not primarily interested in
political matters generally, or political loyalties specifically, their view
gradually changed. The clues for interpreting my behavior were over-
whelmingly in different directions, and presumably the role of Ma Shwe Mi
was more in accord with all that their senses told them about my interests in
the village.

The role was perfectly acceptable to me, but it did have some disruptive
overtones that I would not have predicted. I fully intended that my role
should be a neutral one, for I wished to relate to persons of both sexes and
of all ages, but I did not intend that it should be quite so neutral insofar as
physical appearance was concerned. Rather drastic measures had been
taken in the cutting of my hair en route to Burma. I set out with a fairly
short but still feminine cut aboard a cargo liner which took twenty days to
reach Manila and two months to arrive in Malaya. Somewhere en route the
ship's barber agreed, at my request, to do what he could to remedy my
shaggy appearance, and I emerged with something very close to a man's
cut. Later, in Rangoon, further attempts to repair my appearance left me
with only a few feminine forelocks. "Never mind," I thought. "It will be
less trouble this way." But with my lean, angular appearance, it is not
surprising that the Burmese could not at first easily determine my gender.
To be female means, above all else, to have long, beautifully cared-for hair,
usually worn in a bun at the back and on top of the head for very special
occasions. When this key defining characteristic was lacking in one who
probably looked like a generalized "foreigner" anyway, people inevitably
asked others in Burmese when we met whether I was male or female.
Despite this glaring defect in hair style, my Burmese name and Burmese

dress helped to define me as female, I suppose. I also had several features the Burmese especially admire in the way of feminine beauty. One of these was light skin, of course; another was naturally arched eyebrows, which did not have to be drawn with eyebrow pencil. These were commented upon frequently. A third factor was a long nose, which the Burmese rather liked by way of contrast, if nothing more. In addition, I selected flowered longyis that appealed to their tastes, and I sat with propriety, as a modest, well-bred young woman should. I wore fragrant body lotion, lipstick, earrings which forever amused them because my ears were not pierced, and flowers in my hair whenever I could get them to stay in for any length of time. I was further supposedly very rich. Apparently these combined factors served to make me seem attractive as a woman, at least in the eyes of Burmese women, a number of whom expressed in various ways pronounced jealousy of their husbands' time with me. Such men generally related to me more directly and freely than they could to a Burmese woman under similar circumstances.

I do not know how the Burmese men viewed me as a woman. The adults talked easily with me on almost every subject and the young men of courting age liked to come and visit. They even prepared a dinner of chicken curry for me before I left. At one point I received a proposal of marriage, but this could hardly reflect a general view that I was desirable as a woman or as a wife. It came from the best con artist in the village, a young man who was incorrigibly lazy, who borrowed without repaying his debts, and who viewed himself as something of a great lover, with aspirations for higher status through any means available other than by diligence and hard work.

Since I related equally well to elders, married men, bachelors, and youths of courting age, I suspect that I was viewed very much as Ma Shwe Mi of the song would be viewed—perhaps as a mother figure; certainly as unapproachable sexually, but to be loved and respected otherwise.

I know that there was genuine concern for me as a person and for my safety. I saw this repeatedly in little ways in which support was shown me in the presence of visitors. It was brought home to me clearly and with force the night strangers in Western dress appeared on foot in the village just as the sun began to set. They asked for me, and an alarm sounded in the minds of everyone. No one comes as a stranger to a village on foot in the evening unless he is bent on some mischief.

My interpreter and I were visiting in a neighboring house when one of the young girls of courting age came running, trembling visibly, eyes wide with fear, and out of breath, to tell me that some men were asking for me. The assumption was, of course, that I was going to be kidnapped, and everyone responded with shock and an anguished, "Oh, no!"

The house I was visiting was that of one of the emotionally disturbed persons in the village. He was an old man with marked paranoid tendencies, who feared that others were trying to kill him and all of his sons. He lived with his wife and bachelor son, but despite his vulnerability in some respects, he promptly urged me to move from the veranda where we were sitting and to hide inside. My interpreter agreed that I should do so, and by this time I was sufficiently realistic in my appraisal of the dangers inherent in the Burma situation to acquiesce. At the same time, however, I asked our frightened little messenger to learn the names of these men and to return to tell me. She could not manage this in her fear and ran to her own house to hide. Some time later my cook brought a note addressed to my interpreter. It provided names and asked that we come to talk with the visitors. My interpreter recognized one of the names as being that of an acquaintance from the ministry of health, and we cautiously returned. She immediately recognized her former associate, and we began to relax as we learned that the party had had car trouble on the road. Since the men had heard that she was there with me in this village, they sent a message for help by someone on a bicycle while they came on foot to wait with us, their only personal contacts in the vicinity.

Afterward, in discussing this incident with the villagers, there was great relief and hilarity. Each person involved expressed the degree of his fear and recounted the tales he had told to throw these men off the track. Everyone tried to make them think we were no longer in the village, but their stories were so discrepant that our visitors immediately sensed the nature of their concern and persisted until we made our appearance. Actually they were as fearful of the dangers of being in a strange village after dusk as the villagers were for my safety and that of my interpreter. Under the circumstances these fears were realistic, but the point I wish to make here is the manner in which individuals in the village spontaneously acted on my behalf in the face of a perceived threat. I think that this, as much as anything else, will suggest something of the strength of the emotional ties that had developed during my stay in the village. I am sure that I was, on something more than a superficial level, one of them. In fact, as time passed, the villagers always referred to me in the presence of trusted visitors as "Our Shwe Mi."

Acceptance on a deep emotional level, then, must be one of the key elements in the "irreplaceable satisfactions of field work" of which Professor Cora Du Bois wrote in her letter to me. Such acceptance, however, cannot be experienced or described in isolation. It must be related, not only to its effects upon others, but also to its effects upon the self in the immediate situation and to the self in relation to a very different value system "at home." One implication of such acceptance was a degree of strain that my presence and some of my behavior placed upon the villagers, particularly upon those very close to me.

During the day my schedule was full as I went here and there about the village or into the fields. But during the evenings my home was open to anyone who wished to come to visit. After refreshing baths and dinner, we sat by lamplight on grass mats spread over the veranda to accommodate guests who invariably came to visit. The young came; the old came; they came individually or in groups of varying size and composition. We sat by the hour drinking a delightful smoke-flavored pale green tea. We enjoyed candy and nuts of varieties that were luxuries to the villagers, and we talked. We talked about animals, crops, and religion; politics and responsibility; supernatural spirits and former kings. We talked about the British, the second World War, the Japanese occupation, and independence. We talked of courtship and marriage and the training of children. In so doing, new understandings of Burmese culture fell into place. Some of my most important insights emerged from these evenings, and I think I could not have dispensed with them. They were much too enjoyable on the one hand, too informative on the other.

My generosity in offering refreshments, however, created something of a problem for the villagers. Only a very wealthy (and slightly mad) Burman would have continued this pattern over such a long period. Since I wished to provide food, the villagers felt free to accept it. According to Burmese standards of propriety, however, too frequent visiting and too hearty participation under such circumstances calls forth criticism from others. Those who do not show appropriate reserve are accused in gossip of coming only to eat. Some who came more often than others felt compelled to make clear to me in subtle ways that their visits were because they enjoyed the camaraderie. Others were reluctant to partake of refreshments but felt they would offend me if they did not. Again, in subtle ways, they let me understand this.

For some who had become very close to me as next-door neighbors, informants, and friends a different kind of conflict derived from this situation. These people had a slightly more realistic view of my wealth. They identified with me in this particular matter and felt that some of those who visited really were being somewhat greedy and taking advantage of my hospitality. These gatherings were, in fact, a strain on my budget. My friends sensed this, and they were resentful that the villagers did not show a little more restraint. Their very act of resentment, however, created feelings of guilt and anxiety. They felt that they would be punished in the next existence for wanting to withhold food from others; they would become *peiktas,* supernatural beings with huge bodies and enormous appetites and mouths so small that not even a single grain of crushed rice could enter easily. While this expectation was not an overpowering concern, it aroused sufficient anxiety to have to be dealt with through humor on occasion, in fleeting comment at other times, and eventually through quiet discussion with me.

I am sure that my presence and my behavior in the very fact of my acceptance by the villagers generated many other varieties of strain. These, I suspect, were comparable in some ways to the conflict I began to experience as I truly became more and more Burmese in my thinking and in my movement within the Burmese cultural tradition.

As my work progressed, it was very rewarding to see the patterns of Burmese life assume more definite form. I was somewhat pleased by the sureness with which I was beginning to handle interpersonal exchanges. I was relieved to see order emerging from the confusion of beliefs and behavior to which I had been exposed. I liked these Burmese people and thoroughly enjoyed becoming a member of their community. Slowly a growing feeling of belonging began to compensate for all the frustrations involved in getting settled there.

When my role was established, my acceptance a matter of fact, I began to experience life more fully in Burmese terms. As I was freed from coping with superficial details of interpersonal relationships, I became more sensitive to nuances in communication. Surprisingly, I began to find it increasingly difficult to know what people really meant in certain contexts. For the most part face-to-face relationships in Burma were wonderfully relaxed and delightful experiences. There was much warmth and every suggestion of frankness, sincerity, and support. There was never any suggestion of anger or deception. Repeatedly, however, I found individual positions shifting with circumstance. A person would say one thing in one situation, something else in another. Occasionally he would indicate that a different meaning attached to an earlier statement from the meaning that had been understood. Each time this happened, I found myself wondering if I had misheard on a previous occasion. I began to be quite concerned about the accuracy of my observations. It was not until I better understood the status hierarchy and conceptions of power and authority that I felt more secure that I was, indeed, observing accurately. When I found myself predicting to a degree what people would say on certain subjects in particular situations, I knew that I understood some of the basic ingredients of the Burmese world view. Positions really shifted with circumstance. People did say things which could have one meaning attached in one situation and a different meaning in another setting. They might well have implied both meanings simultaneously. In the light of Burmese assumptions about the nature of man and the world in general, it would have been foolhardy to do otherwise. Granting the assumptions made, there was need for such defensive maneuvering.

What I learned about their world view, essentially, is that there are a great many unpredictable elements in their universe. Although man, nature, and the supernatural have the capacity for both good and evil, the potential for harm from each is so great that one must be constantly on guard against everything from slight hurt to total destruction. In the face of so many unknowns, a great deal of attention and energy must go into the warding-off process. As long as highly unpredictable forces of evil can be thwarted, there is the possibility of good, and there are ways of achieving it. Avoidance and manipulation, for example, are two important means to whatever sense of mastery can be achieved or the degree of control that can be acquired in such a system.

Precautionary measures against harm may be taken in the form of propitiation of various sorts. Aside from this, however, the first rule of self-protection in a threatening universe is simply to avoid offending other beings, whether they be human or other than human. When harm does threaten in a particular situation, it is only sensible to change one's loyalties, one's words, or one's stance as necessary to deflect the danger. As one succeeds in holding off a threatening universe, he is free to manipulate himself in ways that will call forth gifts and rewards from those in more secure positions. The more skilled one is in gaining the support and protection of such persons, the more secure he himself becomes and the more his own status rises. Because one's sense of worth is frequently gained at the expense of others, however, part of the excitement of the game of interpersonal relationships is to put others down while appearing not to offend. This gambit requires, of course, that one be mindful of the disguised intent of others to achieve similar small victories.

This world view seems to produce a great deal of social and verbal ambiguity. Defensive measures require it, but ambivalence is its counterpart. When a person's remarks, for example, may just as easily imply criticism as commendation, there can be no meaningful response until something tips the balance of intention in one direction or another. Energy must be constantly engaged to seek clarifying clues. There is a silent questioning, a continual watchfulness, a frequent testing. Often nothing convincingly decides the issue, and there is vacillation as first one interpretation is made, and then its opposite. A major consequence seems to be a prolonged state of tension, associated with an inability to further organize one's feelings and an immobility in responding to specific words or actions. Part of the danger in organizing the emotions, in fact, may be the degree of affect that is held in uneasy abeyance and that might burst forth in the form of an angry attack. A world view of this sort seems to require a potential for aggressive response despite the social patterns designed to vitiate its need.

Under such circumstances it seems important to find relief from enduring anxieties, and the Burmese have devised many ways of doing this. I was consciously aware of relief from just this sort of tension during some of our livelier evening sessions of joking and laughter. Other ways include the ubiquitous outdoor plays of the Burmese, their games, and their music. Had I stayed longer, I am sure I would have learned more about tension release and anxiety-reducing mechanisms in the Burmese way of life. These have significance especially for the lighter, gayer side of Burmese personality. There are, I am sure, many social forces operating to support the kind of buoyancy that makes it a pleasure to be with Burmese individuals despite the underlying forces I have described.

If those forces do exist, however, and this is the way the system, in fact, works, then those who are accepted as participants in it are compelled to function to some extent in the same manner. It would be impossible to maintain position and respect otherwise.

When I became aware of the double-edged way the Burmese have of relating, I began to meet this challenge by responding in fairly typical Burmese fashion in some respects. To maintain self-esteem, for example, I became much less trusting. I quietly developed an invisible chip on the shoulder and watched carefully to see that no one succeeded in knocking it off. These events did not occur in sequence, of course. In the very process of becoming aware, my own behavior was changing imperceptibly to meet the requirements of the system. This change was perfectly appropriate in context, but when I viewed the Burmese system itself and some of my behavior in it from the vantage point of my own values, I was troubled.

The Burmese world view was not congenial to me. The one I carried with me from a very different way of life was that man has a considerably greater degree of mastery over his own fate than the Burmese assume. I was not happy in the premise that one's fellow man is quite so unpredictable and quite so capable of harm. I disliked having to question motives and to guess at the forces that directed behavior. I was not happy with the knowledge that interpersonal relationships were so very pleasant because they were based ultimately upon a fear of offending. It was not reassuring to know that offense, whether intentional or not, would be met sooner or later with retaliation and that it could take many forms. In brief, from a strictly personal point of view I was not especially proud of what was involved in playing the Burmese game well. I did not like the rules themselves, and I liked even less what they required of me.

In essence, what I have been saying here is that emotional acceptance in the field is basic to the anthropologist's method of participant observation. When the emphasis is upon participation, it provides the means whereby he not only observes some of the subtleties in interpersonal relationships, but experiences them as well. In that very experiencing his own personality is changed somewhat. This is so because to genuinely participate in another cultural system and to relate freely within it means, to a degree, to make the same kinds of assumptions others do, to organize the emotions in a similar fashion, to perceive the world as they do, and to maintain self-esteem at the same points and along the same dimensions they do. This is not a facile process, whereby one uses the self as a surgical instrument to probe for knowledge and then withdraws, to all intents and purposes unchanged by the experience. To some extent it involves alterations in the very structure of the ego.

To be an observer as well involves something more. The intellect may be disengaged more easily than the emotions. For purposes of analysis, one can and must move back and forth as a matter of course, analyzing one's own behavior in the context of two separate social systems. When these two systems are diametrically opposed in some of their most fundamental assumptions, then there may be a sense of conflict about a self, whose major commitment is to one system but in the context of field work is increasingly involved in a very different one.

In the final analysis, my Burmese experience was a powerful source of both satisfaction and frustration, which left me with opposing feelings. I have found it just as difficult to marshal my feelings about the Burmese themselves. How are the spontaneity and pleasures of interpersonal relationships to be reconciled with the deliberate manipulation and basic distrust? To which does one primarily respond? If I could say that the people are wonderful but that it is their value system that disturbs me, I would be more comfortable in my feelings about both. But values are built into personality and motivate behavior, and the ambivalence remains. I can still accept positively only part of my experience in Burma and with the Burmese.

A question remains. If my field experience was so traumatic emotionally, so difficult financially, so constantly thwarting in terms of getting into and maintaining myself in the research setting, so full of conflict at the cognitive level, and so wearing physically, why do I agree with Cora Du Bois that the long run satisfactions of field work are irreplaceable? One reason is that I got through it and accomplished the major part of the study I had planned. Another is that some of the ties I established within the village, and within that technical and diplomatic community I shunned originally, have remained important and rewarding ones. Most importantly, however, that field experience revealed to me, in a way nothing else could, something vital about the relationship of the individual to society and the meaning of culture at the gut level.

The barriers to entering a new cultural system head on are just as formidable as if they were made of bricks and mortar. By grappling with what at first is an unyielding structure and by gradually becoming able to move easily within it, I learned more about the freedom of the individual within culture than I could have otherwise. Because I was also an observer, however, and not just a participant, I could place the meaning of this system alongside the meaning of my own, and I could see a major conflict. By the same token I could include these two kinds of systems among all others to achieve a perspective that, by its very range and depth, allowed me to tolerate with greater equanimity the pressures upon me to conform within my own cultural tradition. Furthermore—and perhaps this is the most salient point of all—I had a much firmer basis for continuing to explore various dimensions of relationships between individuals and societies, belief systems and behavior, interests that have been with me a good long while and shall probably remain with me always.

Reference

USEEM, JOHN, JOHN D. DONAGHUE, and RUTH HILL USEEM. 1963.–"Men in the Middle of the Third Culture," *Human Organization,* 22, 169–179.

Field Work in Five Cultures

ANN FISCHER held the position of professor in the department of anthropology and in the school of medicine at Tulane University. She was codirector of the research project "Family Survey of Metropolitan New Orleans." She wrote a number of papers on Negro family structure as well as on the various cultures in which she did field work. Ann Fischer died in 1971.

Field experience in Truk, in Ponape, in Japan, in New England, and among the Houma Indians provides a rather diverse view of what it means professionally and personally to be a woman in the field. This cultural variation was accompanied by variation in living conditions both within and among cultures. In order to clarify the points that follow, it is necessary to begin with a description of the field work situations. This will be followed by a more detailed consideration of the interplay of culture, living conditions, and being a woman in field work.

Truk, in Micronesia, provided my first field experience. At the time (1949) I had just been married. The field work made it necessary to go alone to the island of Romonum in the Truk Lagoon, while my husband remained at administration headquarters. Romonum was a ten-mile boat trip distant, over what could be very rough water. Except for occasional weekend trips to the base at Moen to visit my husband and some rare junkets with Romonum people to the nearby large island of Tol, I stayed on Romonum for three months. My husband came to Romonum two or three times during those months, and occasionally administrative personnel passed by on official visits. At the end of three months I returned to Moen to stay permanently with my husband in the village of Mwän. The relative isolation on Romonum had aided in acquiring some language ability. We lived in Mwän by the sea with a Trukese couple in a house next to the village meeting hall, somewhat removed from the homes of the Trukese of the village.

During my stay in Mwän I was pregnant. This condition was very useful in terms of my field work—the subject of which was the Trukese mother—since the physiological experience of pregnancy was explained and commented upon by the Trukese about me. The physiological process also brought to mind many questions that I might not otherwise have thought to ask. My husband and I were given much advice about how we should behave under the circumstances.

267

Toward the end of my pregnancy, after eleven months on Truk, we moved to Ponape, about 350 air miles away. In our first year there, my first daughter was born in the small naval hospital in the American colony of Kolonia. We lived in a beautiful, if rather remote, setting, on an agricultural station built by the Japanese. There were myriads of tropical plants and a romantic natural pool and waterfall in which a few of the sacred eels of Ponape swam, along with Ponapeans and Americans not afraid to join them.

After the birth of my daughter we employed two Trukese women to help in the house, and one of these lived in. At home we all spoke Trukese, since my husband held the theory that two languages at one time confuse an infant. I went to work—at first parttime, later fulltime—teaching English to Ponapeans and other students representing the seven islands and seven languages of the Ponape district.

Socially, I often joined my husband in attending feasts held in the various districts of Ponape, as well as participating in the active life of the American colony. Numerous Trukese and Ponapean visitors to our home furnished a rather steady supply of informants.

Although I was able to do some testing in the school setting on Ponape, my only field work, in a remote district, came at the end of our three-year stay on that island. I took my (by then) two young daughters with me to the village of Nan Uh. My husband visited us on weekends, when he was not confined to the base and to the administrative duties of the government offices, and in the last week of a six-week stay in Nan Uh he remained in the field with us. A Ponapean couple and a single Trukese woman lived in the house with us. The house was located next to the district office, a situation very favorable for observation. We left Ponape at the termination of this field work to return to the United States to complete our graduate studies.

My third field work experience, in New England, was quite different from those in Oceania, but not unlike one in Japan that came much later. Our children were of pre-school age. Our house in this New England village was centrally located next to a church. It had a large yard with ample play equipment to attract neighborhood children—the subjects of our study. We lived for a year (1954–1955) in the village and became a semi-detached part of the community. The situation was uncomfortable but very fruitful for a woman gathering field data. I believe it was a much better situation for me than for my husband for a number of reasons to be discussed below.

My fourth field work experience was in a very deprived community of mixed French-Indians in southern Louisiana (summer of 1960). The Houma Indians were my particular field project, and my husband had no plan to study them at all. I rented a house halfway between two settlements of Houma, and in the beginning of the summer's work my husband and children joined me there. As time went by, my family grew quite bored with the situation, as well as physically uncomfortable; we therefore compromised by having my husband return to our home in New Orleans with the children. I would spend four days a week with the Houma, returning to New Orleans for the weekend to type up field notes. My contact with the Houma has been extended if intermittent: even before going to live with them, I had made several field visits to various Houma communities with public-health nurses, and since my stay I have continued to visit them as well as to see some of the people occasionally as visitors to my home in New Orleans.

Our last field work experience was organized by my husband. In this trip to Japan I served as an associate investigator with him. We lived in a Japanese city in a fairly comfortable house outfitted with some American amenities. Our children went by army bus to an American school about ten miles from our home. The closest Americans, with whom I had some contact, were the families of army officers and a Fulbright professor who lived a short walk over a small mountain as well as the American diplomatic community. Since I did not speak Japanese other than sufficiently to get around the city alone, my conversational opportunities were very limited. Yet by the time of this field experience I had become accustomed to living in remote and foreign places. The rich cultural life of Japan was so completely enthralling that I find myself looking back on that year as one of the pleasantest of my anthropological career. I can't attribute this strictly to the fascinating culture, for I think my own development as a field worker had much to do with it.

It is easy to see that these field situations were not very comparable, yet I believe it is possible to use them as a basis for generalizations about women in the field. Though others would certainly not have responded to the field work exactly as I have, perhaps I am representative enough to feel that there may be fundamental reasons why women will react in certain common ways to this kind of experience.

When they enter anthropology in graduate school, I wonder how many women actually think about what it will mean to work in the field. I don't believe I did. For one thing, as a student in college at the time the country was just emerging from the Depression, it was difficult to imagine that money for field work would become available in such quantities as it actually did after the second World War. As was the case with many of my fellow students at that time, my exposure to anthropology had been slight as an undergraduate, and such exposure as it was was in a department of sociology. I did have the good fortune to have Loren Eiseley as a professor, and I was attracted to anthropology as a result of a course in physical anthropology that he conducted at the University of Kansas. I thought of myself in the future as digging up bones and artifacts and, failing an opportunity for this, envisioned a safe harbor in some United States urban area, studying a group of immigrants and taking advantage of my sociology background. Had I realized that the possibility existed of going off alone to the ends of the earth to accomplish my goals, I can't say for sure whether or not I would ever have become an anthropologist.

Some courageous women make field work into a grand game of adventure into new places, and they feel none of the insecurity that a journey into an unknown culture brings out in me, but by and large I think women have many more qualms than do men about leaving their own setting. With a husband, a companion, or a field team the anxieties attending field work tend to be diminished—a touch of home remains. I believe that this generalization applies most strongly to young women who, in the normal course of events in American culture, would be at the stage of raising their families. It is not usual to have an opportunity to have a family in the field, and in this respect my own experience is exceptional. Anthropologists' wives who are not themselves anthropologists often do this, but women anthropologists generally do not. The responsibility for a large drop-out rate for women in anthropology rests perhaps on this one problem. Actually, it is probably easier to keep both family and career viable in many field situations than it is in the United States. For me things fell into place, and I believe they would for others if the profession were willing to accept building a family as the natural course of events and to support women who wish to try it.

I'd like to discuss now an aspect of field work that appears to affect men differently from women and to weave into the discussion my own various experiences in different cultures to illustrate the factors influencing this differential response. In actuality, it is not one single response, but a number of initial reactions to living in another culture that go under the name of "culture shock." Symptoms include depression and concomitant inhibition of activities, rejection of members of the culture studied as beyond the pale in certain respects, and paranoid feelings that one is being cheated, plotted against, or laughed at contemptuously. Even the best of field workers experience it—often to a marked degree.[1]

One might ask whether cultural shock is necessarily a bad thing in relation to field work. Bateson was responsible for calling to my attention that the first few frames in a movie often gave away the main theme. These beginnings take you away from whatever else you may have been thinking about and plunge you immediately into the happenings on screen. Anthro-

1. Malinowski's experience of "culture shock" is documented in his diary and beautifully commented upon by Clifford Geertz, "Under the Mosquito Net," *New York Review of Books,* 9 (4), Sept. 14, 1967, pp. 12–13.

pologists may in a sense be overprepared for entering a culture. Perhaps a certain amount of shock is necessary for good field work. On the other hand, if the tension becomes too great, the field worker is apt to withdraw whenever possible, both physically and psychologically.

At a recent (1967) meeting of the Southern Anthropological Society the difference in the responses of men and women to foreign cultures was brought home to me. Dobyns noted at this meeting that all of the studies of cultural shock discussed at the meeting were studies about women. It seems reasonable that women might feel more cultural shock than do men. The matter of preferring to stay in a familiar environment, as was discussed earlier, plays some part. Another element that creates a good deal of trauma for women abroad is a necessarily great change in ordinary habits when moving into a different culture. American training in housewifery is by and large nonadaptive in the field. Trying to maintain too many standards of excellence in this area of life causes problems. It is possible that there is unwillingness on the part of most peoples to provide women with household service, for since women are the prime tenders of the house in most cultures, people have difficulty comprehending the ignorance of the woman field worker in this matter. Only if this ignorance is thoroughly demonstrated will native women come to the aid of a woman in performing typical feminine chores; I did not know many women who were able to get assistance in cooking in either Oceania or Japan. Most anthropologists can accept, as I was able to, native foods and native sanitation practices. Over a long period of time, however, one misses American food. Men are not expected to cook for themselves in many places, and perhaps they are more tolerant of what is offered them. I was able to have good American-style food on occasion by persistence in teaching cooking to those who helped me and by persistence in avoiding cooking chores myself. In Japan women who worked in our house all began by saying that they could not possibly cook for us, but after a short period of my trying to cook while using them as assistants and their firsthand observation of my ignorance of how to cook in Japan, they almost eagerly disposed of my services. Household tasks can take up so much time—as indeed they do for women in most parts of the world—that little other work is possible in the field if these chores are performed by the anthropologist.

There was variation in both the amount and cause of cultural shock in my various field work experience. Shock was greatest in Truk. Even so, although the physical type was different, before I could understand the language there was a certain feeling of *déjà vu*. The women's character types seemed familiar; there was a "debutante," a "busy housewife," and so on. It was nevertheless difficult to be set down alone in a culture so different from my own and to be unable to make my wishes known with words. This was my first field experience, and I had paranoid reactions as the result of conditions of extreme lack of communication with other humans, even though the Trukese smiled and assisted me in a friendly manner.

The least amount of cultural shock in my field-work experience was in Japan. Once an appropriate entrance is made to the Japanese social system, much opportunity for shock disappears. The formalized process of introduction and escorting of a stranger in new undertakings in Japan is a shock absorber. One knows in advance that proper introduction means that one will be accepted and will receive polite treatment. Again, however, men may be more familiar with the process of moving into new territory, and perhaps they pave the way for themselves more carefully than do women.

The most serious trauma in Japan comes from what American women tend to view as the unfavorable status of Japanese women. This status has been steadily changing since the war, and in any case American women are treated as Japanese expect American women wish to be treated, which softens the blow to the feminine ego considerably. However, the tacit assumption remains that women are inferior to men and, furthermore, that the behavior of American women (partly due to their failure to understand this) is infinitely inferior to that of Japanese women.

It is surprising to learn that field work in one's own culture can be as traumatic for a woman, if not more so, than field work in a foreign culture. This finding, a result of field work in Orchard Town led me to consider more carefully the meaning of cultural shock and to wonder if there isn't more to this phenomenon than can be accounted for simply by being set down in a strange culture. Everyone is familiar with the initial loneliness in a new community that engulfs the American housewife whose husband's employment has necessitated frequent transfers, and this feeling is certainly part of the problem in field work. In the case of the housewife, however, she knows rather exactly how her social life will eventually work out; the field worker does not.

Field technique includes many devices that tend to shorten the period during which one feels at sea and a total stranger. Nevertheless, even with the use of every conceivable method of entering the community quickly, it took six months of living in Orchard Town before I could begin to feel at home there. I suspect that my husband had an even more difficult time than I did, as was certainly never the case in any other of our common field work ventures. I believe that one reason for the difficulty in New England was that the role of participant-observer is very easily equated with some rather unpleasant feminine roles in American culture, such as "busybody." Men are much more ridiculed in the role of busybody than are women, of whom it is more readily expected. In a foreign culture a participant-observer can play the pleasanter role of the "naive child," but not so in American culture. Sociologists have gotten around this problem by taking refuge in the methodology of questionnaire-type instruments; in their situation it is not the field worker but the instrument that becomes too personal. I realized in work in my own culture that fear of offending sensibilities and frustrating the desires of people for privacy had caused me to project American culture onto my other field work experiences and that, as a result, perhaps I was sometimes too timid in pursuing information. The more formalized and less personal the material being gathered, the weaker this feeling of prying becomes.

The feeling of being an intruder into the private lives of one's subjects is greatest in American culture and least in Truk. In Truk living is in the open, and people wander in and out of homesteads during the day. Romonum is such a small island that territoriality has to be kept at a minimum. Trukese hate to be alone and are always happy to have someone with whom to pass the time of day. Americans are completely unthreatening in the area of privacy with which Trukese are particularly concerned. Trukese do not like for the neighbors to know how much food or material possessions they may have hidden away, for then the neighbors are likely to ask for a share or to borrow something. The Trukese who doesn't wish to fulfill the request will deny the possession of hidden things. An American request will readily be filled, with the prospect in mind that a return in greater quantity or quality will soon be made.

Response to the field worker among the Houma Indians was fairly typical of American Indians—a strong suspicion that the overt friendliness of the anthropologist was intended to win their trust, whereupon they would be betrayed. My being a woman lessened their suspicion. It was difficult even for the Houma to imagine that a woman would be acting as a spy to gather information and use it to prosecute would-be medical practitioners or to get control of signatures to dupe the people of their little remaining title to land. Such stories did nevertheless circulate, particularly in factions and families opposed to those who had been friendly to the anthropologist. I am sure that the stories would have been taken much more seriously had I been a man. In some cultures the opposite would doubtless be true; perhaps the situation depends upon the sex of the powerful and the sorcerers in a culture.

The formality in Japanese culture almost eliminates the possibility of feeling an intruder. But the Japanese are also quite ready to examine their own internal life and to report it, perhaps because of their tradition of meditation, poetry writing, and the like. In Japanese movies the verbal reporting at the graveside of a loved relative is a common scene. The wish to know the interior structure of things is well understood in Japan; it goes far beyond the rather cold scientific approach of Americans to introspection. A pattern is an artistic experience as well as a science.

In view of this natural tendency of women to feel something of an intruder outside of her own milieu, the problem of finding an appropriate role in the field is more complex than for a man. Without a respected and useful role the field work grows most tiring. In some cultures the anthropologist is interesting to the informants because a woman in such a situation is rather a curious phenomenon. The curiosity sometimes, but not always, revolves around the sex role. Japanese men sometimes seemed to like to question me about matters about which Japanese women are not likely to be very knowledgeable. I had a very extended visit from a veterinarian who was interested in how much I knew about automobiles (which is only a very limited amount, in fact). He told me that he would be completely unable to discuss this subject with his wife. Some Japanese men think that the spiritual aspects of life in which Japanese women tend to involve themselves are rather silly and decadent. It is sometimes difficult to know whether they actually secretly admire this spirituality but assert their masculinity by belittling it to some extent. Especially during and following adolescence women become experts in one of the fine arts of Japan. Later on, the woman adds an aesthetic overtone even to the practical affairs of the household. American women, in contrast, tend more to expect the atmosphere to follow from the performance of certain duties, and this approach seems more congruent with the Japanese male character. This circumstance may be why American women seem so domineering to the Japanese.

Among the many factors that make it more difficult to create an acceptable feminine role in another culture is the frequent presence of American colonies in most parts of the world. A man may "go native" abroad—and Americans consider it to be appropriate, if not admirable, behavior—but this is not true for women. It matters little what the woman's actual behavior may be in the field, in many situations rumors of her behavior will be readily circulated among both natives and Americans, for she is a most legitimate target of gossip for both groups. There are only a few acceptable roles of American women in this situation; one is "missionary" and another is "schoolteacher." A more modern one is probably "Peace Corpswoman." This latter role, however, is subject, I am sure, to the same sort of problems that the American woman anthropologist confronts in relation to the more conservative Americans living in these communities. Often one has to be concerned, not only with what the informants think of the anthropologist, but also what the other Americans think of her. As anthropologist or Peace Corpsman, one can become an antagonist speaking for the people and against American ways all too easily. It is not a graceful role, even from the point of view of the people being studied or helped (a Peace Corps function). Americans expect American women to uphold American standards within limits. Women in any role who challenged the standards excessively in the Trust Territory were asked to leave if they didn't leave voluntarily after private behavior became public knowledge. Discretion is extremely important when an American standard is broken, and one quickly discovers that there is no protection from either Americans or natives.

One of the reasons for the concern with the behavior of women in the field is that some American authority is often responsible for her safety. The thought is not only that the woman needs protection in terms of possible sexual assault, but also that she is more likely to be attacked in other ways and to be taken advantage of because she is a woman. I believe that women are more vulnerable than men to various problems of self-protection both in terms of their property and their interaction with people. My university has had both male and female graduate students in the field in Colombia, but the same faculty who considered sending a male graduate student a gun to protect himself from marauders on one occasion felt it wiser for a female student to leave the field rather than take a chance on her safety. In this instance she had received a threatening note warning that she would be killed if she did not turn over a certain amount of money in a certain manner. However, she felt that adequate precautions were taken for her safety following this incident, and she wished to remain in the field.

Not only is the protection of women a major concern to American authorities; it is also often important to the people being studied to protect the field worker. One should be certain how far the protection extends, however, before taking a chance on it. Of course the need for protection varies in content from one culture to another; sometimes the important aspect is physical safety, but more often it is protection from physical discomfort, gossip, or psychological isolation. In addition, the presence of a woman may put her hosts in particular jeopardy, and the hosts may take extensive measures to protect themselves.

For example, on Truk the possibility of uncontrolled sexual activity raised a threat to the whole community, and the chief of Mwän village went to some lengths to protect his village from the incursions of American sailors by erecting barriers and guard posts to prevent their entrance into the village. If an American man were injured in a quarrel with a Trukese man over a woman, the chief knew full well that much hard feeling would have resulted. Women do not have this problem because they are not considered sexually threatening to the community. Women do fight over men in Ponape, however—I knew a woman whose ear had been bitten off by the jealous wife of her lover. But usually the concern regarding women is to protect their safety. The Trukese took steps to avoid unpleasant incidents in my case: a woman accompanied me wherever I went. More than once

Trukese men proved to be interested in peeping into American homes at the American base, and on occasions they were rewarded with a jail term for their troubles. It is not possible to impose this sort of punitive reprisal on an anthropologist, and good rapport demands the avoidance of incidents wherever possible.

One of the best protections against sexual incidents can be the lack of knowledge on the part of the woman foreigner of how courtship roles are played in the culture. In Truk, and in Ponape where rape is a virtually nonexistent offense, cooperation must accompany involvement in a sexual problem. The men of this area of Oceania take a certain pride in knowing how to approach women and what responses to expect, and most of them would not risk initiating or continuing a relationship when the proper roles are not played. Although a few sexual incidents did occur between American women and Micronesians, considering the number of people in both groups who were in close association, they were extremely rare. One Trukese of long acquaintance did ask me once, when he was drunk, as to how an American woman might be approached for romantic purposes. Since he was drunk and clearly intending to practice his acquired knowledge on me, I was evasive and managed to escape the situation without hurting his feelings. Even in this case there was no apparent intention of offending me. I think the paramount motive was the hope that some new secrets might be added to his rather extensive love-making accomplishments, for which he was well-known. No doubt he hoped that I might succumb to his charms as did most Trukese women, according to his and others' reports. A great deal of his rather high status centered on these activities. Even though sex is considered to be a battle to be won or lost in Truk, I believe in this case the triumph would have been over his fellow Trukese. There seemed no intent to seriously lower my status.

Though ignorance may at times shield the woman field worker, knowledge is ultimately the best protection, for the various cues to romantic entanglements are different from place to place and take some time to learn. It can be a handicap if one unknowingly gives cues that are incorrectly interpreted.

Concern about sex is certainly a major feature motivating attempts to protect women in the field, but some of the efforts of the Trukese to protect me arose out of their belief in ghosts. The fear that I might be attacked by ghosts was a major concern, even though Americans were said to be immune from such attacks. There was also concern that I might be mistaken for a ghost if I wandered alone into remote villages on the larger islands, where my presence was not expected. At great inconvenience to themselves the Trukese accompanied me wherever I went—if they knew I was going. Once or twice in Mwän village, when my husband was away on a field trip and the Trukese couple who were living with us were slower than I to return from the Base movies, the wise chief seemed to be aware of the situation and stationed himself at a seemly distance to guard the house, coughing occasionally in order not to frighten me and to let me know that he was there.

Truk, Ponape, and Houma cultures emphasized sexual activities enough in daily life to make the anthropologist realize that sex had to be considered in relation to rapport in the community. The Houma live in tight-knit small communities, where gossip about sexual affairs is apt to be more prominent than in larger, more impersonal groups. I was made aware of the problem early in my visits to them. I spent the night at the missionary's home, trying to map out the locations of the various families in the community and listening to his stories about the character of the people. His wife was ill and had gone to bed. Suddenly the missionary got up from his chair, went to the open window, and shouted out a warning to an eavesdropper outside. He then told me that the Houma would assume that the two of us were involved in a sexual intrigue. When my husband was not with me in the Houma community, I felt rather self-conscious about his absence. If I came to the community alone or with a lawyer involved in the problem of school integration for the Houma, I would always go to the home of my closest Indian friend, and she quite willingly accompanied us on visits to other Indians. Nevertheless, it always seemed a mystery to the Houma that a married woman might travel about without her husband, and although no one ever told me so directly, there were dark hints that something might be going on that shouldn't be. After my activities aided in the school integration of the Houma, this feeling that the Houma were not accepting me at face value was somewhat ameliorated. Because my success in this area was immediately known throughout the community, it seemed to clarify and explain my presence to a great extent.

These three cultures—Truk, Ponape, and Houma—have no age limits beyond which an individual may freely carry on activities without having his motives suspected of being sexual. Under these circumstances it is quite a problem to avoid becoming an object of ridiculing gossip if one wishes to move about freely to visit informants.

Protection of my physical well-being and correcting my errors in social interaction were a concern of the Trukese even before I was able to communicate with them. The family among whom I lived on Romonum managed to produce twenty cents to pay the storekeeper when he complained to them that I had misunderstood and underpaid. They made no attempt to explain the situation to me, although they had a long-drawn-out discussion among themselves. When my husband arrived on a visit, I recalled the incident, and he was able to find out about it. Twenty cents was almost half a day's wages in Truk at that time.

On another occasion, when I refused a request by the most powerful man on the island for the cigarettes I had bought as a gift for my host, he simply waited until I had bestowed the gift and then retrieved it directly from the recipient. In this case both my host and I were offended, but my host knew that the better part of wisdom was to give in on the matter. At that time both money and American cigarettes were scarce, and most Trukese had to take to the less desirable alternative of rolling their own cigarettes from home-grown tobacco. Had I been an American man in this situation, I doubt that the incident would have occurred; it represents a case in which people are less worried about how a woman will react to them.

When I discovered that the Trukese would protect me as they would a child in many situations, I sometimes managed to get my own way in what even at the time seemed a rather petulant and childish fashion; at times, though I understood what was going on, I might pretend not to do so if it served my purposes well. Looking back I am ashamed of such behavior.

In New England, also, I found people who were interested in both my own and my project's welfare. The community was somewhat isolated from cultural activities, and our study there stirred intellectual interests in some members of the community. Most women with children were interested in the project, although some of them may have had reservations about participating as informants. I found support from the women of the town who were bound together through a series of organizations that served, among other things, to protect the women from the psychological isolation created by the nuclear family and to promote the good of the community as a whole. There was nothing comparable for my husband, other than the volunteer fire department. The men of the community tended to drive the long distance into the city each weekday, and they had little time or inclination for extensive village social organization. In the women's groups the leadership tended to be remarkably supportive of the anthropologist and her field work, just as they would support the socialization of any new woman into the community. They paved the way for my entrance into many homes and for observation and interview situations. The men of the community showed more disinterest or skepticism about the study, and they certainly never very actively supported it. Women in most communities are accustomed to giving service and can more readily give some sorts of help to a woman than to a man. In addition, the nature of the study—child training—tended to be of less importance to the men of the community.

One of the most insightful aspects of being a woman in the field is the stimulus she offers for comments on what should be her appropriate role in life. Usually people comment on what shocks them most about the field worker's behavior. This reaction might be called counter-cultural shock. Comments are usually directed rather impersonally toward the "Americanness" of the behavior. Women in other cultures often mention envying the life of an American woman, and the Japanese and Trukese women feel that American men treat women better than their own men do, giving this as a reason women wish to intermarry. Japanese men interpret the high rate of intermarriage differently; they feel it to be due to the highly attractive character of Japanese women who, they feel, are irresistible to American men with the misfortune of having lived with domineering American mothers or wives. Trukese comment on the lack of wife-beating among Americans and the more permanent nature of our marriages. Such comments cannot be taken as indicative of any belief in the superiority of American life in these respects, however. Further investigation reveals that on Truk wife-beating indicates affection as well as anger. And in Japan both sexes pride themselves on the subservience of wife to husband. The field worker can easily fall victim to criticizing something an informant has himself criticized concerning feminine life in his country, only to find that in reality the informant doesn't agree.

It is difficult for the American woman field worker to adopt a womanly role in a culture in which women are subservient to men. This problem is accentuated if there is no academic tradition that allows a scholarly role for women. Professional women are not shrinking violets in their own societies, and they are not apt to become so just because the expectation exists in some other culture. Most professional women have been in conflict about the professional role at other points in their lives; carrying out field work in places where women's status is low may serve to renew the conflict. It is very difficult not to disapprove of what seems virtual martyrdom on the part of women in these cultures. The best adjustment the field worker can make is to admire the beauty of these role performances, thus encouraging others to instruct her in how to perform them, but the natural reaction tends to be in the other direction—to try to get the informant to confess that she really detests such a state of affairs. Questions along this line are often not quite comprehended.

In some instances a single woman may find this kind of culture easier to work in than does a married woman. On Truk my absent husband was endlessly pitied by women in their conversations with me. There was no understanding whatsoever that my scholarly commitment might have temporary priority over my husband's needs. On the other hand, a single woman over seventeen would be considered quite an oddity, and the Trukese might feel impelled to right matters in that respect. When my widowed mother-in-law visited Ponape, there were many laments for, and lack of understanding of, her probably permanent unmarried state.

Most of these comments appear intended to force the woman into the role the Trukese feel is appropriate for her. They were quick to mention to my husband that life must be much better for him when I stayed properly at home and tended to his housekeeping chores. And when he would visit me, they would say to him, "Oh, you are really hard up with this state of affairs, aren't you?" Small wonder that at the first opportunity I assumed my proper Trukese position at the side of my husband—who, contrarily, didn't quite approve of my lack of bravery in not staying alone longer in the field. On the other hand, it was assumed to be quite natural for a man to leave for another island and return to his family only when he felt like doing so.

It can be seen that in a culture such as Truk it is difficult to develop a role that is sufficiently conforming to make life comfortable as a field worker. Early in the field a woman can take the role of a child as mentioned above; this is more suited to her than it would be for a man. Later she must become a mother, sister, or dear friend—useful roles in living as a partic-ipant-observer, but not particularly productive in obtaining field work information of the extended interview type over a long period.

The role of a woman is different in the cultures I have studied, and I would like to attempt to make some comparisions in terms of these roles and how they influenced the field work experience. In all cases, however, the generalization holds that a field worker has one strike against her in trying to fit into a community when she enters it alone; this is due to the almost universal feature of women's role—to stay close to home.

A woman on Truk is supposed to be a modest, unassuming servant to her husband and parents as a young adult and a fair arbiter of quarrels and a dispenser of food and work loads as an older mother. Thinking is an activity relegated to men, for women are considered empty-headed and un-able to understand much more than those tasks they have learned to per-form. Early in life girls are taught service tasks, and they learn to behave properly toward superiors; with this skill and knowledge firmly implanted, they are considered more or less ready to face whatever may come.

In spite of these strong behavioral expectations for women, however, the Trukese are quite flexible about the kinds of people they can accept or endure, because, for one thing, living and surviving on small islands demands it, and, for another, they have had immense experience with for-eigners who have ruled them—Spanish, Germans, Japanese and Americans. Sex roles in Truk are fairly sacred, although perhaps less so than in our own society. When sex roles are not properly performed, no very serious sanc-tions are invoked. Wife-beating for acting above the status of a woman, or slight, rather amused ridicule for those few women described as "just like a man" (which includes indulging in such activities as climbing coconut trees or pounding breadfruit) are about the extent of it. Because of this "give" in Trukese culture, women can function there as successful field workers.

My own role developed on Romonum around my introduction as a person who needed to learn language and who would be studying the mothers and children and Trukese culture in the same way that Tom Gladwin, Ward Goodenough, G. P. Murdock, Frank LeBar and Isidore Dyen had done previously. I was brought to Romonum by my husband and Tom Gladwin, who made all the arrangements for my living there. It was clear from the beginning that my role had an institutional charter in the persons of these two American men, who would be concerned if I were treated badly.

The Trukese may have had a few doubts about how their commission to care for my welfare should be carried out, but, if so, they were not apparent. Trukese greatly pride themselves on proper behavior. They began by assigning me to a language instructor—a man, since girls were thought to be far too foolish and giggly to do the job. (There were many comments throughout my stay on my unusual—for a woman—intelligence.) A young girl was supposed to cook my meals and accompany me whenever I stepped from my hut. An older woman supervised this girl's behavior and criticized her loudly when necessary. At this early stage in my work I was a person to be cared for and protected, partly because I was a friend of Mr. Tom's—a long-time resident of Romonum and Truk—but also because I represented the ruling power. Today it is reported that the Trukese are no longer so concerned about American power, which they know to have been superseded by the power of the United Nations. But at that time, I am sure, they treated me as they did partially because of some presumed influence of mine with the powers in effect and partially because of my control of valued trade items. I was a task for them that, if performed well, would bring a little money, valued gifts, and influence at headquarters when needed. There was, to be sure, some sentimental attachment to anthropologists who had preceded me, and thus I was treated not only in a politic fashion, but also with warmth.

My language instructor—an authority on how to teach Trukese to anthropologists, having done so for those who preceded me—also attempted to direct many of my activities during the early part of my stay. If I had allowed him to dominate the work, I believe that my field experience would have been quite different. Instead, I persistently sought out the women, who were my subjects of study. The only men who ever offered information to me were members of the family in which I lived, the teacher, the chief, and my language instructor; otherwise men tended to avoid me. When I visited their homes, a boy or a man would often climb a tree and provide me with a drinking coconut; then I would be left to the women, unless I happened to contribute to the discomfort of a man, which I did on at least one occasion. A man with a headache managed to disrupt my observation period of his wife and infant child by moaning and complaining constantly to his wife. I couldn't speak Trukese at the time, but finally I learned that he wanted an aspirin from me.

There was a marked contrast between the treatment of myself and my husband. When he visited me, my chair (the only one on the island) would be pre-empted for his use, and an informant would squat by his side, spending hours answering his questions. Formal arrangements would quickly be made to demonstrate for him some aspect of Trukese life in which he had expressed an interest. As a result, if our field notes are compared, my husband's record the more formal aspects of culture in exactitude, while mine tend to be a running account of what was happening in the village or in the homes in which I observed. This difference held in most of the cultures in which we did field work together, although in New England I was in a better position to obtain formal interviews than was my husband. The difference in our language ability in Truk could not totally account for the discrepancy, since even after I learned Trukese well, our field notes continued to differ considerably. Our access to data was different in every culture we studied, and although our interests and personalities may have contributed to some of these differences, our sex roles were also a most important element.

My experience in Ponape differed somewhat from that on Truk because of some subtle differences in the Ponapean feminine role. Women do not appear to be so subservient to men on Ponape as they do on Truk. As in the United States, a Ponape woman's status tends to derive from that of her husband; the wife of a higher-status husband will be treated with more dignity than the wife of a man of lower status. During my time in the field in Ponape, because my husband was second in command in the American administration of the island, I was treated with respect in all of my interaction with people, but I felt less free to wander about informally, as I had done on Truk. Ponapeans are industrious people, and their island has rather difficult terrain to exploit, even though food and fish are more plentiful than in Truk. In the settlement where I stayed, long walks up the mountain were a frequent necessity, as were all-day fishing trips. If I came unannounced, a woman might feel the need to curtail her food-getting activities while I was there, even if I protested that I wanted her to go about her business as usual so that I might observe the work. I therefore had to show more care in making appointments at times convenient for my visits. Once a well-meaning acquaintance invited me to go along on a fishing trip in which much of the village participated. Because I was completely incapable of carrying the big nets and running barefoot through the water on the rough coral, the villagers laughed and made jokes about my ineptitude, but they were also angry about the fish I allowed to escape from the ring of nets. As a sop to my hurt feelings, I was given a small boy's job of tending the boat that followed along, but it was soon apparent that I wasn't even able to do that job well. It was easier, given these circumstances, to avoid visiting and simply take advantage of the steady stream of visitors who stopped by while passing on the main road in front of my house. Such pot luck in selecting informants was not always the most satisfactory method of field work.

So long as I was the highest representative of the American colony present in my Ponapean district, I lived the life of Riley. Songs were made up in my honor, and people regularly came in to tell me what a pleasure it was to have me staying in the neighborhood. I began to feel overly important, with all of the attendant pleasures, only to have my ego vigorously deflated when the district administrator and his wife arrived for a visit. Even bigger feasts than had been given me were prepared at this time, and the name of the "Distad's" wife quickly substituted for mine in *my* song, while I was all but forgotten. The next day, of course, I was again sought out. When other Americans visited me, little attention was paid to them. My husband's visits brought forth more invitations to the "kava hour" in the local chief's house than was the case when I was alone in the field. The older people and some higher officials in the village saved their attentions for my husband, but the younger people, even those of high rank, were willing to talk to me at length. My husband's better command of the language and the lack of English among the elders were partially responsible for this situation. On Ponape men sought me out often and many of my extended conversations were with men. Again, this cannot be attributed to my sex, but to the status I had through my husband and as a schoolteacher. I also have the impression that Ponapean women are more impatient than Ponapean men and prefer to be actively engaged in work rather than visiting—in contrast to Trukese women. Men and women interact and cooperate in work more regularly on Ponape than on Truk.

For me, the role of a woman was more enjoyable on Ponape than on Truk because of the greater equality in the relationships between men and women, the devotion of the women to active lives, and the respect that seemed to adhere to many of them in the culture. The Ponapeans treated me as something of a powerful person in my own right, as did the Houma Indians; in Japan and Truk I was treated as an adjunct to my husband. Actually, my power was virtually nonexistent in Ponape, but in any case power often rests on myth. By accident I happened to become a central figure in Ponapean intrigue that turned out tragically. I received credit for having influenced events in which I actually had no part at all. The incident illustrates the exaggerated power the people in the field thought I had.

In a house near my field station lived one of the higher-ranking titled men in the district. He had a young niece, who was visited surreptitiously one night by a Trukese who was in love with her. The titled man disapproved of this courtship because Trukese are immigrants and therefore of low status on Ponape. Some of his relatives pursued the young man, who had hidden in my house on the advice of the Trukese who worked for me. All of this was unknown to me at the time, but in the middle of the night a cigarette tip burning close to the screen next to my bed awakened me, and I called to the couple sleeping in the other room to find out who was standing just outside my house smoking within inches of my face. They were very slow to move (since they knew who it was but did not wish to tell me) and the intruder escaped into the night. Through the next hour or so I could hear a good deal of movement both within and without the house. The Trukese suitor left my house in the early morning hours before dawn and received a serious beating by a gang of young relatives of the offended uncle.

On the following day a high official came to explain the incident to me and to tell me who had been standing outside my window. The guilty boy, a former student of mine, was arrested by the police through no doings of mine. Following this, his family forced him to come to apologize to me, but since I did not press charges, he was released. Weeks later, the other young man, the would-be Trukese suitor, was found drowned in a stream only a few inches deep. The official whose niece was involved was held to be responsible for his death and was to be tried for the beating his relatives had given the Trukese boy, but the trial was delayed for some time. The people of my district said that the reason for the delay was that my name was involved and that the Americans did not want my name brought up in court. Actually, Americans found the, to them, strange court cases of the Micronesians more amusing than anything else, since they were totally outside the system. No one would have cared in the slightest even if it had been necessary for me to testify. The outcome of this whole sorry event was that the district official, the girl's uncle, went insane and committed suicide while being held in jail for the murder of the boy.

The people of the district were apparently very concerned with the effect this might have on my opinion of them and, through me, what my husband and other Americans might think. I received many apologies and a few gifts to appease what they thought would be my anger. I could never obtain a satisfactory answer from them as to why they thought I should be so concerned with this affront. I am sure, however, that one barely conscious reason was the sexual intent with which most Ponapean men enter houses at night. It may be that the peeping boy deliberately awakened me with his cigarette to make me aware of the situation and to cause me to expel the Trukese boy from my house, thus making it possible for the gang to attack him. The Trukese inside my house, on the other hand, feared this possibility and concealed the whole incident from me until morning, when the boy was gone. Other members of the community not involved in the incident considered it a rather mad affair. Whatever the case, all sides misinterpreted both my reaction to the incident and what I would have done at the time had I known what was going on. They also overestimated my influence on the later events. Had I been a man, I believe the gang would never have approached the house at all but might have sent a representative to complain about the refugee. Under such circumstances the matter would have been more openly discussed, and the subsequent murder might not have occurred.

In New England the complications in my role did not grow out of any lack of fit of the anthropologist's role with the larger culture, for though there were no other anthropologists in the town, and only a few women with professional training of any kind, the people were able to place me in some kind of role system through their knowledge of the general culture. In some ways I fitted all too well into the general pattern of women's roles in Orchard Town, and this caused some difficulties in the field work itself. In many respects the community wanted to accept our family on the same basis as any other family, but in some special way we were set apart as people who had not chosen Orchard Town as a place to live permanently. Our familiar roles within the community made it impossible for the people to avoid us as they would door-to-door salesman, for example, or even a public-opinion interviewer whose questions could be answered or refused as one chose. We had to be treated as neighbors as well as investigators—a difficult combination. Neighbors may gossip, but investigators may not. Informants had to be certain which role we were playing at any given moment, and there was a constant shifting back and forth, since neighbors have quite different rights and privileges than do investigators.

Not only my informants, but I myself, found my role confusing in New England. It seemed natural to replace the friends I had left in Cambridge with women from Orchard Town. This created a role conflict for me, for one does not generally "investigate" friends or use them as informants. The informal friendships that women develop in American communities were enticing; they offered me an excellent source of data, which was not available to my husband, but on the other hand, this use of friendship seemed inappropriate. Both I and my friends and informants found our relationships shifting rapidly back and forth between these two sets of roles, but I was never quite able to overcome the resulting strain. Many of the women recognized my problem and tried different solutions to reduce the strain. Individual women tended to prefer one or the other of the role sets—friendship or informant—and tried to keep the relationship organized accordingly. One of my best informants was very creative in the way she handled the situation. As long as I remained in Orchard Town, she considered it both interesting and useful to serve as an informant, but she seldom stepped over into the role of friend. After I left Orchard Town, she shifted into the role of friend, and we have continued to correspond over the years—my study of Orchard Town serving as the basis for our continuing interest and friendship.

This conflict—friend or informant—does not occur in such intensive form in a foreign culture. I have found friends in all of the cultures I have studied, but they have been fewer across language and cultural barriers. Such friendships with foreigners leave deep ties in the field, but the meaning of the tie is almost nonverbalizable. Much of the content of these friendships is in the realm of a feeling of kinship, for the shared experiences have a large degree of difference in interpretation for the two people concerned; an understanding of each other's lives can never be attained to the extent this occurs in friendships within one's own culture.

The Houma Indians are primarily French-speaking; only a small number of the young people were really at home in the English language in 1960. Yet they are a part of American culture and were even acquainted to some extent with Tulane University. By and large they accepted me as a professor, a role they understood as a kind of glorified teacher. I believe that I served them as a means of contact with the mainstream of American life more fully because I was a woman. First, as I mentioned earlier, it was easier for them to trust me; and second it is the role of the women of the group generally to act as intermediators with the general culture. The Houma are shrimp fisherman and trappers; the isolated life entailed by these occupations means that the women and girls are most likely to be the ones to speak English and to contact English-speaking entrepreneurs of all sorts. In most of the homes I visited, the women acted as informants for me. Even when I went with male lawyers to their homes, it was chiefly the women who gave information needed for legal purposes. When men talked to me, my limited knowledge of Louisiana French usually led to the necessity of a woman's repeating in English parts of what the men said; only occasionally would the situation be reversed. One of the interesting features of work among the Houma was the numerous occasions when both husband and wife together talked to me. I have not ordinarily found this to be the situation in other cultures. These pairs have some economic meaning to the Houma—the women sometimes accompany the men on shrimping expeditions. There is a closeness between husband and wife that at times makes them appear almost to have one ego. One of my best Houma friends—a woman—died in Charity Hospital in New Orleans not long after I had spent the summer among these people. I visited her in the hospital many times a week during her terminal illness and found only her children present. Her husband was unable to face her loss, and she insisted that he stay on the bayou so that the sorrow of parting would not be unbearable for either of them. These people found it difficult to understand my presence in the field without my husband; they thought my husband must be very lonely. However, there was none of the Trukese feeling that my husband might be having difficulty without someone to perform wifely chores. Houma men are quite able to fix for themselves the irregularly scheduled meals of seafood and rice.

In Japan my contacts with informants were in large measure in my own home and on social occasions. My husband had a number of paid and volunteer aides in his work, and I kept a running account of what happened in interviews, which he translated. On my own I served as a teacher of English to many Japanese who called at my house to request such service. This instruction was done on an exchange basis—information for language instruction. The two functions of the lessons were easily combined, although perhaps neither was done as efficiently as might otherwise have been the case. By and large the students intended to pay me with money, but all agreed to serve as informants instead. The Japanese assumed that I would be able to spend time in this fashion and were more likely to request instruction from me than from my husband. The classes, however, were often conducted jointly with my husband.

Japanese culture is much more adapted to study by formal methodology than are the others in which I have worked. I was not admitted to the informal life as a woman, as I had been in other cultures. Perhaps it would have been otherwise had I had more language skill, but I doubt it.

The Japanese understood my professional role rather well. In any case, they have some knowledge of an American woman's role, and they allow American women to attend functions to which their own wives might not be invited. This does fit the pattern of the office girl in Japan, who might attend a cherry-blossom-viewing party as an employee of a firm.

I was never entertained alone in Japan, but always in the company of my husband. When we were entertained in Japanese homes, the housewife might act strictly as a proper Japanese wife—serving but not joining the group in conversation unless spoken to—or the party might be planned by the husband for the specific purpose of allowing us to meet his wife and see his home life, and in such a case the wife would be an integral part of the group interaction. I believe that there was some interest in us as a couple on the part of Japanese women, since there is a growing demand in Japan for feminine equality with men, and women enjoy seeing what American husband-wife relationships are like.

My own role in Japan would have been different had I been single, I think. A young girl with a master's degree in anthropology visited us for a few days, and the Japanese professors at the university arranged for her to be escorted and cared for during her stay in the city. Though she spoke Japanese quite well, she was never allowed to venture about on her own.

In conclusion, I think that some generalizations about women in the field can be summarized from these varying experiences:

1. A woman in any culture will be treated differently depending upon her own social arrangements—whether she is single or has a husband and/or children. In any event, avoiding gossip about supposed or real sexual incidents can be very important, especially for women, in maintaining good rapport. Regardless of her social arrangements, there will be some efforts on the part of the community to let her know what proper feminine behavior should be in her case and to press her, albeit gently, into the proper behavioral mold. In terms of field work, this effort can be both aid and handicap.

2. A woman is less feared and is taken less seriously than a man in most cultures. Sometimes this is an advantage and sometimes a disadvantage, depending upon the aims of the field project.

3. An American woman anthropologist will in general experience more cultural shock in the field situations than will a man, but she is more likely to be protected by the people being studied than is a man.

4. A satisfying role in field work is often difficult for a woman to develop, partly because of the lack of professionalization of women in other parts of the world, and partly because of the difficulty in delegating usually feminine chores to others in the field.

5. There is no one way that a woman will be accepted in all cultures. On the other hand, in every culture a woman is approached differently and has access to slightly different kinds of information than does a man. However, the kinds of information she has access to are not uniform across cultures.

References

FISCHER, ANN. 1957. *The Role of the Trukese Mother and Its Effect on Child Training.* Cambridge, Mass.: Harvard University Ph.D. thesis. Also 1952, Trust Territory of the Pacific Islands, Truk, Caroline Islands (mimeographed).

———. 1965. "History and Current Status of the Houma Indians," *Midcontinent American Studies Journal,* Special Issue: "The Indian Today," 6, 149–163.

———. 1966. "Flexibility in an Expressive Institution: Sumo," *Southwestern Journal of Anthropology,* 22, 31–42.

———. 1968. "Reproduction in Truk," *Ethnology,* 2, 526–540.

FISCHER, JOHN L. with the assistance of ANN FISCHER. 1957. *The Eastern*

Carolines. New Haven, Conn.: The Pacific Science Board, National Academy of Sciences, National Research Council in Association with Human Relations Area Files.

FISCHER, JOHN L., and ANN FISCHER. 1963. "The New Englanders of Orchard Town U.S.A." In Beatrice Whiting, ed., *Six Cultures, Studies of Child Rearing.* New York: Wiley. Republished, 1966, as *The New Englanders of Orchard Town U.S.A.,* Six Cultures Series, Vol. V. New York: Wiley.

————. 1964. Chapters and material on New England. In Leigh Minturn Triandis and William Lambert, eds., *Mothers of Six Cultures.* New York: Wiley.

Field Work in Pacific Islands, 1925–1967

MARGARET MEAD was president of the American Anthropological
Association, the Society for Applied Anthropology, and the World Federation for Mental Health. She received countless awards and honorary degrees, and her contributions to the field of anthropology are too numerous
to list here. Her books, especially COMING OF AGE IN SAMOA, GROWING
UP IN NEW GUINEA, and MALE AND FEMALE, have been widely accepted
by professional anthropologists and also by a more general reading public.
She was curator emeritus of ethnology at the American Museum of Natural
History and adjunct professor of anthropology at Columbia University.
Margaret Mead died on November 17, 1978.

A rea and period are two of the significant conditions that must be taken into account even in discussing what would appear to be such a universal as the sex of the field worker. I will be writing here from experience in Pacific island cultures still governed, in all but one instance,[1] by representatives of metropolitan powers with Western standards. In time, however, I cover almost the entire period in which women have gone into the field to do scientific work—that is, from the period in which such an activity was regarded as very unusual and unsuitable to the time when field work is regarded as a necessary activity for a professional anthropologist of either sex. I propose to base my discussion, not only on my own experience, but also on that of colleagues and students and to introduce the topic with a brief discussion of conditions specific to the Pacific islands.

Initially field work in the Pacific was done in areas where government was in the hands of a metropolitan power—Imperial Germany, Great Britain, The Netherlands, the United States, Portugal, Australia, France, or New Zealand. In all of these cases the field worker—and particularly the male field worker accompanied by his wife, and the woman working alone —had the problem of bridging the gulf, in manners and in way of life, between the governmental agents and the "natives" who were to be studied. In all of these cases there were definite social barriers between indigenous populations and white officials, which presented a series of difficulties. Too close fraternization with native peoples—especially residence in their villages and adoption of some features of their way of life, such as food or furniture—was regarded with varying degrees of disapproval, disgust, and suspicion by white officialdom. At the same time the anthropologist, resident in a remote area, was and in most places still is expected to act as a hospitable link in the white network, entertaining the traveler and dropping

1. Bali, when I worked there in 1957–1958.

293

field work for the pleasures of visiting over tea or drinks. The invisible barrier that separated and still separates the world of the white man from the world of the native meant that simultaneous functioning in both worlds was virtually impossible. The most successful field workers have come equipped to participate, properly dressed, in the white world, spending time making friends and gaining allies within the nearest governing station, and prepared, when necessary, to re-enter those communities, even when this resulted in temporarily dropping out of native village life.

The most vivid expressions of this necessity came to me on the Sepik River in 1938, when a pinnace would stop on the bank of the river. My house would be filled with Iatmul people—men, women, and children—whose affairs were of the greatest interest and urgency to me. As figures of white men—identifiably white, not yet individually identified—appeared against the horizon, they looked like paper dolls, unreal figures in an unreal diorama. Then slowly, as they approached, their features would take shape, as known or unknown people, and as they assumed reality, the Iatmul people, a minute ago my closest concern, would assume the flat, nonspecific appearance of paper dolls in their turn. This was the kind of price one paid sometimes, after weeks of speaking and writing and thinking in a native language, involving an almost physical wrench in order to come back to English.

There were also advantages in this castelike society that admitted no blending, for the barrier between a white woman and a group of native people was unambiguous everywhere in the Mandated Territory of New Guinea; warm relationships across a fixed barrier were easier to manage.

Living conditions also provided for the employment of a large number of native domestics. The actual business of living takes a great deal of time; purchase of local foods, arrangement of expeditions back to base for food and supplies, and care of the sick, are all rather routine activities in most parts of New Guinea. A difficult terrain, sometimes involving several days of walking and climbing, and a variety of indigenous diseases make heavy demands on physical stamina. The conditions are not very different from what they were in the 1920's as described in *Stranger and Friend* (see Mead, 1966), by Hortense Powdermaker, who was the first woman to work entirely alone there. The conditions in the 1960's are still very exacting. Ann Chowning and Jane C. Goodale worked in inaccessible parts of New Britain; Nancy Bowers walked long miles and Madeleine Leininger was left, installed by James Watson at sunset, in a completely strange village in the Highlands, where she did not speak a word of the language; and three anthropological wives in the Vayda Expedition to the Mareng braved both illness and very difficult paths and childbirth immediately upon their return. As the peoples closer to government stations have been missionized and educated, the anthropologists have pushed further out into the bush, beyond the limits of propane-gas refrigerators as they were once beyond the limits of primitive kerosene refrigerators. Despite a general change in the ethos of the governmental officials that make somewhat gentler treatment of the native peoples more mandatory, there remain the same problems of the divided life—dependent on the good will of the white people for mail, transport, supplies, medical care, and often safety; and on the native people who live in a different world for the actual fulfillment of one's reason for being there. Field workers who fail to establish adequate relationships with the white world usually suffer heavily for their failure, and those who establish them find the shift between two sets of values, language, ethos, extremely trying.

In field work spanning forty years among the Manus, in the Admiralty Islands (Territory of Papua, New Guinea), I worked in 1928–1929 as a member of a husband-wife team (Fortune, 1931, 1935; Mead, 1930a, 1930b, 1931, 1932, 1934); in 1953 as the mature leader of an expedition with a couple as student assistants (Mead, 1953, 1954a, 1954b, 1954c, 1955, 1956, 1961–1962, 1964; Mead and T. Schwartz, 1960; Schwartz, L. S., 1959; Schwartz, T. and Mead, 1961); in 1964 as an expedition consultant with an anthropological couple already well established in the field (Mead, Schwartz, and Schwartz, 1963–1969); in 1965 by myself; and in 1967 as the guide and consultant of a four-man film team making a feature film for educational television (Gilbert, 1968; Mead, 1965, 1967, 1968). Extracts from the letters I wrote, in which I attempted to make the living conditions vivid for people at home, will most succinctly chronicle the changes.

> Pere, via Lorengau,
> Manus, Territory of New Guinea.
> Via Sydney.
> Jan. 10, 1928

I am alone for the first time. It was more complicated to plan for than Samoa because here we have so much worldly wealth which couldn't be transported about easily. The house is lined with shelves filled with tins and stationery and photographic material. I couldn't leave it and go to a native house to sleep because no native would be willing to sleep here and guard it, for they are very frightened of houses without guardian ancestral spirits.

So I surveyed my household and its retainers. Our usual menage consists of Banyalo, the schoolboy from Rabaul, who is five feet six of sulky uselessness most of the time. Still we keep him because he is useful at working out texts; he's on call in a way that the older men are not and he's responsible enough to be left in charge of the house if we go away in the daytime. He wears a shirt and khaki shorts which impair his character still more. But Banyalo wanted to go to Taui with Reo so he was out of the picture. Then the head cook is Manawai (Bird), a charming, indolent youth of sixteen who was original house boy. Since he has become cook his *laplap*[2] has become incomparably longer, his dignity extraordinary, his aloofness incomparable. But three days ago he had his ears pierced and so is *hors de combat* for five days. Five women of his father's family have come from Loitcha to cook his food over a special fire. He wears tents of pandanus leaf over each ear and looks very solemn and impressed by the fact that his ears are in great danger. Any relaxing of the taboos means a club ear, an unthinkable future to one as vain as he. So he is paddled about in a canoe by smaller boys gravely ministering to his infirmity and only turns up once a day or so to beg newspaper for cigarette papers. Since his ear piercing ceremony, Kilipak "Go to Pak" (an island), has been head cook. Kilipak is possibly thirteen, quick as a flash, son of the ruling family, a natural leader of men. Kilipak's promotion to cook promoted Sotoan, formerly mere kitchen knave who worked for his food alone, to the position of waiter and head valet de chambre. Sotoan is possibly twelve, mild, without authority, deprecatory in manner. And a new "monkey" (P.E.[3] for small boy), who had not haunted the premises before, became assistant valet de chambre. They are so tiny that it takes two to fold a blanket. An even smaller monkey, Kapoli, also joined the forces. So the household headed by a boy of thirteen got under way. The procedure of the absent Manawâi was imitated faithfully by Kilipak; Sotoan strove to take on some of Kilipak's authority as butler and never forgot the vinegar, the quinine, the salt, and the hemoglobin bottles. And Kilipak next organized a band of ten-year-old girls to fetch the firewood which he and his fellow monkeys had formerly fetched for Manawai. Five tiny girls, wearing their little grass tails before and behind, set off in two small canoes, one outriggerless, fastened together to contain the firewood. On their return he shared a tiny bit of his tobacco with them and begged cigarette paper for the whole crew. So by the time Reo left, the child household was in good running order. No one had more than a minimum of work to do, everyone was gay and happy, serious about their tasks, running away to run canoe races while I slept in the early afternoon. For water, wood, and cooking I was well equipped, but now for a sleeping companion.

Our female retainers are three in number, two "wash maries" and my lone "widder" woman, Main. The "wash maries" are two girls of sixteen or so, both engaged to be married soon and able to devote only a small fraction of their time to their work because some man who is

2. *Laplap:* a wraparound garment of European cloth worn by both sexes.
3. P. E.: Pidgin English, now called Neo-Melanesian.

taboo to them is always passing in a canoe, or coming on the little island or coming into the house. All the girls and women wear cloth over their heads in which they can muffle themselves when a taboo relative passes. Married women have only to worry about brothers-in-law and fathers-in-law, but unmarried girls are taboo to all the men of the clan into which they are going to marry. These two girls, Ngaleap and Ngauali, have worked in a most desultory fashion, sometimes not turning up at all. It was a long time before I could get any response out of them, but since Ngaleap trimmed my hair and Ngauali got a thorough blowing up for refusing to wash on the proper day, they have both been devoted. Before that they stalked and sulked and demanded, "Betel, betel," with lowering brows. But Ngaleap is *hors de combat* because one day when they had planned to wash and I declared it unnecessary, they went off to swing on a nearby island. The swings are thirty feet long, long creepers fastened in tree tops. Ngaleap's broke and she fell, not on the water, which would have been quite safe, but on land, and hurt her leg; so she was out of the running. I decided to ask Main, my "widder" woman. She's particularly "lorn" having seen five husbands into the grave and she not yet turned fifty. I pay her three sticks of tobacco a week and it's her business to come and fetch me whenever anything is on foot in the village either in the way of women's industrial activities or of feasts. She demurred heartily from the proposition that she should sleep here but finally consented if she might have Ngauali and another young girl with her. So it was arranged. And yesterday I went off to a turtle feast and a terrible storm came up. All my monkeys kept house in fine style, lowering canvas, barricading doors with the ironing board, etc. I came back to find them thoroughly domesticated and proposing to stay the night en masse. They added that the reason Main was so frightened was that one of her dead husbands belonged to this division and she was afraid he would catch her. So I sent word to Main she needn't come. In the end Ngauali turned up and slept by my side, while five monkeys made a room of canvas on the veranda and sang their frightened little selves to sleep, waking up at intervals to declare that a ghost was nearby. In the evening which, owing to the storm, had all the appearance of a shut-in night at home, I gave them pencils and papers and they did their first drawing. I'm starting with the older ones, so that the little children will draw under conditions similar to those surrounding small children's spontaneous drawing in our culture—that is, after having seen older children draw. At their own request they took new paper and their pencils to bed with them and were up at dawn drawing away. The arrival of a man with fresh fish finally recalled the cook to his duties and the day began. It's altogether a jolly household, infantile, happy, with Kilipak, a genius at organization, at the head. I am as much a figurehead as an English queen when it comes to practical arrangements.

Pere Village, Manus
Territory of Papua & New Guinea
July 2, 1953
written at Patusi Patrol post,
S.C. Manus

I am writing in a temporary camp on top of a high hill above the old village of Patusi, looking down on the site of the old village of Peri (now spelled Pere again), where the small high islands where the women once dried their grass skirts and the children hung their swings and the little flat islands which were once meeting grounds and feasting places now stand, empty and green, defining a vanished way of life. At present I am sharing a deserted and somewhat dilapidated semi-European house, roof of sago thatch, floor of plywood (left over from American occupation), with some seventy natives. The rest of the villagers are scattered about in a few semi-broken-down houses designed for police boys and station staff . . . a few are sleeping in canoes at the foot of the hill and a few of the sick are in the village of Patusi, now on land about two miles away.

We are here because a volcano has suddenly appeared between the islands of Lou and Balowan about twenty miles away, spouting beautiful white smoke—a prelude in this country to ashes and lava—up into an innocently pellucid sky.

Back in Pere
July 6, 1953

On Saturday we received news from the DC that the vulcanologist who had been flown over Rabaul had examined the situation and pronounced the volcano benign. It seems like a contradiction in terms: We had had a long chatty evening, on top of our hill, with the fifty-some people who were still left with me in the big house telling stories of the war, of the coming of "All America," of the move from the old place. Finally Pokanau deigned to remember that his grandfather had told him of a tidal wave in his father's childhood. Then Manawai, who was one of our first boys, and interrupted his activities to have his ears pierced, came to say they had decided to have three weddings the next day! And then Kilipak brought letters from Mbunei from the DC saying the alert was over and we could go back. All night people kept waking up, lighting lamps, looking for the dawn, and soon after dawn a fleet of canoes took us back to the village which had not—as we all feared—been destroyed. Not a single thing had been stolen, everything lay like the buried houses of Pompeii, but not buried, quite safe among these disciplined and careful people. And there were three weddings in the Church, and now each young couple, free to talk together, to eat together, to go about together in public, freed of all the old irksome taboos and exploitation, can sit down comfortably in a section of the house which is their very own.

From my verandah I have a view of the mountains, and it is two minutes' walk to a view of the open sea. There are houses on three sides of me, some six feet away, people practically look out of their windows into mine, but this is excellent for field work, and since my five days on the mountain I am no longer distressed by the children's screams in the night; this is learned behavior, an aggressive assertion of their dislike of waking up, or desire to sleep with a different parent, etc. All day the children play in white sand of the square, which in the early morning is pockmarked with the holes of giant crabs. Although the houses lack the style of the old village, on the whole it all seems more beautiful. There were lovely sunsets and fair moonlight nights in the old Pere, but the angry voices, the strident drums, the shouting and the turmoil somehow spoiled the tropical landscape. Now the air is filled on a Sunday afternoon with the sounds of the ukeleles strummed very softly and with children playing singing games. Spotlessly clean naked babies are brought to have their eyes washed out with boric acid.

There is much too much to do, of course. I realize now that part of the sense of overwork in Tambunum in 1938 was because I had a fluent command of Pidgin English and a general understanding of the culture and a start on the language. This meant an immediate flow of activity which—combined with trying to reproduce the work which Made Kaler (our Balinese secretary) and I had done together—was very tiring. The same thing, only worse, has happened here, for here I have both Pidgin and Manus, and a knowledge of most of the grown people; people can be identified to me at once, I don't have to stop to have a kinship term explained, but this means that the mass of information, combined with endless reminiscing, anecdotes about everything that has happened in the last 25 years, assume rather alarming proportions, and my typing up gets way behind itself. I don't dare use tape because there is no chance to work over and revise, or if one does, it takes as long.

> Back in Pere
> October 2, 1953

And certainly it is easier for me personally to feel committed to an endeavor of heartbreaking difficulty than to a mere desire to maintain the status quo, however balanced and charming that status quo—as in Bali. Also, this degree of sympathy and warmth that comes with long acquaintance is hard to overestimate. I used to feel I knew many of the people with whom I worked, and often I did know them—people like Faamotu in Samoa, and Made Kaler in Bali, and our Arapesh boys. But this is different, possibly because they are—from our point of view —not too gifted with ways of being articulate in personal relations, and the long detailed knowledge of the past replaces a capacity for introspection. But, when Karol Matawai, tall, violent, unruly, comes in with eyes flashing, determined to press a point of pride home, which will end with ten people going to jail on a charge which no one really wants to enforce—neither government nor natives—I find my efforts to reason with him are so tempered with the memory of the way he felt in my arms as a baby, of the way he cried the day he pried his father out of a ceremony to beg a red balloon from him, that there is no irritation in my voice, and my pleading succeeds. And then, because I know Kilipak —his older brother—I knew which plea will reduce his angry pride, and if I can make him see how his younger brother's reputation will suffer, this will prevail over all his cocksure determination to have his own way.

Problems of participation, of where one should interfere and where not, take on a different color when the people themselves are as anxious for guidance on Roberts' Rules of Order as for quinine to stop malaria. The tendency toward suicide and depression which comes with the increased internalization of conscience, and self-blame for thoughts as well as for acts, also involves the anthropologist in a new kind of therapeutic participation.

Of course, those of us who worked in New Guinea have always done everything we could to save life and limb, but before the antibiotics our capacities, as lay people, were much more limited. And now the request for help in school, help in meetings, and help in "getting a clear idea of the road ahead," are asked in the same voice in which they once asked us to tie up a cut. All this results in one's turning rapidly over in one's mind: what will it be necessary to say to the most promising and most crucial young man in the village, who is still alive because he tried to hang himself with a piece of rubber tubing left over from the war which fortunately broke? How to combine "You are the descendant of Korotan, you are a member of the clan which is the root and strength of this village, of all the Manus, the clan that is the *lapan* (the aristocrats) of all the people—you are the one who has lived close to Pokanau, the man who still remembers the old genealogies, and you have learned these too, you who best understand the new, who write better than anyone else in the village, who had the energy to organize and keep a school going without any help or materials from anyone. You are the link which will bind the past and the future together—without you the hopes of this village will lie scattered and broken." How to combine all together so that he will be able to conquer his self-destructive wounded pride and despair and decide to live? All this requires a complete involvement—perhaps involvement is always measured by one's relative ability to act and to understand—such as I used to achieve in trying to revive a drowned child or reduce a teething baby's fever. But it's curious and wonderful to watch the way a changing ethic means a changing type of participation.

The main trouble in life is women; they don't know what to do about women. Marriage as an exclusive, unique relationship is very difficult to handle; the search for replicating situations keeps them in a continuous state of jealousy and suspicion. Their notion of physiological processes is the continuous eventuation—eat, digest, excrete, marry and have children who grow. Their darkest suspicion of women is that they are continuously resorting to abortion, and they resent the woman's unique control over gestation, delivery, and lactation. Rather, like the Japanese, they feel it would be a good world if there were no women in it.

Under the old system women controlled childbirth, childbearing, and the seances through which the ghosts spoke; all of these functions have been taken away from them; it is the men who write rules about infant welfare. Great emphasis is placed on the emancipation of women, that they have the right to marry whom they wish, and that their husbands should help them with the children, but this is accompanied by increasing masculinization—women play a more active role in fishing (shooting fish with an odd combination of musket and fish spear, swimming under water), swim for shell, act as boats crew, are the economic supports of their households far more than in the past. Where the New Guinea men would like to exercise women's procreative functions, the Manus would simply like to eliminate women altogether and have readymade babies which they could care for and shape to their will.

The shaping is very gentle—I have seen no other society where there is less bullying of children simply because they are smaller, weaker, more ignorant, or less controlled. But the mother's task is to give the child the strength to stand vis-à-vis an adult; she teaches it to walk by kicking some ball-like object away from her, after which it totters. She does not feed it unless it yells, she responds to its anger with a similar yell or slap, she is permitted no tenderness, and men in turn neither respect nor evoke tenderness from their wives. The new regime of marriage by choice will, they believe, correct the bad marital relations, and it remains to be seen whether this change, imposed at a late age, can correct them.

> Bulletin Letter from Peri Village
> Manus Island, Papua and New Guinea
> October 23, 1964

I have hesitated whether or not to write a bulletin letter, but it seems there are so many small details that will otherwise have to be repeated over and over before I can start to talk about this trip. I live here, literally neck-deep in the past. For example, today Lokus, who was one of my little houseboys in 1928, and Ted's cook in 1953, and is now again our chief cook and factotum—a mild, shy little man of about fifty, but I feel him as frail and old, and his hearing and eyesight are going—Lokus came to tell me that his wife had gone to Mok to mourn for her sister's

husband, and "You remember, Piyap, the time we came back on a
canoe from Lou, in 1929, it was Litauer's canoe, he was my wife's
father." Every event is tied firmly into the shared past, and I am supposed to remember as well as they do, each detail of the long past.
Faces are somewhat harder this time, especially for the men who were
in their teens in 1953—the old people again recall their childhood faces,
and I can place them by bypassing 1953 and going back to 1928. The
old women embraced me and wailed, because they are old and will
soon die, and my boys—now men of fifty—now treat me more as an
age mate and talk solemnly of the many, many years we have lived—
such a long, long, long time. The kind of aging that we never see is all
about me, toothlessness leading to fallen cheeks and mumbling words,
people who are like walking skeletons. The other impression is one of
literally mobs of children. The village has again increased in size as the
nearby village of Patusi has moved in, packing their houses in the small
bits of remaining space and along the shore so that the whole village is
crowded and untidy. Pig keeping has come back, and the pig pens stand
again on posts over the water. The village now faces out toward the
open sea, so that all day, from before dawn till dark, there are ever
changing patterns of silhouetted figures out on the reef.

Life here on the surface is more comfortable than on my previous
visits. We have two houses: Ted and Lola have the house that the former
young schoolteacher, Peranis Cholai, had built for himself. Our latrine
has a handsome "bridge" built of great old planks, the "bones of Big
Manus," the canoe they were building in 1953. Intermittently, when all
the various parts of battery, generator, bulbs, etc., work, we have electric light, just enough to make the old-style pressure lamp seem unbear-
ably dim. I'd think my intolerance of the old-style lamp was age except
that Ted and Lola also find it impossible to work by.

During this six weeks in the village I have been in the village but not
of it, for life is not set up so that the people come and go freely as they do
when I am here working alone. Ted and Lola are working with single
informants, taking texts and making tapes, in contexts where a mob of
looklooks is a real disadvantage. So informal contacts with the village
are discouraged; people come on messages, we are invited to meetings,
people bring us fish or carvings, but no small children come and go, and
the women stay away and are—in a new word that has come recently
into Pidgin—"worried." Next year I shall spend a few weeks here by
myself, with a house stripped down to bare essentials in which a crowd
will do no harm, and establish a last set of close contacts on what may
well be my last visit. But it is so much easier to leave and plan to come
back again that I may not say it will be my last visit. Within the enlarged village—of some 400 people—those who were children in 1928
are still closest to me, the friendships with newcomers in 1953 seem
slight in comparison.

Letter from Peri
From my eleventh field trip
December 19, 1965

This year I am living in a brand-new house in a brand-new village, with all the excitement of being the Christmas host for the last Christmas that the whole Paliau movement [see Schwartz, T., 1962] will ever hold as exclusively their own. Paliau's dream that all of the people of Manus should be within one political unit has come true, in form at least. The old enmities, especially between adjacent villages, still smolder, ready to burst into angry speech and blows over an injury in a soccer match. The Missions and the Mission villages are still not quite sure whether Paliau is a leader who is slowly bringing his thinking and his people closer to theirs or whether he is after all Henry VIII and John Wesley rolled into one. The village is new: sparkling with paint on the houses of those who could somehow beg, borrow, importune, or in the last resort, buy some corrugated iron; or decorated with patterns woven in the bamboo of traditional materials. After two months of quiet, when small boys rolled hoops and had them confiscated by the school committee, the village is humming with the sounds of the returned adolescents—ukeleles, every radio and record player newly supplied with batteries; well-dressed young people parading up and down or abandoning their school finery to play rough-and-tumble games with each other. Within some houses "rooms" have been built especially for the visiting children, varying from a room in which bed, chair, and bench, all made by hand, are arranged to make a perfect schoolboy's room, with a nicely made bed, pictures of the Beatles on the wall, schoolbooks on the table, schoolbag hung in the window, to a mere corner of a large barnlike room, where a suitcase with a couple of books on top signals the return of a schoolchild. But however poor or however elegant the preparations, the village is alive with the delight of the visitors: the schoolchildren and those who have become teachers in faraway parts of New Guinea, sometimes all alone in some small bush school among alien people only a few years away from cannibalism and headhunting. So the tales they bring are mixed: stories of boarding school, of examinations and prizes won in scholarship or sports, and stories of the extraordinary customs of the people in the interior of New Guinea, who never really wash but only lift up a little water from a stream, and who think that fish are snakes. And which is harder for them to assimilate and understand—a savage way of life, which in many respects is like that of their own grandfathers, now so enthusiastically abandoned, or a way of life which belongs to the modern world, the world of the planes that fly overhead and the news that comes over the radio? For news of themselves comes over the radio too; yesterday morning came the announcement: "At the first meeting of the new Council in Manus, Mr. Paliau Moluat, member of the house of assembly, was elected president."

It is a kind of paradigm of what is going on all over the world, as grandparents and parents settle for what part they themselves can play, and what must be left to the comprehension of the children.

For the first time since the field trip to Samoa, I am all alone. All alone, it is true in a known culture, among people who trust me as one of themselves, whose past I know better than they do; all alone with the mass of assurances that I will be able to do the job I came to do. I measure all the factors that make this trip extremely easy for me: a house built for me by people who know I am likely to break my ankle, equipment all set up from the Schwartz' trip here, a kerosene ice box (unknown luxury), medicines to deal with diseases that were not so long ago intractable, a knowledge of the language and a detailed knowledge of the people—their relationships, their dispositions, their capabilities. And I realize that even so, with all that, which no beginner has, field work is a rather appalling thing to undertake. Nowhere else is a scientist asked to be vis-à-vis, and also a part of, a total human society and to conduct his studies *in vivo,* continually aware of such a complex whole. Perhaps the task of the psychiatrist is comparably difficult—as the psychiatrist is asked to take in, hold in mind, respond to, and respond to his responses to, whole individuals including those parts that are normally veiled from other eyes . . . and not only one such whole, but several. . . . And we do give our young anthropologists many aids, categories into which they can arrange the behavior that they witness, as "mother-in-law avoidance," "ambilateral kinship," "slash and burn agriculture," "nucleation." But if they are to be good field workers they know these tools are as preliminary as the cameras they hold in their hands, meaningless if uninformed by a vivid sense of what is really going on here, now, in this particular culture. And today we give the field worker a whole battery of methods, techniques, tools from which he must choose; more than he can use, just as the vivid ongoing life of a community is more than he can possibly cover in the same detail, with the same vigilance, with the same attention. So as he works he must choose, shape, prune, discard this and collect finer detail of that, much as a novelist works who finds some minor character is threatening to swallow up the major theme, or that his hero is fast taking him out of his depth. But unlike the novelist—except when the novelist feels, as I believe they sometimes do, possessed by characters that have a life of their own—he is wholly and helplessly dependent upon what happens, on the births, marriages, deaths, quarrels, entanglements and reconciliations, depressions and elations, of his small community. True, we have such dependencies in a theatrical company, in a baseball team, on an expedition to the Arctic, and will have it when teams go into space. This is the dependence on one's own team, as whole individuals engaged in an engrossing undertaking—which is the other side of field work, when one works, as I have worked most of my life, with others—

the total result dependent upon the insights, the state of mind and health, the preservation of or breaks in communication among the members of the group. This is engrossing and exacting also, but these are the fortunes of working as a member of a group of your own kind of people, speaking the same language, sharing the same culture, usually nearly of an age. A primitive community, or an isolated peasant community, of another culture than your own is an entirely different matter. You sit at night, with three or four hundred people asleep around you, the whole village silent, and wonder what is going to happen: will the baby about to be born die or be deformed in some strange way; will the mother die and precipitate a whole set of reprisals and recriminations; will a big man die; will a quarrel break the community in two; will a child drown or a canoe break up at sea? So closely are the people knit together that any event will affect the whole; an unexpected absence or illness, an unexpected visitor, and the whole equilibrium is changed. One must be continually prepared for—anything, everything, and perhaps most devastatingly, nothing. For it is events which reveal the forms in which one is interested, for the account of which one is responsible. This existence vis-à-vis a whole community, and a community of a totally different culture, where no slightest lift of an eyebrow or curl of a lip means what it would mean in our own, is the central experience of field work in a living culture. And viewing it from the experience of forty years and eight different cultures, I think we demand a great deal. The wonder to me is not that young anthropologists fail, but that so many succeed.

I've been counting over also the difference between the sustenance that a young anthropologist receives from the uniqueness and historic importance of his work among a primitive people and the position of the latter-day field worker, working with equal commitment and intensity within a culture contact situation. The traditional anthropologist has the wonderful knowledge that everything he records will be valuable—the shape of a flute, the pattern of a cat's cradle, the plot of a myth, the names of the sun and the moon and the stars, a gesture of assent or greeting, a recipe for cooked sago, the method of counting betel nut. All of it is unique, all will vanish, all was and is grist to some fellow anthropologist's mill. Nothing was wasted. He had only to record accurately and organize his notes legibly, and whether he lived or died, what he did would make a contribution. With this, of course, went the responsibility to record many things in which he was not personally interested. But the rewards were immense; in a way, one could not fail. Then, second, if one had a problem, the challenge of possible failure, contrapuntal to the assurance of usefulness and success, was there too; any field may prove to be the wrong place to do the task one comes to do. But also there was the certainty that, if one surrendered fully enough to the culture, it would itself inform one's further choices and provide new problems, home-grown for the field worker's perception. There were rewards for the individual who liked to work alone, just one mind required to take in a culture that had been hundreds, perhaps thousands, of years abuilding and was now before him incorporated in a community of both sexes, all ages, and many diverse temperaments. All the skills he could employ as a scientist plus all the skill he could draw on as an artist were needed here; and he was accountable to no one except to the actuality before him. Those of us who like best to work in close cooperation with others could have the excitement of participating in a team of two or three or four, or perhaps a series of minds of those who had gone before or might come after, as a kind of orchestral realization of the complexity to be studied. These were, and are, the special rewards for the traditional field worker. And with the practitioners of other difficult occupations—psychiatry, space flight, undersea exploration—he shared the delight of using all instead of part of himself.

But my work this field trip not only highlights all of these rewards, but also underlines the difference between traditional anthropological work and work with any group who have come under the continuing influence of contemporary world culture. The uniqueness is no longer a property of what is studied, so that the field worker can rely on certain results if he be only honest and industrious. The uniqueness now, in a study like this, lies in the relationship between the field worker and the material. I still have the responsibility and the incentives that come from the fact that because of my long acquaintance with this village I can perceive and record aspects of their life that no one else can. But even so this knowledge has a new edge; this material will only be valuable if I myself can organize it. Where for traditional field work another anthropologist familiar with the area can take over one's notes and make them meaningful, here it is only my individual consciousness which provides the ground on which the lives of these people are figures. And this makes me acutely aware of how I have always worked with two incentives: an incentive to write up my work, carefully, legibly—which usually meant typing—in the field, so it would be usable in case I died, and the incentive to be sure not to take risks which would interfere with my writing it all up myself, which after all I could do better than anyone else.

But how different this all is from the problems that confront the student who must go out, taking all the physical and psychological risks of field work, to study *another* Caribbean village, or *another* Indian village, not yet uniquely in possession of the lives of any group, deprived of the sharp perceptions provided by an integrated, unknown primitive culture, struggling to work out the dimensions of some problem—without which funds would not have been forthcoming, fearful that the result will be "just another community study"; possibly entangled in the modern devious net of intelligence, counterintelligence, conflicting loyalties; and beset by the small difficulties of hard water and lack of plumbing and light, which were far less of a trial to a generation who had grown up with kerosene lamps.

Finally, there is the way in which, if one works in a culture where the people become literate, one's own work becomes part of their sense of their own history. For the most part anthropologists have treated this negatively, either insisting on the anthropologist's obligation to protect the people themselves or the chances of future field workers or deploring the effect that the publication of religious secrets has had on the relationship between a tribe and its anthropologists. Very few have written for the people whom they have studied, yet now the books that I have written are becoming part of the consciousness of the Manus people, particularly of the people of this village. The names of the old men who died before they were born can be supplied with visual images: the changes through which their parents have gone are there before their eyes. After the unique experience when, under Paliau's leadership, the whole village, old and young, moved together to a new form of life, they now have the unique experience of keeping their past, in visible and detailed form, and a form that is respected by the world into which they are moving as teachers and civil servants. Then one contrasts this odd outcome of the state of anthropology with the conditions in Iran, where the pre-Moslem part of their history was part of our history, but not of theirs, so that I, as a child, read about Cyrus the Great, but my contemporaries in Iran did not. And it resolves itself into a new puzzle, whose history is best for whom, which is I suppose one of the things that Tolkien [1954–1956] is talking about.

The distinction between working in a Manus village such as Peri and work in New Guinea is primarily the difference between being on the seashore and being in the interior. Field work in the swamp villages at the mouth of the Sepik and on Manam Island where Camilla H. Wedgwood (1934) worked has many similarities. Working in the interior of one of the large islands, such as New Ireland or New Britain or the interior of the Great Admiralty, has many things in common. If one works near the seashore, one is working with people with sophistication and a wider range of experience; if one works in the interior, the people tend to be land-bound, in ideas as well as in facts. Papuan languages are harder than Melanesian languages to learn to speak. If one lives in villages that have very recently been brought under control, as the Mundugumor (see Mead, 1935) had been, certain precautions are necessary so as not to arouse recently suppressed headhunting temptations. If one works in a village where food is very scarce, the problem of drawing on that food supply for oneself and imported assistants becomes acute, and the need to supplement it, if possible, becomes important. But aside from considerations like these, I should say that all areas of New Guinea and the surrounding islands present pretty much the same problems: transportation and food, maintaining a balance between some relationship to the official white community and to the native villages, the extreme chanciness of which events will occur while one is there, the small size of the villages, which results in a great deal of extrapolation from single cases.

For contrast, I include excerpts from letters from four New Guinea mainland villages: the Arapesh village of Aliatoa, the Mundugumor village of Kinakaten on the Yuat River (now called the Biwat), the Tchambuli village on Aibom Lake (now called Chamberi), and the Iatmul people of Tambunum Village on the Sepik River. The first three trips followed each other within a period of thirty-three months, so that the state of the Territory was the same throughout, although from outside we heard of the closing of the banks in the United States and the Japanese invasion of Manchuria, which Australians feared might mean a call-up to military service.

Aliatoa, Wiwiak, New Guinea
January 15, 1932

I stayed at a plantation owned by the Cobbs while Reo went inland to scout about. The chances of getting our stuff moved in looked very poor. The country is mountainous, there are only native trails, running up perpendicular cliffs or along the beds of streams. The natives have practically everything which they need of white goods, knives, blankets, kettles. They cannot be compelled to carry, and they don't like carrying. Reo was pretty hopeless at first, but he went about from one village to another, unearthed their darkest secrets which they wished kept from the government, and then ordered them to come and carry. This for some villages, and the others came by contagion. Reo came back to the Cobbs not knowing whether any carriers would turn up or not, but the next day eighty-seven came. In all it took about 250 to get our stuff up here to Aliatoa, which is three days from Wiwiak, the government station, and two days from the Cobbs. Mr. Cobb lent us six strong boys from his plantation line to carry me in. We had brought one of those string hammocks and they strung it on a pole and laced me, with banana leaves over me to keep out the sun and rain, for all the world like a pig. It was a little sea-sickish being handed up and down some of the mountains, but it was a great improvement on walking. Reo had only been in this village overnight. He had made a speech telling them that he approved of all their old customs and that if we came to live here the village would always be full of matches and salt—the two great desiderata. So they said we could build a house and Reo marked out a place the right size in the spot they assigned to us and told them to build a house. Then he left a boy in charge of all our stores, piled up in two natives' houses, and came down to get me. We didn't have an idea whether we would find a house here or not, but when we got here they had the framework up and the floor down, a big fence about the whole open space, and the village paths were spread with sage-leaf thatch shingles. We lived in a native house for a week while they finished the house.

It's such a delightful climate that difficulties are compensated for by a temperature which has never touched eighty since we've been here. I'm in better health than I've been since before I went to Manus. In the long intervals of peace, when there are only a few people in the village, we have even quiet days, ending up with a game of deck tennis before dinner. It's an amusing culture with very nasty institutions—like female infanticide, menstrual huts, rather cruel initiations, etc., but in spite of these, a happy, casual, good-natured people.

Collecting, too, has its difficulties. In the House Tamberan, the sacred men's houses, are carved figures, which are named and charmed into a high state of dangerousness. When Reo went into the interior, he marked some for purchase. Their owners carried them here, done up like little pigs in pieces of stiff bark; they came by the little side roads which are taken by women who are tabu, and by hunters who wish to get home secretly with their kill, and by people who want to buy pigs and who fear if others see them go they may say, "I hope he doesn't find a pig to buy." They arrived in the village. Reo put them in the storeroom. Immediately came a storm of protest from our boys. If they ate any food from that room, they would waste away and die. The place where our house stood was hot enough because a big House Tamberan had stood there, and these carvings were awfully hot and everyone would be ill. Then came a delegation from the village saying it was not safe to keep those carvings in a house where there were women and children, they must be put in the village House Tamberan. Very well, we were only too willing, for I had been forbidden to go into the storeroom lest I see these mysterious images. But who were to carry them? The men-o-bush were still here, but they were tired and sulky because they had been paid only twice what they had been promised; no one in the place would touch the dangerous things, so Reo had to carry them himself up and down the village from which the women had all been barred within their houses. Then the secret of the exorcising leaf was bought dearly from the men-o-bush, and the store and house carefully broomed. The worst is yet to come, for we have no idea how we are going to get the incubuses to the coast or whether all the Cobb boys will run away if they are brought to the plantation. While they were being carried, I hid in a native house with a woman who spent her time showing me an abortive drug and commenting sharply on the fact that the men could not see the drug, that they could not even hear the name of it. Thus feminine self-esteem was avenged. . . .

Then there was the night last week when Amito'a and I dyed skirts. This is one of the occasions when the women get back at the men. No men or children can come near, no smell of cooked meat, no knife which has ever touched meat, no feather headdresses can come near. The very sound of men's voices will spoil the dye, just as the sound of women's voices will anger the Tamberan and as the touch of a woman's hand may spoil hunting gear. We squatted in a wind-swept little leaf shelter and watched the great pot, its top covered with pads of big green leaves, boil over with a bubbling fluid which gradually turned blood-red. And once some boys talked, and the skein of sago threads which was being put into the pot caught fire. And Amito'a's husband stayed with Reo until night (midnight) and, just to reassert his masculine superiority, told Reo all about the nice brain soup which the warriors used to drink, brewed from the scooped-out brains of the enemy, although up to now they had been denying any touch of cannibalism. So Baimal danced about the room, illustrating the savage delight of war, for Baimal is always light and airy even when his talk is of death, and Amito'a and her sister-in-law, Ilautoa, squatted by the watched pot, and said, "We feed pigs, we make grass skirts, we dance, two by two we go for the firewood, two by two we bring the water, two by two we dye our grass skirts." And the wind howled and ruffled the thatch, and I enjoyed it, in spite of the smoke in my eyes.

We are becoming steadily more disassociated with the outside world. We had stopped Rabaul's forwarding our mail because we thought we were leaving, so we have had no mail for two months nor will get any for another month. The mainspring of my watch is broken. The only radio news we have heard refers to events which we don't understand, for the most part. It is like being on board a ship, condemned to a few hundred feet of moving about, and knowing that practically nothing can possibly happen. Recently the district officer and medical assistant passed through and were hung up here for two days. After they left we were both ill; the impact of white people, sitting about, more food than we usually eat, and possibly onions which we hadn't tasted for six months, was too much for us. I am more convinced than ever that the way to do field work is just never to come up for air until it is all over, but of course it's luck to have a spot healthful enough to make it possible.

I repeat my cry for reading matter, old magazines preferably. Novels aren't good, for one is tempted to finish them, which is bad. On a magazine one can ration oneself to one article or story a day.

I even begin to wonder what the date is. These people have names for moons, like "the moon when we get bananas from a deserted yam garden," but as everybody plants at a different time, no two families' moons are alike. As they say, "You count the moon but we just know their names," and all they really know are names which can be applied when appropriate to the moon which is up at present, and no two families have the same calendar. They think it's very odd that we should think a moon would have only one fixed name.

Kinakaten, Yuat River
New Guinea, 1932

In the minds of the most suburban Rabaulite, and in the minds of the wildest bush native, the Sepik stands for mosquitoes, crocodiles, cannibals, and floating corpses—and I can assure you we have seen them all. We are not on the Sepik itself—that is Bateson's stamping ground [see Bateson, 1932]—but on a tributary eighty-seven miles from the mouth of the Sepik which runs east into the Madang area. This river is called the Yuat. It is parallel to the Little Ramu, where Thurnwald worked [see Thurnwald, 1916] and about half a day further up. The mosquitoes have not been exaggerated; they are the most amazing, determined, starving crew imaginable—the natives can tell at a glance whether they have had a full meal and are likely to make a nasty bloodstain on one's clothes—but most of them never had a full meal and are fighting for just one before they die. It took us about a week to study out the various ramifications of the mosquito problem: it has a clothing, an architecture, a closet economy all its own. For instance, you can't keep anything in suitcases, for the mosquitoes get in the cracks and, when you go to find something, attack by the thousand. Air-proof boxes, if you swish the air all about while opening them, will do. But the best plan is to spread one's possessions thin over endless shelves, so that everything can be found and grabbed before more than a hundred wounds are sustained. Bathing except at midday has to be done with a whisk in one hand. Reo has of course discarded shorts, and I have evolved a costume which looks like a beach parade but serves very well, an ordinary dress and pajamas legs—fortunately Reo had a lot of old ones in pastel shades, so I can even evolve color schemes. This with a large straw hat—for short strolls a helmet isn't necessary—make me feel slightly ridiculous but protected. The too-long pajamas bell over one's shoe tops. Then one can't sleep in a room, for all the mosquitoes will go and hide in the corners during the day, having been disappointed of the feast which they glimpsed through the net. Even two boxes placed near each other give them somewhere to hide. So we have a huge veranda, with the mosquito room standing in the middle of it, and our beds at one side. Away at the back is a dressing room; one side is a store, most of it is just great open spaces, for air and safety. The mosquito room is a box, nine by ten by ten feet, made of copper wire and uprights which bolt together. The door closes with a pulley made of a box of cartridges. There is a box with two drop-hinged ends, thrust through the wire, and one boy cautiously inserts a dish and drops his trap door, then the inside boy opens his side and whisks out the dish. The floor is made of a ground sheet, and one has to use ash trays inside and not pour the tea grounds through the floor, which seems ridiculous faddishness in New Guinea. Inside there is just room for a table, two straight chairs, and two easy—our old ones—chairs, a box for papers, a tiny bookcase for glasses, my work basket, etc., and at all four corners hang native net bags containing our slender supply of reading matter, mending, etc. For once you go in, you don't want to open the door if you can possibly help it. It means living in horribly small quarters and climbing over each other all the time, and clearing away work so that the table can be laid, but it represents heaven none the less.

So the mosquitoes deserve their reputation; as for the rest, the crocodiles do eat people quite often, they make drawing water from the river at night a dangerous matter, they provide the art motif and a great model crocodile actually swallows the initiates, and most important of all, one can cook with the whites of crocodile eggs. "Making corn fritters with crocodile eggs among the cannibals." They were all cannibals until about four years ago; boys of twelve have eaten human flesh and they show merely a mischievous and merry glee in describing their previous diet, but the idea of eating rats fills them with shuddering nausea. And we've had one corpse float by, a newborn infant; they are always throwing away infants here, as the fathers object to observing the tabus associated with their survival.

The natives are superficially agreeable, but we suspect them of being Melanesians nonetheless, with all the Melanesian's natural nastiness. They go in for cannibalism, headhunting, infanticide, incest, avoidance and joking relationships, adultery, and biting lice in half with their teeth. Also their language is simply ridiculously easy—has hardly any grammar at all. I've hardly had to try to learn it, it's so simple. But the women's grass skirts are quite gorgeous, and at dusk and dawn when there are deep shadows on the water and everyone comes out for a stroll, I like them very much. The village extends along the edge of the river and is under water in the wet season. At one end of the village is the chief man with ten wives, while his rival at the other end has nine. These harems are not primarily designed to minister to a Turklike lust, but rather are up-and-coming tobacco-growing concerns, work all done by the women. None of the women has ever seen a white woman before and I am sure I shall start a suffrage movement among the more distant villages who find me "talking place," [4] an accomplishment of which the first white man certainly did not boast.

4. "Talking place": speaking the local language.

Aibom Lake, Sepik District,
New Guinea
February 1, 1933

Here we are on a lovely lake, not quite black, but crowded, with lotuses. The people are gentle and polite and slip between one's fingers. They have some of the complexity of the Big Sepik but speak a gender language again, and it is probably all a veneer. There are about 400 of them within a half hour's walk of each other, they have some thirteen house tamberans, and we've already seen a big feast. The three localities are so jealous of each other that the only way to get a house built was to have two built, and so we now have two houses which they are completing in their own good time, but strictly in step. And the next dilemma is which one to live in; one has the better view, but the other, more adjacent usable buildings; one has the higher roof, the other the straighter floor. And we have told them that when there is a big feast in one half, we will live there, and vice versa. Meanwhile each hamlet sends spies to the other so that the work will keep abreast, and I fret and fret over the delay at really getting organized and settled. But it is really a beautiful place, far the most beautiful in which we have been; we can go swimming in the lake, or canoeing on the lake; the roads are not so rough that I cannot walk over them easily even at night; the people are in many ways like the Samoans and therefore most intelligible to me and very attractive.

Tambunum Village, Sepik River,
New Guinea, June 24, 1938

This building a house in the field is such a funny business; one is limited by time, by the materials available, by the skill of the natives, by the size and layout and condition of the site. One wants to build a place in which to live with a maximum of comfort and a minimum of effort. The comfort is all a matter of few steps, having everything inside the mosquito room which may be needed inside and everything outside which will be needed outside—for every slip-up means opening the screen door and letting in mosquitoes.

There are five islands, as the diagrams show: the big mosquito room; the small mosquito room, in which I receive women and children and in which Gregory works with single informants occasionally; the bed, which is an eight-foot square platform, on which a six-foot mattress is set, entirely surrounded by a big net, always tucked in, with a white canopy over it to keep out some of the dust and some of the insects (at that one spends five minutes picking up caterpillars, small spiders, swallow-tailed nits, mosquitoes, flies, borers, etc., which are always to be found speckling the bed when one climbs in); the storeroom, in which Tomi has lined all of the tinned goods, as to whether they are singletons or have a large number of "one talks" (members of the same group); and the bathroom, which is our pride and joy, with its cement floor that drains and a broad shelf made of real planks (tops of kerosene cases) on which bottles will stand up, and a water tank, Dutch style, made of an oil tin, begged from a schooner and chopped in half with an axe. But aside from the question of comfort and expedition in the matters of bathing, dressing, and eating, the house has to be primarily considered as a combination laboratory, observation post, fort, outpost, dispensary, and gathering place. There must be room for people to gather without breaking or spoiling or pilfering anything. There must be a place in which to do medicine which has a wall dividing the audience from the operating theater; there must be blank surfaces on which children can put their papers to draw, and a shelf on which their clay modeling can be displayed; there must be from all points a view of a road or a bit of beach or another house, which can be utilized with the long lens; there must be ways of dividing visitors into informants and mere *looklooks,* seats for the real visitors to sit upon, newspaper and tobacco for them to smoke. There must be small trade ready at any moment to buy a fish or a coconut brought by a daring three-year-old. It's all a little like planning how to live comfortably in a show window and at the same time keep up continuous observations of the crowd that gathers outside. But we are excellently placed; our veranda stands where the main road ran, and the main road now curves around it, and everyone stops to look over the fence. This is the main women's road; the men's road goes by on the beach side of the house, and important processions of self-conscious males carrying shell valuables or shamans in trance, hunting for suspicious-looking shadows of sin, stand out in conspicuous silhouette. Baangwi's house is about four feet from the edge of our house, and his brother's house stands at the end of the little dip of land in which we live. Here there is a wide cleared space where the children play games and make drawings in the dust. The kitchen also stands on the main road, and from its flimsy shelter I can watch events outside, and have a boy dictate the abuse which is raging outside, without the boy's being too embarrassed. Baangwi is our landlord and nearest neighbor; he is a charming person, graceful, high-spirited, decorative, with an endless range of styles of doing his hair, and a fine angry oratory at five thirty in the morning, when he discovers that someone has robbed his fowl's nest. He believes in his culture, accepts its bombast as real and its rules, which are only meant to insult other people, as applicable to himself, and so he plays his roles with a conviction which most Iatmuls lack.

They are a gay, irresponsible, vigorous people, always either laughing or screaming with rage. The two types of behavior are more or less alternative and seem to give them about equal satisfaction. Children learn to yell for every satisfaction, and later they decide it was the yelling they enjoyed. When anyone loses his or her temper, the by-standers stand about, grinning from ear to ear, feeling reassured that this is a world in which people can lose their tempers HARD. They enjoy anger more than any people I have ever seen. For they are not cruel, or stingy, or greedy. They have no infanticide, they look after their poor and orphaned, they share food and betel and tobacco with a lavishness which the state of their food supply hardly justifies, and they lose their tempers all over the place, without guilt or shame. It's a world in which one has to keep raising one's voice in order to be heard at all.

> Tambunum Village, Sepik River
> New Guinea, August 12, 1938

The whole rhythm of our lives, of the lives of everyone in the village, including the ghosts and the shamanic spirits, is at present dependent upon the slight variations in the height of the river which mean it is or is not possible to shoot crocodiles. This is the lowest water in five years, the first time that the people have been sufficiently in the good books of their capricious shamanic spirits to be allowed to find an abundance of meat for the death feasts which will be made at high water. For hun-dreds of square miles land that is usually dotted with lakes, cross-cut with canals, and itself a mere squashy quagmire, has dried up, and the people go and burn it off in great patches, laying bare the remaining sorry little puddles in which the crocodile and turtles and fish are plung-ing about. Then the whole hunting group takes part in the actual croco-dile hunt. They go and camp for days while this is going on and only return to the village when there is a death or a quarrel or when their supplies of worked sago run out.

Last month we joined one of these camping parties. We fastened another little canoe—about fifteen feet long—beside our canoe which carries the outboard engine, and with three boys and four days' supplies we started on the three-hour trip downstream which ultimately, after going up a long canal, brings us to a place which, seen from the village, is up-river.

As soon as we turned into the canal, we began to meet canoes; the canal was a busy little village street, where the Sepik is a great lonely empty track, which a whole fleet of canoes could never crowd—first a canoe with men armed with hunting spears and containing nothing ex-cept lumps of firewood, then canoes of children out gathering lotus flowers, and merrily chewing on lotus rhyzomes, while some of the girls had braided the long white rhyzomes into belts from which they chewed bits at intervals.

We found our party camped on a little ledge of dry ground about six yards wide, about twelve feet above the stream, and sloping off into some of the newly dried grass country, over which one could look for miles. The people had built no shelters at all but merely stood their cylindrical basketwork mosquito bags up along the bank and used the trees on which to hang up baskets of food, rain capes, and other bits of personal gear.

Our own camp was simply a large piece of canvas set up like a tent on a few pieces of light elephant grass, with a mosquito net under it. But no sooner had we got comfortably inside it in the evening than strange shouting and bellowing began, men of importance standing up and ordering the moon to come out, so that there would be no rain. Then our two shamans went into trance and began stamping and gesticulating up and down, among the fires and the smoke frame, the pitched mosquito bags, and the little wooden stools, the women who were just finishing cooking, or trying to turn or stow away their fish. The shamans have to pretend to be reasonably *non compos mentis,* and so they pitched about, knocking their heads against hanging baskets occasionally, but doing much less damage than I did, embarrassed by an electric torch, a notebook, ignorance of the ground, and a strange interpreter just roped in at a moment's notice to dictate the shamans' shouted incomprehensibilities. The smoke stung one's eyes, the mosquitoes bit and bit, the interpreter wearied, one stumbled over crocodile tails and put one's foot into the side of baskets—all with the assurance that the written record would certainly turn out to be illegible. Finally after an hour of this we went to bed, and then in the night it poured.

Next morning it was a shivering disgruntled company which listlessly gathered up its wet belongings and prepared to move camp to another spot. The next day they were to go to an appointed market where their smoked fish and turtles would have got them enough carbohydrate food and betel nut for ten days. But just as the camp was finally breaking up, an old man and an old woman, both of whom were planning to make death feasts for which their clan was hunting in this communal way, had a quarrel, and the old woman threw away the crocodile that she had been given. Someone brought it down the stream and laid it on the bank, and later one of the hunters went and sang mournful totemic songs of it, as it was his totemic thing, a water thing, thus inappropriately left on land. And everyone was so dispirited and angry over the quarrel and the rain that they abandoned next day's market and any further hunting and went home. And so did we.

These peoples with whom I worked in the 1930's are the most primitive of any included in this book, and the peoples of New Guinea with whom contemporary field workers make first contacts today are equally primitive, as far as basic culture is concerned, but sophisticated in different ways.

They have seen airplanes, and they become almost at once part of a much faster-moving culture-contact situation. Boys go away to school rather than to indentured labor; patrol officers come in to register people for voting rather than for head taxes. The equipment available for the field worker is a tremendous improvement over the equipment available forty years ago. Otherwise little has changed. Life in interiors was difficult then and, where there are no roads, is difficult now. Travel by canoe and small boats was, and still is, hazardous. There is always the possibility of an earthquake or a volcanic upheaval or a hurricane. The business of living—getting where one wants to go, getting supplies and mail and film in and out, building a house, training helpers—takes up a great deal of time. Usually medical work is added to all of these other problems.

But there are also many compensations that are lacking for the field worker in more complex cultures or in cultures where more Europeans or educated members of the same culture are nearby. In New Guinea people accept women as friendly. They are an expressive people, in terms familiar to Europeans, and present none of the stylized resistance in demeanor and facial expression found among American Indians. They are culture-conscious, in the sense that they know their own local culture and language to be different from their neighbors'. They are therefore not shocked to find themselves objects of study; instead, they are flattered that the field worker is taking the trouble to learn their customs and their language. In most parts of New Guinea people had heard, even when I first went there, of some village that had been studied by an anthropologist, and they were eager for their turn. I never encountered any opposition or suspicion, though there were things which they of course could not understand. The Manus of 1928 had no notion of altruism, and their theory of our presence was that we were taking pictures of them that Europeans would consider, and pay for, as pornography. They know that the Mission and the missionized natives considered some of their customs lewd and salacious.

The primitiveness of the scene intrudes most, not in the treatment one receives from the people, but in the state of the food, the housing, illness and death. Hazards are mainly hazards from members of other tribes, the insane, accidents, and illness. Before the new malarial suppressants, one might have malaria as much as a third of the time. A scorpion bite might disable one for weeks. In Tambunum on the Sepik River 10 per cent of the deaths came from death adders, and there were no known antivenom serums to deal with them. A broken bone may mean a long painful journey to the nearest doctor, many days away. There are obscure skin diseases and unidentified fevers and dysenteries. But the illnesses do not compare in intensity with the illness one gets in India, or even in Mexico. The painfulness of bush life is mild compared with the jungles of Latin America, where

Zunia and Jules Henry (1944) worked. The discomforts in a hot climate hardly compare with the rigors of traveling with a nomadic people in a cold climate, as Ethel John Lindgren (1934, 1938) did among the Lapps—where she was suspected of being a government spy, with the result that she could not take notes—or with the problems faced by Warren and Nina Swidler (Swidler, 1968) two years ago among the nomads of Baluchistan, where she could only take what she could carry on a camel. I have never heard of any difficulties encountered by women in New Guinea that were not due to problems of transport, food, illness, or loneliness. I have never heard of a case where their presence was resented or where their motives were deeply suspected. There have been some ambiguous encounters of anthropologists in New Guinea, but in each case Europeans were involved, to resent claims on their hospitality or to fantasy too close an intimacy between anthropologist and natives, which meant letting European status down. An informant was murdered in the Berndts' back yard; they were horrified by New Guinea savagery, as was Kenneth E. Reed (1965). But one can also be repelled by Polish canons of pride and betrayal or by Greek anarchy, by subtle forms of cruelty as well as by accounts of cannibalism or necrophilia.

It is easier to describe how the various people with whom I worked looked to me than how I looked to them. In Samoa I had the advantage of youth and high status. The American fleet had come in while I was in the port, and I had been the guest of the admiral. Among the very rank-conscious Samoans I was able to raise the rank of the other Americans with whom I associated. They knew that I was writing a book, and they thought themselves a very suitable subject. They considered my interest in children and adolescents lamentable but helped by my size; I was five feet two and weighed 100 pounds; since I was smaller than their young girls, the association with children was somewhat more forgivable. They chaperoned me carefully. They taught me to dance and to speak the courtesy language, and they were proud of their pupil. Our relationships were gay and lacking intensity, and yet I felt that in later years, if I had wanted to go back, the family who adopted me initially would have welcomed me and fed me and cared for me if I were ill.

In Manus I arrived as a newly married woman who had never borne a child, still thin and slight and looking, in their words, "still a young girl." They were appalled at the idea of a woman all alone among strangers, with no male relative to turn to, and one of our principal informants proclaimed himself my brother to whom I could flee if my husband beat me. They knew that I could not swim, and they were always watchful about the state of house floors or when I was in a canoe. Where the Samoans had provided social protection, the Manus provided primarily physical safety.

The Arapesh encountered me first when I was trussed up like a pig and had to be carried into the mountains because the ankle I had broken in Manus never became very strong again. To them I was someone who could not walk, marooned on a mountain top, while they ranged far and wide carrying heavy loads and heavy babies. I found them temperamentally very congenial, although intellectually they were very exasperating. I was treated as kin by the whole village, and babies were taught to trust me by endless repetition of kinship terms: "She's your father's sister, good! good! good!" Whenever I was alone, the women came and sat with me, singing softly in the chilly evenings, and they trusted me to dispose safely of the dangerous bandages that might deliver them into the hands of sorcerers. The men trusted me not to betray any of their secrets to the women. Only once was there an episode of repudiation. Baimal, the chief painter of the village, was making a bark painting and I recorded it, as he painted, in a miniature copy in water color. He was attracted by the clean brightness of the little copy, but he was angered that it was done by a woman; muttering "Women! Women!" he left the village for several days. When I left Manus the first time, I did not cry, although the people beat the death tattoo on the slit gongs, but in Arapesh, when the long trek down to the beach started at dawn, everyone cried.

The Mundugumor were the fiercest people with whom either of us had worked; they were cannibals just a few years removed from raiding. I walked among them in the village, but we did not let a group up into the house [5] for fear that old habits might reassert themselves; after all, a head is a head. The people used me as an excuse for not fighting, but they accompanied their noisy quarrels with threats of "Just you wait until there is no white woman in the village, and then you'll see."

Among the Tchambuli I slipped into the women's world very easily; a group of women were dancing when I arrived, and I joined the dance. Soon I was being offered partly smoked cigars and given babies to hold. In neither Mundugumor nor Tchambuli did we stay long enough to form ties as close as we formed among the other peoples we had studied.

The Balinese presented a sharp contrast to all of these other South Sea people. They were used to some contact with Europeans who came to Bali, not only to govern, but also to paint and study the music and simply as delighted tourists. Europeans as spectators of their dancers were familiar to them, but any kind of human contact, warm or cold, they found frightening. When I showed sympathy over the illness of a child, they simply withdrew, faces smiling but elbows so tense that the babies in their arms cried as their mothers spoke with meticulous courtesy, covering their fright. It was

5. The house was built high above the ground on posts, a confined space out of view of the village.

not until I learned how to theatricalize my every word and gesture, to caricature and overact every genuine bit of feeling, that I could set the Balinese at ease. They brought their babies to be given medicine, they came to listen to the phonograph or to beg for old tin cans, but they remained distant, accepting us rather than welcoming us. Pictures taken in the field show the extent to which I adapted to the style of the people with whom I was working. In photographs taken in Bali I look disassociated, sitting among a people each of whom was separated from the others. In Samoa the pictures show me dressed up, sitting and standing to display my Samoan costumes and rank; in Manus I am alert and tense, half strangled by a child clinging around my neck; in Arapesh I have become as soft and responsive as the people themselves.

The Iatmul in 1938 presented a contrast to the Balinese and to all the other trips. I arrived knowing something of the language and a great deal about the culture, firmly placed as the wife of an anthropologist who belonged inside the system. They took me in, tested me, periodically provoked me with tall tales, and made me so much a part of their life that twenty-nine years later, when I returned, they picked up the threads again. But this was also true in Bali after twenty years; house boys now grown men picked up the camera box and the tripod and set about reinstating their old tasks.

In all three cases—Manus, Bali, and Iatmul—when I returned many years later, I found that the people remembered and enjoyed the intensive months that we had shared together, as they taught me and helped me and I attended to every detail of their lives. I believe the best generalization I can make is that all of them, in their very different ways, enjoyed making their culture conscious, articulate, and visible. I have never been back to Arapesh, but in the summer of 1968 I met Saharu, who had been my devoted small attendant in 1932, and he made me a present of a new Australian dollar and wept because he and I were both still alive. Something about the discrepancies between the experiences that lie between the first time I worked with them and the time when I return seizes their imagination, makes them meditate about the nature of the world, the changes in the world, their age and mine. It is almost as if the fact that I have aged so much more slowly than they have, so that men twenty years younger than I are shrunken and senile, is some kind of measure of the difference between living in a culture and being a recording spectator. "We had forgotten all this," said Kutan looking at the pictures that I brought back, "but you had them all the time."

We may now turn to more general considerations. As every going human society is composed of both sexes and a range of ages, the age and sex of a field worker becomes immediately important. If one is to practice the kind of involvement in the local community that permits one to sample the full range of types of interaction, then one's own stance must be clear. On occasion field workers have attempted to evade this basic condition; to insist on having no clear biologically defined position within the local structure; to be treated as a "child of clan" but acknowledge no clan position; to insist, though a woman, on witnessing ceremonies forbidden to women; or to insist, though a man, on witnessing events forbidden to men. At the worst, as in William Jones' insistence on hiding and watching a birth (Jones, 1907), this could mean death; at the best it means a blurring of one's sensitivity. It is done at a price, with some loss of a sense of self and confusion for those with whom one works.

There were two major situations in which I found a biologically defined situation really constricting. The first was in Manus in 1928, when, because I had not yet borne a child, I was forbidden to see childbirth. The second was in Bali, where the beginning and end of life are sacred because they are closest to the fringes of the recurrent other world. As the mature married state is at the very nadir of ceremonial purity, I was often debarred from ceremonies at which only young girls and old women were permitted. Later, in Manus in 1953, endowed by the people with fewer years but greater seniority than my actual age of fifty-three, I experienced the privilege of accompanying a group of men out fishing, for example, without the chaperonage and circumspection which had been a constant source of slight irritation on my first field trip at the age of twenty-three to Samoa, where I was never left unattended for a minute.

Actual beauty is less important than the attitudes a woman has toward her own looks. The beauty is happy about her looks and expects other people to enjoy them too; she is likely to have an ease that will carry her along even among people who do not in fact value her particular features. The older woman without any especially appealing features and no nonsense about her may also have an easy time both with officialdom and with primitive people. And sometimes ambivalences that are troubling in civilization may be resolved in the field. Very small women may be able to capitalize on their size if they want to work with children; very tall women get themselves treated as if they were men; prim, spinsterish women assume a post-menopausal age they have not in fact reached; youngsters smarting under the indignities of youth assume unexpected authority. But as a rule, it is ease in one's own body, willingness to be watchful about dress and manners, and a capacity to feel and look "at home" wherever one is that counts most.

It may be said categorically that any age and either sex is to some extent a handicap in studying a whole culture if one must work alone. Ideally a three-generation family, including children highly trained to understand what they experience, would be the way to study a culture; such a method is neither practical, in terms of field work personnel, nor tolerable in small communities, where a married couple is often almost too heavy a burden on the physical and personal resources of the people. Without either a full or partial complement of others at the same time or over time, the best that the single field worker can do is to preserve his own position very clearly and, to the extent that it is possible, imaginatively reconstruct—in conversation and remote observation—what a member of the other sex, or someone older or younger, would be able to see, touch, feel.

All this is complicated in several specific ways for a woman field worker alone. A woman alone in the field has greater freedom than a man alone in traditional situations where there has been limited contact with Europeans, and that mainly male. A tribal people will be jealous of their women, or will offer them to male visitors in ways that are hard to resist, but tribal women do not fear that a woman anthropologist will take their men. Tribal men are constrained by the caste barriers that accompany first culture contact from making any personal approaches to a woman of superior status of another race. There are, of course, exceptions to this, among sophisticated peoples whom Europeans have found sexually attractive; there may be men who have encountered European prostitutes or have been objects of attention from European women. This is particularly true in Polynesia, where the kinds of culture contact that have occurred mean that Polynesians will not hesitate to approach a European woman, and women field workers may be tempted into inappropriate friendships. But in general, the position of a European woman in a Pacific village situation is relatively secure, compared with that of a man. The people will protect her, according to her known status, as they would one of their own. At the same time, as long as she observes the outward forms appropriate to a member of her sex, young men will tell her a great deal about ceremonies that she would not be permitted to witness if they are once certain that she will not repeat what she knows to their women. A male anthropologist may occasionally establish a comparable relation to an old post-menopausal woman, but in general women's affairs are more body-linked and more guarded than the ceremonial secrets of the men. The fact that an anthropological field worker is a man is less easily masked—for the village women, that is—than is the fact that the strange, remote, equipment-burdened anthropologist is a woman for the men. Subject always to the peculiarities of each culture, women field workers have an easier time the older they look or are willing to look. The pretense of virginity in women who have been married is particularly dangerous, and on the whole all signs of maturity, previous marriage, and motherhood are valuable assets, lowering the anxiety of the male community charged with protecting or defending any women in their midst. A woman working alone, especially an older woman, may therefore expect to be able to get more of the culture than a man working alone. This is of course very fortunate, for a great deal of what is usually regarded as culturally important in most societies is almost exclusively the affair of men. The circumstances that cause intellectual women to be bored at dinner parties when relegated after dinner to conversations with wives who are interested only in babies, servants, and bargains holds in primitive societies also. Where there is high rank, women of rank may be interesting informants, as in Bali and Polynesia. Where women are important religious practitioners and so play a role in the community, the woman medium or ceremonial specialist may be very interesting. But in general, wives and mothers are as limited in their interests in one kind of society as in another. If the woman field worker is primarily interested in child care and personal relations, this is not such a handicap, but if she is concerned with matters of politics, economics, and ceremony, women are seldom as good informants as men; they are not accustomed to attend, in a concentrated way, to any line of thought; their children tug at their legs, their babies cry to be fed, and their husbands beat angry tattoos if their wives are away from home too long.

Women field workers may be divided into those with deeply feminine interests and abilities, who in the field will be interested in the affairs of women, and those who are, on the whole, identified with the main theoretical stream of anthropology in styles that have been set by men. Women with feminine interests and especially an interest in children are also likely to marry and so are less likely to go into the field except when accompanying their husbands. In practice, therefore, we have tended to have women who are more oriented toward feminine concerns working with their husbands or only temporarily deeply concerned with field work, or somewhat masculinely oriented women, independent, bored by babies at home and abroad, working alone, and using male informants.

Field work is in most cases lonelier for women than for men. Women's activities are more restricted; contacts with other Europeans have to be managed with more skill and tact. Where a male field worker can afford a night on the town in an outstation, a woman—especially a woman who is a stranger in an area—cannot. Only long habituation and knowledge make it advisable for her to go on expeditions to other villages, where the living conditions are unknown, or to venture out in the middle of the night when sounds of a brawl occur. Relief from village life can take the form of hunting or fishing for men; accompanying women who weed and gather shellfish on the shore is more back-breaking and less refreshing. Furthermore, where men may chafe under continence enforced by the exigencies of field work, what women miss deeply are strong personal relationships and tenderness. This can be somewhat compensated for if one works a great deal with babies and small children; this is a resource that male field workers who also miss tenderness can seldom take advantage of because usually where the babies are, there are the women also.

Without exception it seems sound advice for both male and female field workers to form no relationships modeled on primary relationships among the people whom they are studying, taking no one for child, parent, spouse, sibling, or lover, however partial and fictive such relationships may be. Simulated primary relationships draw too heavily on the field worker's own culture and distort and dim the observers' capacity to maintain that necessary distance that is both warm and limited, affectionate but not passionate, friendly but not partisan. Fictive relationships that are not simulations of primary ones permit the field workers to experience the formalities of the culture they are studying. The field worker has to be free not to love too much and to dislike those individuals whom he or she finds ethically or aesthetically repulsive. This rather rudimentary requirement seems to have been obscured for some of the field workers of the 1950's, who seem to have mixed the demands for good interracial behavior at home with some imaginary demand that one should like, or even love, any people who are subjects of anthropological inquiry (see Mead, 1959). The earlier requirement that one should fully respect the members of another culture, no matter how primitive, is a simpler one to fulfill and more scientifically and ethically sound. Trying to love, or even like, a whole group of people, regardless of their differing personalities and endowments, is as much an insult, although a less damaging one, as disliking a whole people for ethnic reasons.[6]

6. Some recent events highlight these particular points. Irving Wallace has a genius for nosing out the unpleasant; his attribution of suppressed racism to his fictional anthropologists in *The Three Sirens* (1963) undoubtedly echoes some indiscriminate professional attitudes about emotional integration among some of the young anthropologists he interviewed. I have also been struck by the horror some contemporary anthropologists have expressed because Malinowski, who has been outstanding among anthropologists, in describing primitive culture as worthy of respect and appreciation, should have also expressed—in his private diary (1967)—annoyance and repudiation of his native informants and even used a contemporary epithet to describe their color. After one has been aggravated for days by broken promises, slovenly work, churlish refusals —which at some time accompany almost all prolonged field work in small communities —the tendency to blow off steam and condemn everyone roundly in private, in correspondence or diary, is a good safety valve and not a suitable topic for moralistic recriminations. That Malinowski, as a German- and English-educated Polish aristocrat, could penetrate the delicate fabric of Trobriand culture is a fact of profound importance for the whole world, one important contribution to the post-second World War climate of opinion in which peoples of every race have been treated as worthy and capable of nationhood.

A third indication of this curious attitude of field workers of the 1950's and 1960's showed up in the discussions in Marian Slater's symposium held at the 1966 annual meeting of the Association for the Advancement of Science, in which field workers testified—I can find no better word for it—to their boredom with, aversion to, or sentimental regard for members of primitive or urban proletarian communities. One does not go to a primitive community to satisfy one's demands for sophisticated twentieth-century conversation or to find personal relationships missed among one's peers. Those who would do the first are fatuous; those who would do the second risk endangering the reputations and work of their more disciplined colleagues.

On the other hand, although women field workers are more personally lonely, they may also more easily live as part of the households of others or set up households of their own; and in so doing they may have better food, better health and more of a semblance of an active, normal social life. Men alone in general do a poorer job of setting up a household, eat less well, and establish a narrower range of relationships. There is, however, the danger that in the post-second World War world women will be so used to life without servants and so lacking in any knowledge of how to manage them that they will fail to take advantage of a household setting as a way of attracting a group of different ages and both sexes around them and so making their households part of the community of households within which they live.

Women field workers tend to be handicapped by either an inadequate knowledge of the equipment they need to use—typewriters, tape recorders, cameras—or by a kind of reversed masculine protest that makes them resent the fact that they should have to use screwdrivers or monkey wrenches. The fact that at least half of the men who go into the field are equally ignorant and inept when it comes to tools doesn't help very much. Many women tend to feel somehow abused by the intractability of material things. The importance of mastering any technology that is to be used—for either sex, but especially for women alone—cannot be overemphasized.

Women alone in the field are also more likely to be preoccupied with present or possible future personal relationships than are men. There is a kind of freedom from the demands of a personal life in deeply engrossing field work that is more likely to appeal to a married man—temporarily free from demands to care for the children or to buy a new car—than it is to women, who hope to retain a fiancé or find a husband. Married women, except in later life, hardly ever go into the field alone. Women are more personally vulnerable in the field, more affected by news of illnesses and death and rupture of relationships at home, and therefore more likely to become rundown, ill, or depressed or to break off their field work prematurely. Such conditions combine with memories of the doubts of their professors, who questioned whether they would ever really become anthropologists, or the fury of those male professors who put their special faith in a woman student and feel betrayed if she dares to marry or have a baby.

For women, more than for men, age, sexual experience, marital status, previous or expected motherhood, acceptance or rejection of spinsterhood, maturity, and post-menopausal zest loom larger than they do for men. In predicting the success of a male field worker, bio-sociological conditions are less significant. Just because field work alone is a lonely business, women tend to feel that their loneliness is imposed on them, while men who can feel they have elected lonely adventurous paths are less likely to be sensitive and resentful when the loneliness presses too hard.

Because the aim of field work is to encompass a whole, and as many parts of that whole in as much detail as possible, field teams are successful to the extent that the skills and capacities, temperaments and interests of the team members are complementary, asymmetrical, and noncompetitive. A husband-and-wife team, or a team in which there is a great discrepancy of age, whether of the same or opposite sex, works better than a team of two men or two women of the same age. Each piece of knowledge that either member of the team acquires speeds up the learning of the other or others. If this is accepted enthusiastically, without rivalry, then any team of whatever composition, but especially one contrasted in sex or age, will be able to do, not twice, but four or five times as much work as one person working alone. However, differential self-esteem and competitiveness are very likely to accompany any field work and are particularly likely to complicate a relationship between man and wife. Field work is individualistic; ideally each young anthropologist wants to write a whole book about the whole culture.

Some of the grant-giving institutions have come to distinguish between wives and working wives, reserving the latter term for those women who may be regarded as scientists in their own right. Legitimately, then, the term "wife" should be reserved for women who, however skilled or however highly educated, are primarily interested in their husbands' careers and who go into the field with the same intention of ministering to their husbands' success as if those same husbands were physicians or politicians or astronauts, following careers that require rather special displays of devotion and endurance on the part of their wives. The only trouble with this distinction is that, in practice, many highly trained and originally committed women, quite capable of doing first-class work on their own, are reduced instead to the combined role of secretary and technical assistant, at rates cheaper than such functions command in the marketplace, when secured in the form of the wife of one's bosom. It would take more than the fingers of both hands to count the cases where the price of continued marriage has been the consent of the wife trained in anthropology to complete intellectual obliteration, selfless typing, proof-reading, the making of bibliographies.

This should not be regarded as a wholesale indictment of anthropologists as husbands, but it is true that marriages between anthropologists are peculiarly subject to the vicissitudes of socially cultivated attitudes in men who cannot tolerate independent intellectual activities on the part of their wives. Women anthropologists are continuously tempted into endogamous marriages, for this is indeed the way in which both the hopes for private happiness and field work can be met. Men are equally tempted by the convenience of having a wife for whom the field is a privilege instead of a cross. But such marriages for women with independent intellectual abilities are both particularly hazardous and particularly rewarding. The most difficult cases are those in which an original partnership has been accompanied by high romantic hopes, gone down in disaster, and in which the husband, going on to another partner has, without acknowledgement, appropriated the work of the former mate. Here I speak not out of my own experience, but of the experiences of many other women field workers.

Perhaps no other endogamous marriages, except those of two committed foreign missionaries or two stars of show business, present quite as many hazards. The members of a good anthropological team in a difficult field location are as interdependent as two trapeze artists or, to pick a loftier simile, as Alfred Lunt and Lynn Fontanne. It is, in retrospect, quite impossible to disentangle the threads of their expert perceptions, so as to say whose insight was more significant or who got the first clue to some unsuspected aspect of the culture. Even tape-recorded conversations cannot catch the nuance of an almost uttered thought that nevertheless feeds and nourishes the growing insight of the other. And it may also be added that the kind of marital accord that sustains a lifetime of shared field work may be of so involved a quality that one member of a team who worked so perfectly in step cannot survive the death of the other.

Where marriages between anthropologists are based on marked contrast in temperament and tempo, as is for many reasons most desirable, there is a further hazard in the way in which the cultural style, the physique, and the habitat of a people may lock into the preferences of one of the pair and repel the other. In this way an unstable balance between spontaneity and control, a need to dominate and a need to be dominated, an uncertainty of sex identification in both, a longing for violence and an absolute repudiation of violence, a love of the sameness of a slow-flowing river and a sense of infinite boredom with such a fenlike landscape, may all become the basis of a new tension.

Ruth Benedict (1934) wrote of culture as "personality writ large." A whole culture—especially small, isolated, exaggeratedly distinctive cultures, such as those of New Guinea—may have, in a most extreme degree, the stimulating or devastating effect that a friend who brings out a contrast in temperament may have on the balance of a marriage. Both field workers are concentrated on the culture, both are working minute by minute with members of that culture; everything—dreams reported by informants and dreams of one's own, fears of sorcery, threats of death, styles of work, loyalties, treacheries and betrayals—will exacerbate such differences. And to a considerable degree they cannot be guarded against, except in marriages that are already so stable, so inured to the hazards of field work, that the precautions are no longer necessary. These different perceptions may in turn become the basis for reports on the culture that may contrast, as do those of Freuchen (1931) and Rasmussen (1931) on the Eskimo, and perplex those who think of field work as the emotionless and objective performance of carefully arranged and personally neutral routine activity. Just as each child complicates a marriage in terms of its sex and its temperamental similarity or contrast to one parent or the other, so a whole village intensely observed and related to, tuned to one emphasis often at the expense of another, acts as an amplifier of latent antagonisms.

This is true to a limited extent in any anthropological marriage, but it is accentuated in field work that is focused—as mine has been—on problems of personality and culture. Such field work, like clinical work in psychology and psychiatry, requires that the practitioner work as a whole person. But unlike the psychotherapist, who can restrict his total insights to the consulting room and turn them off altogether when dealing with members of his family and colleagues, such an anthropologist has to learn to be a whole person all of the time, twenty-four hours a day in the field and out of the field. This adds intensity to all personal relationships—those with informants, with other team workers, with one's teachers and students and colleagues. It is probable that women have a higher toleration for such continuous personal involvement, if only because they have identified as children with their mothers who, as wives and mothers, were necessarily displaying it. Women working in the field with children do not have to identify with the children but can enter the world of women and children, by identifying with the women who are mothers. Male field workers who are interested in children, such as male psychotherapists working with children, have to enter the world of women and children by identification with the children as their mode of understanding, and this involves psychologically expensive regression. In the field, therefore, culture and personality studies make fewer demands on women in the work itself, but heavier demands in all attempts at intellectual cooperation among those who are related to each other as real or fictive husbands, lovers, friends, parents, or children.[7]

Field work will be hard for women who are not willing to put their whole personalities into it. On the whole it is harder, I believe, for women who have made a masculine identification in childhood, who do not enjoy women and children, and who are impatient with the small continuous

7. The violence of some of the internecine in-fighting that goes on within anthropological circles can be explained by the incestuous overtones of such intense relationships. Anthropologists of my generation still regard all other anthropologists, including those whom they have never met, as kin, toward whom one may express all the ambivalence generated by close family ties and toward whom one is also totally obligated to provide succor *in extremis*. As the profession grows so much larger, this sense of kinship becomes harder to establish, and it may be that it will survive only in the extraordinary bad manners of anthropological reviewers who will imitate their elders' style without recognizing that that style was accompanied by the kind of unquestioning willingness to help appropriate to those who regarded themselves as members of one large family.

demands made by strangers on each other in isolated places. (But such women may be able to tolerate solitary field work better than do women who have lived their whole lives in intense relationships with others but fail to establish it in the field.) For those women who enjoy intense involvement at every level, all the time, night and day, anthropological field work as a member of a team whose members one loves is undoubtedly one of the best ways of cheating time and compounding delight and of living several lives in the course of one lifetime. Each culture so lived is a separate whole life.

References

BATESON, GREGORY. 1932. "Social Structure of the Iatmul People of the Sepik River," *Oceania*, 2, 245–291 401–453.

BENEDICT, RUTH. 1934. *Patterns of Culture*. Boston and New York, Houghton Mifflin; reprinted 1961, Houghton Mifflin, Sentry edition 8.

FORTUNE, REO F. 1931. "Manus Religion," *Oceania*, 2, 74–108.

————. 1935. "Manus Religion," American Philosophical Society, Memoir 3; reprinted 1965, Lincoln: University of Nebraska Press, BB 303.

FREUCHEN, PETER. 1931. *Eskimo*. Translated by A. P. Maerker-Branden and E. Branden. New York: Grosset and Dunlap.

GILBERT, CRAIG, producer and director. 1968. *Margaret Mead's New Guinea Journal;* 16 mm, 90 min., sound, color. New York: National Educational Television.

HENRY, JULES, and ZUNIA HENRY. 1944. *Doll Play of Pilaga Indian Children.* Research Monograph No. 4. New York: American Orthopsychiatric Association.

JONES, WILLIAM. 1907. *Fox Texts.* (Publications of the American Ethnological Society, Vol. 1) Leyden, Late E. J. Brill.

LINDGREN, ETHEL J. 1934. "Field work in Social Psychology in Eastern Asia." In First Congres International des Science Anthropologiques et Ethnologiques, London, 1934. London: Institute Royale d'Anthropologie, pp. 152–153.

————. 1938. "An Example of Culture Contact Without Conflict," *American Anthropologist*, 40, 605–621.

MALINOWSKI, BRONISLAW. 1967. *A Diary in the Strict Sense of the Term.* New York: Harcourt, Brace.

MEAD, MARGARET. 1930a. *Growing Up in New Guinea.* New York: Morrow. Reprinted 1968, New York: Dell, Laurel edition 3270.

————. 1930b. "Melanesian Middlemen," *Natural History*, 30, 115–130.

————. 1931. "Living With the Natives of Melanesia," *Natural History*, 31, 62–74.

————. 1932. "An Investigation of the Thought of Primitive Children, With Special Reference to Animism," *Journal of the Royal Anthropological Institute*, 62, 173–190.

————. 1934. *Kinship in the Admiralty Islands,* Anthropological Papers of The American Museum of Natural History, 34, Part 2.

————. 1935. "Part Two: The River-Dwelling Mundugumor." In Sex and temperament in three primitive societies. New York: Morrow. Reprinted 1968, New York: Dell, Laurel edition 7777.

————. 1953. *"Manus Revisited."* In *Papua and New Guinea Scientific Society, Annual Report and Proceedings, Port Moresby, 1953.* Port Moresby: Papua and New Guinea Scientific Society, pp. 15–18.

————. 1954a. "Cultural Discontinuities and Personality Transformation," *Journal of Social Issues,* Suppl. Ser. No. 8, 3–16.

————. 1954b. "Manus Restudied: An Interim Report," *Transactions of The New York Academy of Sciences,* Ser. 2, 16, 426–432.

————. 1954c. "Twenty-Fifth Reunion at Manus," *Natural History,* 63, 66–68.

————. 1955. "Energy Changes under Conditions of Cultural Change," *Sociometry and the Science of Man,* 18, 201–211.

————. 1956. *New Lives for old.* New York: Morrow. Reprinted 1968, New York: Dell, Laurel edition 6333.

————. 1959. "Cultural Factors in Community-Education programs." In Nelson B. Henry, ed., *Community Education.* National Society for the Study of Education, 58th Yearbook, Part 1. Chicago: University of Chicago Press, pp. 66–96.

————. 1961–1962. *New Lives for old.* Horizons of Science Series, I, No. 6, 16 mm, 20 min., sound, color. Princeton, N. J.: Educational Testing Service.

————. 1964. *Continuities in Cultural Evolution.* New Haven, Conn.: Yale University Press. Reprinted 1966, New Haven, Conn.: Yale University Press, paperback Y–154.

————. 1965. "New Guinea Revisited," *Redbook Magazine,* 124 (4), 6–12.

————. 1966. "Anthropologist in the Field." Review of *Stranger and Friend* by Hortense Powdermaker. *Holiday,* 39, 113–115.

————.1967. "Letter From the Field: Return to New Guinea," *Redbook Magazine,* 130 (1), 20–27.

————. 1968. "Filming Life and Death in a New Guinea Village," *Redbook Magazine,* 132 (1), 46, 50–52, 54.

————, and THEODORE SCHWARTZ. 1960. "The Cult as a Condensed Social Process." In Bertram Schaffner, ed., *Group Processes.* Transactions of the Fifth Conference, October 1958. New York: Josiah Macy, Jr., Foundation, pp. 85–187.

————, THEODORE SCHWARTZ, and LOLA SCHWARTZ. 1963–1969. "A Field Study in Cultural Systematics, New Guinea." NIH (National Institute of Health) grant MH 07675 to American Museum of Natural History. Mimeographed.

POWDERMAKER, HORTENSE. 1966. *Stranger and Friend.* New York: W. W. Norton.

RASMUSSEN, KNUD. 1931. *The Netsilik Eskimos: Social Life and Spiritual Culture.* Report of the Fifth Thule Expedition 1921–1924, Vol. 8, Nos. 1–2.

READ, KENNETH E. 1965. *The High Valley*. New York: Scribner.

SCHWARTZ, LENORA S. (Lenora Foerstal). 1959. *Cultural Influence in Perception*. Unpublished Master's Essay, Stella Elkins Tyler School of Fine Arts of Temple University. Philadelphia.

SCHWARTZ, THEODORE. 1962. *The Paliau Movement in the Admiralty Islands, 1946–1954*. Anthropological Papers of The American Museum of Natural History, 49, Part 2.

———. 1963. "Systems of Areal Integration: Some Considerations Based on the Admiralty Islands of Northern Melanesia," *Anthropological Form* 1, 56–97.

———, and MARGARET MEAD. 1961. "Micro- and Macro-Cultural Models for Cultural Evolution," *Anthropological Linguistics*, 3, 1–7.

SWIDLER, WARREN W. 1968. "Technology and Social Structure in Baluchistan, West Pakistan." Ph.D. Thesis. New York: Columbia University.

THURNWALD, RICHARD G. 1916. *Bánaro society*. American Anthropological Association, Memoir 3.

TOLKIEN, J. R. R. 1954–1956. *Lord of the rings*. London: Allen and Unwin; Boston: Houghton Mifflin.

WALLACE, IRVING. 1963. *The Three Sirens*. New York: Simon and Schuster. Reprinted New York: New American Library, paperback T 2523.

WEDGWOOD, CAMILLA H. 1934. "Report on Research in Manam Island, Mandated Territory of New Guinea," *Oceania*, 4, 373–403.

Wife, Widow, Woman: Roles of an Anthropologist in a Transylvanian Village

DIANE FREEDMAN holds several positions that reflect her interdisciplinary interests. She teaches courses in research and critical thinking at Temple University, in folk dance at Swarthmore College, and in anthropology in adult education classes. In addition, she runs recreational folkdance groups for a variety of community organizations whose members range in age from children to senior citizens. She is continuing her research in dance and gender roles, studying a second Eastern European language, and planning field work with dance groups in ethnic communities in the United States and Eastern Europe.

Introduction[1]

I am an anthropologist, a dancer, and a widow. These three aspects of my life intersect like the circles of a Venn diagram, with one aspect never free of the influence of the others. My focus here is on my professional role as an anthropologist in the field and on the impact of my husband's death on this role. By reflecting on my two field-work situations, I hope to re-create the emotional context through which the variations in role expectations that I experienced as a wife and a widow can be understood.

I was seventeen years old when I met my late husband, Robert, in 1965. It was the beginning of my university education, and I was enjoying new experiences on emotional, physical, and intellectual levels. As my mind embraced new concepts of anthropology, my body strove to master a variety of dance styles. Robert was my dance teacher. We matured together, building our emotional attachment on a sound foundation of shared interests and experiences. We married three years later, after I had completed my baccalaureate degree. The fusion of my anthropological and dance interests has its roots in this period of my life, and it is inextricably tied in with the emotional euphoria of a mutual lifetime commitment.

My interest in Romanian dance developed in the years that followed through my participation in recreational folk dance groups as both dancer and teacher. Simultaneously, I trained as an ethnographer in the culture and communication program of the anthropology department at Temple University, in Philadelphia.

1. I first went to Romania on a grant from the American Council of Learned Societies for language study. My research in the first year was supported by the Department of Anthropology, Temple University. My second year was spent as an Exchange Scholar on a program of the International Research and Exchange Board (IREX). My Romanian affiliation in the first year was the Universitatea Babeş-Bolyai, in Cluj-Napoca. In the second year, as an IREX exchange scholar, I was affiliated with the Consiliu Naţional pentru Ştiinţă şi Technologie. My thanks to all of the above institutions, whose generous support made my research possible.

While learning about studies of nonverbal communication, I began to consider the study of dance from a communications perspective. My choice of Romania as a field site allowed me to augment my dance knowledge and experience in the context of a professional research problem: the study of the meaning of dance as a form of communication between men and women (Freedman 1983). Romania was a good place to investigate this problem because of the persistence of folk traditions, including dance, in the country's rural areas. In addition, both Robert and I were somewhat familiar with Romanian music and dance styles.

When I decided on long-term field work as part of my graduate training, there was never a question as to what my private circumstances would be. Robert and I did not consider a prolonged separation. Robert's profession as a high school physics teacher allowed him the flexibility of an extended leave of absence with the assurance that a position would await him on his return. Together we excitedly prepared for our trip to Romania, with the understanding that while Robert would assist me if he could, he would not undertake a detailed study of the language, and he would thus not be part of the intensive interviewing process. Speaking for him, as I must, I'm sure that his expectations included the idea of a year of relative leisure during which he could relax and catch up on reading while I did my work.

We did spend the year together in the field, but it was the last year we would spend together. Robert's illness abruptly ended our stay. He died of cancer six months after we returned home.

The following year I resumed my work, returning to the field as a widow. During the first month of my return I was still in mourning. According to village custom, after the first anniversary of my husband's death my mourning state was ended; in the eyes of the villagers my civil state was then changed to that of an eligible single woman. The three different statuses of married woman, widow in mourning, and single woman were responded to by the villagers in different ways. During my first stay I faced some problems common to all ethnographers and some others that were unique to my position as a woman ethnographer attempting independent research in an Eastern European country. My return had unexpected consequences. When I returned to the village, I experienced differences in my relations with villagers which I could only attribute to my changed social status. Each of these different interactions was conducive to collecting certain types of data. My field work was therefore enriched by the experience of participating in the society in a variety of social roles.

The First Year

Our arrival in Romania was fraught with difficulties. We were independent researchers, lacking a government grant. Although we had been officially accepted as students in a summer language-training program, we had no official

Romanian sponsor. Our lack of a sponsor was in direct contrast to the situation of other foreigners entering the country, most of whom were met at the airport by an official of their sponsoring organization, led through the intricacies of customs, and driven to lodgings that had been reserved for them.

Lacking such an escort, we negotiated the rough waters ourselves. Since we had known that receiving packages would be nearly impossible, we had brought everything we would need for the year along with us. Somehow we persuaded the customs officials that our huge suitcase of film was legitimate and that we carried no pornographic books in our collection. Emerging from the ordeal of customs, we discovered that the taxis were gone and that all the hotels were full. Further intense negotiations were required before we could arrive in the city and settle in a "full" hotel. On top of everything else, a slight cold that I had been nursing before our departure had become a severe eye-and-ear infection during the twelve-hour plane ride from New York to Bucharest. Sick, disillusioned, and depressed, I collapsed into bed on our first night in Romania. Things had to get better. So far, our excursion had seemed like a nightmare.

We first sought help from the officials at the American embassy. They advised us to give up and go home, commenting on the futility of trying to do independent work in Romania. We were to receive the same advice from many sources. Finally realizing the extent of our persistence, the embassy suggested that we try to make a connection with the Ministry of Education through one of the universities. With this plan in mind, we left Bucharest for the Summer Language Training Institute in southern Transylvania.

During our summer of language training we decided to locate our research in northern Transylvania, an area with well-preserved folk traditions. We were encouraged in our research plans by several Romanian academicians who had come to the institute to lecture to the language students. With renewed energy and expectations, we left the institute for Bucharest, expecting to spend a few weeks sorting out details and then to head for Cluj-Napoca, a large city and university center in Transylvania. We had not counted on the overwhelming complexity of the Romanian bureaucracy, including the section with which we had to deal, the Ministry of Education.

The next two months were even more difficult than our first few days in the country had been. We made daily pilgrimages to the ministry to try to secure permission for our research. There, we competed for the attention of the officials with hundreds of other foreign students, most of whom were on state scholarships to medical school. It took several days of just watching the students' behavior for us to learn how to even get into the office. Once in, we received complex and often contradictory answers. We were sent out again, only to return the next day for the same ritual. It was our most discouraging time in Romania, and we often did contemplate giving up and going home, as everyone we had contacted expected us to do.

A breakthrough finally occurred: I would be permitted to stay if I would pay in hard currency the equivalent of university tuition. The catch was that since I was the principal researcher, Robert was technically my dependent. While this was a reversal of our roles at home, the situation did not bother Robert. He was certainly not threatened by the idea that I was the primary researcher, since he did not pretend to an academic interest in my work; his interest in the field was personal and was totally connected to our relationship. We did not even consider the question of which one of us was to be the team's chief until we became entangled in the red tape of Romanian bureaucracy.

The bureaucrats could not conceive of a male dependent. They insisted that Robert also pay tuition in order to remain in the country with me. The obvious sexual bias of this expectation finally moved our embassy contact to intercede on our behalf through her contacts in the Ministry of Education. Within a few days our respective statuses as student and dependent were confirmed, and our "permissions" were prepared, signed, and stamped with the official seal. Relieved, we finally left Bucharest for Cluj.

In our continuing naïveté we thought that our bureaucratic problems were behind us and that we could now concentrate on our work. Not so. While life was considerably more pleasant in Cluj than it had been in Bucharest, we were still far from our goal of finding, and settling in, a village.

"Permissions" given at the national level had to be checked and double-checked at the levels of both the province and the *comună,* an administrative unit comprising a group of villages. Once we had chosen our village, the major roadblock became the question of housing. According to national law, no foreigner may stay overnight in the home of any Romanian citizen. We had thought that my status as a student would supersede this rule, but the local officials were still uneasy about our proposal to live with a village family. Their counterproposal was for us to live in a tourist hostel ten kilometers from the village.

Finally, I had to state my case in a formal presentation to the minister of culture at the provincial level. A professor who had worked in the village in which I wanted to live was present to comment on my unusual request. The provincial officials, all of whom lived in the capital city of the province, questioned both my need and my desire to actually live with the peasants in the village. I believe that they were sincere in their opinions that I did not know what I was getting into, that I underestimated the hardships of village life, and that I would not last very long in the discomfort of a Romanian winter in a village house. In addition, the model of field work with which they were familiar was that of a series of brief trips to the field site to collect information on specific topics. Long-term field work focusing on broad ethnographic goals is not an Eastern European academic tradition. Despite their reservations, however, the provincial officials approved my research proposal. We proceeded with our plans to move to the village. It was now mid-November, five months after our arrival in Romania.

We had visited the village of Cimpoi[2] a few months earlier in our initial search for a field site. We had gotten off the bus in the center of the village on a rainy Sunday afternoon and had been greeted by a policeman who gave us two pieces of information that we later learned were incorrect: first, that there was no dancing in the village on a rainy day, and second, that women should not go into the bar, which was the only public place in the village where we could escape from the rain. Consequently, our initial visit was very brief; we left on the return bus.

Despite this first unpleasant experience, we chose the village of Cimpoi for our research. It met our criteria for a research site because it had a rich, well-preserved folk tradition, especially in music and dance. It was also sufficiently modernized that living conditions were unstrained, with large, electrified houses located near transportation. A road running through the village assured us of access by bus or car throughout the winter months. Cimpoi is located in the region of Țara Oașului ("country of Oaș"). It is an isolated region, and because of this isolation the local dialect differs in both pronunciation and some vocabulary from standard Romanian. Our first few months in the village were spent adjusting to these differences.

Village officials, in conjunction with representatives from the provincial government, helped us to find appropriate accommodations. We rented a comfortable room with a separate entrance in the house of a childless couple who lived near the center of the village. Since the woman was hesitant about cooking for us (explaining to me later that she did not know what we would like), officials helped us to arrange for a daily meal to be brought from the local high school. We made all other food preparations ourselves.

Our unpacking process resembled that described by Friedl earlier in this volume. The villagers assumed that we were wealthy, like all other foreigners. Their assumptions were supported as they watched us unpack what we considered to be the bare essentials for living. Among our luggage were gifts for informants, including fabric. The brightly colored fabric, in red, yellow, or green with floral designs in contrasting colors, was highly prized for making the full-sleeved blouses and wide skirts for the women's Sunday clothes. I had no intention of giving it all away on our first day, although that was clearly what they wanted me to do. The fabric was examined and commented on by the assembled women. It was apparent that those present expected to be the recipients of most, if not all, of this newfound bounty.

We felt that we were in a delicate situation. I had to assure the women that they would indeed receive some of the goods, but I reserved for myself the right to decide the time and the manner of the distribution. Everyone appeared to be satisfied. We were to learn, however, that this first experience was only the beginning of what would come to be a complex problem.

2. I have changed the name of the village to protect the anonymity of my village contacts.

The villagers saw us as potential brokers for material objects that were difficult for them to obtain. After they got to know us better, we were faced with a steady stream of requests. The requests came from both villagers and officials as well as from both our close associates and people whom we had barely met. A variety of items was requested, including clothing, automobile parts, and household appliances. Later, when we purchased a car, we were asked to give people rides to both near and distant destinations.

Our responses to these requests were generally negative; we tried to explain that we were not capable of fulfilling their expectations. This was true in the sense that our limited funds did not allow for extraneous purchases. From the Romanians' perspective, however, our position was not conceivable. They were aware of the existence of dollar shops for tourists in which goods unavailable on the Romanian market could be purchased for hard currency. Since it was illegal for them to have such currency in their possession, the only way for them to obtain such goods was through intermediaries such as us. Eventually we did make a few of these purchases, but the constant pattern of requests and denials was wearing on us and was the cause of much of our anxiety about alienating our village hosts.

Another potential source of alienation was the question of religion. Before leaving for Romania, I had wondered how to present our religious identity. Colleagues whom I had approached for advice on this question were divided in their opinions. The options were those of being direct and honest with the villagers, explaining that we were Jewish, or of being discreet about our religious affiliation. We had considered the latter option because of the known history of anti-Semitism in the area since its occupation by Germany during World War II. The Jewish families who had lived in Cimpoi before the war had been deported, and none had returned. While many of our informants remembered a variety of incidents from wartime about which they were willing to talk, the question of the fate of the Jews was never discussed with us.

Knowing something of this history before we entered the village, I was reluctant to disclose our Jewish identity. Yet I was also reluctant to blatantly lie to the villagers, bearing in mind my hope that they would not lie to us.

On our first Sunday in the village we went to church, still undecided about how to present ourselves. Since the spatial arrangement of the congregation in church is sex segregated, Robert and I were not together, nor could we even see each other. We stood in the family places of our hosts; Robert was in the front of the church with the married men, and I stood with the married women behind the group of men and older boys. Without any conscious decision on my part, I watched closely the actions of the women around me and mimicked them. It must have been in the back of my mind then that this would be the course of least resistance and the one least likely to get me into trouble. I was as unfamiliar with the Romanian Orthodox church customs practiced by the villagers as I was with the Roman Catholic rites practiced by my neighbors back home. At the conclusion of the service the members of the congregation filed out in front of the priest, who blessed each one with the sign of the cross on his or her forehead. I was similarly blessed, and noticed, by the priest. When I met Robert outside, he reported that he had just stood there trying to look attentive during the service but had not participated in any other way.

The day after our church appearance we were invited to a meeting with the priest in his home. The village priest was a young man with an attractive, educated wife and two precocious young daughters. He was well liked and deeply respected by the villagers, who were very proud of both him and his family. One room of his home was decorated with traditional folk costumes of the region, hung museum-style on the wall.

Our discussion began with friendly exchanges but came quickly to the point: our religion. Since I had only been in the village for a week, my language skills were barely minimal. The discussion took the form of a question-and-answer session: Were we Eastern Orthodox? No. Roman Catholic? No. The priest then listed all of the Protestant sects that he could think of. With each negative reply he became more concerned. Finally he ran out of types and looked at us questioningly. It was now or never. I volunteered a single word, "*Evrieu*," thus announcing to him and to the rest of the village that we were Jews. We waited for the response. The priest broke into a smile, much relieved, saying "Judaism is a religion, too!"

Also relieved that this question was now settled, we participated in a halting discussion on religion. The priest wanted to know why I had made the sign of the cross during the service. I said that I had thought that it was the proper thing to do in church. He said that it was not necessary for me to do that, but that I was welcome to come to church any time. Every time I did go to church and join the processional to be blessed, he blessed me as he did all the others, but with a slight smiling acknowledgment of mutual understanding.

When we returned to our hosts' home the discussion was repeated at a different level, for the villagers were concerned less with categories than with belief. What did it mean to be a Jew? What did we believe in, and what beliefs did we deny? My answers to these questions were based on the broadest interpretations of doctrine. They would certainly not be accepted in an Orthodox interpretation of Judaism, but they were consonant with my own rather ecumenical belief system. My answers satisfied our hosts, who concluded that whatever we were was acceptable as long as we also went to church.

The village officials responded in yet another way to the information about our religion—Were we Jews, or were we Americans? In their worldview these appeared to be mutually exclusive categories. We tried to explain that it was possible to be both, but I'm not sure that we ever succeeded. Given the choice, we emphasized our civil rather than our religious status. This emphasis was reinforced when the officials learned that neither of us had ever been to Israel.

Only later in my stay did I appreciate the significance of our first interview with the priest. Romania's official political ideology rejects religious participation. The churches flourish in spite of, rather than because of, any political support they may receive. Members of the Romanian Communist Party are restricted from entering any church for any reason. While this rule is relaxed for villagers, it is strictly enforced for party officials and for anyone connected with government work, such as teachers. Our early appearance in church must have been a sign to the priest and villagers that we were not trying to ally ourselves with an official position on religion. The priest's further relief when we finally explained ourselves can be interpreted in this light. For him, our being Jewish was preferable to our being either atheists or members of one of the proselytizing sects that were frowned on by both the government and the Orthodox church. By declaring that we were Jews, we labeled ourselves as people who were not espousing an official party doctrine on religion.

These early discussions on religion were our first attempts at prolonged conversation with our hosts. My language skills were minimal, and Robert's were practically nonexistent. Gradually we increased our competence. I began to participate in the daily activities of the women while they cooked, sewed, and gathered together to talk in one another's kitchens. As a married woman myself, I could trade questions with them on the vicissitudes of married life. Details of their own lives were made available to me which would have been reserved had I been unmarried. Since, in the villagers' view, marriage confers womanhood, all unmarried females were considered to be girls. While the villagers recognized that girls seeking higher education often postpone marriage beyond the customary village age of sixteen, an unmarried "girl" of twenty-seven would have had a much harder time gaining acceptance into the women's community.

One of the topics that the women were most interested in was birth control. The women knew that I had been married for eight years and yet had no children. I explained that this was by choice and that we had decided to delay having children until I had finished my education. They wanted to know my methods, and upon hearing for the first time about oral contraceptives, they expressed the hope that I could procure the same for them. I repeatedly denied this possibility and tried to explain the complexity of the situation. Nevertheless, they continued to ask—not only for contraceptives but also for some "medicine to bring back the flow."

Their problem must be understood in the context of Romania's pronatalist policies. Government policy does more than encourage births; it also forbids any attempt to artificially limit them. Both birth control and abortion are illegal. The obvious result of these laws, in Romania as elsewhere, is a large number of illegal abortions, with dire consequences for many women. The village women knew much about abortion and its consequences, hence their desire for some other form of limiting their pregnancies. We understood and shared with one another the frustration that something so easily available to me should be denied to them. However, in this situation there was nothing I could do. Their only means of limiting births, short of sexual abstention, was controlled by their partners, who could choose whether or not to acquiesce to the women's desire for coitus interruptus.

My contact with men was more restricted than was my contact with women. This restriction was due in part to the culturally prescribed separation of the social and economic roles of men and women. There were fewer occasions for me to interact with men, and the resulting lack of familiarity imposed a reserve on the relationships I did develop. This social distance was intensified by the fact that I did not participate extensively in the evening gatherings of friends and relatives. During these gatherings, cross-sex joking helped to mediate the separation between the sexes.

While participation in these gatherings might have been beneficial to my work, I balanced the benefits with my need to spend some time alone with Robert. After a full day of speaking and thinking in a foreign language, I was happy to retire to our small room to write notes, play backgammon, or just speak English. Robert's presence allowed me some respite from the constant pressures of field work. He gave me the kind of escape that a solitary field worker could not have experienced.

There was another reason for our avoidance of the evening gatherings of our hosts. By preference, neither Robert nor I was even a mild social drinker. Robert's tolerance for liquor was greater than mine, but he did not drink for recreation. By contrast, in the village—especially during the long, quiet winter months—communal drinking was the primary leisure activity for the men, and they were often joined in this by the women.

Village hospitality dictated that anyone invited into the house be offered a glass of *ţuica*, a local and particularly powerful variety of fruit brandy. There were three producing stills in the village, one of which was managed by our host. In late fall and early winter, after the harvest, farmers would bring in their produce and return later for the finished brandy. As a consequence, our house was always well supplied with drink and served as a social center through which the business was transacted. We were often invited to join in these interactions. What the local people understood, however, and we did not was the method of polite but firm refusal. The custom was for the host to fill the glass and watch closely until it was emptied (preferably in one shot). It was refilled immediately. Hosts would continue to urge drink on their guests beyond the point of saturation, even if the results were disapproved of later in gossip about how much brandy so-and-so consumed.

In our first meeting with our host, both of us were urged to drink far more than either our desire or capacity would dictate. When Robert became sick after drinking, we began to realize the extent of the problem. Social, political, ritual, and economic interactions were contextualized by the exchange of liquor; our participation in this exchange would have to be curtailed if we were to survive the field experience. After several similar encounters during the time in which we were familiarizing ourselves with the village, we learned how to refuse drinks without causing offense. Women were not expected to be able to drink as much as men, so I had an easier time than Robert did. Once we purchased a car, it became easier still, since everyone recognized the legal necessity for not touching even a drop of liquor if one would soon be driving. Nevertheless, we sometimes avoided social encounters because the effort of refusing drink was just too wearying for us. This peculiarity of ours probably contributed to the villagers' perception of us as young and inexperienced.

Village men viewed a man's ability to drink as an important part of his masculinity. I imagine, although I have no direct evidence for this assertion, that Robert's reputation among the men suffered slightly because of his disinclination to drink. This was probably offset by his high status as a teacher and by the villagers' practice of continually reminding one another that our customs were different from theirs. From my perspective, Robert's reputation among the men was more than balanced by his reputation among the women, who noted with approval that he usually did not drink to excess and that when he was drunk he never became violent or even verbally abusive (traits common enough in their husbands). From these comments on Robert's behavior I could begin to see the characteristics that women most valued in men, characteristics that I later elicited in interviews with young girls who were in the process of choosing their future husbands. It intrigued me that those attributes most negatively valued by the women were those considered important by the men.

While the villagers knew that our own household customs differed from theirs, we were expected to conform somewhat to the ideal pattern of the sexual division of labor. In this pattern, household and garden tasks are the domain of the women, and heavy agricultural work and the care of large animals are left to the men. Women are ritually prohibited from some tasks, such as milking sheep. In general, however, custom rather than rigorous sanction dictates the daily work routine. Our household was different, since Robert had neither land to till nor animals to tend. As a result, he did more than half of our housekeeping. Villagers were scandalized by our customs on this issue. We tried to keep our arrangements private, but privacy is nearly impossible in a situation in which literally every trip to the outhouse is observed by the neighbors.

Our water came from a well located in the courtyard, and nearby lay a long pole with a hook on which a bucket was slung, lowered, and pulled up. Throughout the winter the pole was covered with a glaze of ice, making the job tricky, at best. This job was customarily done by women, but whenever I attempted it the result would be about one-fourth of a bucket of water. Since Robert had no such problem, he was designated as our water retriever. While the men sometimes drew water, they never did it routinely. Men's reactions to our system were divided. Some thought it amusing, while others felt that Robert was degrading himself by doing women's work. The women, in contrast, considered it a positive sign of Robert's concern for me. Even the women, however, had limits of custom beyond which they would not be drawn. When they realized that Robert was also washing clothes, I was advised that he should do this in the house and that I should then hang the clothes outside; otherwise, my reputation as a good wife would suffer. From these comments on our behavior, I learned about the villagers' expectations both for us and for one another.

The focus of my work was dance as a medium of communication between men and women. My own interest and training in Balkan dance had led me to work in Romania. One of the principles of Labananalysis, the analytic movement system that I had studied, is that direct kinesthetic experience is necessary in order to fully comprehend a movement style. All of these considerations motivated me to learn the village dance. I asked girls to coach me in the dance steps, just as they would coach their younger sisters. Through their corrections of my mistakes, I began to develop a kinesthetic awareness of the movement style which could later be compared to an analysis of films recorded during village dance events. While I did learn the basic steps of the dance, I never fully mastered the style. My dance lessons always took place in the privacy of a girl's home; I did not choose to dance in public. On one occasion, however, I did participate in the Sunday dance. The situation was embarrassing because of the inappropriateness of my participation.

On our first visit to the Sunday dance, Robert and I were accompanied by an entourage of village officials and family members of our hosts. We knew nothing on that first day about the rules of participation in the dance. We were not planning any filming; we wanted only to get a feel for the activity and to see what the responses to us would be. This was to be our first public appearance in a village event.

The village officials were trying to accommodate to what they perceived to be our wishes. Throughout our stay in the village, they tended to view our interest in customs and folklore as equivalent to that of tourists. They acted as though all we required was to participate minimally in a colorful event and to have our participation dutifully recorded on film so that we could take the photo home as a souvenir. Clearly, this kind of participation in village society posed no threat, in comparison with my habit of constantly asking questions about almost everything. Our interest in the Sunday dance as a public event was therefore encouraged.

It is within the context of this official encouragement of our public activities that our embarrassment at the first dance must be understood. The officials, who were neither knowledgeable about nor sensitive to the villagers' unspoken rules on dance participation, assumed that we wanted to dance. While I had expressed an interest in learning the dance, I did not intend to dance publicly for some time, if ever. Nevertheless, we were strenuously urged by the officials to join the couples dancing on the floor. Robert steadfastly refused. I thought that his refusal would get us out of it, but I underestimated the officials' persistence.

Finally, one of the older men was drafted into escorting me onto the floor. His discomfort was matched by my own.

Each dance set is played for about ten minutes. Partners dance face-to-face, with the woman's hands on the man's shoulders and his arms around her waist. They shift to a hip-to-hip position for the turns. The dance is composed of four structurally different motifs, or step combinations. Some of them are slow and are done in place, while others require vigorous movement and turning, with the man totally controlling the movements of his partner. Young girls like to wear colored stockings and undergarments that match their blouses, so that when their skirts flare out during the fast turns the display is color coordinated.

As my partner and I both knew that I had no notion of how to perform, he avoided the faster and more acrobatic movements. We danced sedately and extremely self-consciously under the watchful eyes of the village officials and of all the others who had come to watch the dance. At the conclusion of the dance it is customary for the man to lift his partner a few inches off the ground. Throughout the dance I was wondering if my partner would attempt this lift. As the music ended, we both gratefully let go of each other. No lift was attempted, and we quickly returned to our places. I expressed my gratitude to the officials for the opportunity but said that I had much more to learn before I could again participate in the dance. They seemed to agree.

Only later did I learn how truly inappropriate our dance participation had been. The man with whom I had danced had not participated in the Sunday dance for years and did not particularly enjoy dancing, even on those occasions when it was common for older men to dance. The Sunday dance was not such an occasion. As part of the courtship ritual of the village, among the men it is limited to bachelors and young married men. Married women continue to dance past the time when their husbands have stopped, measuring their attractiveness by the frequency with which they are invited to dance by the younger men. The man has total control over both his decision to participate in the dance and his choice of a partner, for once a woman or girl is asked she cannot refuse the invitation without severe social sanction. My dancing was doubly inappropriate for the lack of initiative and choice by my partner, who was coerced into the move out of deference to the wishes of the village officials. Since everyone involved understood the situation, there were no negative sanctions placed on either of us. The power of official intervention became clear to me through my reflection on this incident. I began to wonder about the extent to which our interactions with villagers were dictated by informal but official comments to them about how to deal with us.

My understanding of the complexity of the rules surrounding participation in dance events was built up over several months of attending dances and interviewing people on related topics. I was gradually building a model of a gender-based social organization that is expressed in dance style. I was also interested in learning something about dance styles from other regions. To this end, Robert and I decided to attend a dance competition in southern Romania.

The festival was a yearly competition of *Călușari,* groups of ritual healers who use intricate dance patterns in their curing ceremonies. The groups are assembled during the weeklong festival of Whitsuntide (*Rusalii*), which occurs fifty days after Easter. One of our American colleagues was studying these groups, and we filmed the dances in conjunction with her work (Kligman 1981). We spent an exciting weekend watching and filming the beautiful dances and the clownlike and ribald antics of the dramatic personae who are part of these ritual groups. Since we were away from our own place of work and were not directly concerned with research in this area, the constant pressures of collecting data were absent. Our stay was almost a vacation. It was also our last bit of field work together.

Toward the end of the weekend, two events occurred which would later become symbols to me of the end of our stay in Romania. As we were filming the last few performing groups our camera equipment began to malfunction. We suspected that the motor was burning out, and we made arrangements to send it to Bucharest. We were not too concerned, since we were planning a vacation from the field in the next several weeks and our work would thus not be hindered by the camera's absence.

The second event was the onset of Robert's illness. Toward the end of the weekend, Robert began to feel weak and listless. At the time, we attributed his condition to fatigue. We decided to postpone a trip to Bucharest and return immediately to the village. We hoped that once we were back in the village, Robert could enjoy a period of rest and relaxation which would lead to his recovery.

The thirteen-hour drive, which had seemed so adventurous a few days before, was grueling for Robert in his weakened condition. We were glad to be back in our village home, but it soon became apparent to us that Robert needed more than a simple rest. He continued to weaken, and a yellow tinge appeared on his skin. To the villagers, his skin color was a sign of hepatitis, a common disease in Romania, dreaded because of its long period of isolation and recovery. As our village friends looked into Robert's eyes and gave their diagnosis, they assured me that although the disease was unpleasant it was one that was understood by their physicians and from which recovery was usually certain. At the time, the faint suggestion that Robert could have a disease from which there was no recovery seemed ludicrous to me.

We returned to Cluj and sought the help of an Israeli friend who was studying medicine. He referred us to a doctor whom he had met and whose discretion he trusted. The need for discretion arose from the uncertain nature of what we were facing. If the villagers' diagnosis was indeed correct, the accepted treatment was a prolonged stay in the hospital. From our perspective, a hospital stay was as likely to preclude as to promote recovery. We therefore had to see someone who had a realistic view of the country's current medical practices and the bureaucracy involved in them as well as a potential sympathy with our position. This doctor, who happened also to be Jewish, was such a man.

Avoiding the entanglements of red tape, he saw us immediately and ordered X rays and blood tests. The results, he informed us, were inconclusive. Robert's fatigue was due to severe anemia, which had to be treated at once. No hepatitis was detected, but an unusual mass had shown up in the chest X ray. Only further exploration could disclose its nature.

It was at this point that the candor of our newfound friend was most appreciated, for we were in such a state of confusion that we did not know what step to take next. The doctor explained to us that the diagnostic procedures used to determine the nature of the illness were complex. Although he had excellent medical facilities at his disposal, he thought that perhaps those available in the States would be more complete. He therefore suggested to us that we go home, if possible. We returned to the village, packed a few belongings, and left the country within the next week. Our intention was to return to the field as soon as Robert recovered.

During the following year I existed in a liminal state, in a shaky transition between past expectations and future uncertainties. When we returned home in July, all thoughts of my research were abandoned as I used all of my energy to cope with Robert's illness. I had to learn how to function effectively in a culture entirely new to me, that of medical experts. Refusing to accept the futility of a fight against a large, inoperable, malignant tumor, I sought out medical researchers working on still untested therapeutic techniques. But my persistence was unrewarded. Six months of intensive therapy did not stem the course of the disease. Robert died in December 1976.

Shortly after his death I returned to teaching, still unsure about my future. It took a few months for my mental inertia to wear off so that I could even begin to think of making plans. Even now I'm not sure when I became aware of the certainty of my future course. It seems as though it just became apparent to me one day that since I had left my field work in the middle, I had to return to it.

The timing of my return to the field the following fall was based on several considerations. I had been awarded a grant from the International Research and Exchanges Board (IREX) for the fall of 1976 to support my continuing research plans. When I was unable to take advantage of this grant, the people at IREX graciously arranged for it to be held for a year. Another consideration in my decision was the focus of my research on dance in courtship and wedding rituals. I had to be established in the village by the winter wedding season or else postpone my work for another year. My return to Romania in the fall of 1977 was thus motivated by both research and funding opportunities.

I anticipated that returning to the village alone would be traumatic, but I reasoned that, considering everything else, I could handle it. While this was my conscious decision, I was still hesitant to leave the comfort and emotional support of my family. I decided that the transition from home to field would be easier if it was not so abrupt, so I planned to stop in Kenya to visit friends on my way to Romania.

The Nandi, among whom my friends were working, are a patrilineal group of farmers and herders living in western Kenya (Oboler 1985). Among these people it is customary for a young widow to remarry within her late husband's lineage. At the time of my arrival I had been a widow for nine months. The Nandi solution to my problem was clear: I should join my friends' household as a second wife. While I had been trained to study, analyze, and understand differences in social systems, I was not quite prepared for such a direct application of other customs to my own life. Nor was I prepared to understand the subtlety with which living in a different culture affects the field worker. As field workers we immerse ourselves in the natives' culture, but we must also be aware that their solutions are appropriate only in their own cultural context.

Among the Nandi, I was an outsider, with little understanding of either the people or the culture. The visit reinforced my sense of the exotic and my own feeling of foreignness. When I returned to Romania, this feeling abated. I was back in a country where I knew the language and had some sense of understanding the people. Because of this stark contrast, I deluded myself into believing that my return to the village was almost like coming home. In retrospect I believe that this was just a defense mechanism to help me during the difficult transition back to my work.

The Second Year

My second arrival in Romania was quite a contrast to the first. As an official exchange scholar, I was met at the airport and ushered through the formalities to my waiting accommodations. I still had to spend a few weeks in Bucharest negotiating the formal approvals I needed for my work, but my official status made this process much easier than it had been earlier. Several more weeks were spent in Cluj, ironing out the details of my stay with the local officials. Finally I was ready to return to the village. I now had to be "reincorporated" into the village in the new status of widow.

During the first few months of my second stay I was still in mourning. As a descendant of Eastern European Jews, I shared with the villagers the custom of recognizing an official mourning period of one year. In the village, being in mourning meant that I wore black in public and refrained from participating in any music, dance, or other festivities. This was not a hardship for me for two reasons: first, I personally accepted this symbolism as meaningful within my own worldview, and second, most of this period coincided with Advent. In Romanian villages, weddings and other dance occasions are prohibited during this ritual period before Christmas. My work was thus not restricted by my abstinence from the dance or other festive events.

The first thing the villagers noticed upon my return was the change in my appearance. When I had first met them I had had very long hair, a trait highly valued on their scale of physical beauty. Early in my first stay I had learned to tie my hair in a *conci,* a braided knot that is worn only by married women. I continued to wear my hair that way throughout my first stay. Both my ability to make the knot and my desire to wear it were a source of surprise and pleasure to village women.

When Robert died I cut my hair. For me this was a personal symbol of the end of one part of my life. Village women also use hairstyle as a sign of mourning: they let their hair hang loose and unbraided for the duration of the mourning period. When the period is over, however, they return to wearing their former style. They never cut their hair, and the length and thickness of it is evident in the size of the knot that can be seen protruding from under a woman's headscarf.

The women were shocked at what they considered to be a very drastic decision on my part. Why had I cut my hair? Didn't I realize that the period of mourning would soon be over? Surely, I would marry again soon. What of my hair when I remarried? Wasn't I sorry that I had done such a thing? And so on. The consensus seemed to be that by this act I had further removed myself from village custom. Since I could no longer look like a village woman, my actual identity as an outsider, a "lady" from the city, was more evident.

In response to my widowhood, both men and women were empathetic. We traded questions on the nature of death, grief, and mourning in our respective cultures. I was frequently asked to recount the details of my husband's illness. A new dimension of shared experience encouraged an increased contact with older women. A change in my relationships with villagers came about because of slightly altered perceptions (both on my part and theirs) that our lives were not as different as the surface contours would suggest. Their notion of America as a land of unlimited possibilities was diminished by their realization that the saying they used among themselves to cope with the events of the world applied to me as well: *N'ai ce să fac* ("There's nothing you can do").

For me, the repetitive recounting of my story was a great emotional strain. Everyone I knew, and many people I didn't know, had to hear all the details of Robert's illness and death. In the telling and retelling, the older women especially tried to share with me stories of their own sorrows. The problem was that I really did not care. In retrospect, I see that I could have collected all kinds of information about illness, death, and dying, but that was the last thing I wanted to hear about at that time. Consequently, I didn't write down a single note about these stories, and eventually I even tried to avoid conversations that I thought might turn in that direction.

Another difficulty that I had with these early conversations was that they invariably turned to my future: Of course I was still young; of course it was good that we hadn't had any children; of course I would marry again soon; of course my life would soon be back on track. In public I cheerfully agreed with all of these assumptions, while privately I doubted them all. The disparity between the content of my daily conversations and the reality of my daily thoughts was difficult to mediate. My highly charged emotional state certainly affected my ability to work during the first few weeks of my return to the village. Finally everyone had heard the story, and we got around to talking about what I wanted to talk about. I am reminded here of a comparison to Friedl's chapter in this volume, for in the early part of my second stay the village women were certainly better interviewers than I, the interviewer, was.

The fact that I had returned to the village brought about changes in my relationships with people which were not related to my changed status. I was now renewing old friendships rather than trying to start new ones, and the intensity of some of the relationships changed accordingly. Another change occurred because I was now unaccompanied. Being alone, I sought out people for companionship as well as for interviews. Apart from my change in civil status, this was the biggest difference between my two field experiences. It meant that most of my waking hours were spent in the company of one or more of the villagers.

The first anniversary of my widowhood was spent in the village amid the gaiety of the Christmas season. I was thankful that it was a time of intense activity, with little leisure time for contemplation. Once my period of mourning was officially over, my civil status changed to that of an eligible young woman. Because of this change, I could participate in a wider variety of village events.

I had been working with one of the young girls on information about customs and spells for attracting men as husbands and dance partners. Since I was now single, it was appropriate for me not only to learn about these customs but also to participate in them. My timing was also appropriate, for the village girls believed that midnight on New Year's Eve is the most propitious hour for soliciting supernatural guidance. I was invited to participate in this ritual with the young girls; from their perspective I, too, was in need of attracting a man.

My host family had been more solicitous about my well-being since I had returned to the village alone. When I announced my intention to leave the house at midnight on New Year's Eve, they tried rigorously to persuade me to stay home. There had been some uneasiness over my previous evening outings, since my family feared dangers from loose dogs, drunken men, and wandering spirits (in that order). Their uneasiness on this occasion, however, had to do with the specific night of New Year's Eve. I did not understand it, and my hosts did not give me any reasonable explanation. Despite their objections, I was resolved not to miss the opportunity of participating in a magical rite with the young girls.

Months later I learned that the problem had been with my return to the house rather than with my departure from it. According to tradition, the welfare of the household for the next year depends on the sex of the first person to cross the threshold after midnight on New Year's Eve. A man or boy brings good luck to the household; a woman or girl brings bad luck. When my decision to leave at midnight became clear to my hosts, they arranged for a neighbor boy to enter the house before my return. In this way they insured the well-being of the household for the next year and at the same time avoided conflict with me. The incident now serves to remind me of my lack of a total understanding of the events I was experiencing.

In my role as a single woman I had more opportunity to mingle with the young girls than I had had previously. I spoke with them about work, school, boys, and forthcoming marriage plans. Most girls are married by the age of sixteen, but a few of them manage to put it off for one or two years longer. The girls were reticent to disclose to me their favored choices for future husbands, since the final decision is contingent on a suitable financial arrangement that is worked out by the parents of the prospective bride and groom. Public announcement of the couple's intentions before the conclusion of the negotiations would leave the individuals and their families open to possible embarrassment if something should go wrong. Because of this possibility, individuals may choose the season in which they will be married before they actually decide on their future spouses.

In one instance I was invited to be a ritual sponsor, or godmother, at the wedding of one of my young friends. I was pleased to be asked and readily agreed. Godparents were traditionally chosen by the groom and his family at the time of his wedding, but recent custom has allowed for a second couple to be chosen by the bride. As I was the bride's choice, I was to be part of the second, or the lesser, godparents. The role involves both social and economic obligations to the couple and their future children. It is usually filled by someone with either a kinship or a social connection to the parents of the marrying couple.

One problem with my fulfilling this role was that godparents come in pairs. Since I had no husband, there was no one who could serve with me as god-father. I was at a loss for a suggestion as to who my partner should be. My hosts suggested that I find a male colleague and bring him to the village for the wedding, but this solution was not feasible. I thought that perhaps a married male relative of the bride would do, but this also seemed somehow inappropriate. Finally, I thought that the whole idea had been scratched. I left the village for a few days and returned to find that the groom's unmarried brother had been selected to serve with me as godparent.

All problems had been resolved, or so I thought. Two days before the wedding, concern arose among my host family about the legitimacy of my participation in the wedding. They knew that I was Jewish. They also knew that my religious affiliation was more signiñcant to the priest than it was to them. They urged me to go and talk with him about the wedding. Their apprehensions were justified. The priest informed me that since I was not Catholic, my name could not be inscribed in the church book as the religious sponsor at a wedding. When I pointed out that I was representing the side of the bride and that the godparents chosen by the groom could be the official sponsors, he agreed that I could participate informally in the church ceremony.

I did participate actively in this wedding. I went on the rounds of the village to invite the guests, helped the women prepare huge quantities of food for the feast, and danced in the girls' circle surrounding the bride as she was ritually separated from her natal home. Along with the groom's brother, I attended the couple during the church ceremony, placed the crown of marriage on their heads, and pinned my gift of scarves to the bride's headdress, to be displayed before the entire village. Finally, after making our financial contribution, the groom's brother and I danced with the bride in her new home, in the final dance through which she is ritually incorporated into the family of her husband. As I went through these stages of separation, transition, and incorporation, my own transitional state was emphasized. I wondered what form my own reincorporation would take.

This wedding marked the beginning of my participation in village dance events. While I did not dance at the weekly courtship dances for the young people, I did sometimes dance at weddings when I was not busy recording other types of data.

I was studying dance as part of the courtship process, gathering data to support the hypothesis that dance is an important medium of communication between the sexes. While I was trying to sensitize myself to all of the nuances of the rules for dance participation, it took me a long time to realize that these rules were being applied to me as well. The following episode is an example of the kind of trouble in which I sometimes found myself. The problems were a reflection of my changed relations with the men of the village because of my new status as a single woman.

I went to as many village weddings as possible, even if I was not acquainted with the participants. Most people knew of my presence in the village, whether or not they knew me personally, and they were pleased to have me photograph their festive events. At this particular wedding, no one I knew was present. I talked a bit with the bride and her attendants, did some filming, and watched the proceedings. The traditional dance sequence for weddings was that the female friends and relatives of the bride would encircle her with a dance before she left home for the church ceremony. This wedding differed from others in that rather than dancing in a circle around the bride, the wedding guests danced together as partners. One of the older men asked me to dance, and I accepted. A while later, he asked me again. While I knew that dancing twice with the same man is improper in the Sunday courtship dance, I did not think that the rule applied to dancing at weddings. I again agreed to dance with him. He was drunk and having a good time; I was also enjoying myself. I danced with a few other men before the end of that phase of the wedding. When the groom's party came to lead the bride to the church, we all left the house. I did not return after the ceremony.

At home, my hosts questioned me about the wedding and about who had attended. I did not know the names of anyone except the principal participants, but I described the man with whom I had danced and learned that he was from another village. I thought nothing more about my participation in the wedding. Unfortunately, others did.

I was included in the rumor network of the village only to the degree that my hosts and a few close friends would tell me what was being said. A few days after the wedding, I was startled to learn that I was the center of village gossip. A woman had accused me of having an affair with her husband. She turned out to be the wife of the man with whom I had danced at the wedding. While I had often heard such rumors of illicit behavior, I was taken aback by the kind of evidence on which they could be started.

My hosts were not surprised. They advised me that any contact with a man, particularly a stranger, was open to such interpretation. Now that I was single, a conversation on the bus or street, an exchange of pleasantries, or a smile could all be interpreted as signs of an illicit relationship (by the women) or as invitations to one (by the men). It was not only my single status that encouraged these interpretations but also the fact that I had already been married. In the villagers' thinking, once a woman's sexual appetite has been stimulated it does not abate. Both men and women therefore assumed that I was looking for a partner. This interpretation was emphasized because of my participation in the dance. Throughout the first part of my stay I was happily ignorant of this problem. Once I became aware of it, I felt a strain in all of my relationships except those with the young girls.

A related problem arose in discussions about my future. Villagers felt that I needed a husband. The existence of a young widow in the village is both a threat to the women and a temptation to the men. This fact was emphasized to me not only by my own situation but by gossip about a village woman of my age who had also been recently widowed. Since the customary age of marriage for young men, especially educated ones, was later than that for girls, there were still a few unmarried men of my age (at that time, I was twenty-eight) in the village. It was not unknown for people from this area to marry Westerners.

The subject of my choice of a future husband was therefore an underlying theme in all joking interaction with me. Amid all the jokes there was more than a hint of seriousness: Why shouldn't I marry a man from the village? Village men are handsome. Village men are strong. Village men are hardworking. I heard these comments from both men and women, even though in other contexts women would tell me that not one in a hundred of the village men made a good husband. More than the issue of my welfare was at stake in these discussions. Almost everyone in the village had a friend or relative in the States. Some of these people were recent emigrants, while others had left Romania years ago. No matter how tenuous the relationship, it was always referred to with pride. Marriage of a villager to a foreigner was one way in which other villagers could increase their contacts with people in the West.

The implications of my discussions with both the men and the women were clear: I should remarry quickly, regardless of my lack of financial need, and among the village men there were plenty of eligible candidates. Even as an outsider, I felt this pressure to conform to the social norms of the village, and I'm sure that the pressure on me was more indirect than that on village women in similar situations. The other young widow whom I mentioned did remarry, within a year after I left the village.

Conclusion: The Social and Political Contexts of Field Work

In their daily lives, villagers must juggle the demands of conflicting role obligations. They must contribute to the functioning of their households, demonstrate solidarity with a gender-based social group, placate the supernatural, maintain economic and social status within the community, and survive the seemingly random application of little-understood national laws to local and personal affairs. The presence of a foreign researcher in their midst can only complicate an already complex situation. For example, through me the village women learned of contraceptives about which they had known nothing, yet they were powerless to obtain them. I was also in a situation of role conflict, since the things that my hosts wanted me to do to reciprocate their hospitality were sometimes contrary to national laws.

As foreigners it is our duty to know and respect local customs as well as national laws, even if our native contacts do not. This necessity is even more critical in a place such as Romania, where the national government shows intense interest in the daily activities of its citizens. When rules are transgressed, sanctions are applied. In Eastern Europe, these sanctions are not placed on the researcher, who at worst may have to leave the country. The sanctions, when applied, affect the people with whom we work. As ethnographers, it is our obligation to be aware of our impact on those whom we choose to study.

In politically sensitive times, international events can and do impinge on the lives of individuals—villagers and researchers alike. Laws regulating contact between Romanians and foreigners, particularly those from the West, are strict, and penalties for infringement are harsh. Romanians are constrained to report all conversations with foreigners to authorities. As noted earlier, foreigners cannot remain overnight in Romanian homes. While these restrictions may be lifted for ethnographic researchers, the exemption is discretionary.

Once I was settled in the village, there were few restrictions on my research activity. I was urged by officials to avoid certain topics of conversation and to limit my filming to traditional events. Access to village records was denied to me in the first year, but I did obtain access in the second year through my affiliation with a national research organization. I was somewhat restricted in comparative work, since the housing law prevented me from remaining longer than a day in any other village in the region. While I could speak with anyone, I was sure that the people I interviewed were, in turn, interviewed about me. I could only hope that their contact with me would bring no negative consequences.

My interviews focused on rituals of courtship and marriage and on the social context of gender relations. During both stages of field work I questioned people on family relations, the sexual division of labor, and power and influence in the domestic and public spheres. I observed and participated in weddings and interviewed ritual specialists on stages of separation, transition, and incorporation in these rituals. Using these techniques I developed an interpretation of the meaning of dance in these ritual stages.

Ethnographers recognize that it is easier to get some types of information than others. The roles in which we find ourselves may also influence the kinds of information we can obtain. While I was never actually excluded from getting any specific type of information, each of my three roles was conducive to developing certain sets of relationships, which then influenced the data that I collected.

As a married woman it was easy for me to talk with other married women about the problems and pleasures of marriage. They were as curious about me as I was about them, and we could share information on our respective situations. Most of my information on family relations and the balance of work patterns in the household was collected during my first year of work. When I returned as a widow, I was inundated with stories of sickness, which, as I have already mentioned, did not interest me. I also learned about the social restrictions of being a widow and the limits of proper behavior for a woman in that category. I heard stories about other widows' plans to remarry, and I learned for the first time of magical rites to help find a second spouse, rites that were also used by men.

Later in my second stay I had more in common with the young girls than with the women. Villagers perceived me as younger than my actual age for two reasons: I was still a student, and I was childless. The young widow whom I mentioned earlier had three children. Yet I, like her, was vulnerable to village gossip. After the incident in which I danced with a stranger at a wedding, my behavior and reputation with men became a focus of village gossip. Once this problem about my reputation with men surfaced, my relations with both men and women were strained. Because of this strain I was more comfortable with the girls.

From that point my behavior was interpreted differently; friendly interactions were seen as indications of illicit behavior. My need for friendship and approval led me to participate in gatherings where cross-sex joking was common, and I was often the focus of the jokes. I interpreted these events on a surface level, as jokes in a friendly spirit. But the underlying theme was more serious than I realized at the time. I did not understand the extent to which they had included me in their system. My psychological need to be accepted and to feel at home overshadowed the reality of my being in a different system and led me to misinterpret some of its cues. Since there were some cultural features that I shared with the villagers, it was easier and more convenient for me to forget about our differences. I succumbed to the danger of emphasizing similarities rather than clarifying differences.

My village hosts taught me much about their lives and their culture, yet there was much about them that I did not understand. Through the process of interpreting the data that reflect the joint interaction of our lives, I learned equally about them and about myself.

Ethnographers are not like chameleons. We cannot change our personalities to fit our field situations. We can learn more about who we are when we see ourselves through the double-sided looking glass of our ethnographic lens. Our data result from the cumulative experiences of our interactions with our informants. Over a period of three years, I interacted with the villagers in three separate social categories: those of wife, widow, and single woman. These three types of interactions gave me a variety of perspectives from which to understand village culture. The varying experiences helped me to develop a more complex model of men's and women's roles in the village social organization than interviewing alone would have done. Although my experiences resulted from personal tragedy, they gave me a unique opportunity for varied participation in village society. My understanding of the rules on which the society is based was enhanced by this opportunity.

The few difficulties that I experienced in my work were a result of both the sensitive nature of the international political situation and the significance of my own social role as a basis for the interpretation of interpersonal relations. These difficulties were outweighed by the cooperation of my village hosts, who responded good-naturedly to both my inquisitiveness and the lack of sophistication in my efforts to live by their rules. Without their help and support, which went beyond the bounds of social hospitality, my work would not have been possible.

References

FREEDMAN, DIANE C. 1983. *Dance as Communicative Code in Romanian Courtship and Marriage Rituals*. Ph.D. dissertation in anthropology, Temple University. University Microfilms.

KLIGMAN, GAIL. 1981. *Căluş: Symbolic Transformation in Romanian Ritual*. Chicago: University of Chicago Press.

OBOLER, REGINA. 1985. *Women, Power, and Economic Change: The Nandi of Kenya*. Stanford: Stanford University Press.

The Return of Redwoman: Field Work in Highland New Guinea[1]

RENA LEDERMAN has been teaching courses on economic and political anthropology, Pacific cultures, the anthropology of gender, and the anthropology of knowledge at Princeton University since 1981. A revised version of her Ph.D. dissertation (Columbia University) will be published as the book WHAT GIFTS ENGENDER: SOCIAL RELATIONS AND POLITICS IN MENDI, HIGHLAND PAPUA NEW GUINEA.

1. This essay was drafted five years ago, shortly after I returned from my first field trip. Revising it recently, I updated my ethnographic analysis and incorporated some observations I made when I returned to Mendi in 1983. But I did not make explicit reference to the growing literature on ethnographic writing and reflexive anthropology (many significant examples of which came out while I was in the field: for reviews, see Clifford 1983; Marcus and Cushman 1982), although this essay is in fact a contribution to those efforts, as well as to an anthropology of gender. My central concern here is not with research techniques, nor is it autobiographical. I aim to describe the *process* of my anthropological knowledge in a way that acknowledges its affinity with my Mendi hosts' own processes of understanding. I aim to highlight the simultaneous mutuality and autonomy in the social relationships of field work and to suggest something of the wider sociopolitical context of those interactions.

W hat does it mean to study "gender" in a society outside of our own
historical tradition? The cross-cultural study of gender is a vivid instance
of the challenge all anthropological field workers face, regardless of their interests. None of us can help using our own cultural categories—gender, kinship,
economy—as a means of entry into other worlds of meaning. But how do we
learn to recognize when those familiar interpretations impede our further progress? Familiar orchestrations of meaning are compelling, and while they can
rarely be silenced altogether (nor necessarily should they be), they must be muted
in order for one to distinguish them from unfamiliar alternatives. By means of
this description of my field-work experiences, I hope to suggest how this ability
to hear alien themes develops. I will not argue that the differences we perceive
come to be denied or blurred during field work. Rather, field work creates the
potential for intensive sociability between people with different presuppositions
about the world, and as such it makes possible a kind of mutual understanding
and translation that acknowledges the distance that separates lives lived in New
York or Boise from those lived in New Guinea.

I first want to describe a chronology of adjustments as my husband, Michael
Merrill,[2] and I made our way to the Mendi Valley, in the Southern Highlands
Province of Papua New Guinea (P.N.G.).[3] Later, I will consider these same

2. Despite his own ongoing involvements, including work in labor education and historical
research on eighteenth- and nineteenth-century American rural society, Mike ran off to Mendi with
me, participated in the research, and proved that one does not have to be an anthropologist in order
to understand these things.
3. Research was conducted in the Mendi Valley, part of the Southern Highlands Province of
Papua New Guinea. New Guinea is the name generally used to refer to the whole of the large
continental island located due north of Australia in the South Pacific. The island is divided politically
in half, the western part—Irian Jaya—having been relinquished by the Dutch and annexed by
Indonesia in the 1960s. The eastern part—now called Papua New Guinea—was originally colonized
by Britain (Papua) and Germany (New Guinea). It was unified after World War I under Australian
colonial administration, which continued until 1975, when the country gained its independence. The
Mendi Valley is one of many high-mountain valleys in the country's densely settled central cordillera.

361

themes as they specifically bear on the difference being a woman makes in Mendi.

Getting to the Field: Competence and Familiarity

Even for other anthropologists, the name "Papua New Guinea" conjures up exoticism or (sometimes the same thing) "real" anthropology. It was with some anticipation, therefore, that Mike and I disembarked after our Qantas flight from Sydney, Australia, to Port Moresby (the national capital of P.N.G.). We had already been on the road for several weeks by this time, and both of us were looking forward to the shock of the unfamiliar. We were greeted instead by asphalt, by English-speaking taxi drivers, and by a kind of heat similar to that which we had left behind in New York not long before.

We spent three weeks in Moresby, from the end of September to mid-October 1977, living in a guest house near the University of Papua New Guinea. There, we practiced *Tok Pisin* (Melanesian pidgin, the lingua franca), met a handful of Mendi students who told us a bit about our destination, and commiserated with two anthropologists from Canada who were also on the brink of field research. We made trips into the center of town to buy things that we had been warned (needlessly, as it turned out) might not be available in Mendi town: Coleman lamps, canvas boots, drugstore supplies. Evening discussions with various members of the university's Department of Anthropology and Sociology concerning local student strikes, academic politics, and people and events elsewhere in P.N.G., in the United States, and in the world were frustratingly familiar. Consequently, once our contacts had been made and our accommodations in Mendi town arranged by phone, we were ready to go.

Mendi town is the headquarters of the Southern Highlands Province, the last Highlands area to have been brought under Australian administrative control when P.N.G. was not yet independent. Whereas the Australians had established a political and economic presence in most other Highland valleys during the 1930s (coastal New Guinea having been under colonial rule since the late nineteenth century), this did not happen in the Mendi Valley until 1950.

Since then, the people of Mendi and the rest of the province have experienced important transformations. Local political autonomy was undercut by means of an enforced ban on clan warfare, and provincial and national government links were established in the countryside, supported by a growing network of roads and by air-transport connections to other parts of the country. A plethora of evangelical missions from the United States and Australia arrived. Governmental, mission, and private commercial projects (e.g., tea plantations, sawmills, and retail stores) were initiated. A system of rural community schools and medical-aid posts, run by Papua New Guineans, was established. A number of high schools were built in the various subprovincial centers, and a provincial hospital was built in Mendi town.

Despite all of these changes, the Southern Highlands Province is one of the least Westernized in the country. The province's particular colonial history is at least partly responsible for this situation. For example, very little land has been alienated from indigenous clan control. While the Mendi people have a reputation for cultural "conservatism," or resistance to externally induced change, they are not particularly unusual in this. Following the general Highland pattern (Brown 1978), the vast majority of the Mendi live outside of town in fairly densely settled rural communities, growing the sweet potatoes and raising the herds of pigs which are the productive basis of a social and political life carried on quite apart from provincial institutions.

To assert that the Mendi, like other Highlanders, have not embraced Western-style political and economic change is not to imply that they have no historical experience of their own (Lederman 1986a). While the legitimacy of indigenous and introduced sociopolitical and economic relations is likely to be a contested issue for some time to come, for now the Mendi have been selectively adapting foreign things to their own structure of uses—for example, they have been incorporating cash along with older valuables such as pigs and pearlshells into the gift exchanges that accompany marriages, mortuary ceremonies, and clan-sponsored political events.

Our ten-seat Beechcraft plane flew quite low as we approached the Mendi town airstrip. As we ended our two-hour early-morning flight from Port Moresby we could see a rock quarry and the Southern Highlands branch of the Highlands Highway below us, as well as footpaths, grass-thatched rooftops, and fenced sweet-potato gardens planted in rows of mounds. The town is located at the southern, low end of a V-shaped valley that extends about twenty-five miles northward. At 5400 feet above sea level, the morning air was cool and almost sickeningly sweet-smelling. We were met at the airstrip by Dr. John Millar, superintendent of the provincial hospital and the sort of thoughtful and unconventional person we would have wanted to know even if we had not all been thrust together—as we were to be—in an out-of-the-way corner of the world. John drove us and our luggage to a one-room, prefabricated bungalow near the high school, normally reserved as a residence for teachers or government employees but unoccupied just then. He dropped us off and headed for the hospital, leaving us to our own devices.

Our bungalow was set amid tall and wispy casuarina pines, characteristic of the Highlands, near a winding stone- and flower-banked road. I set to work unpacking my books and papers, creating a familiar workspace as a way of suppressing the feeling of falling into a void. I was the only anthropologist in town—a role (not quite a job; this was dissertation research) whose essence appeared to be to find out what was going on but never to be part of it, whatever it was. I had received lots of anecdotal advice in the States, Australia, and Port Moresby about how other anthropologists in P.N.G. had found a rural village in which to live and how they had identified helpful local leaders (called "big-men" in the anthropological literature) without whom, they swore, they could never have done their research. I had received advice about the proper positioning of my outhouse, about various brands of tape recorders, and about a variety of elaborate note-taking and indexing regimens. These details were both crucial and beside the point. All advice ended with an obligatory coda that, of course, one's situation was always unique, and one therefore had to be flexible. Given that one's identity is socially constructed and that Mendi social constructions were the subject of my investigation, no one could tell me beforehand exactly *who* I was to be. What anthropologists were thought of by expatriates and others in town, how the rural Mendi with whom I would eventually be living would interpret my work, what kind of participation in local life would be possible or necessary—all of these things were vague.

Meanwhile, Mike was attracted by familiar noises coming from the nearby high-school basketball court. If I was unsure about what I ought to be doing, he at least knew the rules of *that* game (and, being a good head-and-shoulders taller than the tallest Mendi student, he had reason to expect success). He came back in an hour or so, convinced by the experience that things would fall into place.

In fact, things fell into place with remarkable speed, so much so that I found myself apologizing for it in my letters home. If I had embarked for another part of the United States, I might have legitimately expected that initial periods of disorientation in the wake of new places and people would give way quickly to the recognizable and the taken-for-granted. I had not expected that this would occur in Port Moresby (which, for all its asphalt, is a Third World city, and not White Plains, New York), in Mendi town (a frontier community of a few thousand residents), and, finally, in the rural community in which we would ultimately settle. Still, amid massive evidence to the contrary, we both came to find our surroundings familiar by finding familiar things (basketball games in various guises) in our surroundings. We imagined we recognized our new world because we saw images of the world we had left behind reflected on its surface; this was a way of maintaining the necessary sense of competence which gave us the confidence to make decisions and to act. This sort of competence was transcended to a degree, but only slowly and not entirely consciously.

Our first month in Mendi was spent in perusing provincial government documents and in following up leads concerning likely communities in the northern part of the valley in which to live. Mike also spent time working on a writing project he had started before we left the States, and I began to study the Mendi language, with the help of students from the high school. Since I was interested in learning about how the Mendi organize their *mok ink* (pig kill) festival,[4] I asked teachers at the high school, government officials, and others familiar with the area whether they had heard which Mendi clans had announced intentions to hold the event during the next year. After about three weeks, I had learned of two localities with *mok ink* plans, visited each of them once, and considered their logistical, sociological, and aesthetic advantages and disadvantages at length. As it turned out, all of this really did not matter, since the two localities were both part of one clan alliance planning one *mok ink*.

In the end, the decision was made for me by the people I met. Perhaps the most important of these was Paki Nali, a twelve-year-old first-year high-school student with shining eyes. Paki, whom I met in the course of my attempts to study the Mendi language, determined to adopt Mike and me as soon as he had an inkling of what our plans were. He touted the advantages of Wepra, his place, and he claimed that if we were foolish enough to choose Kuma, the other place, our house would sink into the boggy ground and we would be miserable. What is more, he said that his father, Nare, was a leader and would arrange "everything" for us if we chose Wepra.

We first met Nare on our second visit to Wepra, about three hours' north of town by foot. He was with a large group of people, all keening over the body of his brother's young son, who had just died. I hesitated to approach him in this context, but Paki insisted. Nare came out of the crowd to greet us. Speaking in very clear pidgin (with which Mike and I were still not completely at ease then), he explained what was happening in simple terms. He told us to come back to talk with him next week, after the boy was buried. Our meeting with Nare, and the beauty of the place, convinced us to settle in Wepra.

Nare was, in fact, a leader. Both for this reason and others having to do with his wide experiences outside of Wepra, he was able to make our transition to the village almost easy. He organized the building of our house and provided a house site ten paces from his own dwelling. He selected my first field assistants for me; a married man named Mel and Mel's teenage brother Tolap, both clansmen of Nare's wife, Nande. Mel and Tolap helped us until we left Wepra in 1979. Both Mel and Nare were unusual in the extent of their experience with the world outside of Mendi. Both reached out to meet Mike and me more than halfway in the beginning, easing our transition to village life and almost conspiring with us to preserve our fragile sense of purpose and competence.

---

4. In Mendi, a *mok ink* (pig festival) is organized and sponsored by an alliance of clans (*sem onda*, autonomous political/territorial groups). It involves about five years of preparations, which culminate in a massive pork distribution that involves the slaughter of hundreds of pigs. The festival is a practical demonstration of the ability of a loose federation of political allies to coordinate their productive work and their intergroup policy. While clan alliances may sponsor other sorts of events more frequently, the *mok ink* is the most spectacular demonstration of the political viability of *sem onda* in Mendi nowadays.

Mel, who had had no formal schooling and who knew no English, had lived for seven years during his late teens and his twenties in Port Moresby, working in the P.N.G. army cafeteria. He had returned to Wepra around 1972 at the request of his father, who thought that Mel had been away too long and ought to get married. Mel was not comfortable with the competitive ethic of rural social relations, which require a considerable amount of wheeling and dealing and backroom politicking in preparation for ceremonial events (see Lederman 1986b). He would get morose when the time of major clan ceremonies approached. While he participated adequately, there were times when he seemed to prefer to escape into the orderly and slightly abstracted research routine I had developed. His identity was very much associated with his relative cosmopolitanism, which he enjoyed showing off by punning in pidgin and demonstrating his knowledge of the eight other P.N.G. languages he had picked up on his travels, or describing other parts of the country he had seen.

During our first real conversation with him, only three days after we had moved to our new house in Wepra, he asked about President Nixon and the war with the "communists" in Vietnam, and about Black people in the United States. He had learned about these things from a Black American soldier he had gotten to know, and who had impressed him, during his stay in Port Moresby in the late 1960s and early 1970s. This conversation was at once fascinating and extremely disorienting for Mike and me, sitting in our woven basket of a house, perched on a hilltop right at what we had foolishly imagined was finally the edge of the earth.

While Mel's ability to reach out to us reflected something of his ambivalence about village life, Nare's empathy had more positive roots. Nare had been Paki's age in 1950 when the Australians had first set up administrative headquarters for the Southern Highlands at Murump (the indigenous name for the site of what is now Mendi town). Nare and his mother and brothers were immigrants to the Mendi Valley, refugees from tribal wars in their home area to the southeast of Murump. They were living near Murump at the time and only later moved to Wepra, when Nare's mother married a Wepra man (her first husband having been killed in the fighting). Nare was intrigued by the strangers. He struck up a friendship with a police officer, a native of coastal New Guinea who was then stationed with the new colonial administration for the Southern Highlands in Mendi town, and learned to speak pidgin. The officer enrolled Nare in a medical orderly training program.

In the program, which was his only schooling, Nare learned to read and write pidgin. During his training he toured the Highlands on inoculation patrols and worked in hospitals in Madang, on the north coast of P.N.G. Later he helped to build a medical-aid post at Wepra. He had been running this post for nearly twenty years when we met him in 1977.

He and his wife, Nande (about whom I will have some things to say later), adopted Mike and me into their household, shared with us, and expected us to do the same. Nare's sensitivity to our needs was not due simply to his familiarity with other white people. Our behavior and his relationship with us had no parallel in his earlier experiences.[5] But being an immigrant to Wepra himself, Nare felt that he understood personally our difficulties as outsiders. Unlike Mel, Nare enjoyed thinking about, organizing, and participating in tribal ceremonies. He was a "big-man" because of his wide network of exchange partners (whom he could draw on when he needed pigs, pearlshells, or money for ceremonial transactions) and because of his influence over collective clan decision-making. He had worked hard to prove himself a true member of his adoptive community.

More generally, I think that the same sensibility that had led Nare to strike up a friendship with the police officer when he was a boy also enabled him to empathize with us. Apart from whatever immediate benefits he imagined would accrue to him from our presence in his house compound, he was genuinely curious about us and wanted to understand how we were similar to or different from him. We were, in fact, as much "specimens" for his investigations as he was for mine. Despite his enjoyment of and commitment to village life, Nare, like Mel, knew what it meant to live between two worlds. He was sensitive to his own ignorance about the world outside Mendi, and he was anxious to participate with his accustomed mastery in the changes that were coming.

Nare's concern with evaluating the alternatives was reflected in many of the conversations we had with him. I think we all agreed that there were advantages and disadvantages to both ways of life. For example, we had a series of inconclusive discussions about where white men's money comes from. Nare wanted to know how it is made and how its production is controlled, and he found it hard to believe that P.N.G.'s currency is truly its own. These concerns were related to another discussion about gambling magic. In that discussion, I insisted on talking about "luck," whereas Nare speculated about "sorcery" (*tom*) and other means of intelligent human control over the cards (these divergent positions deriving, perhaps, from my theoretical and his practical interest in the matter).

While he was interested in money (which he used in ceremonial exchanges), Nare was not convinced of the merits of business relative to the rural gift economy. He often got into arguments about this with his brother Peter, who lived in town and worked there as a skilled auto mechanic. Peter wanted to start a business, but as yet he had little support (financial or otherwise) from his village relatives, who had been involved in *mok ink* preparations for the past several years. Peter felt that the complex organizing effort involved in festival preparations was a waste of time and that labor and resources would be better spent in setting up a profit-making garage, which he could manage. Nare admit-

---

5. For example, he and other villagers we met remarked that "Australians" do not eat with native people, whereas we did so as a matter of course.

ted that in business one could accumulate valuables, whereas after a ceremonial wealth display such as the *mok ink* one gave away as gifts everything that had been borrowed from one's exchange partners or that one had produced for the event, and therefore one did not end up ahead financially. But, Nare argued, many of those working in town were selfish and lazy by village standards; their earnings were spent mostly on items of personal consumption, such as food and clothing. In contrast, rural ceremonies involve long-range planning, hard work, and skill and yield social returns not only in individual prestige but also in political organization. Mike and I sympathized with Nare's analysis.

Similarly, in comparing the ways in which each society mourns the death of friends and kin, we agreed that Mendi practices made much more sense. Whole communities mourned together, and public expressions of intense feeling were valued and were turned to constructive social ends through gift exchange. This was in vivid and sobering contrast to the privatization of feelings Mike and I had experienced during the death of a close friend shortly before we had left the States for P.N.G., and it was our single most important lesson.

In this way, we spent many months of evenings around our cooking fire with Nare after a long day, talking about here and there. It was in this context of deepening friendship that his and our own very human need to understand strange things in familiar terms, and for accustomed reasons, began to break down. In this deeply known context, Mike and I could not completely ignore the ways in which the apparently comprehensible parts of Nare's life (and those of other people with whom we become close) fit together with other parts and in ways we did not yet understand. As a friend, Nare could not be analyzed into pieces but had to be confronted whole. We were forced, in this way, to face his way of life as a whole too. In comparing our lives as totalities, we began to understand our differences. Achieved with difficulty, if at all, such control over the analytical imagination is very hard to sustain at a distance.

Getting to the Field: Research and Strangeness

We carted our trunks and supplies up to Wepra from Mendi town with the help of John Millar and his four-wheel drive Toyota to the place where the road gave out, and the rest of the way with the help of numerous neighbors-to-be. While we were still engaged in putting the finishing touches (doors and windows) on our house, I once again worried about inventing a routine and a role into which Mike and I might fit. I was most concerned that Nare and the others should think well of us, but I did not know by what standards we would be judged.

During the first couple of weeks, nothing much happened in the Wepra neighborhood for us either to observe or participate in. Just hanging around seemed unproductive, since there was no "thick of things" in which one might find oneself in this settlement of dispersed farmsteads. Most daily activities—gardening, gift exchanges, discussions of events—took place in people's houses and yards rather than in some central, public place. Generally, the only occupants of the ceremonial ground—a large clearing in the social center of Mendi communities where parades and large public meetings are held on occasion, and around which several of the "men's houses" were grouped[6]—were men playing cards and groups of children.

I had explained to Nare that I wanted especially to understand the work that went into the preparations for a *mok ink* and the other major festivals but that I also needed to talk with everyone about garden work, gift-exchange partnerships, and other mundane details of life. I told him that I wanted advice concerning what he and other members of the community thought important for me to know and to write about. Whether as a result of these words or of his own line of thought, Nare decided that I ought to hear the stories that old men and women tell. For starters, he showed us three special, "heirloom" pearlshells that he owned and invited a very old man who lived up the hill from our house to tell us about them. But the stories—full of references to battles fought and other intrigues that had occurred a generation or two earlier, and during which the shells had periodically changed hands—were barely comprehensible to me. My "informants" had no idea how ignorant I was; the amount of tacit knowledge presupposed in the epics was vast. The stories and their telling were definitely "anthropological" (and, finally, *un*familiar), but I was not ready for them (but see Lederman 1986a).

I was encouraged through this experience to assert some control over the progress of the research, and I drew up a set of censuslike questions. After discussing them with Nare and Mel to make sure that they made sense and were not impolite, Mike and I began visiting people's houses in the early mornings, asking our questions and at the same time familiarizing ourselves with Wepra's neighborhoods. However, I soon became frustrated with this routine as well. Because of the dispersed layout of the community, I felt I was spending more time walking than talking. I was often discouraged by the difficulty I had in getting around Wepra's steep and slick footpaths.

I also felt obvious and intrusive. I would arrive at a homestead, hoping to

6. The Mendi and other Highlanders traditionally build two kinds of houses: "men's houses" and "women's houses." In Mendi, women's houses are places where women and children sleep and where pigs are stalled at night and on those days when they are not let out to forage for food in bush areas. Men often eat with the rest of the family in their wives' houses, and they sometimes sleep there as well. Most men build houses of their own, where they can talk and eat with male guests and where they often sleep. The separation of male and female sleeping quarters is related to beliefs held by the Highlanders about the dangerous polluting effects on men of contact with female menstrual fluids.

ask the resident adults my list of questions in an efficient manner. But instead, the whole family—plus any overnight guests from other communities—would invariably gather around exclaiming that the "Redwoman" (*ten mboli* in the Mendi language; "red"—*mboli*—is the term the Mendi use to refer to "white" people) had arrived and clucking sympathetically about my muddy boots and trousers. In the babble, it was difficult to ask a straight question, much less to get a simple answer. People always offered me roasted sweet potato, pulled out of the ashes of their morning fire. Besides making it difficult to hold pen and notepad, this offering also caused me to wonder how I was ever to right the balance. A series of formal interviews with a fair percentage of community residents was to be a necessary complement to the more informal historical and event-oriented investigations I had planned. But I could not imagine interviewing everyone in this way, taking or declining their food month after month; my debts would become too burdensome. As it stood, my rounds were neither proper visits nor proper research.

A more reciprocal arrangement had to be devised. While both Mike and I also attended events and visited with people informally throughout our stay, by our second month in Wepra we were conducting most formal interviews at our own house, usually in the late afternoons. We would talk with one or two people at a time about a set topic while huge cauldrons of rice and vegetable stew simmered on our cooking fire. Over the course of a year or so, I worked out a series of interviews concerning marriage and mortuary gift exchanges, personal exchange parternships, land-tenure rights, and so on. All of these were aimed at gathering background information that would have emerged only sporadically and unsystematically in ordinary conversations. While this information was common knowledge to longtime residents, it was essential to any comprehension of contemporary and past events and relationships. During and after the interviews we would all eat together, and the talk would often continue informally, turning to matters of more immediate concern to my guests.

This routine satisfied my own personal and research needs. As it turned out—and luckily for me—it also meshed well with certain Mendi expectations. For one thing, many of the topics about which I wanted to know also interested my guests. For another, this pattern of visiting—in "private" and accompanied by a meal—fit rather well with people's normal behavior. On a deeper level, residing and eating together are central idioms of "kinship" in Mendi, where kinship is an achieved social relationship only partially created out of the given fact of birth. That everyone in the community ate with us at our house helped to establish us rapidly as members of the community, and it was remarked upon numerous times during our stay. Our action opened the way for more intimate social relationships and, therefore, for our first real confrontations with the unfamiliar aspects of Mendi life. For example, it was only after we had eaten together in this way that our neighbors felt that they could draw us into their gift-exchange networks, the real cement of personal interaction and of the indigenous economy in Mendi. And it was only after we began eating with everybody that Nare, Nande, and other members of our immediate family began warning us about the causes and contexts of sorcery, a subject fundamental to any understanding of Mendi politics. My interviewing routine started as a means of anchoring my day around something familiar and productive, but it led us to the heart of some puzzling differences between our own and Mendi social relations.

At the same time, interviewing and the more obvious research work (such as mapping gardens) marked both Mike and me as different from our neighbors, defining our strangeness in our behavior. While Mike resisted accepting the gulf, I was resigned from the outset to the fact that I would never "become Mendi," acting and living just like other members of the community. I think that the difference in our expectations had a lot to do with the difference that being male or female made there, an issue to which I will return soon. In any case, Nare, Mel, and many of the other people we got to know did not require such a transformation from us—they *needed* us to be different. All of us needed to puzzle over our differences more than we needed to abolish or ignore them. Still, people appreciated that we conformed to certain basic Mendi standards of properly "human" behavior: we laughed and ate with everyone, became close with some people through gift exchanges, mourned the deaths that occurred during our stay in the community, and contributed to collective ceremonial wealth displays.

Incorporation and Acceptance

I have been describing both how Mike and I learned on our preexisting framework for understanding the world as we made a transition from New York to Mendi and the conditions that made another stance possible. It is important to stress that this adjustment was reciprocal. Anthropologists and other travelers are not the only ones whose structures of meaning are challenged by intercultural contact. How the Mendi and other Highlanders experienced the coming of whites to their land was similar to Mike's and my experience in settling in Wepra in at least this way; they too incorporated unusual events into preexisting cultural structures with remarkable ease. By means of their myths of origin, they assimilated the coming of whites to Mendi just as they have assimilated Western wealth into their nonmarket forms of exchange and styles of consumption. Similarly, they accepted Mike and me into one of their communities without great disruption to their lives. How they did this reveals something about their culture—its openness to change and the creativity of its metaphoric extension of meanings to new situations.[7]

Early in our stay in Wepra, we asked to hear the legends that people often tell one another around their fires at night. One story was deemed particularly appropriate for us, and consequently I recorded several versions of it on tape. The story was remarkable because it was the only one regularly accompanied by an unsolicited exegesis. It went like this:

A man named Sunda Kowil lived in the high country far to the north of Mendi. One night Sunda Kowil went hunting marsupials in the forest. After much effort, he found a place where the animals had been feeding. He sighted and shot one, but it got away, taking his arrow with it. He built himself a shelter in the forest and spent the night there, determined to do better the next evening. However, the next night he had the same bad luck, and the same again for a third night.

He decided to change his tactics, and he made preparations on the fourth day for tracking his prey. When his arrow was stolen once again, he followed its trail of blood southward for several days into the Mendi Valley.

Still tracking his marsupial, Kowil came upon a large house. He went closer to have a better look. In a nearby burial ground, he saw many young women crying near a fresh grave. He went back to the house and approached a young woman who was alone inside. He asked her what had happened, and she explained that she and her sisters had recently lost all four of their brothers, the last of which they had just buried that day.

Kowil returned to the site of the grave, now deserted, and exhumed the body to discover that it was not a man but a large white pig. He returned to the house with the pig-brother's body. The woman he had talked to earlier looked on while he sealed various holes and cracks in the house, which was in disrepair, and then built a fire [of which the women apparently had no previous knowledge]. He then started to singe the bristles off the pig, preparing it to be cooked. The woman protested, but he assured her that he knew what he was doing. He butchered the carcass and cooked some small pieces of meat with a green, which he offered to the woman. She refused, saying it was her brother and therefore inedible. He insisted, and she took a small bite. Liking the taste, she ate several pieces with relish.

Just then, the other women returned to the house. There were ten black-skinned women, like the woman to whom Kowil fed the pork, and one red-skinned woman with a strong will. When all of the women were inside the house, he closed all the exits, locking them all inside with him. Only the red woman was suspicious and escaped through a hole he had overlooked.

Sunda Kowil built a large fire, and the house soon filled with smoke, blinding the women, who stumbled about feeling for the exit. To calm them,

7. Roy Wagner (1972) writes of the innovation of meaning in his ethnography of the Daribi, another New Guinea people (see also Sahlins 1981; Wagner 1981[1975]).

he fed them all sorts of good food, including pork, which they had never eaten before. Finally, after all the eating, they complained that they had to go outside to relieve themselves.

At that time, women were not as they are now. They had no vaginas or anuses. Kowil had noticed that in order to relieve themselves they would rub against the spine of a banana leaf located near the house. Thinking about this earlier, he had prepared the banana leaf by placing sharp bamboo on its spine. When the women went out to urinate after their meal, they rubbed themselves on this sharp edge, cutting themselves open and becoming as they are today.

Kowil married the woman he had first spoken with and soon she was pregnant. At first she bore a grass, and in subsequent pregnancies she bore other animal and vegetable species. Finally, she bore a human infant: a boy. Sunda Kowil warned her not to nurse it, but to feed it water from a gourd he showed her. But she refused, asking him, "Why do I have breasts, if not to nurse a child?" He advised her to seek out a forest tree fruit when she became hungry, but she replied, "Why do I have hands, if not to plant the food we will eat?" It is said that as a result of the woman's actions people have to work for their living.[8]

Male informants analyzed the story like this: "Now those for whom Sunda Kowil made the fire—the black-skinned people—that's us, Papua New Guineans. The red woman who left, she ran off and bore you all [whites, called *tenol mboli,* or 'red people,' in Mendi]. Sunda Kowil made fire for us. We don't have electricity, or 'power,' in our houses. We do not sleep in cold houses like you do but build fires in ours to keep us warm at night. Your houses are cold. You build no fires. Look, you live like the women did before Kowil came. The red woman left and bore you all. That is why Europeans don't have to work very hard with their hands. And because the black woman did not listen to her husband's advice, we Papua New Guineans plant gardens, chop firewood, and do other kinds of hard work."

Everyone insisted that the myth derived from precolonial times; however, exegeses like the one just given were admittedly a recent innovation. They were telling us that our existence had been anticipated even before any of us arrived. The story hints at an explanation for the differences and inequities between Papua New Guineans and whites at the same time that it asserts a common origin for us all. What is more, the "red woman" who went off and became the progenitor of the "Europeans" was originally from Mendi. It follows that her descendants have returned home to their matrilateral kin, just as many Mendi are currently

8. A similar story is associated with the Melpa *Amb Kor,* or Female Spirit Cult, in Mt. Hagen, to the northeast of Mendi (see A. Strathern 1970). The symbolism of "red" and "black" is complex. In Mendi it is used to distinguish same-sex siblings in several myths, and it has acquired an additional "racial" meaning only recently (whites are called "red" people—*tenol mboli*—in the Mendi language).

reestablishing ties with their own matrilateral relatives in distant Highland communities with whom they had lost touch during the days of tribal fighting.

By 1977, when Mike and I arrived, the Mendi had assimilated much more than the simple existence of whites. Like other Highlanders, they had incorporated many items of Western manufacture into their own socioeconomic system, a fact with implications perhaps as great as that of Kowil's wife's unfortunate choices. The transformation of Western commodities into gifts—whose exchange constitutes social relations basically antithetical to those of a capitalist economy—has thus far been part of an efflorescence of the indigenous political economy. While the motion is hardly one-way (see Gregory 1982), from a rural perspective the signs of cultural autonomy or integrity and the expansion of familiar possibilities are apparent, and the signs of dependency and subordination to the logic of a foreign sociopolitical structure are less clear.

This confidence was revealed in the particular way in which the residents of Wepra incorporated Mike and me into their community. While Nare and Nande included us in their household (sharing the pork gifts they received from their exchange partners and kin, for example), we were not given any clear kinship identities. We were treated just like indigenous immigrants, neither kept categorically outside the system nor accorded any special privilege. According to the standard procedure, we acquired a general association with the clan of our local sponsor, but membership in such groups is achieved gradually in Mendi. It is not an all-or-nothing fact of one's social identity.

More than anything else, eating together and exchanging gifts of wealth are the bases upon which the Mendi build personal relationships. For instance, early in our stay Mike was told that if he really wanted to become *Kurelka* (the Wepra clan name), he would have to live in Wepra for a long time indeed and to contribute to Kurelka projects, such as the *mok ink*. Over the course of our stay, we did contribute frequently, both privately to our growing network of exchange partners and publicly to clan displays. The degree to which we had achieved insider status can be measured by the reciprocal aid we were given when we organized a feast prior to our departure in 1979. Not only were our direct requests for aid answered but we also received many unsolicited gifts, enabling us to organize a feast about which the whole community felt proud.

In common with other Highlanders, the Mendi are used to accepting immigrants into their communities. War refugees, maternal kin, and other outsiders are incorporated without fuss into their clans, since a large membership is valued. Kinship in the Highlands is thus not merely a matter of who one's parents or ancestors were but is achieved through long-term cooperation and joint participation in rituals, ceremonies, and the like. It was therefore understandable that our entry into the Wepra community should have caused no great disruption. It is also understandable that real membership in the community would be the product of a lifelong commitment and involvement. When we left in 1979, our commitments were insufficiently proven, our incorporation only provisional. Our departure, which our neighbors treated as they would a death, was more disruptive than our arrival.

I was able to return for three months during 1983, demonstrating a measure of good faith, and I plan to return again in the future. However, the practical difficulties—finding funds, coordinating a trip with one's responsibilities at work and to one's family—raises troubling questions about the anthropological endeavor, especially when it is carried out in a society that places a premium on densely articulated social relationships.

On Being a Woman in Mendi

The interrelated processes whereby I both learned about Mendi gender relations and lived as a woman in Mendi recapitulate all that I have described thus far. As with field work generally, so too learning about gender in Mendi required moving from a reliance on familiar interpretations to a perception of difference and an ability to translate it with sensitivity, a movement sustained by the tension between identification and distance.

When I first planned research in P.N.G., my interest was primarily in laying to rest static models of Highlands political economies and only secondarily in understanding male/female relations. During the late 1960s and the 1970s, agrarian production in the Highlands was analyzed as an equilibrated, conservative ecological system. Based on studies of societies on the Highlands "fringe," pig-kill festivals similar to the *mok ink* were interpreted as adaptive mechanisms, functioning like thermostats to control the potentially destructive natural expansion of pig herds (see Rappaport 1968).

As a general interpretation of Highlands agriculture, this framework came under attack in the mid-1970s. It appeared that in central Highland societies, pig herds are managed more actively by their owners; Highlanders control the size of their herds by means of breeding and trade, and they actively increase them *in order* to stage pig festivals. They maintain large herds and tolerate a degree of ecological pressure for years before actually killing their pigs. In fact, the history of the central Highlands has in part been a history of the expansion of intensive, ecologically innovative production systems geared to the support of large herds of domesticated pigs (Golson 1982), a process of expansion which is still under way in some places (Boyd 1985).

Thus, we still faced the explanatory void that the ecological models had been meant to fill. Why were these events held, and what sorts of factors determined their scale and frequency? The festivals were interesting as spectacular products of sociopolitical systems that were known to be decentralized and participatory in organization. It seemed to me that one had to situate an explanation for the festivals within a wider study of the social relations that made them possible. I decided to focus not simply on the aims of leaders during festivals but also on the relationships between leaders and ordinary people and between men and women.

The sexual division of labor appeared to be particularly relevant. Highlands production systems emphasize the sweet potato, cultivated intensively by means of sophisticated techniques. Sweet potatoes are the staple food of humans, and they are also fodder for large herds of pigs which, with sweet potatoes, are the main products of the indigenous agrarian economy in Mendi and neighboring Highland societies. Along with pearlshells and modern Papua New Guinea currency, pigs are central to the wealth exchanges that take place during marriage and mortuary ceremonies and that help reproduce both personal and intergroup relationships there.[9] My ethnographic reading taught me that while both men and women are engaged in garden production, women are largely responsible for the daily work of cultivating sweet potatoes and looking after pigs. The literature I read implied that while women control the production and distribution of sweet potatoes (making decisions about planting and harvesting, for example), men control the allocation or use of pigs and other forms of wealth. As participants in policy-making meetings (from which women are excluded), men control the scheduling of those festivals (such as the *mok ink*) which are held "in the clan name"—arguably a focus of public life for both men and women—during which pigs and other valuables are displayed and exchanged.

Put another way, men appear to dominate what anthropological observers recognize as formal "politics" in the Highlands. They monopolize leadership positions, which are achieved by means of oratorical and organizational skills and the ability to mobilize wealth through exchange-partnership networks for public distribution.[10] Political control over the scheduling of festivals might have implications for an understanding of the relations of production if the scheduling shapes the intensity of garden work. I hoped to explore whether women's

9. These distinctions reflect indigenous conceptual categories. In particular, the Mendi distinguish the personal relationship of "exchange partners" (*twem ol*) from the collective relationship of common clan (*sem onda*) membership. In an economic system that discourages the personal accumulation of wealth in favor of its giftlike distribution, exchange partners are personal friends who reciprocally depend upon one another for valuables whenever one of them needs some in order to participate in a ceremony or to help another partner. While exchange partnerships are dyadic, clan membership is collective, or "corporate." Clans are named groups that are associated with bounded territories and conceived of as having a transgenerational existence. Clan membership defines a person's rights to garden land and house sites and his collective responsibilities. In contrast, a person's exchange-partnership network defines an aspect of his personal autonomy from his clansmen.

10. Leadership is not inherited, and there are no formal offices that must be filled. Each group may have many "leaders," and all face the possibility of having none. "Big-man" (*ol koma*) is a descriptive term applied after the fact of demonstrated accomplishment.

exclusion from this form of political control might be a condition of the "exploitation" of female labor (see Lederman 1980).

Anthropological accounts of gender ideology and of the relationships between Highlands women and men, and especially between wives and husbands, highlight antagonism. Whether men consider women actively "dangerous" or passively "polluting"—attitudes that vary from region to region—the overall assessment on the part of anthropological observers was of female subordination. Ritual symbols value maleness over femaleness, and idioms of social-group continuity and unity are agnatic, emphasizing male ancestors and relations among "brothers."

Until recently, women have not figured as anthropologists' main informants in Highlands research, despite the fact that a reasonable number of anthropologists working there have been women. Anthropological accounts have depended on the attitudes, explanations, and descriptions of Highland men. These accounts have also paid disproportionate attention to male-dominated activities. Male anthropologists found speaking with Highland women difficult. Given the anthropological (and Highland male) emphasis on public clan ceremonies, women have seemed not to be where the interesting action is. Thus, as a result both of their informants' influence and of biases reflecting the values of their own societies, many field workers interested in sociopolitical questions appeared to have concluded that speaking with Highland women was not worth the effort. In any case, field work is a difficult enough business, and much could be learned without female instruction.

While the implications of the choices field workers made in the past have only begun to be explored, during the past decade projects in which women, gender relations, and gender symbolism are in the foreground have gained legitimacy in Highlands research (and anthropology generally). In any case, at the time of my first field work the existing anthropological literature, with its account of sexual antagonism and female subordination, worried me. If Mendi women's behavior was restricted, would mine be as well? Would being married underline my femaleness, preventing me from escaping a narrowly female role if I wished to escape it, or would my status as a white outsider predominate? Would I have as much trouble speaking with Highlands women as male anthropologists had, or would I be able to speak *only* with women?

Since I was interested in the relationship between the organization of agricultural production and the politics of ceremonial exchange, and since I imagined that these were largely sex-segregated domains, I was anxious to be able to speak with both men and women. Without that ability, I felt that I would not understand the ways in which male and female interests (e.g., with regard to the "proper" uses of pigs) diverged.

My research strategy was initially shaped, with contradictory effect, by my fears concerning how to present myself and by my sensitivities about my status and autonomy, born of my experience as a woman in the States. I was concerned with not aligning myself clearly with either the men or the women (as I understood the difference then): I did not go gardening right away with Nande, nor did I insinuate myself into the men's houses, normally off-limits to women. I hoped to take advantage of whatever ambiguity my outsider status afforded, sidestepping the issue of my own gender and commitments for a while, if possible.

While it did not make me "male" in Mendi terms, this strategy of emphasizing my anomalousness limited my contact with Mendi women during the first couple of months in Wepra, during which I was establishing a research routine. As I have shown, women did not figure prominently in our entrance into village life. Paki chose to introduce Mike and me not to his mother but to his father, and for good reasons—Nare spoke fluent pidgin at a time when I could not have understood any Mendi, whereas Nande, like other Mendi women, spoke pidgin poorly (although she did understand quite a bit of it). What is more, only a man had the power to give us land and to organize a work party to build a house. Nare chose male assistants for us, though we held open the possibility of adding a woman to the staff later on.

More because of my personal need to assert autonomy than because of any research strategy, I was concerned with letting Nare and others know from the outset that Mike and I had come to Mendi because of *my* work and *my* grant money. I asserted that I had to be consulted concerning any personal- or public-wealth contributions people might want the two of us to make. To my surprise, Nare and the other men did not appear at all troubled by this arrangement. Other things, however, made more of an impression. Later on, after they knew both Mike and me better, some of our male friends admitted that when we had first visited Wepra to discuss the possibility of living in the village, they had thought it odd that I (the woman) had done most of the talking. Women are not "orators" in Mendi (nor in the Highlands generally), and they are not expected to speak out to strangers as I had done.

Mendi ideas about men and women contain subtleties, of which I was then unaware, which were capable of accommodating my deviations. As time progressed, my neighbors were able to translate aspects of my behavior into their own terms (in ways that I will describe further on). Without realizing it, and even despite myself, I was being placed—as was my relationship with Mike. Throughout our stay, unmarried young men and women especially enjoyed hearing about our exotic American marriage and courting customs. My accounts—which were biased in favor of descriptions of egalitarian sex roles—were a means of explaining myself to them. However, our young assistant, Tolap, revealed how our behavior was reinterpreted in terms of Mendi ideas about gender. After months of spending his idle hours sleeping, eating, and gossiping around our house, one day he asked Mike whether Mike and I were not in fact brother and sister rather than husband and wife. When Mike asked him how he could think such a thing, Tolap answered, "You two don't fight."

Now, while that observation was not entirely accurate, it did reveal something about gender categories in Mendi. For all the anthropological discussions of "sexual antagonism" in Highland New Guinea, turned out that in Mendi antagonism is not derived from a categorical opposition between "men" and "women" as such but instead is engendered by other sorts of structural contradictions.[11] *Alliances* between "brothers" and "sisters" are as characteristic of male/female relations as is the *antagonism* characteristic of "husbands" and "wives." The qualities of women as "sisters" are generally valued. Thus, gender is not a unified dimension of difference in Mendi.

Because of my initial research decisions, my first concrete understanding of what Mendi women were like came from my relationship with Nande, Nare's wife. She was a remarkably hard-working woman. While most women look after perhaps five pigs, Nande cared for between twenty and thirty of them at a time. She had forbidden Nare from taking a second wife, as Mendi big-men are wont to do, because she wanted full joint credit with him for their accomplishments. Nare, for his part, was confident in her ability and in her dedication to their reputation. He also believed that his own success depended on a harmonious, cooperative household. He disapproved of men who had more than one wife, since the potential for favoritism and conflict was great. Nare's views on the matter were demonstrated early in our stay when we spoke with him about our desire to buy one of the pigs in his herd to fatten up and slaughter upon our departure. Nare insisted that we discuss the matter with Nande. He told us that the pigs were not his alone and that since Nande would be looking after the animal for us, she ought to make the final decision concerning the transaction. At the time, I did not know whether these words reflected Nare's Westernized attitudes about husbands and wives or whether it could be taken as a "Mendi" value. Did Mendi women "own" pigs? Were husbands and wives "supposed" to cooperate in decisions concerning the allocation of household wealth?

Despite her evident self-confidence and her prominence in Wepra, and also despite her particularly elaborate and ramified kin connections (which constituted the basis for the success of Nande and Nare's household in mobilizing wealth for ceremonies, as Nare himself pointed out), Nande fit a number of expectations I had formed concerning Highlands women based on my pre–field work reading. Nare was the one who represented the household to the world at public gatherings. He stood up to make explanatory speeches as he distributed pork or pearlshells at clan affairs. What is more, Nande would not have taken over that position for anything (as she made clear to me during the anxious moments

11. The spouse/sibling contrast parallels the distinction I described in note 9 between exchange partnerships (paradigmatically established in marriage) and clan membership.

before the ceremonies began). She had a point. As Mike was to learn, distributing pork is a harrowing affair, and one which many Mendi men themselves do not relish.

Consequently, knowing Nande did not challenge my assumptions about sex roles in Mendi. She was extraordinary, but her relationship with Nare still seemed to fit the woman-as-producer/man-as-transactor pattern found in other Highland societies.[12] About other women and their relationships I did not know. At first I was unsure as to what to interview women about and needed more informal contact. In particular, I imagined asking them detailed questions about the pigs they cared for and about their garden work. D'Arcy Ryan, an anthropologist who had done research in Mendi during the 1950s, had mentioned in his Ph.D. thesis that Mendi women were involved in the distribution of their own bride-wealth—a fact that held some interest, given notions then fashionable among anthropologists about women being "exchanged" in marriage—and I intended to learn more about it. But I was uncertain about women's involvement in exchange generally, a fact which would be relevant to an understanding of women's economic autonomy and involvement in "public" life. Would I discover any woman-to-woman wealth transactions? In other parts of Melanesia, women make gifts to one another of items in which men do not transact; would there be "women's wealth" in Mendi?[13]

I wondered especially about the conflicts that husbands and wives might have over the disposal of pigs. Would such conflicts reflect contradictions between male and female conceptualizations of their "property rights?" What about systematic differences in their personal ambitions and political interests? Why was Nande not interested in publicly distributing pork from the pigs she had worked so hard to raise? Conversely, why was Nare driven to do so, despite the stress such a performance entailed? I wondered in what contexts I would be most likely to learn about female idioms concerning personal and social value and power. Nande and Nare aside, would talking with women about conflicts and alternate systems of social value get them (or me) in trouble with their husbands?

During our first months of field work, in the course of collecting census information from men concerning their currently outstanding gift-exchange obligations ("debts" and "credits"), I was surprised to find that they regularly mentioned female exchange partners. Women routinely controlled pigs, pearlshells, and money. Were women, then, "transactors" in Mendi? If so, they were unusual among the Highlanders known to anthropologists.

After I had lived in Wepra for a time, then, I became aware of several

12. Transactor/producer is a cultural contrast reflecting indigenous ideas about men and women in Mt. Hagen (M. Strathern 1972).

13. Annette Weiner (1976) describes women's wealth transactions in the matrilineal Trobriand Islands.

paradoxes. As I have noted, the sexes are not neatly polarized in Mendi, but antagonistic and hierarchically organized gender idioms are central to political discourse there. Women are not simply subordinate to men, but at the same time there are social situations in which "femaleness" is denigrated. The analytical problem was to distinguish which paradoxes reflected merely my own confusion and unfamiliarity with the society and which reflected real contradictions in Mendi culture.[14]

Mendi men denigrate women as often as they speak of women's strengths and of the importance of male/female cooperation. But expressions of male superiority and control often occur in contexts in which they appear to make little sense or where, at least, they have little practical effect. For example, one day a male friend of ours remarked that we ought to have sweet potatoes planted in the small garden behind our house, and he volunteered his wife then and there for the task. I was skeptical and asked him if he hadn't better discuss the matter first with his wife, but he insisted that everything was under control: "She hasn't any say in the matter." Several hours later his wife joined us all at our house for a visit, but with no intention of doing any more planting that day. As the afternoon wore on she sat, drawing on a homemade cigarette and playing with her small daughter, while her husband began to plant the sweet potato runners, stopping periodically to exclaim in disgust at her laziness.

Our young bachelor acquaintances insisted that they would never tolerate such a situation but would beat their future wives into obedience. However, when one of these men got married during our stay, he appeared to lose much of his resolve. For one thing, like other Mendi women I know, his wife demonstrated that she was prepared to defend herself physically if need be. Another (and more significant) reason was that she was also in a position to leave her husband to look after his pigs himself, since she could always return home to her natal territory, which was nearby. Unlike women in some other Highlands societies where alliances between brothers-in-law are common, Mendi women are strongly supported by their brothers and their other kin, who will readily take them in for extended periods and back their demands for compensation for any injury or insult they have suffered. One of Mel's sisters stayed with him for well over a year in this way.

It seemed that men "talked tough" and asserted their dominance but could not compel their wives to obey them. Even when women appeared to obey, they often restated the reasons for their actions in terms of their own desires, denying the truth of the men's denigrating descriptions of them and frequently belittling men in turn (though it always seemed to me that they did so with humor and detachment, not with assertions of dominance and control).

---

14. For an excellent discussion of the paradoxes of "gender thinking" in a Highlands society, see the work of Marilyn Strathern (1972, 1976).

All of this insubordinate female feistiness was appealing to me and (once again) "familiar." I was encouraged by these observations and decided to try interviewing women in my house in the late afternoons, just as I had been interviewing their husbands. Despite Mike's and our male assistants' presence and participation in the work, these discussions went smoothly. Interviewing women did present some new complications. Women would come over to talk only after their pigs had returned home from the bush for their evening meal, and exactly when they would show up was unpredictable. They also brought with them all of their young children, so these gatherings were boisterous. It is also more unusual for women to go visiting in the evenings than it is for men. Men often spend evenings together with other men, while women are more frequently found individually in their own houses then. But by the time we started interviewing women at our house (about two months into our stay in Wepra), our habits were well known. Our intention to speak with all the adults in the community—even women—was accepted by our male friends (though some thought it redundant), and it was heartily approved by Nande and other of our female acquaintances.

The interviewing went so smoothly that I wondered why other Highlands researchers had had any problems at all in talking with women. Part of the answer may be that Mendi was more sexually egalitarian than some of the other Highlands societies where anthropologists had worked. Then too, I had assumed that women were going to have important things to tell me, and consequently I had simply determined, one way or another, to talk with them. Mike's ease in talking with women (whether I was present or not) may have derived from his relationship with me, although it sometimes seemed that the unmarried young women even preferred him!

From our interviews with women and from many more informal observations, I began to understand the relationship between Mendi women's autonomy and their restrictions and to relax my grip on my initial assumptions concerning production, property, and power. I puzzled over cases that seemed to probe the rules. Why was it that social handicaps (such as immigrant status) could be successfully overcome by men who desired to become clan leaders, whereas those few women who also wanted to distribute pearlshells and make speeches but who had no such handicaps were barred from these activities? Why was it that most women asserted little interest in participating with men in these ceremonies, while men felt compelled to participate whether they wanted to or not? Why could women exchange wealth in some contexts and not in others? Why did "brothers" and "sisters" typically get along well but "husbands" and "wives" did not? I slowly learned that I could not pick out those pieces of the puzzle that appealed to me simply because they were familiar. Although it provided an entrée, that sort of comprehensibility was false; Mendi gender relations and ideology are "strange" insofar as our analytical categories cannot elegantly make sense of them. Female "insubordination" in Mendi has different roots, and therefore a different meaning, from analogous behavior at home. If Mendi men were "sexist," they had invented a kind of sexism different from ours. Understanding once again required a difficult process of viewing things whole, fixing one's gaze on the uncategorizable facts as well as on the seemingly familiar ones.

I have written about this problem elsewhere (Lederman 1980, 1986b) and can only provide an outline of my interpretation here. I found that whereas in the States many women have created a sense of their collective interests against men and against pervasively patriarchal institutions, in Mendi the interests of men and women are not polarized in this way. Men and women are differentially involved in two kinds of social relations in Mendi: although both men and women participate with autonomy in exchange partnerships, only men are true members of clans. The distinction between exchange partnerships (*twem*) and clanship (*sem*) does not correspond neatly to any of ours: not to the distinction between "public" and "private" domains, to that between "family" and "economy/polity," nor to that between "internal" and "external" social spheres.[15]

On the one hand, the interests of men and women diverge in the context of clan ceremonies, which are the practical means by which men create solidary associations and in which expressions of male dominance have real meaning. In daily life, this divergence of interest is expressed in the relationship between husbands and wives: while husbands seek to participate in local clan affairs, the affiliation of wives is with a different group residing elsewhere. On the other hand, in the context of personal obligations among exchange partners living in many communities, men and women cooperate. Here, in fact, "gender" is not an issue at all. These nonclan contexts are not infused with gender symbols and are neither male-dominated nor female-dominated. They are, however, important both for an understanding of Mendi experience as it is culturally constituted and for the structural analysis of Mendi social relations. These contexts are arguably as important as the more visually spectacular clan exchange ceremonies upon which anthropologists working elsewhere have legitimately focused their attention. While male-dominated institutions are not as pervasive in Mendi as they are elsewhere, and while Mendi women appear to have relatively wide scope for action in a domain itself valued by both men and women, at the same time women are excluded from other domains that men, at least, value highly. Mendi men consider their wives to be their colleagues, opponents, or servants, and they say they dominate them even when they do not. Mendi women say that they belong to both their husband's and brothers' clans or to neither, practically in the same breath. Like ours, Mendi gender ideology is contradictory. Its contradictions, however, are different from the ones with which we struggle.

15. See note 9.

Being able to talk with women as well as with men and learning about the Mendi's relative egalitarianism considerably eased my anxiety about how to present myself. While I continued to explain my behavior with reference to American customs, I felt less inhibited about acting, from time to time, like a Mendi woman. I went gardening with Nande, and we became close. I sat with other women at pork distributions and enjoyed their running commentaries on the performances of the men. Despite these things, full identification was not possible. It was not until I had returned to New York and had begun to sort through my notes and experiences that I started to understand why I had not been able to "be myself" in Mendi. Explicitly and actively "translating" myself into Mendi terms would have first required an understanding of the rules of acceptable female behavior in Mendi and also of what is meant by the alternative possible plays on—and violations of—the rules. This has only begun to be possible since my return trip to Mendi in 1983.

A few of the younger women gave me a hint about the role I might more actively adopt. Observing my behavior (and perhaps thinking about my accounts of how things are done in America), they placed me in that "deviant" female category reserved for ambitious, opinionated Mendi women with many exchange partners and projects of their own apart from their husbands and with reputations for talking out loudly. Called "strong willed" (like the red-skinned woman in the Sunda Kowil story), they were frequently admired and a little feared by other women and tolerated by the men, who alternately criticized or praised them in private.[16] Some such deviant status was appropriate to me, since that is the status I hold at home as well, although the particular character of my familiar deviations are different from the Mendi ones I would have had to adopt. To accept the place that Mendi society offered me would have meant signaling at least a provisional acceptance of the full range of Mendi values, including those that defined that place as deviant. In retrospect I realize that my initial detachment was a refusal to even provisionally accept a package that I did not understand.[17]

While I felt that I had to hold myself apart, Mike felt that he fit in rather well. He was not restricted from any of the more obviously valued aspects of Mendi life. What is more, the decentralized, nonauthoritarian, and participatory

16. I am not at all sure about how such women were treated in precolonial times of tribal warfare. While I believe that men were less tolerant of them, there is evidence that the women were not simply suppressed.

17. During a return visit to Mendi in 1983, I was able to use—or at least to play with—such alternative idioms and styles. The point here is that while the "female" role, if such a thing exists, may not itself be deviant or critical, there are particularly Mendi types of social criticism available to women (and to men). Learning another cultural style, like learning a new language, opens the way to new experiences, even to a new world. If, in the process, one is faced with joining the "opposition," it makes sense to do so only if one believes that there is something of value at the core of that experience. One thereby signals one's belief that a particular way of life is worth criticizing in *indigenous* terms, perhaps even worth transforming within its *own* structures of belief.

style of political relations emphatically available to men was extremely appealing to him. He went to the bush to hunt for birds and to fell trees for firewood, and he learned to use his ax (if not his bow) with skill. He gained a reputation for being a surefooted and strong walker. He assisted when Nare distributed pork and officiated at our own distribution at the end of our stay. There were even times when he seemed to forget that he did not fully understand Mendi conventions and could not simply "be himself" any more than I could. The trouble this caused is a story he will have to tell, not I. The point, however, is simply that we both learned that "being oneself" is not natural; who we are is constructed out of and against sets of social conventions. Being able to express oneself requires much more than learning a verbal language or even a style of nonverbal mannerisms. It requires adopting a new idiom of contexts, relations, and subtle but deeply felt convictions.

Comparison and Commitment

I have focused on only one thread of the many constituting my experience of field work, and it traces a pattern that others (whether anthropologists or not) may recognize. Doing field work heightened my awareness of human possibilities and deepened my belief that social life is everywhere a changing product of human creativity (if not exactly human control). The experience was at least a dramatic vantage from which to reflect on homegrown conventions, alternatives, and transformations; afterward, these appeared to be neither natural nor the only ones possible.

But this vantage has risks. While it may improve one's critical sense, it may simultaneously heighten the ambivalence one might have about one's own culture. With field work, I took myself out of my own society without putting myself squarely into another one. In Mendi, I was a sympathetic outsider who did not altogether want to be an insider. The qualified empathy that my field work engendered stood in the way of a sense of commitment, since it prevented a wholehearted adoption of an insider's perspective and even a kind of "ethnocentrism" (by which I mean a single-minded belief in one structure of value). Part of the trauma of returning home to New York (and the smaller trauma that Mike and I experienced every time we spent a day in Mendi town) had to do with a sharp perception of alternative, imperfect worlds. Was it a matter of choosing between them (or perhaps choosing which fight to join)?

This vantage and its risks are not peculiar to anthropologists. Many of the Mendi I know confront a similar problem in their daily lives. One evening in July 1983, I was speaking with Alin, the wife of Nare's eldest son, as we poked at the embers of my cooking fire. Our conversation drifted from village events and personalities in general to her own particular frustrations, as a woman who had had six years of formal schooling, with a life that had thus far been restricted to a rural village. She had thought of becoming a nurse, but her brothers had worried too much about the dangers of her living in town or in another district in order to obtain the necessary training, and her new husband's parents needed her to help them with both gardening and pig tending. Alin commented to me that several of her clansmen were living and working in Mendi town, Mt. Hagen, or even Port Moresby, but very few women had done this—and to top it all off, women's work in the village is harder than men's. I asked her why this was so. She sat back, thought for a moment, and smiled, saying, "Well, I don't really know, but there's an old story about a man, Sunda Kowil, who went hunting marsupials in the forest . . ," and she proceeded to recount the same story that I summarized earlier in this chapter.

Like the men who had told me versions of the Sunda Kowil story, Alin blamed Kowil's wife for contemporary conditions. But in contrast to the male exegeses I had heard, Alin used the story *not* to explain the relationship between whites and Papua New Guineans *but rather* to highlight a message about inequality in the rural sexual division of labor.

While I suspect that they have been critical of their roles in earlier times, too, Mendi women today are sensitive to constraints on their autonomy in new ways. Just as the political basis for male clan action has been altered, if not necessarily weakened, by the existence of provincial and national governmental institutions, male/female relations are in a state of flux because of women's involvement in schools, missions, and marketing. These sorts of innovations may eventually bring the terms of local discourse closer to the universalizing ones favored by many Western feminists. For the present, to assimilate Alin's criticisms and those of her friends into our terms would risk misconstruing their meaning and import (as Sexton's 1982 study of a new women's association in the Eastern Highlands implies). That is, many important changes are unintended consequences of the *persistence* of old practices and frameworks of understanding in new conditions, rather than being cultural or structural transformations. For example, in the past Mendi women usually controlled the allocation of the garden produce they planted. Nowadays, with the possibility of selling vegetables in town for money, they are able to accumulate large quantities of a kind of wealth that men also value. Given the personal autonomy that women are acknowledged to have anyhow in Mendi society and also their involvement in exchange partnerships, this situation may encourage men to devise strategies for linking women's interests more closely to clan ceremonies and clan politics. This would provide women with the same nonmarket uses for money that men now have as a means of keeping money in the rural system (compare A. Strathern 1979; M. Strathern 1981).

Mendi women and men (like other Papua New Guineans) are comparing two ways of life, as I was, but with much more at stake and therefore with less detachment. In both cases, what is necessary is a structural imagination, one that pays attention to the ways in which the parts of each form of experience are articulated. It was this sort of imagination which I think Mike, Nare, and I were fostering during our months of fireside conversations in the late 1970s (conversations of the type that I really only began with women like Alin in 1983), listening and translating and arguing with one another. Anthropology encourages that kind of imagination, and it makes possible the transformation of an ethnocentric sureness that our own ways of doing things are right into at least the *possibility* of a commitment chosen in awareness of the full shape and significance of other actual or possible alternatives.

Acknowledgments

My research in Papua New Guinea was supported in 1977–79 by a National Institutes of Mental Health predoctoral research fellowship and a National Science Foundation predoctoral grant, and in 1983 by grants from the American Philosophical Association and from Princeton University, for all of which I am thankful. I would also like to thank Michael Merrill; Glen Petersen, Rayna Rapp, Abraham Rosman, and Marilyn Strathern for their comments on a draft of this chapter.

References

BROWN, PAULA. 1978. *Highland Peoples of New Guinea*. New York: Cambridge University Press.

BOYD, DAVID. 1985. "We Shall Follow the Fore: Pig Husbandry Intensification and Ritual Diffusion among the Irakia Awa, Papua New Guinea," *American Ethnologist*, 12(1):119–136.

CLIFFORD, JAMES. 1983. "On Ethnographic Authority," *Representations*, 1, 118–146.

GOLSON, JACK. 1982. "The Ipomoean Revolution Revisited: Society and the Sweet Potato in the Upper Wahgi Valley." In A. Strathern, ed., *Inequality in New Guinea Highland Societies*. New York: Cambridge University Press.

GREGORY, CHRIS. 1982. *Gifts and Commodities*. London: Academic Press.

LEDERMAN, RENA. 1980. "Who Speaks Here?: Formality and the Politics of Gender in Mendi, Highland Papua New Guinea," *Journal of the Polynesian Society*, 89, 479–498.

———. 1986a. "Changing Times in Mendi: Notes towards Writing Highland New Guinea History," *Ethnohistory*, 33(1) (forthcoming 1986).

————. 1986b. *What Gifts Engender: Social Relations and Politics in Mendi, Highland Papua New Guinea.* New York: Cambridge University Press.

MARCUS, GEORGE, and RICHARD CUSHMAN. 1982. "Ethnographies as Texts," *Annual Review of Anthropology,* 11, 25–69.

RAPPAPORT, ROY. 1968. *Pigs for the Ancestors.* New Haven: Yale University Press.

SAHLINS, MARSHALL. 1981. *Historical Metaphors and Mythical Realities.* Ann Arbor: University of Michigan Press.

SEXTON, LORRAINE. 1982. "Wok Meri: A Women's Savings and Exchange System in Highland Papua New Guinea," *Oceania,* 52(3):167–198.

STRATHERN, ANDREW. 1970. "The Male and Female Spirit Cults in Mount Hagen," *Man,* 5, 571–585.

————. 1979. "Gender, Ideology and Money in Mount Hagen," *Man,* 14, 530–548.

STRATHERN, MARILYN. 1972. *Women in Between: Female Roles in a Male World.* London: Seminar Press.

————. 1978. "The Achievement of Sex: Paradoxes of Hagen Gender-Thinking." In E. Schwimmer, ed., *Yearbook of Symbolic Anthropology.* London: C. Hurst.

————. 1981. "Self-Interest and the Social Good." In S. Ortner and H. Whitehead, eds., *Sexual Meanings.* New York: Cambridge University Press.

WAGNER, ROY. 1972. *Habu: The Innovation of Meaning in Daribi Religion.* Chicago: University of Chicago Press.

————. 1981 [1975]. *The Invention of Culture.* Chicago: University of Chicago Press.

WEINER, ANNETTE. 1976. *Women of Value, Men of Renown.* Austin and London: University of Texas Press.

Selected Bibliography

compiled by Srila Sen

ADAMS, RICHARD N., and JACK J. PREISS (eds.). 1960. *Human Organization Research*. Homewood, Illinois: The Dorsey Press.

BARRY, HERBERT III, MARGARET K. BACON, and I. I. CHILD. 1957. "A Cross Cultural Survey of Some Sex Differences in Socialization," *Journal of Abnormal Social Psychology*, 55:327–332.

BECKER, HOWARD S. 1958. "Problems of Inference and Proof in Participant Observation," *American Sociological Review*, 23, 652–660.

BERREMAN, GERALD D. 1962. *Behind Many Masks: Ethnography and Impression Management in a Himalayan Village*. Ithaca, New York: Society for Applied Anthropology.

BLAU, PETER. 1964. *Exchange and Power in Social Life*. New York: Wiley.

BOWEN, ELENORE SMITH (pseudonym). 1954. *Return to Laughter*. New York: Harper & Row.

D'ANDRADE, ROY G. 1966. "Sex Differences and Cultural Institutions." In Eleanor Maccoby (ed.), *The Development of Sex Differences*. Stanford: Stanford University Press.

DU BOIS, CORA. 1937. "Some Psychological Techniques and Objectives in Ethnography, *Journal of Social Psychology*, 8, 285–301.

———. 1944. *The People of Alor: a Social Psychological Study of an East Indian Culture*. Minneapolis: University of Minnesota Press.

———. 1951. "Culture Shock," in *To Strengthen World Freedom*. Institute of International Education. Special Publication Series, No. 1:22–24.

EHRLICH, JUNE SACHAR, and DAVID REISMAN. 1961. "Age and Authority in the Interview," *Public Opinion Quarterly*, 25, 39–56.

EULAU, HEINZ. 1968. "Values in Behavioral Science: Neutrality Revisited," *Antioch Review*, 28, 160–167.

FISCHER, ANN, and PEGGY GOLDE. 1968. "The Position of Women in Anthropology," *American Anthropologist*, 70:337–344.

FORD, C. S., and F. BEACH. 1951. *Patterns of Sexual Behavior*. New York: Harper & Row.

FRIEDMAN, NEIL. 1967. *The Social Nature of Psychological Research: The Psychological Experiment as a Social Interaction*. New York: Basic Books, Inc.

GEERTZ, CLIFFORD. 1968. "Thinking as a Moral Act: Ethical Dimensions of Anthropological Fieldwork in the New States," *Antioch Review*, 28, 139–158.

GOLD, RAYMOND L. 1958. Roles in sociological field observations. Social Forces, 36, 217–223.

HAMMOND, PHILLIP E. (ed.). 1964. *Sociologists at Work: Essays on the Craft of Social Research.* New York: Basic Books, Inc.

HEISS, JEROLD, and DENNISON NASH. 1967. "The Stranger in the Laboratory Culture Revisited," *Human Organization,* 26, 47–51.

HENRY, FRANCES. 1966. "The Role of the Fieldworker in an Explosive Political Situation," *Current Anthropology,* 7, 552–559.

HERSKOVITS, M. J. 1948. "The Ethnographer's Laboratory." In M. J. Herskovits (ed.), *Man and His Works.* New York: Knopf.

JONGMANS, D. G., and P. C. W. GUTKIND (eds.). 1967. *Anthropologists in the Field* (Non-European Societies, 6) Assen: Van Gorcum & Co., N. V.

JUNKER, BUFORD H. 1960. *Fieldwork: An Introduction to the Social Sciences.* Chicago: University of Chicago Press.

KLUCKHOHN, FLORENCE R. 1940. "The Participant-Observer Technique in Small Communities," *American Journal of Sociology,* 46, 331–343.

LÉVI-STRAUSS, CLAUDE. 1964. *Tristes Tropiques: An Anthropological Study of Primitive Societies in Brazil.* New York: Atheneum (paperback).

LEWIS, OSCAR. 1953. "Controls and Experiments in Field Work." In A. L. Kroeber (ed.), *Anthropology Today.* Chicago: University of Chicago Press.

LIEBOW, ELLIOTT. 1967. *Tally's Corner.* Boston: Little, Brown; pp. 232-256.

LOMBARD, G. F. F. 1950. "Self-Awareness and Scientific Method, *Science,* 112, 289–293.

LUNDBERG, CRAIG C. 1968. "A Transactional Conception of Field Work," *Human Organization,* 27, 45–49.

MALINOWSKI, BRONISLAW. 1961. *Argonauts of the Western Pacific.* New York: Dutton; pp. 5–25.

———. 1967. *A Diary in the Strict Sense of the Term.* New York: Harcourt, Brace.

MEAD, MARGARET. 1940. "The Mountain Arapesh II Supernaturalism," *Anthropological Papers* (American Museum of Natural History), 37, 317–451.

———. *An Anthropologist at Work: Writings of Ruth Benedict.* Boston: Houghton-Mifflin Co.

MERTON, ROBERT K. 1962. Foreword. In Bernard Barber, *Science and the Social Order,* rev. ed. New York: Collier Books (paperback).

NADEL, S. F. 1951. *The Foundations of Social Anthropology.* New York: The Free Press; pp. 35–74.

NASH, DENNISON. 1963. "The Ethnologist as a Stranger: An Essay in the Sociology of Knowledge," *Southwest Journal of Anthropology,* 19, 149–167.

———. 1968. "Book Review: *Anthropologists in the Field,*" *American Anthropologist,* 70, 768–770.

OBERG, KALERVO. 1954. *Culture Shock.* The Bobbs-Merrill Reprint Series in the Social Sciences.

OLESEN, VIRGINIA L., and ELVI WAIK WHITTAKER. 1967. "Role-Making in Participant Observation: Processes in the Researcher-Actor Relationship," *Human Organization,* 26, 273–281.

PAPANEK, HANNAH. 1964. "The Woman Fieldworker in a Purdah Society," *Human Organization,* 23, 161.

PAUL, BENJAMIN D. 1953. "Interviewing Techniques and Field Relationships." In A. L. Kroeber (ed.), *Anthropology Today.* Chicago: University of Chicago Press.

————. (ed.). 1955. *Health, Culture and Community.* New York: Russell Sage Foundation.

POWDERMAKER, HORTENSE. 1967. *Stranger and Friend.* New York: W. W. Norton.

RICHARDS, A. I. 1939. "The Development of Field Work Methods in Social Anthropology." In F. C. Bartlett et al. (eds.), *The Study of Society.* London: Kegan Paul, Trench, Trubner & Co., Ltd.; pp. 272–316.

ROSE, ARNOLD (ed.). 1952. *Human Behavior and Social Processes.* Boston: Houghton-Mifflin Company.

ROSENTHAL, ROBERT. 1966. *Experimenter Effects in Behavioral Research.* New York: Appleton-Century-Crofts.

SCHULTZ, ALFRED. 1964. "The Stranger." In Arvid Brodersen (ed.), *Collected Papers;* Vol. II, *Studies in Social Theory.* The Hague: Martinus Nijhott; pp. 91–105.

SCHWAB, WILLIAM B. 1965. "Looking Backward: An Appraisal of Two Field Trips," *Human Organization,* 24, 372–380.

SCHWARTZ, MORRIS, and CHARLOTTE SCHWARTZ. 1955. "Problems in Participant Observation," *American Journal of Sociology,* 60, 343–353.

SIMMEL, GEORG. 1950. "The Stranger." In Kurt Wolff (ed.), *The Sociology of Georg Simmel.* New York: The Free Press.

VIDICH, ARTHUR J. 1955. "Participant Observation and the Collection and Interpretation of Data," *American Journal of Sociology,* 60, 354–360.

VIDICH, ARTHUR J., J. BENSMAN, and M. R. STEIN (eds.). 1964. *Reflections on Community Studies.* New York: Wiley & Sons, Inc.

WARD, ROBERT E., FRANK BONILLA, JAMES COLEMAN, HERBERT HYMAN, LUCIAN PYE, and MYRON WEINER (eds.). 1964. *Studying Politics Abroad: Field Research in Developing Nations.* Boston: Little, Brown.

WAX, ROSALIE H. 1952. "Reciprocity as a Field Technique," *Human Organization,* 11, 34–37.

WHYTE, WILLIAM F. 1955. *Street Corner Society.* Chicago: University of Chicago Press.

————. 1957. "On Asking Indirect Questions," *Human Organization,* 15, 21–23.

WOOD, MARY MARGARET. 1934. *The Stranger: A Study in Social Relationships.* New York: Columbia University Press.

Supplemental
Selected Bibliography

(Field Work, Women, and
Cross-Cultural Orientation)

compiled by Stephen E. MacLeod

AGAR, MICHAEL H. 1980. *The Professional Stranger: An Informal Introduction to Ethnography*. New York: Academic Press.

ARDENER, SHIRLEY, NICOLE GOWARD, and JACQUIE SARSBY. 1984. "The Fieldwork Experience." In R. F. Ellen (ed.), *Ethnographic Research: A Guide to General Conduct*. New York: Academic Press.

BEATTIE, JOHN. 1965. *Understanding an African Kingdom: Bunyoro*. Studies in Anthropological Method. New York: Holt, Rinehart, and Winston.

BECK, LOIS, and NIKKI KEDDIE (eds.) 1978. *Women in the Muslim World*. Cambridge, Mass.: Harvard University Press.

BELL, COLIN, and HOWARD NEWBY. 1977. *Doing Sociological Research*. New York: The Free Press.

BELL, DIANE. 1983. *Daughters of the Dreaming*. Melbourne: McPhee Gribble Publishers/George Allen & Unwin.

BERREMAN, GERARD D. 1962. *Behind Many Masks: Ethnography and Impression Management in a Himalayan Village*. Monograph No. 4. Ithaca, New York: Society for Applied Anthropology.

BETEILLE, ANDRE, and T. N. MADAN (eds.) 1975. *Encounter and Experience: Personal Accounts of Fieldwork*. Honolulu: University Press of Hawaii.

BOURGUIGNON, ERIKA. 1980. *A World of Women: Anthropological Studies of Women in the Societies of the World*. New York: Praeger.

BOVIN, METTE. 1966. "The Significance of the Sex of the Fieldworker for Insights into the Male and Female Worlds," *Ethnos*, 31 (supplement), 24–27.

BOWEN, ELENORE SMITH. 1964. *Return to Laughter*. New York: Doubleday & Co.

CASAGRANDE, JOSEPH B. (ed.). 1960. *In the Company of Man: Twenty Portraits of Anthropological Informants*. New York: Harper & Row.

CESARA, MANDA. 1982. *Reflections of a Woman Anthropologist: No Hiding Place*. New York: Academic Press.

CHAGNON, NAPOLEON A. 1974. *Studying the Yanomamo*. Studies in Anthropological Method. New York: Holt, Rinehart, and Winston.

CHAMOUX, MARIE-NOELLE. 1979. "Women in Social Anthropology in France: Some

Points of Reference," *L'Homme,* 19 (special issue, *L'Anthropologie des Sexes*), 223–233.

CHIÑAS, BEVERLY L. 1973. *The Isthmus Zapotecs: Women's Roles in Cultural Context.* Case Studies in Cultural Anthropology. New York: Holt, Rinehart, and Winston.

CLARKE, M. 1975. "Survival in the Field: Implications of Personal Experience in Field Work," *Theory & Society,* 2 (1):95–123.

CLOUDSLEY, ANNE. 1981. *Women of Omburman: Life, Love and the Cult of Virginity.* 2d ed. London: Ethnographica.

CRAPANZANO, VINCENT. 1980. *Tuhami, Portrait of A Moroccan.* Chicago: University of Chicago Press.

DE LAGUNA, FREDERICA. 1977. *Voyage to Greenland: A Personal Initiation into Anthropology.* New York: W. W. Norton.

DOUGLAS, JACK D. 1976. *Investigative Social Research: Individual and Team Field Research.* Sage Library of Social Research, vol. 29. Beverly Hills: Sage Publications.

DUMONT, JEAN-PAUL. 1978. *The Headman and I: Ambiguity and Ambivalence in the Fieldworking Experience.* Texas Pan-American Series. Austin: University of Texas Press.

DWYER, KEVIN. 1982. *Moroccan Dialogues: Anthropology in Question.* Baltimore, Maryland: Johns Hopkins University Press.

EASTERDAY, LOIS, et al. 1977. "The Making of the Female Researcher: Role Problems in Fieldwork," *Urban Life,* 6 (3):333–348.

EMERSON, ROBERT M. 1983. *Contemporary Field Research.* Boston: Little, Brown & Co.

EMERSON, ROBERT M. 1981. "Observational Field Work," *Annual Review of Sociology,* 7, 351–378.

EPSTEIN, ARNOLD LEONARD. 1967. *The Craft of Social Anthropology.* London: Tavistock.

FISCHER, ANN, and PEGGY GOLDE. 1968. "The Position of Women in Anthropology," *American Anthropologist,* 70 (2):337–343.

FREILICH, MORRIS (ed.). 1977. *Marginal Natives at Work: Anthropologists in the Field.* Cambridge, Massachusetts: Schenkman.

FRIEDL, ERNESTINE. 1975. *Women and Men: An Anthropologist's View.* Basic Anthropology Units. New York: Holt, Rinehart, and Winston.

GANS, HERBERT J. 1968. "The Participant-Observer as a Human Being: Observations on the Personal Aspects of Field Work." In Howard S. Becker, et al. (eds.), *Institutions and the Person.* Chicago: Aldine.

GARTRELL, BEVERLEY. 1979. "Is Ethnography Possible: A Critique of African Odyssey," *Journal of Anthropological Research,* 35, 426–446.

GEORGE, ROBERT A., and MICHAEL O. JONES. 1980. *People Studying People: The Human Element in Fieldwork.* Berkeley, Los Angeles, London: University of California Press.

GLAZER, MYRON. 1972. *The Research Adventure: Promise and Problems of Field Work.* New York: Random House.

GOLDE, PEGGY, and DEMITRI B. SHIMKIN (eds.). 1983. *Clinical Anthropology: A New Approach to American Health Problems?* Lanham, Maryland: University Press of America.

GOLDE, PEGGY (ed.). 1970. *Women in the Field: Anthropological Experiences*. Chicago: Aldine.

HAMMERSLEY, MARTYN, and PAUL ATKINSON. 1983. *Ethnography, Principles in Practice*. London: Tavistock.

HAMMOND, PHILLIP E. (ed.). 1964. *Sociologists at Work: Essays on the Craft of Social Research*. New York: Basic Books.

HATKIN, NANCY J., and EDNA G. BAY (eds.). 1976. *Women in Africa*. Stanford: Stanford University Press.

HENRY, FRANCIS, and SATISH SABERWAL (eds.). 1969. *Stress and Response in Fieldwork*. Studies in Anthropological Method. New York: Holt, Rinehart, and Winston.

HILL, CAROLE E. 1974. "Graduate Education in Anthropology: Conflicting Role Identity in Fieldwork," *Human Organization*, 33 (4):408–412.

HUNT, JENNIFER. 1984. "The Development of Rapport through the Negotiation of Gender in Field Work among Police," *Human Organization*, 43 (4):283–296.

INTERNATIONAL CONGRESS and ANTHROPOLOGICAL and ETHNOLOGICAL SCIENCES (Ninth), Chicago, 1973. *Women Cross-Culturally: Change and Challenge*, edited by Ruby Rohrlich-Leavitt. The Hague: Mouton; Chicago: distributed by Aldine, 1975.

JACOBS, SUE-ELLEN (ed.). 1974. *Women in Perspective*. Urbana, Illinois: University of Illinois.

JOHNSON, JOHN M. 1975. *Doing Field Research*. New York: The Free Press.

JONGMANS, D. G., and P. C. W. GUTKIND (eds.). 1967. *Anthropologists in the Field*. Assen, Holland: Van Gorcum.

JOSEPH, ALICE. 1949. *The Desert People: A Study of the Papago Indians*. Chicago: University of Chicago Press.

JULES-ROSETTE, BENNETTA. 1980. *Rethinking Field Research: The Role of the Observing Participant*. Washington, D.C.: American Anthropological Society.

JUNKER, BUFORD H. 1960. *Fieldwork: An Introduction to the Social Sciences*. Chicago: University of Chicago Press.

KESSLER, EVELYN S. 1976. *Women, An Anthropological View*. New York: Holt, Rinehart, and Winston.

KIMBALL, SOLON T., and WILLIAM L. PARTRIDGE. 1979. *The Craft of Community Study: Fieldwork Dialogues*. University of Florida Monographs (Social Sciences), No. 65. Gainesville: University of Florida Press.

KIMBALL, SOLON T., and JAMES B. WATSON (eds.). 1972. *Crossing Cultural Boundaries: The Anthropological Experience*. San Francisco: Chandler.

KUNG, LYDIA, LINDA GAIL ARRIGO, and JANET W. SALAFF. 1984. "Doing Fieldwork." In Mary Sheridan and Janet W. Salaff, (eds.), *Lives: Chinese Working Women*. Bloomington: Indiana University Press.

LAMPHERE, LOUISE. 1977. "Anthropology," *Signs*, 2 (3):612–627.

LAWLESS, ROBERT, VINSON H. SUTLIVE, JR., and MARIO D. ZAMORA (eds.). 1983. *Fieldwork: The Human Experience*. Library of Anthropology. New York: Gordon and Breach.

LÉVI-STRAUSS, CLAUDE. 1961 (1954). *Tristes Tropiques: An Anthropological Study of Primitive Societies in Brazil*. New York: Atheneum.

LURIE, NANCY OESTRICH. 1966. "Women in Early Anthropology." In June Helm
MacNeish (ed.), *Pioneers of American Anthropology*. American Ethnological Society Monograph No. 43. Seattle: University of Washington Press.

MALINOWSKI, BRONISLAW. 1967. *A Diary in the Strict Sense of the Term*. New York:
Harcourt, Brace & World, Inc.

MARTIN, M. KAY, and BARBARA VOORHIES. 1975. *Female of the Species*. New York:
Columbia University Press.

MATTHIASSON, CAROLYN J. 1974. *Many Sisters; Women in Cross-Cultural Perspective*.
New York: The Free Press.

MCELROY, ANN, and CAROLYN MATTHIASSON (eds.). 1979. *Sex-Roles in Changing
Cultures*. Occasional Papers in Anthropology, No. 1. Buffalo: Department of Anthropology, State University of New York at Buffalo.

MEAD, MARGARET. 1959. *An Anthropologist at Work: Writings of Ruth Benedict*.
Boston: Houghton Mifflin Co.

————. 1972. *Blackberry Winter: My Early Years*. New York: William Morrow.

————. 1977. *Letters From the Field, 1927–1975*. New York: Harper & Row.

MURPHY, YOLANDA, and ROBERT F. MURPHY. 1974. *Women of the Forest*. New York:
Columbia University Press.

NAROLL, RAOUL, and RONALD COHEN (eds.). 1973 [1970]. *A Handbook, of Method
in Cultural Anthropology*. New York: Columbia University Press.

O'BRIEN, DENISE, and SHARON T. TIFFANY (eds.). 1984. *Rethinking Women's Roles:
Perspectives From the Pacific*. Berkeley, Los Angeles, London: University of
California Press.

PAPANEK, HANNA. 1964. "The Woman Fieldworker in a Purdah Society," *Human
Organization*, 23 (2):160–163.

PASTNER, CARROL MCC. 1982. "Rethinking the Role of the Woman Field Worker in
Purdah Societies," *Human Organization*, 41 (3):262–264.

PELTO, PERTTI J., and GRETEL H. PELTO. 1973. "Ethnography: The Fieldwork Enterprise." In John J. Honigman (ed.), *Handbook of Social and Cultural Anthropology*.
Chicago: Rand McNally.

PETTIGREW, JOYCE. 1981. "Reminiscences of Fieldwork Among the Sikhs." In Helen
Roberts (ed.), *Doing Feminist Research*. London: Routledge & Kegan Paul.

POWDERMAKER, HORTENSE. 1966. *Stranger and Friend: The Way of the Anthropologist*. New York: W. W. Norton.

QUINN, NAOMI. 1977. "Anthropological Studies of Women's Status," *Annual Review
of Anthropology*, 6, 181–225.

RABINOW, PAUL. 1977. *Reflections on Fieldwork in Morocco*. Berkeley, Los Angeles,
London: University of California Press.

RAPP, RAYNA. 1979. "Anthropology," *Signs*, 4 (3):497–513.

REITER, RAYNA. 1977. *Toward an Anthropology of Women*. New York: Monthly Review
Press.

ROMANUCCI-ROSS, LOLA. 1976. "With Margaret Mead in the Field: Observations on
the Logic of Discovery," *Ethos*, 4 (4):439–448.

ROSALDO, MICHELLE Z. 1980. "The Use and Abuse of Anthropology: Reflections on
Feminism and Cross-Cultural Understanding," *Signs*, 5, 389–417.

ROSALDO, MICHELLE Z., and LOUISE LAMPHERE (eds.). 1974. *Women, Culture and*

Society. Stanford: Stanford University Press.

RUBY, JAY (ed.). 1982. *A Crack in the Mirror: Reflexive Perspectives in Anthropology*. Philadelphia: University of Pennsylvania Press.

RYNKIEWICH, MICHAEL A., and JAMES P. SPRADLEY. 1976. *Ethics and Anthropology: Dilemmas in Fieldwork*. New York: Wiley.

SANDAY, PEGGY REEVES (ed.). 1976. *Anthropology and the Public Interest: Fieldwork and Theory*. Studies in Anthropology Series. New York: Academic Press.

SANJEK, ROGER. 1978. "The Position of Women in the Major Departments of Anthropology, 1967–1976," *American Anthropologist*, 80 (4):894–904.

SCHATZMAN, LEONARD, and ANSELM L. STRAUSS. 1973. *Field Research: Strategies for a Natural Sociology*. Englewood Cliffs, New Jersey: Prentice-Hall.

SHAFFIR, WILLIAM B., ROBERT A. STEBBIUNS, and ALLAN TUROWETZ (eds.). 1980. *Fieldwork Experience: Qualitative Approaches to Social Research*. New York: St. Martin's Press.

SLATER, MARIAM K. 1976. *African Odyssey: An Anthropological Adventure*. Garden City, New York: Anchor Press/Doubleday.

SPINDLER, GEORGE D. (ed.). 1970. *Being an Anthropologist: Fieldwork in Eleven Cultures*. Case Studies in Cultural Anthropology. New York: Holt, Rinehart, and Winston.

SPRADLEY, JAMES P., and BRENDA J. MANN. 1975. *The Cocktail Waitress, Women's Work in a Man's World*. New York: John Wiley & Sons.

SRINIVAS, M. N., A. M. SHAH, and E. A. RAMASWAMY (eds.). 1979. *The Fieldworker and the Field: Problems and Challenges in Sociological Investigations*. Delhi: Oxford University Press.

STACK, CAROL B., et al. 1975. "The New Scholarship: Review Essays in the Social Sciences—Anthropology," *Signs*, 1 (1):147–159.

STOCKING, GEORGE W., JR. (ed.). 1983. *Observers Observed: Essays on Ethnographic Fieldwork*. History of Anthropology, vol. 1. Madison: University of Wisconsin Press.

SUDARKASA, N. 1973. *Where Women Work: A Study of Yoruba Women in the Marketplace and in the Home*. Ann Arbor: Museum of Anthropology, University of Michigan.

———. 1977. "Women and Migration in Contemporary West Africa," *Signs*, 3 (1), 178–189; also in Wellesley Editorial Committee, ed., *Women and National Development*. Chicago: University of Chicago Press.

———. 1981 [1976]. "Female Employment and Family Organization in West Africa," reprinted in Filomina C. Steady, ed., *The Black Woman Cross-Culturally*. Cambridge, Mass.: Schenkman Publishing Co.

———. 1982. "Sex Roles, Education and Development in Africa," *Anthropology and Education Quarterly*, XIII (3), 279–289.

THURSTON, ANNE F., and BURTON PASTERNAK (eds.). 1983. *The Social Sciences and Fieldwork in China: Views From the Field*. AAAS Selected Symposium no. 86. Boulder, Colorado: Westview Press.

TIFFANY, SHARON W. 1978. "Models and Social Anthropology of Women: A Preliminary Assessment," *Man*, 13 (1):34–51.

———. (ed.). 1979. *Women and Society: An Anthropological Reader*. Montreal and St. Albans, Vermont: Eden Press Women's Publications.

———. 1979. "Women, Power, and the Anthropology of Politics: A Review," *International Journal of Women's Studies*, 2, 430–442.

———. 1982. "Women in Cross-Cultural Perspective—A Guide to Recent Anthropological Literature," *Women's Studies International Forum*, 5 (5):497–502.

TURNBULL, COLIN M. 1961. *The Forest People*. London: Jonathan Cape.

VIDICH, ARTHUR J., JOSEPH BENSMAN, and MAURICE R. STEIN (eds.). 1964. *Reflections on Community Studies*. New York: Harper & Row.

WARREN, CAROL A. B., and PAUL K. RASMUSSEN. 1977. "Sex and Gender in Field Research," *Urban Life*, 6 (3):349–370.

WAX, ROSALIE H. 1983. "The Ambiguities of Fieldwork." In Robert M. Emerson (ed.), *Contemporary Field Research*. Boston: Little, Brown & Co.

———. 1971. *Doing Field Work: Warnings and Advice*. Chicago: University of Chicago Press.

———. 1952. "Field Methods and Techniques: Reciprocity as a Field Technique," *Human Organization*, 11 (3):34–37.

———. 1979. "Gender and Age in Fieldwork and Fieldwork Education: No Good Thing Is Done by Man Alone," *Social Problems*, 26 (5):509–523.

———. 1960. "Reciprocity in Field Work." In Richard N. Adams and Jack J. Preiss (eds.), *Human Organization Research*. Homewood, Illinois: The Dorsey Press.

WEINER, ANNETTE B. 1976. *Women of Value, Men of Renown*. Austin and London: University of Texas Press.

WHYTE, WILLIAM F. 1955. *Street Corner Society*. Chicago: University of Chicago Press.

WOLF, MARGERY. 1985. *Revolution Postponed: Women in Contemporary China*. Stanford: Stanford University Press.

WOLF, MARGERY, and ROXANE WITKE (eds.). 1975. *Women in Chinese Society*. Stanford: Stanford University Press.

Women in Anthropology: Symposium Papers, 1977 and 1978. Sacramento, California: Sacramento Anthropological Society, 1979.

Women in Anthropology: Symposium Papers, 1979 and 1980. Sacramento, California: Sacramento Anthropological Society, 1983.